The heraldic device on the front page was given to.
I had wanted a something unusual for the sign on my new Christian book store, and could not find any thing on the net or in the library. I got real frustrated and Said" All right God what do you want!!" The result is what you see. The meaning of is as follows.

1- The lions are King David and King Jesus the Lion of Judah

2- The Green Field of the Shield represents the Earth

3- The Red Diagonal Strip represents the Shed Blood of Jesus.

4- The Star in the Center of the Shield is the Star of Bethlehem.

5- The Lamb on top of the Shield is the Slain Lamb Jesus the Christ

6- The Banner in the Lions rear feet say that "The truth will set you free."

Verses that Say in the kingdom of God.
A book of short bible studies
By

James B. Hoffman

Plus
by permission

A Joyful Marriage Fortress
By
Terry Scerine

Books by James B. Hoffman from Dog Ear Publishing:

"Sin and Life in the Kingdom of God"
and
"Versus that Say in the Kingdom of God"

Coming soon

"Spiritual Warfare in the Kingdom of God"

© 2011 James B. Hoffman
All Rights Reserved.

No part of this publication may be reproduced, stored in a retrieval system, or transmitted, in any form or by any means, electronic, mechanical, photocopying, recording, or otherwise, without the written permission of the author.

First published by Dog Ear Publishing
4010 W. 86th Street, Ste H
Indianapolis, IN 46268
www.dogearpublishing.net

dog ear
PUBLISHING

ISBN: 978-145750-108-1

This book is printed on acid-free paper.

Printed in the United States of America

		Explanation of the front cover	i
		Forward	vii
		Authors note	ix
#2→	1	The Christian life	1
	2	The Kingdom of God	13
#3→	3	The Call to Holiness	20
	4	Herod Slaughters the babies	40
	5	Faith not Fasting	41
	6	Concerning Divorce	42
	7	Jesus' Prayer in the Garden	43
	8	What is Tithing	44
	9	Incorrect Translations	46
#4→	10	Being Born Again (salvation)	49
	11	Blasphemy Against the Holy Spirit	62
	12	Do We Judge Others	65
	13	The Rock of the Church	69
	14	This is the True Body	81
	15	Prayer	99
	16	Predestination	103
	17	Divorce of the Nation of Israel	107
	18	Jesus in the Grave	111
	19	The Lie of Mary Remaining a Life Long Virgin or Without Sin	114
	20	Saved by Faith and Grace	115
	21	The Baptism of the Holy Spirit and His work in your life	121
	22	The Father Calls all Men	134
	23	The Lie of born in sin, guilty of sin, or with a fallen nature	136
	24	The Blood	148
	25	Obeying Natural Government	152
	26	The Lie of Once Saved always Saved	154
	27	The true prophet of God	161
#1→	28	Healing	176
	29	The Lord's supper, Communion	186
	30	The words of Jesus as they relate to the natural nation of Israel and the natural Jew	188
	31	The anti-christ who, what, where, and when	221
	32	A short study on sin	225
	33	A Joyful Marriage Fortress	227

FORWARD:

Summer, 1972; the Lord blesses me with His choice of the man who is to fill the empty places in my life. We've had many years of living, loving and growing together. Praise God! He's not through with us yet!

It has often been said on my side of the family, "If you don't want to hear the truth, don't ask Jay". Even before Jay came to walk closely with the Lord, he was a man who valued truth. Once (I think it was our second date) he accidently broke a thermometer hanging on the garage of an elderly man and instead of doing what many would have done (forget about it – who will know?) he went to the man and explained what happened. That impressed me, gave light on his character, and truthfully was one of the reasons I said "yes".

When Jay first came to the Lord, and in his zeal as a new Christian, he used the truth of the Word as a hammer to try and reach others for the kingdom. God lovingly, patiently, led him to understand that "hammers come in many sizes" and the size of the hammer depends on the task. The Spirit now chooses the 'hammer' and Jay wields it obediently, in love to his Lord.

Jay is passionate about the ' truth of the Word' getting to all people so they can stand in righteousness and wield the Sword of the Spirit to gain victory for the kingdom and the saints of God.

If you seek truth, desire a closer relationship with Jesus, would be a warrior for God; if you desire victory in your life, to walk in freedom, healing; and if you desire to KNOW where you will spend eternity, then read this book.

It is vital that you read with the eyes of the Spirit, the eyes of the heart; seeking truth as a dying man fights for life!

May our Lord bless His truth to your understanding.

Yours in the love of Jesus
Sharon Hoffman

Authors Note:

I want to thank you for buying this book of short bible studies. The proceeds will go for the work of bringing Jesus to all who need Him.

I wish to thank my wife Sharon for her understanding of my being involved with this work to the exclusion of most of my house-hold chores or at the very least being late doing them. One chore I did not neglect is cooking, I like to eat. Sharon also did the final edit of this manuscript.

I must, as in my First book **"Sin and life in the Kingdom of God"**, ask you to read all of the scripture and commentary on any one subject before making up your mind about it. The only way to know what God intends for us to know is to find out everything that He has to say about it. I Check out all the verses in the either the New Testament, the Old testament, or both. If you will do this you will know the truth.

There are NO contradictions in the bible. Get the WHOLE STORY. Do not take **anyone's** word, mine included, about what the bible teaches. Check it out for yourselves. Use the Greek and Hebrew dictionaries to see what the original words mean. The Strong's Concordance is a good first level starting point. Let God, through the Holy Spirit, confirm, to you, every thing you read or are taught before you accept it into your heart as the truth of God the Father.

Is not your salvation more important to you than to some pastor, priest, or teacher? Listen to them, they may have it right, but make sure that what they say and or teach is what the bible says and means. Again check it out for yourself! Listen to the Holy Spirit, it is His Job to bring all truth to you.

You are responsible for your own salvation. The leaders of your church can not get you to heaven, only you can do that by Jesus' shed blood removing the guilt of sin from your conscience, thereby making you sin free. It is your choice to stay that way, and you will if you desire to spend eternity with God the Father, the Son, and the Holy Spirit.

You will note that the last study / book in this book is not by me. I have included this book on God's plan of Marriage because it is very important for the survival of Christian marriages and is used the by permission of Terry Scerine the author.

Many thanks for buying this book of short bible studies, and may God open your mind and heart for a full and complete understanding of His works.

All scripture is from the King James Version unless otherwise noted.

In Christ
James B. Hoffman

The Christian life

Luke 17:20 And when he was demanded of the Pharisees, when the kingdom of God should come, he answered them and said, The kingdom of God cometh not with observation: 21 Neither shall they say, Lo here! or, lo there! for, behold, the kingdom of God is within you.

The kingdom of God is now. It is not as in some men's concept, a future physical kingdom on the earth. You cannot see it. It is a spiritual kingdom that started at the resurrection of Jesus and is forevermore. The only way to enter into it and stay in it is to repentant and to stay sin free. The only, prepaid ticket, is by Jesus' work on the cross. There is no other way into this 'spiritual kingdom'.

Mark 4:26 And he said, So is the kingdom of God, as if a man should cast seed into the ground;

This seed, the death and resurrection of Jesus, grows into a ripe plant that has many groups of seeds, the individual Christians, and each of these seeds produce many more seeds. This is how the body of Christ grows.

John 3:5 Jesus answered, Verily, verily, I say unto thee, Except a man be born of water and of the Spirit, he cannot enter into the kingdom of God.

John 3:6 That which is born of the flesh is flesh; and that which is born of the Spirit is spirit.

The water represents the word of God, and the Spirit represents the Holy Spirit by which your spirit is renewed (born again) to God the Father. All this is by Jesus' shed blood and your free will choice to be born again and remain sinless. Again how could this be a natural physical kingdom?

John 5:24 Verily, verily, I say unto you, He that heareth my word, and believeth on him that sent me, hath everlasting life, and shall not come into condemnation; but is passed from death unto life.

This is the how we get in and have the reward of being in the kingdom of heaven. It is the only way to have fellowship with the Father and Jesus, and the indwelling of the Holy Spirit. Again there is NO other way to heaven. You have passed from the dead works of your sin to the revival of your spirit (by your choice to remain sinless) and into life with the Father and Jesus.

John 6:27 Labor not for the meat which perisheth, but for that meat which endureth unto everlasting life, which the Son of man shall give unto you: for him hath God the Father sealed.

Meat that rots is the false teachings of the world that will be done away with at the end of the age. The Meat that is pure with no rot is of God; it is to know and understand that we must walk sin free by the word and the commandments of God.

Here is a call to all men to enter into the kingdom of heaven. Give up the works of the world and work for God!   You could also say live for Jesus, not the world!

John 6:47 Verily, verily, I say unto you, He that believeth on me hath everlasting life.

This would be life in the spiritual kingdom of God, not some reworked earth with Jesus sitting on an earthly throne taking animal sacrifices for the forgiveness of sin. This is a lie of Satan being taught in man's church today; such teaching is a slap in the face of Jesus. We must check out all that is told to us by the word of God so we don't fall into the trap of Satan's teaching that sounds good, but does not conform to the bible. So, again, check out every teaching very carefully in the bible. To 'believe' has many meanings to it: that Jesus did die on the cross and was resurrected to life, that His shed blood removes the guilt of your sins from you, that the kingdom of God is spiritual, that Jesus is lord and master of all creation, that you must be baptized in water, have faith in all that Jesus is, that you must repent and ask forgiveness for you sins with a broken heart ETC, ETC. Quite a large word? EH!

John 14:6 Jesus saith unto him, I am the way, the truth, and the life: no man cometh unto the Father, but by me.

You can not get into the kingdom of heaven any other way or by any other road! No other religion offers this choice to the world. No other religion offers any form of salvation by the removal of sins from your conscience which then makes you sin free, unless you sin again. If you fall back into sin you must again ask for forgiveness to get back into the Kingdom. Yes I mean that one un-repented sin will get you kicked out of the kingdom, but then again Gods' mercy allows you to repent and ask forgiveness as many times as necessary to keep you in the Kingdom. Jesus is the ONLY key to the door of heaven. Again only Jesus is the way of and to the light of the Father. There is NO OTHER WAY!

Romans 13:8 Owe no man any thing, but to love one another: for he that loveth another hath fulfilled the law.

To owe someone is to have hard feelings toward them, especially if you can not pay. To operate in love is to walk sinless with Jesus in the Kingdom of God. If you are in sin do you not owe God the Father a repentant attitude and broken contrite heart?

1 Corinthians 15:50 Now this I say, brethren, that flesh and blood cannot inherit the kingdom of God; neither doth corruption inherit incorruption.

See, I told you the Kingdom of God is Spiritual! If flesh and blood can't inherit it then the only other thing to inherit it is your spirit. You can not get into the Kingdom of God in sin, it is only for Gods' holy and spiritually pure, sinless children.

This is the same for the false concept of inheriting sin. You can't. Your spirit, which is given from God, is not made and given in corruption and sin. Sin, or more rightly the guilt of sin, resides in your conscience (as shown in **Hebrews chapter 9: 1-15)**, which is part of your spirit. It does not reside in your flesh as some major churches teach.

Again read **Hebrews chapters 9 & 10**. Do you really think God would give you a defective spirit? Again the kingdom is only for the spiritually pure, which is what babies are. Babies "LEARN" to sin while growing up. In the Thayer's lexicon it says that sin is a learned habit. **Eph. 2:3**. II says by nature children of wrath. (the word Nature in Eph 2:3, means a learned habit). These babies are not held accountable for sin until they come of age (the understanding of the moral consequences) at which point they are held responsible for their sin, at which point they then need Jesus to get back to being spiritually pure. You must understand that you learn morality, you are not born with the knowledge of good and evil.

See **JOHN 7:7**. This shows that before John was old enough to know and understand the law of God that he was not held accountable for breaking the law or you can also say sinning.

Ephesians 5:5 For this ye know, that no whore monger, nor unclean person, nor covetous man, who is an idolater, hath any inheritance in the kingdom of Christ and of God.

Sinners don't get in, it does not matter if you were once saved. If you fall back into sin you've lost it all and are on the way to hell. Your only chance is to repent and ask forgiveness. Just because your sin is not listed in this verse doesn't mean this verse does not apply to you in your sins.

Matthew 10:38 And he that taketh not his cross, and followeth after me, is not worthy of me.
Luke 14:27 And whosoever doth not bear his cross, and come after me, cannot be my disciple.

To pick up your cross is to walk as Jesus walked, sinless and holy. It is not dragging around a couple pieces of wood nailed together. It's a spiritual command not a physical one. This means that Jesus must be first in your life. He must be above all else including your family and all things of the world, period.

Matthew 12:30 He that is not with me is against me; and he that gathereth not with me scattereth abroad.

To be with Jesus is to be sinless. If you're not for Jesus you are against Him. If you sin you love your sin more than you love Jesus. Simple EH! If you are in sin you will be scattered away from the Kingdom of God, and will not go to heaven unless you repent.

John 5:14 Afterward Jesus findeth him in the temple, and said unto him Behold, thou art made whole: sin no more, lest a worse thing come unto thee.

This is the first person Jesus tells to stop sinning, and this is before He went to the cross. Have you stopped yet? Question: Why would Jesus command us to do something we were unable to do (stop sinning)? In this regard to this command we 'are able' to stop sinning! It is a free will choice every time we sin. Now you must understand that Jesus is no respecter of persons and that He remains the same forever. This` command is for all people of all time . So obey ! Stop sinning!!

John 8:10 When Jesus had lifted up himself, and saw none but the woman, he said unto her, Woman, where are those thine accusers? hath no man condemned thee? 11 She said, No man, Lord. And Jesus said unto her, Neither do I condemn thee: go, and sin no more.

This is the second person that Jesus told to stop sinning before He went to the cross. Do you really think that Jesus would order us to stop sinning if it were not possible? This is a command! It is for all Christians! Do you think Jesus was just kidding? Have you stopped yet?

John 8:34 Jesus answered them, Verily, verily, I say unto you, Whosoever committeth sin is the servant of sin.

When we become born again and sin free our master is Jesus. If you sin again you have changed masters from Jesus to Satan, and have put yourself back onto the road to hell. It is a free will choice you make. No one makes you sin, or stop sinning. To get back your holiness (sinlessness) you must repent and ask (in spirit and truth) forgiveness for your sins of the Father in Jesus name. Then you will be on the straight and narrow road to Jesus and the Father again. The Father will forgive as many times as necessary to get you to heaven, The catch or hook is that you MUST ask!!

John 14:15 If ye love me, keep my commandments.

John 14:21 He that hath my commandments, and keepeth them, he it is that loveth me: and he that loveth me shall be loved of my Father, and I will love him, and will manifest myself to him.

How can this be more clear ? One of the most important commandments is that you stop sinning and be holy as He is holy. The opposite is also true, if you are in sin you are not holy and you are not saved. If you DON'T keep His commandments you then hate Jesus and love your sin. Is not one of His commands "Go forth and <u>sin no more</u> lest a worse thing happen to you"?

John 14:23 Jesus answered and said unto him, If a man love me, he will keep my words: and my Father will love him, and we will come unto him, and make our abode with him.

"Keep my words" is the same as keep my commandments! Again the opposite is true! If you disobey the commands of God, the Father and Jesus will no longer make their abode with you , and you will be separated from God by your choice. You will not be able to come back to God until you repent with a broken heart. It's kinda hard to get your mind around the fact that if you <u>don't love</u> Jesus and stop sinning, then you <u>hate Him</u> in your sinfulness. You might say that you love your sin more than you love Jesus. Both of these statements are true and scriptural.

John 15:6 If a man abide not in me, he is cast forth as a branch, and is withered; and men gather them, and cast them into the fire, and they are burned.

This is the result of sinfulness! HELL! The only way to abide in Christ is to be sinless, and stay that way.

John 15:9 As the Father hath loved me, so have I loved you: continue ye in my love.

A command to remain sinless and Holy. How can you love something when you drive it away by sin? Don't misunderstand, it is you who will drive Jesus and the Father away from you by your sin. God does not leave by His choice.

Romans 6:22 But now being made free from sin, and become servants to God, ye have your fruit unto holiness, and the end everlasting life. 23 For the wages of sin is death; but the gift of God is eternal life through Jesus Christ our Lord.

When you are made sin free, by your choice, you become HOLY. If you return to sin you will have to start all over again unless you don't want to go to HELL! This gift of being sin free is "only" from Jesus.

Romans 8:13 For if ye live after the flesh, ye shall die: but if ye through the Spirit do mortify the deeds of the body, ye shall live. 14 For as many as are led by the Spirit of God, they are the sons of God.

To live after the flesh is to remain in sin; your spirit is killed by your sin. The only way to bring your spirit back to life is to die to sin and live sinless for Christ. To be led by the Holy Spirit you must be born again, remain sinless, and be baptized in the Holy Spirit.
        1-2-3 what could be simpler?

Romans 13:14 But put ye on the Lord Jesus Christ, and make not provision for the flesh, to fulfil the lusts thereof.

To "put on Jesus" is the same as "pick up your cross daily". It is to walk sinless, to be perfect, to be holy, to walk as Jesus walked. If you don't you are disobeying the commands of Jesus and are destined for hell as a sinner. Do you think you are living as Jesus would have you live? If you can't say yes you have a real problem.

1 Corinthians 10:21 Ye cannot drink the cup of the Lord, and the cup of devils: ye cannot be partakers of the Lord's table, and of the table of devils.

Here it says that you can not be Holy and a sinner at the same time. It alludes to the fact that one sin separates you from Jesus, the Father, and the Holy Spirit. As you are the holy temple of God, do you really think that God will share you with the devil by staying with you when you sin? To say it again: God can not abide sin and will leave you until you ask forgiveness and repent. Jesus is your master as long as you remain sinless, but one sin changes your master back to Satan. Is this what you want for your life??? Are you a 'YO YO' Christian who is in and out of the kingdom constantly?

1 Corinthians 15:57 But thanks be to God, which giveth us the victory through our Lord Jesus Christ.

This is Gods' answer to the world that is full of sinfulness. This is our way out! The way to get rid of sin, to stop sinning, to be holy, to be pure, to be without spot or wrinkle, to live forever in glory with Jesus. BELIEVE and come to Jesus in truth and spirit. Claim the victory! Do it now! Ask forgiveness and repent!!!

1 Corinthians 16:22 If any man love not the Lord Jesus Christ, let him be Anathema*Maranatha**

If you don't love Jesus you are cursed. Jesus said in John 14 :15 "If ye love me, keep my commandments". *You are cursed if you sin, and **Think about it are the meanings for the Greek words above.

2 Corinthians 7:1 Having therefore these promises, dearly beloved, let us cleanse ourselves from all filthiness of the flesh and spirit, perfecting holiness in the fear of God.

A call to be holy and pure by remaining sinless, and choosing to stay that way. How can the modern man's church say we are still sinners after being cleansed of sin by the blood of Jesus? Does your church teach that Jesus' blood only "covers" sin? This is a lie of Satan. This allows you to continue in sin and feel good about yourself, instead of having a broken, contrite, sinless heart for Jesus. By the way check out **Heb. chapter 9** about Jesus' blood and how it removes the guilt of your sin from your conscience.

2 Corinthians 10:5 Casting down imaginations, and every high thing that exalteth itself against the knowledge of God, and bringing into captivity every thought to the obedience of Christ;

This is one of the tools God has given to us to use. It helps you to remain sinless. Just having a thought (temptation) that is worldly does not mean it is a sin. As long as you capture (in Jesus' name) that and any other tempting thoughts, and reject them in Jesus' name you will stay sinless and in obedience to Christ. This means that you do not act on this thought or dwell on it, you MUST reject it in Jesus name.

The "new age" worldly people use the word "imagine" as a mantra to get you into their world of sin. It is true that this is a very powerful word and it works. They say if you can imagine something you can do it. This is used by Satan to get you to believe the lie that "you can be as God yourself". If you can be as God then why do you need Jesus? It is their way of teaching and thinking which is a lie of the greatest magnitude. The only truth in this world comes from Jesus!!

Galatians 5:9 A little leaven leaveneth the whole lump.

Be careful one sin will ruin your day, it will keep you out of heaven. To remain holy, pure, and walking with Jesus and the Father you must not sin. To remain in the kingdom of God you must remain sinless. It's not three strikes and your out, but only one. A very small, inconsequential, false teaching will, (if you let it) lead you away from the truth of Jesus. Be careful and check out everything with the bible. If you can not confirm any teaching by the bible reject it. Even this bible study book.

Ephesians 4:24 And that ye put on the new man, which after God is created in righteousness and true holiness.

This is what you are after going through the cross of Jesus a new man, HOLY, RIGHTEOUS, and WITHOUT SIN. Stay that way and you will spend eternity with Jesus and the Father.

Colossians 2:6 As ye have therefore received Christ Jesus the Lord, so walk ye in him:

What can be easier to understand? You are born again, that means to walk as He walked which is "sinless". This is picking up your cross every day as Jesus did, and walking as He walked, obeying the Father.

Colossians 3: 8 But now ye also put off all these; anger, wrath, malice, blasphemy, filthy communication out of your mouth.9 Lie not one to another, seeing that ye have put off the old man with his deeds;10 And have put on the new man, which is renewed in knowledge after the image of him that created him:

BE HOLY WITHOUT SIN!!!!!!!!! Be Christ like. That is if you want to go to heaven in glory and reside with the Father. Or do you think Jesus is just pulling your leg???

1 Thessalonians 2:12 That ye would walk worthy of God, who hath called you unto his kingdom and glory.

Do you not think that walking worthy is the same as walking sinless and holy? Not walking holy is the opposite of walking holy, and if you're in the kingdom with one, then you're out of the kingdom with the other. Ya think?

1 Thessalonians 3:8 For now we live, if ye stand fast in the Lord.

To live is to be spiritually alive, and to stand fast is to resist sin thereby remaining holy. To sin is to die spiritually.

1 Thessalonians 4:7 For God hath not called us unto uncleanness, but unto holiness.

No comment is need here. I hope!

1 Thessalonians 5:19 Quench not the Spirit.

To quench the Holy Spirit is to be in sin. The command here is not to sin. If, by some chance you decide to sin you will quench the Holy Spirit causing Him to leave you to Satan. God does not share. Believe it! Your life depends on it!

1 Thessalonians 5:22 Abstain from all appearance of evil.

This goes beyond just saying "don't sin". It says don't even look like you're in sin.

1 Timothy 6:14 That thou keep this commandment without spot, unrebukeable, until the appearing of our Lord Jesus Christ:

The commandment is to "love your brother as you love yourself." Without spot and 'unrebukeable' means that you must stay holy by remaining sinless until you see Jesus, either at your physical death or at the second coming.

2 Timothy 2:16 But shun profane and vain babblings: for they will increase unto more ungodliness.

I'll tell ya, James was right. The hardest thing to control is your tongue. If you can control it you've come a long way toward walking in a sinless holy condition. Remember what comes out of your mouth can never go back in. It cannot be unsaid.

Hebrews 10:23 Let us hold fast the profession of our faith without wavering; (for he is faithful that promised;)

This is a call to and for Holiness? Without wavering means to act and live in and by faith.

Hebrews 12:4 Ye have not yet resisted unto blood, striving against sin.

This is what Jesus did praying in the garden right before He was arrested. God loves Jesus. God is no respecter of persons. God loves all equally. So God expects you to obey as Jesus did, even to resisting to the extent of shedding your own blood. The really neat thing is that God will not allow you to be tempted beyond what you can resist.

I was once complaining and groaning to God about some sin in my life that I thought I could not control. He answered me, in a voice that was unmistakable and said ,"Have you shed blood yet"? I knew immediately what He meant and I quit complaining at that moment and have not yet complained again about sin not being under my control, and never will. PTL

Hebrews 12:14 Follow peace with all men, and holiness, without which no man shall see the Lord:

Read what it says, believe what is says, do what it says, and you will go to heaven. Do I really need to explain this??

James 1: 14 But every man is tempted, when he is drawn away of his own lust, and enticed. 15 Then when lust hath conceived, it bringeth forth sin: and sin, when it is finished, bringeth forth death.

You can see the path of temptation to full blown sin and spiritual death. This is the result of just that one sin. Think how hardened you become after a lifetime of sin. So don't wait, come to Jesus now!

James 4:17 Therefore to him that knoweth to do good, and doeth it not, to him it is sin.

The definition of sin. To know the good and to **not** do the good is sin. You can say right or wrong in place of good or bad. Can you see that this is a choice of doing the good, or doing the bad? Just not doing the good is sin. Nothing makes you sin but you. The devil did not make you do it! Here you can see that babies or young children can NOT be sinners because they have no moral understanding of the moral consequences of their actions, of good or bad, right or wrong.

1 Peter 1:15 But as he which hath called you is holy, so be ye holy in all manner of conversation;16 Because it is written, Be ye holy; for I am holy.

You can see by the many verses that say 'be Holy' that God is really serious about this subject. To be Holy means to stop sinning. You can not have fellowship with God if you are a sinner, even if you were once saved. There is only one way to get back into God's grace and that is to ask forgiveness and repent of your sin. *There is no such thing as a sinning or carnal Christian. You either is or you ain't!*
No middle ground with God, He is a red light God. His way or hit the road Jack. CLEAR?

1 John 2:6 He that saith he abideth in him ought himself also so to walk, even as he walked.

Another command to walk sin free, be holy as Jesus is holy, walk in the same way Jesus walked with God's love for all mankind. How can we do any less? Let's say if you abide with Him(JESUS) then your are sinless, and if you don't abide with HIM (JESUS) you are a sinner ! Is this clear?? It only takes 'one' unrepented sin to get you kicked out of the kingdom and keep you out. You must repent and ask forgiveness to get back in.
See **1 John 1:9** .

1 John 5:18 We know that whosoever is born of God sinneth not; but he that is begotten of God keepeth himself, and that wicked one toucheth him not.

Be holy and sin not. This is our call to the born again life . If you sin you are no longer holy, you are spiritually dead, and you are out of the kingdom. You have, by sinning, made to be of no avail your being born again. You must now repent and ask forgiveness and start again in your walk with Jesus. By keeping yourself holy you're making the choice to stay sin free and in the kingdom of God. God will protect you from Satan as long as you stay holy by obeying and continuing in His commandments. Satan CANNOT attack or harm you as long as you remain in God's care. This means sin free in Jesus.

2 John 1:9 Whosoever transgresseth, and abideth not in the doctrine of Christ, hath not God. He that abideth in the doctrine of Christ, he hath both the Father and the Son.

This verse tells us what happens if we are not walking in holiness, and what happens if we are walking holy, without sin. Are you in or out??

3 John 1:11 Beloved, follow not that which is evil, but that which is good. He that doeth good is of God: but he that doeth evil hath not seen God.

Make no mistake, this is a call to holiness. It confirms James 4:17 as a definition of sin: Which is "to know the good and do it not". So do good and thereby be holy.

Jude 1:21 Keep yourselves in the love of God, looking for the mercy of our Lord Jesus Christ unto eternal life.

To remain in the love of God is to be holy and without sin in your lives. Jesus is the "ONLY" way to eternal life with God the Father. The 'mercy' means that you can ask forgiveness as many times as you need to get to the point of not wanting to sin, and then stop sinning. Do this by your choice.

Matthew 18:20 For where two or three are gathered together in my name, there am I in the midst of them.

This is the way true members of the body of Christ should meet. Not in some man's building on the corner, one or two days a week, with hundreds or even thousands of people! How can you, in these so called mega-churches, know who your brothers and sisters in Christ are? Or even know what they believe in? How can you be in accord or of one mind with someone you don't even know? How can the, so called, leadership of men / pastors even come close to knowing who you are and what you need from Jesus? The proper gatherings are in homes, rented buildings, Etc., and should be a common occurrence on any day or days of the week. No any one man is in charge as Jesus is the head, but all have a part in the worship, prayer, and teaching. Christ should be on our minds and out our mouths every day constantly.

Luke 11:17 But he, knowing their thoughts, said unto them, Every kingdom divided against itself is brought to desolation; and a house divided against a house falleth.

There is no division in the true body of Christ. It can not split and form a new body / church. With over 2000 different Christian church denominations in the world, which one is the true Body of Christ? There is only one true head (Jesus) and there is only one true Body (the truly born again). There are only two kinds of religious bodies in the world :
1- Those owned and run by Satan.
2- Those owned and run by Jesus.
Is Jesus the head of your church or is it some pastor or governing board?

Ephesians 4:3 Endeavouring to keep the unity of the Spirit in the bond of peace. 4 There is one body, and one Spirit, even as ye are called in one hope of your calling;

One body, one mind, one church, one Spirit, one Son, one Father, one God. With no division. All in agreement with Jesus as the head.

Luke 12:8 Also I say unto you, Whosoever shall confess me before men, him shall the Son of man also confess before the angels of God: 9 But he that denieth me before men shall be denied before the angels of God.

When you witness for Jesus He tells all of heaven that you are a good and faithful servant. One way to deny Jesus is to refuse to witness for and about Him. Another way is not to come to Him in spirit and truth. THEN you are an anti-Christ!

1 Corinthians 10:17 For we being many are one bread, and one body: for we are all partakers of that one bread.

We are one in Jesus, no divisions, one truth, one mind, one body, one head, one gospel, one Jesus, one Father, one Spirit, one God. Does this describe your church ? Is your church in agreement with other churches? Are you one with Jesus, or do you play just a little in the world?

1 Corinthians 10:21 Ye cannot drink the cup of the Lord, and the cup of devils: ye cannot be partakers of the Lord's table, and of the table of devils.

You cannot be a sinner and a Christian at the same time. Is this not clear? One sin puts you at the devils table, and repentance brings you back to the table of the Lord God. You CANNOT eat at both tables at the same time. We are here on the earth to learn to stop sinning, and to come to Jesus and the Father by our free will love for them. It is said there will be no sin and no temptation in heaven. No sin is by our choice and no temptation is by God's command. Yes you can sin in heaven, but you won't want to. I do not believe that God takes away our free will when we are saved or when we die and go to heaven. Did not Satan sin in heaven, and was he not kicked out for that sin?

2 Timothy 2:15 Study to shew thyself approved unto God, a workman that needeth not to be ashamed, rightly dividing the word of truth.

Study and learn what the word of God says, and God will smile on you. If you don't the world will ridicule you for your lack of knowledge. How can you answer questions from a sinner or your Christian brothers if you don't know and understand scripture?

2 Timothy 3:12 Yea, and all that will live godly in Christ Jesus shall suffer persecution.

As long as you remain sinless with Christ the world will make you suffer in one way or another, if not outright killing you. This is also called trials and tribulations.

James 4:7 Submit yourselves therefore to God. Resist the devil, and he will flee from you. 8 Draw nigh to God, and he will draw nigh to you. Cleanse your hands, ye sinners; and purify your hearts, ye double minded.

This is very clear! By resisting the devil (temptation) you remain sinless and Satan cannot harm you. God will protect you from all harm. Remember what the conditions are that you must obey. A double minded man does not know even what direction he walks in. You cannot be in Gods kingdom and Satan's kingdom at the same time.

A double minded man will try this. It's called a middle of the roader, a fence sitter, and so on.

1 John 2:5 But whoso keepeth his word, in him verily is the love of God perfected: hereby know we that we are in him.

The 'word' of God commands us to be sinless, there by we are made perfect. We as born again, made by choice sin free, Christians have the sure and certain knowledge that we are saved and going to heaven as long as we remain sin free. Or "IF"(**1 John 2:1**) we sin, we then ask (**1John1:9**) forgiveness and repent, and get on with our walk in the light of Jesus the Christ. This word 'IF' tells us that sin is a choice and not something we 'have to do'.

1 John 3:18 My little children, let us not love in word, neither in tongue; but in deed and in truth.

I guess you could say that "actions speak louder than words".

1 John 5:19 And we know that we are of God, and the whole world lieth in wickedness.

I've been telling you how wicked the world is, here's the verse that tells you this. This is why we are called out of the world, to be a set aside people and not to take part of anything in or of the world. Jesus must be absolutely the first and foremost of all things in your life. This means 'everything' in your life! No excptions!!

The Kingdom of God

Matthew 3:1 In those days came John the Baptist, preaching in the wilderness of Judaea, 2 And saying, Repent ye: for the kingdom of heaven is at hand.

Matthew 4:17 From that time Jesus began to preach, and to say, Repent: for the kingdom of heaven is at hand.

Luke 16:16 The law and the prophets were until John: since that time the kingdom of God is preached, and every man presseth into it.

Matthew 10:6 But go rather to the lost sheep of the house of Israel. 7 And as ye go, preach, saying, The kingdom of heaven is at hand.

Matthew 13:24 Another parable put he forth unto them, saying, The kingdom of heaven is likened unto a man which sowed good seed in his field: 25 But while men slept, his enemy came and sowed tares among the wheat, and went his way. 26 But when the blade was sprung up, and brought forth fruit, then appeared the tares also. 27 So the servants of the householder came and said unto him, Sir, didst not thou sow good seed in thy field? from whence then hath it tares? 28 He said unto them, An enemy hath done this. The servants said unto him, Wilt thou then that we go and gather them up? 29 But he said, Nay; lest while ye gather up the tares, ye root up also the wheat with them. 30 Let both grow together until the harvest: and in the time of harvest I will say to the reapers, Gather ye together first the tares, and bind them in bundles to burn them: but gather the wheat into my barn. 31 Another parable put he forth unto them, saying, The kingdom of heaven is like to a grain of mustard seed, which a man took, and sowed in his field: 32 Which indeed is the least of all seeds: but when it is grown, it is the greatest among herbs, and becometh a tree, so that the birds of the air come and lodge in the branches thereof. 33 Another parable spake he unto them; The kingdom of heaven is like unto leaven, which a woman took, and hid in three measures of meal, till the whole was leavened.

Matthew 13:44 Again, the kingdom of heaven is like unto treasure hid in a field; the which when a man hath found, he hideth, and for joy thereof goeth and selleth all that he hath, and buyeth that field. 45 Again, the kingdom of heaven is like unto a merchant man, seeking goodly pearls: 46 Who, when he had found one pearl of great price, went and sold all that he had, and bought it.

Luke 13:18 Then said he, Unto what is the kingdom of God like? and whereunto shall I resemble it? 19 It is like a grain of mustard seed, which a man took, and cast into his garden; and it grew, and waxed a great tree; and the fowls of the air lodged in the branches of it. 20 And again he said, Where unto shall I liken the kingdom of God? 21 It is like leaven, which a woman took and hid in three measures of meal, till the whole was leavened.

John 12: 24 Verily, verily, I say unto you, Except a corn of wheat fall into the ground and die, it abideth alone: but if it die, it bringeth forth much fruit.

John 18: 36 Jesus answered, My kingdom is not of this world: if my kingdom were of this world, then would my servants fight, that I should not be delivered to the Jews: but now is my kingdom not from hence.

The kingdom came into being at the death on the cross and the resurrection of Jesus, it is a spiritual kingdom that is now and forevermore. Are you in it? The kingdom of God started growing like a seed planted, and will continue to grow until the second coming of Jesus. The planted seed is Jesus and the Holy Spirit waters (the word) it by guiding us, the saved of Christ, into all truth(the expanding kingdom).The leaven that spreads through the whole lump of dough is representative of the body of Christ spreading through the whole world thereby expanding the Kingdom as leaven expands the dough.

Matthew 13:47 Again, the kingdom of heaven is like unto a net, that was cast into the sea, and gathered of every kind: 48 Which, when it was full, they drew to shore, and sat down, and gathered the good into vessels, but cast the bad away. 49 So shall it be at the end of the world: the angels shall come forth, and sever the wicked from among the just,50 And shall cast them into the furnace of fire: there shall be wailing and gnashing of teeth.

Here is the reward of those who are in and those who are not in the kingdom of heaven. This is the reward that you have chosen, by your free will to remain a sinner or a saint. We have two choices in our lives: to stop sinning and enter the Kingdom, or remain in the sinful world as a sinner and ride the train to hell. Notice that the sinners are taken out and burned first.

Matthew 16:28 Verily I say unto you, There be some standing here, which shall not taste of death, till they see the Son of man coming in his kingdom.

Luke 9:27 But I tell you of a truth, there be some standing here, which shall not taste of death, till they see the kingdom of God.

The Kingdom started at the resurrection so all who were alive at that time saw the Kingdom of Heaven. It is a "spiritual Kingdom" NOT a physical kingdom here on the earth for a thousand years. The thousand year millennium is an unnumbered amount of years from the cross to the second coming of Jesus. The word in the Greek for millennium is a plurality, it means thousands.

Matthew 19:14 But Jesus said, Suffer little children, and forbid them not, to come unto me: for of such is the kingdom of heaven.

Mark 10:15 Verily I say unto you, Whosoever shall not receive the kingdom of God as a little child, he shall not enter therein.

Luke 18:17 Verily I say unto you, Whosoever shall not receive the kingdom of God as a little child shall in no wise enter therein.

Ephesians 5:1 Be ye therefore followers of God, as dear children;2 And walk in love, as Christ also hath loved us, and hath given himself for us an offering and a sacrifice to God for a sweet smelling savour.

You must have the faith and the innocence of little children to get into the kingdom of heaven. Our innocence comes from repenting and asking forgiveness. The innocence of children comes from being born that way. Born sinful is a lie of Satan to keep you in bondage. The faith for your salvation is in your nature, that is given by God. As baby baptism is not in the bible, the only way a baby can go to heaven is for it to be sinless (Or you can say innocent).

Matthew 19:23 Then said Jesus unto his disciples, Verily I say unto you, That a rich man shall hardly enter into the kingdom of heaven.

Mark 10:23 And Jesus looked round about, and saith unto his disciples, How hardly shall they that have riches enter into the kingdom of God! 24 And the disciples were astonished at his words. But Jesus answereth again, and saith unto them, Children, how hard is it for them that trust in riches to enter into the kingdom of God!

Luke 18:22 Now when Jesus heard these things, he said unto him, Yet lackest thou one thing: sell all that thou hast, and distribute unto the poor, and thou shalt have treasure in heaven: and come, follow me.

To get into the Kingdom of Heaven you must put Jesus FIRST in your life, all else must be secondary. This is the treasure you receive along with fellowshipping with God the Father for eternity.

Matthew 26:29 But I say unto you, I will not drink henceforth of this fruit of the vine, until that day when I drink it new with you in my Father's kingdom.

Mark 14:25 Verily I say unto you, I will drink no more of the fruit of the vine, until that day that I drink it new in the kingdom of God.

Luke 22:18 For I say unto you, I will not drink of the fruit of the vine, until the kingdom of God shall come.

Luke 24:41 And while they yet believed not for joy, and wondered, he said unto them, Have ye here any meat? 42 And they gave him a piece of a broiled fish, and of an honeycomb. 43 And he took it, and did eat before them.

John 21:12 Jesus saith unto them, Come and dine. And none of the disciples durst ask him, Who art thou? knowing that it was the Lord. 13 Jesus then cometh, and taketh bread, and giveth them, and fish likewise.

Acts 10:40-41 Him God raised up the third day, and shewed him openly; Not to all the people, but unto witnesses chosen before of God, *even* to us, who did eat and drink with him after he rose from the dead.

Jesus did eat and drink after His resurrection, before He rose to heaven to rule and reign. This is proved by the verses shown above. The kingdom is now and forever a spiritual kingdom and not a physical kingdom to come with Jesus ruling on a throne in the rebuilt temple in Jerusalem for a thousand years.

Luke 17:20 And when he was demanded of the Pharisees, when the kingdom of God should come, he answered them and said, The kingdom of God cometh not with observation: 21 Neither shall they say, Lo here! or, lo there! for, behold, the kingdom of God is within you.

The kingdom of God is not now nor will it be, as in some men's concept, a future physical kingdom on the earth. You cannot see it. It is a spiritual kingdom that started at the resurrection of Jesus and is forevermore. The only way to enter into it is to repentant and stay sin free.

Mark 1:14 Now after that John was put in prison, Jesus came into Galilee, preaching the gospel of the kingdom of God, 15 And saying, The time is fulfilled, and the kingdom of God is at hand: repent ye, and believe the gospel.

The kingdom of heaven is for all those who come to God through Jesus. This is why Jesus started teaching that the Kingdom was "at hand". It did not come into being until the resurrection.

Mark 4:26 And he said, So is the kingdom of God, as if a man should cast seed into the ground;
The seed grows into a ripe plant that has numerous seeds, and each of those seeds produce many more seeds. This is how the body of Christ grows. Jesus was the seed of the spiritual kingdom of God. His death, three days in the grave, and resurrection was the planted seed which has grown into the body of Jesus.

Mark 16:15 And he said unto them, Go ye into all the world, and preach the gospel to every creature.16 He that believeth and is baptized shall be saved; but he that believeth not shall be damned.17 And these signs shall follow them that believe; In my name shall they cast out devils; they shall speak with new tongues;18 They shall take up serpents; and if they drink any deadly thing, it shall not hurt them; they shall lay hands on the sick, and they shall recover.

These are the marching orders given to the body of Christ. Do you march to them?

John 7:38 He that believeth on me, as the scripture hath said, out of his belly shall flow rivers of living water.

This is witnessing the gospel of Jesus (the word) to the world of sinners by believers. Contrary to what most people would have you believe, Christianity is not a "private religion". Those who don't talk about Jesus are the same as the Pharisees who rejected Jesus by putting Him on the cross. Are you a believer or a Pharisees? Have you put Jesus on the cross to get rid of Him? Are you ashamed of your life or just of Him? Surprise, He will not go away no matter how much try to hide!

John 3:5 Jesus answered, Verily, verily, I say unto thee, Except a man be born of water and of the Spirit, he cannot enter into the kingdom of God.

John 3:6 That which is born of the flesh is flesh; and that which is born of the Spirit is spirit.

The water represents the word of God, and the Spirit represents the Holy Spirit by which your spirit is renewed (born again) to God the Father. All this is by Jesus' shed blood and your free will choice to be born again. Again, how could this be a natural physical kingdom?

John 5:24 Verily, verily, I say unto you, He that heareth my word, and believeth on him that sent me, hath everlasting life, and shall not come into condemnation; but is passed from death unto life.

This is the how to get in, and have the reward of being in the kingdom of heaven, in fellowship with God the Father and Jesus. It is the only way to have fellowship with the Father and Jesus. Again there is NO other way to heaven. You have passed from the dead works of your sin to the revival of your spirit and into life with the Father and Jesus.

John 6:27 Labour not for the meat which perisheth, but for that meat which endureth unto everlasting life, which the Son of man shall give unto you: for him hath God the Father sealed.

Meat that rots is the false teachings of the world that will be done away with at the end of the age. The meat that is pure with no rot is the word of God, and by this word we walk. Know and understand that we must walk sin free by the commandments of God. Here is a call to all men to enter into the kingdom of heaven. Give up the works of the world and work for God!

John 6:28 Then said they unto him, What shall we do, that we might work the works of God? 29 Jesus answered and said unto them, This is the work of God, that ye believe on him whom he hath sent.

This is the first work we must do. BELIEVE IN JESUS!!!! To believe in and to be saved by Jesus means that either we MUST obey all of His commandments, or out you go! Do it Gods way or don't bother. Gods way is simple, stay sin free. It's in the bible, read it!

John 6:47 Verily, verily, I say unto you, He that believeth on me hath everlasting life.

This would be life in the spiritual kingdom of God. It is not some reworked earth with Jesus sitting on an earthly throne taking animal sacrifices for the forgiveness of sin. This is a lie of Satan being taught in man's church today. This teaching is a slap in the face of Jesus. We must check out all that is told to us by the word of God.

John 14:6 Jesus saith unto him, I am the way, the truth, and the life: no man cometh unto the Father, but by me.

You can not get into the kingdom of heaven any other way or by any other road! No other religion can or does offer this choice to the world. No other religion offers any form of salvation by the removal of sins from you conscience. Jesus is the ONLY key to the door of heaven. Only Jesus is the way of and to light. There is NO OTHER WAY!

John 17:1 These words spake Jesus, and lifted up his eyes to heaven, and said, Father, the hour is come; glorify thy Son, that thy Son also may glorify thee: 2 As thou hast given him power over all flesh, that he should give eternal life to as many as thou hast given him.3 And this is life eternal, that they might know thee the only true God, and Jesus Christ, whom thou hast sent.

The Father gives citizenship in His Kingdom to all who come, of their free will, to Jesus. This is your entry point to eternal life in the Kingdom of heaven. Again there is ONLY one true God(the Father, the Son, an the Holy Spirit). All, and I mean <u>ALL</u>, others are false!

Romans 13:8 Owe no man any thing, but to love one another: for he that loveth another hath fulfilled the law.

To owe someone is to have hard feelings toward them, especially if you can not pay. To operate in love is to walk sinless with Jesus in the Kingdom of God. If you are in sin do you not owe God the Father a repentant attitude and broken contrite heart?

1 Corinthians 6:9 Know ye not that the unrighteous shall not inherit the kingdom of God? Be not deceived: neither fornicators, nor idolaters, nor adulterers, nor effeminate, nor abusers of themselves with mankind,10 Nor thieves, nor covetous, nor drunkards, nor revilers, nor extortioners, shall inherit the kingdom of God. 11 And such were some of you: but ye are washed, but ye are sanctified, but ye are justified in the name of the Lord Jesus, and by the Spirit of our God.

Are you guilty of any of these sins? I hope not if you want to spend eternity with Jesus in the kingdom of God. God's mercy will allow you to repent as many times as is necessary to get you to stop sinning and remain Holy. (**1JH 1: 9**)

1 Corinthians 6:10 Nor thieves, nor covetous, nor drunkards, nor revilers, nor extortioners, shall inherit the kingdom of God.

Ah! Sinners don't get into the Kingdom! What makes you a sinner in your mind ? Is it one, two, or more sins? Well we have to go by what the Word says and not what you think or what some man's church has taught you. The bible says if you sin you're a sinner. To put it bluntly ONE sin makes you a sinner and gets you thrown OUT of the kingdom. I'll tell you again how it works. First you are not born in sin(**John 9:1-2**) or with a fallen nature that makes you sin. It is always a choice to sin (**James 4:17**) . We have free will don't we? You become a sinner when you make the choice for that first sin after you become a moral person (which is: coming to the understanding of the ramifications of doing a right or wrong thing). At that point you become a sinner and you need Jesus. After you repent and ask forgiveness of Jesus, you are then no longer a sinner as Jesus' 'Holy and Pure Blood removes your sin from your conscience **(Hebrews 9:14)**. After this there is NO sin in you. You are now "made by choice" a sin free Christian. "If" you sin again (**1John2:1**) you are now a sinner, but God's mercy(**1John 1:9**) allows you to ask forgiveness and repent as many time as you need to get to the point of not sinning any more.

1 Corinthians 15:50 Now this I say, brethren, that flesh and blood cannot inherit the kingdom of God; neither doth corruption inherit incorruption.

See I told you the Kingdom of God is Spiritual! If flesh and blood can't inherit it then the only other thing to inherit it is your spirit. You can not get into the Kingdom of God in sin because it is only for Gods' holy and spiritually pure children.

This is the same for the false concept of inheriting sin. You can't. Your spirit, which is given from God, is not made and given in corruption and sin. Do you really think God would give you a defective spirit? Again the kingdom is only for the spiritually pure, which is what babies are until they come of age and start being held responsible for their sin, then they need Jesus to get back to being spiritually pure.

Again this is a free will choice we must make; one way or the other. It can be nothing but a CHOICE, and again only we can make it. No one can do it for us, such as having our babies baptized. How can a baby make a moral choice for Jesus?

Ephesians 5:5 For this ye know, that no whore monger, nor unclean person, nor covetous man, who is an idolater, hath any inheritance in the kingdom of Christ and of God.

Sinners don't get in, it does not matter if you were once saved. If you fall back into sin you've lost it all and are on the way to hell. Your only chance is to repent. Just because your sin is not listed in this verse doesn't mean this verse does not apply to you in your sins.

Revelation 3:7 And to the angel of the church in Philadelphia write; These things saith he that is holy, he that is true, he that hath the key of David, he that openeth, and no man shutteth; and shutteth, and no man openeth; 8 I know thy works: behold, I have set before thee an open door, and no man can shut it: for thou hast a little strength, and hast kept my word, and hast not denied my name.

Jesus has, by His work on the earth, opened the door to the kingdom of Heaven for all who would come to Him in repentance. No one, not even Satan, can keep you from going through that door to eternal life with the Father. You are the only one who can make the choice to go through it either way, in or out, saved or sinner. Which are you?

The Call to Holiness

Leviticus 19:2 Speak unto all the congregation of the children of Israel, and say unto them, Ye shall be holy: for I the LORD your God am holy.

Matthew 5:48 Be ye therefore perfect, even as your Father which is in heaven is perfect.

Be sinless, holy, and perfect! Is this not a simple command from God? Do you believe God or do you believe some man who says you can never be holy while on this earth? Where else are you going to get holy? Do you think you can go to heaven without being holy? Do you believe that you can make yourself good enough to go to heaven? It is only through Jesus and His work on the cross, and resurrection from the grave that we have any chance at all, and it's a slim chance at that. Did not Jesus ask if He would find any true faith when he comes back for the second time?

So when do you think your going to get holiness? When you get to heaven? Your only chance to go to heaven and be with the Father is to become holy first. You can only do this by going through Jesus' shed holy blood to have your sins removed from you, and stop sinning as Jesus commands. That's it, no other way, no other plan.

You know time is short either to death or the second coming, so get saved now. Why take a chance on hell???????

Matthew 10:38 And he that taketh not his cross, and followeth after me, is not worthy of me.

Luke 14:27 And whosoever doth not bear his cross, and come after me, cannot be my disciple.

To pick up your cross is to walk as Jesus walked, sinless and holy. Not dragging around a couple pieces of wood nailed together. It's a spiritual command not a physical one.

John 8:12 Then spake Jesus again unto them, saying, I am the light of the world: he that followeth me shall not walk in darkness, but shall have the light of life.

Walk in the light (Jesus) with no darkness(sin) in you. Jesus is also called the word (**John 1:1**), so as you walk in the light of Jesus you walk in obedience to His word. Can you see this? Do you not think that this means that as long as you walk hand in hand in the light and commands of & with Jesus that you are sin free?

Matthew 12:30 He that is not with me is against me; and he that gathereth not with me scattereth abroad.

To be with Jesus is to be sinless. If you're not for Jesus you are against Him. If you sin, you love your sin more than you love Jesus and there by are against Him. Simple EH! If you are in sin you will be scattered away from the Kingdom of God.

Matthew 13:12 For whosoever hath, to him shall be given, and he shall have more abundance: but whosoever hath not, from him shall be taken away even that he hath.

Luke 19:26 For I say unto you, That unto every one which hath shall be given; and from him that hath not, even that he hath shall be taken away from him.

To have is to be sinless in Christ. To have not is to be in sin and even lose your chance of salvation at death or the second coming.

Matthew 15:13 But he answered and said, Every plant, which my heavenly Father hath not planted, shall be rooted up.

You must be in the Kingdom of heaven to not be rooted up. To be rooted up is to be thrown into hell. This is by your choice, not to come to repentance, by remaining in sin. The plants that are planted by God the Father are in the ground and growing because of their free will choice to do all things as God commands. The good plants are wheat, the bad plants are tares (sinners).

Matthew 16:24 Then said Jesus unto his disciples, If any man will come after me, let him deny himself, and take up his cross, and follow me.

Picking up your cross means to come out of the world and live to and for Christ, holy and sinless. You can not be made to do this. It is your free will choice. In fact Jesus says to "count the cost" of giving up the world and walking sinless. It is a life and kingdom changing decision that we all on this earth must make.

Matthew 19:21 Jesus said unto him, If thou wilt be perfect, go and sell that thou hast, and give to the poor, and thou shalt have treasure in heaven: and come and follow me.

Mark 10:20 And he answered and said unto him, Master, all these have I observed from my youth. 21 Then Jesus beholding him loved him, and said unto him, One thing thou lackest: go thy way, sell whatsoever thou hast, and give to the poor, and thou shalt have treasure in heaven: and come, take up the cross, and follow me.

Holiness and perfection comes from being sinless, or you can say putting Jesus first in your life. This means giving up all that is in the world, obeying the commandments of God, and walking hand in hand with Jesus.

Mark 9:50 Salt is good: but if the salt have lost his saltness, wherewith will ye season it? Have salt in yourselves, and have peace one with another.

A lack of salt is sin in your life. Salt is used to preserve food, so does the lack of salt preserve your life and your walk with Jesus? How can this be more clear? Can you say: "I'm salty".

Luke 11:35 Take heed therefore that the light which is in thee be not darkness. 36 If thy whole body therefore be full of light, having no part dark, the whole shall be full of light, as when the bright shining of a candle doth give thee light.

Be 100% full of light, which means be sinless and holy before God. You can not be a fence sitter. You are either in or out, in sin or without sin. Which are you, in the light of Jesus or the darkness of the world?

John 1:23 He said, I am the voice of one crying in the wilderness, Make straight the way of the Lord, as said the prophet Esaias.

"Make the way straight" is a call to holiness. You can not fellowship with Jesus unless you have made yourself straight by going through the cross and becoming sinless.

John 2:21 But he spake of the temple of his body.

We are the temple of God, the born again of Christ, and have the Holy Spirit residing within us. There are no more worldly buildings that God the Father will reside in. He ripped the veil of the holy of holies top to bottom, thereby showing that He, God, would not reside in a building ever again. He also sent the Roman army to destroy Jerusalem and the temple in 70 A.D. so there could be no doubt about what God meant by ripping the veil in half.
See **Daniel 9:26**.

John 5:14 Afterward Jesus findeth him in the temple, and said unto him, Behold, thou art made whole: sin no more, lest a worse thing come unto thee.

This is the first person Jesus tells to stop sinning, and this is before He went to the cross. Have you stopped yet? Question: Why would Jesus command us to do something we were not able to do? Now you must understand that Jesus is no respecter of persons and that He remains the same forever. So that command is for all people of all time .

1 Corinthians 8:12 But when ye sin so against the brethren, and wound their weak conscience, ye sin against Christ.

To sin against a brother is to sin against Christ, as any sin is, which means you have lost your holiness. Now you have to ask forgiveness from your brother and from the Father through Jesus.
John 8:10 When Jesus had lifted up himself, and saw none but the woman, he said unto her, Woman, where are those thine accusers? hath no man condemned thee? 11 She said, No man, Lord. And Jesus said unto her, Neither do I condemn thee: go, and sin no more.

This is the second person that Jesus told to stop sinning before He went to the cross. Do you really think that Jesus would order us to stop sinning if it were not possible? This is a command! It is for all Christians! Do you think Jesus was just kidding? Have you stopped yet?

John 8:21 Then said Jesus again unto them, I go my way, and ye shall seek me, and shall die in your sins: whither I go, ye cannot come.

If you die in your sins you go to hell. This is the result of not following the commandments of Jesus to stop sinning and be holy as He is holy. Seeking (seeking while in sin and not repenting and asking forgiveness is a waste of time you can not find Jesus in this manner) and repenting are two different things. Only by repenting can you follow Jesus to heaven. If you don't repent and ask forgiveness you cannot follow Jesus.

John 8:34 Jesus answered them, Verily, verily, I say unto you, Whosoever committeth sin is the servant of sin.

When we become born again and sin free our master is Jesus. If you sin again you have changed masters from Jesus to Satan, and put yourself back onto the road to hell. This is a free will choice you make. No one makes you sin, or stop sinning. To get back your holiness (sinless) you must repent and ask forgiveness of your sins of the Father in Jesus name in spirit and truth. Then you will be on the straight and narrow road to Jesus and the Father.

John 12:35 Then Jesus said unto them, Yet a little while is the light with you. Walk while ye have the light, lest darkness come upon you: for he that walketh in darkness knoweth not whither he goeth.

John 12:46 I am come a light into the world, that whosoever believeth on me should not abide in darkness.

This is another command to walk sinless and in the light of Jesus. The result of walking in darkness, with sin, is that you have no direction in your life. You will just stumble around in the darkness, getting nowhere except to hell.

John 14:15 If ye love me, keep my commandments.John 14:21 He that hath my commandments, and keepeth them, he it is that loveth me: and he that loveth me shall be loved of my Father, and I will love him, and will manifest myself to him.

How can this be more clear ? One of the most important commandments is that you stop sinning and be holy as He is holy. The opposite is true, if you are in sin you are not holy and you are not saved. If you DON'T keep His commandments you then hate Jesus and love your sin. Is not one of His commandments "Go forth and sin no more lest a worse thing happen to you"?

John 14:23 Jesus answered and said unto him, If a man love me, he will keep my words: and my Father will love him, and we will come unto him, and make our abode with him.

"Keep my words" is the same as keep my commandments! Again the opposite is true! If you disobey the commands of God, the Father and Jesus will no longer make their abode with you, and you will be separated from God by your choice. You will not be able to come back to God until you repent with a broken heart.

It's kinda hard to get your mind around the fact that if you <u>don't love</u> Jesus and stop sinning then you <u>hate Him</u> in your sinfulness. Or you might say that you love your sin more than you love Jesus.

John 15:11 These things have I spoken unto you, that my joy might remain in you, and that your joy might be full.

The only true Joy is being in Jesus and this is only accomplished by being sinless. You will have no joy in your heart without Jesus in your life. Oh you will have some happiness but it is not the same as true JOY from God.

John 15:6 If a man abide not in me, he is cast forth as a branch, and is withered; and men gather them, and cast them into the fire, and they are burned.

This is the result of sinfulness! HELL! The only way to abide in Christ is to be sinless.

John 15:9 As the Father hath loved me, so have I loved you: continue ye in my love.

A command to remain sinless and Holy. How can you love something when you drive it away by sin? Don't misunderstand, it is you who will drive Jesus and the Father away from you by your sin. God does not leave by you His choice, He leaves by your choice to fall back into, just even one, sin.

John 15:12 This is my commandment, That ye love one another, as I have loved you. 13 Greater love hath no man than this, that a man lay down his life for his friends. 14 Ye are my friends, if ye do whatsoever I command you.

John 15:17 These things I command you, that ye love one another.

You are the friend of Jesus if you obey Him by living your life in His kind of love. The definition of God's kind of love or Charity is: **1 Corinthians 13:4 Charity suffereth long, and is kind; charity envieth not; charity vaunteth not itself, is not puffed up,5 Doth not behave itself unseemly, seeketh not her own, is not easily provoked, thinketh no evil; 6 Rejoiceth not in iniquity, but rejoiceth in the truth; 7 Beareth all things, believeth all things, hopeth all things, endureth all things. 8 Charity never faileth:........**
Do you not think that it is very important to show your love for Christ by not sinning? Is this also loving your neighbor as you love yourself? If it was not so important why would Jesus say it so many times? Do you think that being in un-repented sinfulness is acting in love?

Romans 6:2 God forbid. How shall we, that are dead to sin, live any longer therein? 3 Know ye not, that so many of us as were baptized into Jesus Christ were baptized into his death? 4 Therefore we are buried with him by baptism into death: that like as Christ was raised up from the dead by the glory of the Father, even so we also should walk in newness of life.

5 For if we have been planted together in the likeness of his death, we shall be also in the likeness of his resurrection: 6 Knowing this, that our old man is crucified with him, that the body of sin might be destroyed, that henceforth we should not serve sin.

When we are reborn into the Spirit of God, by repentance with a heart broken for Jesus, our sin is removed from our conscience. We are then a new creature and all things are made new. Our spirit is reborn into fellowship with the Father God. We are now made, by our choice, dead to sin and reborn to holiness. This is what it means to be baptized into the death of Christ and to be raised up a new man in Christ as Christ was raised up to everlasting life. The command here is to remain sinless by NOT serving sin, or by not letting sin be your master.

Romans 6:12 Let not sin therefore reign in your mortal body, that ye should obey it in the lusts thereof. 13 Neither yield ye your members as instruments of unrighteousness unto sin: but yield yourselves unto God, as those that are alive from the dead, and your members as instruments of righteousness unto God. 14 For sin shall not have dominion over you: for ye are not under the law, but under grace.

Don't sin ! Stop sinning! Resist sinfulness! Be Holy! How many ways can you say it? Nobody makes you sin, not even the habitual sin you have learned from birth. It is a free will choice that you make every time you are tempted. To sin or not to sin that is the question! If you sin you will lose the Grace that God has given you and the only way to get it back is to repent. You died to sin by going through the cross and were made alive in Jesus. The law has no power over you as long as you stay sinless under God's grace: grace from the Greek means "Gods continuing influence in your life and the resulting reflection of that grace in your life".

Romans 6:22 But now being made free from sin, and become servants to God, ye have your fruit unto holiness, and the end everlasting life. 23 For the wages of sin is death; but the gift of God is eternal life through Jesus Christ our Lord.

Being made sin free, by your choice, you become HOLY. If you return to sin you will have to start all over again if you don't want to got to HELL! This gift of being sin free is "only" from Jesus. It is your choice to accept it. You must understand and accept Jesus' work on the cross, or Jesus does not accept you. There is no work you can do to make payment for your sins!! Jesus made final and complete payment for you and everyone else in the world past present and future.

Romans 8:13 For if ye live after the flesh, ye shall die: but if ye through the Spirit do mortify the deeds of the body, ye shall live. 14 For as many as are led by the Spirit of God, they are the sons of God.

To live after the flesh is to remain in sin. Your spirit is killed by your sin. The only way to bring your spirit back to life is to die to sin and live for Christ. To be led by the Holy Spirit you must be born again, remain sinless, and be baptized in the Holy Spirit. 1-2-3 what could be simpler?

Romans 12:1 I beseech you therefore, brethren, by the mercies of God, that ye present your bodies a living sacrifice, holy, acceptable unto God, which is your reasonable service. **2** And be not conformed to this world: but be ye transformed by the renewing of your mind, that ye may prove what is that good, and acceptable, and perfect, will of God.

Do you think that being sinless is not possible? God calls it a reasonable service. How hard can it be? Or do you think that God just throws out commands for the "hell of it" to see what you'll do? This is no joke, be sinless, be holy, be separated from the sinful world, be of Jesus or burn in Hell.

Romans 12:10 Be kindly affectioned one to another with brotherly love; in honour preferring one another;**11** Not slothful in business; fervent in spirit; serving the Lord; **12** Rejoicing in hope; patient in tribulation; continuing instant in prayer; **13** Distributing to the necessity of saints; given to hospitality. **14** Bless them which persecute you: bless, and curse not.

This is being holy in all that you do and all that you are so you don't live in and of the world. Love your neighbor, give of your substance, do no one any harm, in other words be an honest, hard working, morally correct, child of God.

Romans 12:21 Be not overcome of evil, but overcome evil with good.

Do not fall back into sin, witness Christ, be an example to all of what a Christian should be, and bring sinners out of their sins by witnessing the good news of the Gospel to the repentance of sin to the Father in heaven by Jesus' shed blood. This is what over coming evil with good is and how to do it.

Romans 13:9 For this, Thou shalt not commit adultery, Thou shalt not kill, Thou shalt not steal, Thou shalt not bear false witness, Thou shalt not covet; and if there be any other commandment, it is briefly comprehended in this saying, namely, Thou shalt love thy neighbour as thyself. **10** Love worketh no ill to his neighbour: therefore love is the fulfilling of the law.

The commands of God ! Walk in the love of God! Walk in Holiness! Be without sin! What else is there to say? Obey!!

Romans 13:14 But put ye on the Lord Jesus Christ, and make not provision for the flesh, to fulfil the lusts thereof.

To "put on Jesus" is the same as "pick up your cross daily". It is to walk sinless, to be perfect, to be holy, to walk as Jesus walked. If you don't you are disobeying the commands of Jesus and are destined for hell as a sinner. Believe me this verse is a command to holiness.

1 Corinthians 6:18 Flee fornication. Every sin that a man doeth is without the body; but he that committeth fornication sinneth against his own body. **19** What? know ye not that your body is the temple of the Holy Ghost which is in you, which

ye have of God, and ye are not your own? 20 For ye are bought with a price: therefore glorify God in your body, and in your spirit, which are God's.

The command is to flee from sin, don't sin, stop sinning. This is telling you that fornication is a special class of sin that is especially bad. This is any form of sexual sin out of the normal husband and wife sexual union and is deviant. Jesus paid a horrible price for our salvation, so don't DISRESPECT Him or your own body by sinning. We are the Holy temple of God. Would you drive God out of His temple by sin? Think about it!

1 Corinthians 10:13 There hath no temptation taken you but such as is common to man: but God is faithful, who will not suffer you to be tempted above that ye are able; but will with the temptation also make a way to escape, that ye may be able to bear it.

You now have no excuse to sin. If you love Jesus you will stop. There is NO sin that you can not resist. God Himself does not allow you to be tempted beyond what you can resist.
<u>There are two ways to resist sin:</u>

1- With the help of Jesus, the power of the Holy Spirit in your lives, and the limitations that God the Father puts on any temptation that comes your way.
2- Your own will. It's called freedom of CHOICE. You make this choice every time you are tempted to sin.
So there you have it "You don't have to sin". You sin because you like it, you love your sin more than you love Jesus or you would stop. You could say you love your sin and HATE Jesus.

1 Corinthians 10:21 Ye cannot drink the cup of the Lord, and the cup of devils: ye cannot be partakers of the Lord's table, and of the table of devils.

Here it says that you can not be Holy and a sinner at the same time. It alludes to the fact that one sin separates you from Jesus, the Father, and the Holy Spirit. As you are the holy temple of God, do you really think that God will share you with the devil by staying with you when you sin? To say it again: God can not abide sin and will leave you until you ask forgiveness and repent.

1 Corinthians 14:20 Brethren, be not children in understanding: howbeit in malice be ye children, but in understanding be men.

To understand the gospel as a mature Christians you will hold no anger or malice such as a immature child would. Distilling this down means that you must be holy with understanding.

1 Corinthians 15:56 The sting of death is sin; and the strength of sin is the law.

Sin is spiritual death and ultimately physical death. The law tells us what is sin and the law is written on all men's hearts. The law will judge you for good or evil, obeying or disobeying, breaking or keeping . There is no excuse for sinning. You, as a moral person, know right from wrong, good from bad. We must continue doing good and rejecting the bad if we are to stay in the kingdom of God.

1 Corinthians 15:57 But thanks be to God, which giveth us the victory through our Lord Jesus Christ.

This is Gods' answer to the world that is full of sinfulness. This is our way out! The way to get rid of sin, to stop sinning, to be holy, to be pure, to be without spot or wrinkle, to live forever in glory with Jesus. BELIEVE and come to Jesus in truth and spirit. Claim the victory! Do it now!

1 Corinthians 16:22 If any man love not the Lord Jesus Christ, let him be Anathema*Maranatha**

If you don't love Jesus you have cursed yourself. Jesus said in John 14:15 "If ye love me, keep my commandments". *You are cursed if you sin. **Think about it!!!

2 Corinthians 6:1 We then, as workers together with him, beseech you also that ye receive not the grace of God in vain.

In vain means that God's grace is without effect in your life (by choice). What a waste for it to have been given to you. If you ignore your God's given grace you will fall back into sinfulness. God's continuing grace in your life is the power that you need to help you stay sinless. Use it, pay attention to it, stay holy.

2 Corinthians 6:14 Be ye not unequally yoked together with unbelievers: for what fellowship hath righteousness with unrighteousness? and what communion hath light with darkness? 15 And what concord hath Christ with Belial? or what part hath he that believeth with an infidel? 16 And what agreement hath the temple of God with idols? for ye are the temple of the living God; as God hath said, I will dwell in them, and walk in them; and I will be their God, and they shall be my people.

We, the called out holy people of the Body of Christ, have no business hanging around with worldly people (sinners). We are light and they are darkness. WHERE DO YOU HANG AROUND? Do you use the excuse of "I'm just witnessing"? Witnessing is not hanging around with sinners. Are you partaking of their sins, showing that you are as worldly as they are. Witnessing is telling them about Jesus and what He did for them and showing them a holy life by example. This statement by Paul also includes all who say they are of the Body, but have doctrines of demon's that are not in and of the bible, they deny parts of the bible as not for today, or that it was only for the Apostles. Do not be unequally yoked with them .

2 Corinthians 6:17 Wherefore come out from among them, and be ye separate, saith the Lord, and touch not the unclean thing; and I will receive you, 18 And will be a Father unto you, and ye shall be my sons and daughters, saith the Lord Almighty.

Again we who are sinless and in the Body of Christ are called out, separated from worldly people (sinners). "Touch not the unclean thing" literally means do not touch or fall into the sins of the world. We are the holy temple of God. What do we have to do with the world and sinners? We are God's family, holy and pure, living with Jesus and the Father in His Kingdom, not living for worldly pleasures. What do you think Gods means "I will be a Father to you", and what are the conditions for this father hood? Will He still be your Father if you touch the things of the sinful world?

2 Corinthians 7:1 Having therefore these promises, dearly beloved, let us cleanse ourselves from all filthiness of the flesh and spirit, perfecting holiness in the fear of God.

A call to be holy and pure by remaining sinless, and choosing to stay that way. How can the modern man's church say we are still sinners after being cleansed of sin by the blood of Jesus? Does your church teach that Jesus' blood only "covers" sin? This is a lie of Satan. This allows you to continue in sin and feel good about yourself, instead of having a broken, contrite, sinless heart for Jesus. By the way check out **Heb. chapter 9:14** about Jesus' blood and how it removes the guilt of your sin from your conscience.

2 Corinthians 10:5 Casting down imaginations, and every high thing that exalteth itself against the knowledge of God, and bringing into captivity every thought to the obedience of Christ;

This is one of the tools God has given to us to use. It helps you to remain sinless. Just having a thought (temptation) that is worldly does not mean it is a sin. As long as you capture (in Jesus' name) that and any other tempting thoughts and reject them in Jesus' name. This will allow you to stay sinless and in obedience to Christ. This means that you do not act on this thought or dwell on it, you MUST reject it in Jesus name. The "new age" worldly people use the word "imagine" as a mantra to get you into their world of sin. It is true that this is a very powerful word and it works. They say if you can imagine something you can do it. This is used by Satan to get you to believe the lie that "you can be as God yourself". If you can be as God then why do you need Jesus. Their way of teaching and way of thinking is a lie of the greatest magnitude.

2 Corinthians 13:9 For we are glad, when we are weak, and ye are strong: and this also we wish, even your perfection.

Paul tells the Corinthian Church that they must be perfect which means holy, pure, without sin. Do you think that this is for all who are in the body of Christ or just for those who Paul sent this letter to?

Galatians 5:1 Stand fast therefore in the liberty wherewith Christ hath made us free, and be not entangled again with the yoke of bondage.

Being in liberty with Jesus is the same as being sinless as Jesus was. Jesus has given us the way to get out of sin by making us free of the guilt of sin in our conscience. The command here also is: don't fall back into sin. "The yoke of bondage" is sin.

Galatians 5:9 A little leaven leaveneth the whole lump.

Be careful one sin will ruin your day, it will keep you out of heaven. To remain holy, pure, and walking with Jesus and the Father you must not sin. To remain in the kingdom of God you must remain sinless. It's not three strikes and your out, but only one.

Galatians 5:24 And they that are Christ's have crucified the flesh with the affections and lusts.25 If we live in the Spirit, let us also walk in the Spirit.26 Let us not be desirous of vain glory, provoking one another, envying one another.

This is how we as members of the body of Christ have to live or it's out of the kingdom and into the big bad world. Holiness is being sin free and thereby free of sin. By following the guidance of the Holy Spirit who convinces us of sin in our lives, and by this convincing we then convict ourselves. If we're smart we will then repent. One of the ways that we do this is to love (with God's kind of love) our neighbors and brothers. Not the ushee–gushee kind of hugee–kissee kind of love that you see in the main line churchs of man today.

Galatians 6:1 Brethren, if a man be overtaken in a fault, ye which are spiritual, restore such an one in the spirit of meekness; considering thyself, lest thou also be tempted.

Help restore a brother to Christ in the love of Christ with the understanding that you too may be tempted to sin by his sinfulness. Do not fall to this temptation! Stay <u>HOLY</u>. Help your brother by reminding him/her that Jesus still loves them and expects them to show their love for Him by repenting and asking forgiveness, and from then on walking in <u>holiness</u> by remaining sinless.

Galatians 6:7 Be not deceived; God is not mocked: for whatsoever a man soweth, that shall he also reap. 8 For he that soweth to his flesh shall of the flesh reap corruption; but he that soweth to the Spirit shall of the Spirit reap life everlasting.

So be holy! Don't "soweth" to your carnal desires (get back into sin). By sowing to your carnal (learned) nature you are opening yourself up to more and more sin of the world, and the more you sin the harder your heart becomes toward Jesus and repentance. I've been guilty of this, and it is really hard to come back. You need to make a concerted effort to win back your life with Christ. By staying holy you will have overcome the world and all it's sinful pleasures, and you will have your feet set firmly on the narrow road to heaven and glory with the Father. By the way, do you really want to "mock" the biggest, most powerful being that ever was or will be by spitting in His face? That's what you do when you sin!

Ephesians 4:17 This I say therefore, and testify in the Lord, that ye henceforth walk not as other Gentiles walk, in the vanity of their mind,18 Having the understanding darkened, being alienated from the life of God through the ignorance that is in them, because of the blindness of their heart: 19 Who being past feeling have given themselves over unto lasciviousness, to work all uncleanness with greediness.

Don't be as the rest of the world and walk with your head, mind, and heart in darkness, seeing and doing only what pleases you. How simple can it be? Turn to God and walk in His light. Do you see the command here? Be sinless, be holy, be without spot or wrinkle. Open your eyes, see the truth. Open your ears, hear the truth. Open your heart, understand the truth.

Do this and you will see, hear, and understand God.

Ephesians 4:24 And that ye put on the new man, which after God is created in righteousness and true holiness.

This is what you are after going through the cross of Jesus —HOLY, RIGHTEOUS, and WITHOUT SIN. Stay that way and you will spend eternity with Jesus and the Father.

Philippians 1:21 For to me to live is Christ, and to die is gain.

To live to Christ is to be holy and pure. To die is to die to sin, resist temptation, stop sinning. To gain is the glory and grace of God and is the result of dying to sin.

Philippians 2:14 Do all things without murmurings and disputings:15 That ye may be blameless and harmless, the sons of God, without rebuke, in the midst of a crooked and perverse nation, among whom ye shine as lights in the world;

Be an example to the world by the goodness and straight forwardness of your life in the body of Christ. This can only be done with the power of the Holy Spirit in your life. By listening to the guidance of the Holy Spirit and following it you will not do all the things of the world that seem natural to all those who are in the sinful world. You will be morally correct, holy, and sinless if you do as the Holy Spirit commands you to do.

By the way, the baptism of the Holy Spirit is not received automatically at salvation. It is a separate experience. See the study on the Baptism of the Holy Spirit further on in this book. You do receive the holy Spirit at salvation as an, you might say, engagement ring promising the wedding of the bride of Christ at the second coming.

Colossians 1:21 And you, that were sometime alienated and enemies in your mind by wicked works, yet now hath he reconciled 22 In the body of his flesh through death, to present you holy and unblameable and unreproveable in his sight:

You have been saved, now you must remain holy and sinless (stop sinning) to continue in your walk with the Father and Jesus. Learning to stop sinning is one reason that we are on the earth for 80 + years.

After all, we learned to sin from birth and continued in sin after coming to a moral understanding of our actions. Sinning(by nature children of wrath) is a learned habit according to Thayer's Greek lexicon. See **Eph.2:2-3.** If you continue to sin after your salvation you will lose all that you have gained by being born again unless you repent and again gain entry into the Spiritual kingdom of heaven.

That you sin by your "inherited sin nature", and that you have no choice but to continue in sinfulness is a major lie taught in man's church. This teaching of the modern church is of Satan!! To sin is a choice that you make every time temptation comes up.

See **James 4:17** It says that sin is a choice. **James** in Chapter 1, verses 1 through 16 explains how temptation turns into full fledged sin that leads to spiritual death.

Colossians 2:6 As ye have therefore received Christ Jesus the Lord, so walk ye in him:

What can be easier to understand? You are born again, that means to walk as He walked which is "sinless". This is picking up your cross every day as Jesus did, and walking as He walked obeying the Father. So must we walk the same road ,which will lead to heaven as long as we, as Jesus did, obey the commands of the Father in Heaven. By the way all of these commands are in the bible, if they're not they're not from God the Father.

Colossians 3:1 If ye then be risen with Christ, seek those things which are above, where Christ sitteth on the right hand of God. 2 Set your affection on things above, not on things on the earth.

Focus on the things of God, Jesus, and Heaven. Do not have any care for things of the world such as wars, natural disasters, or the pleasures of the world. God will provide all that you need and protect you from all harm. This comes with the understanding that you are doing it God's way not your way. What the unsaved are doing around you should be of no account to you. Are we not called out of the world? Do we not live in the spirit and not in the carnal flesh. Are we not to be a holy, called out people set aside for God? Are we not dead to the world and alive to Christ??

Colossians 3: 8 But now ye also put off all these; anger, wrath, malice, blasphemy, filthy communication out of your mouth.9 Lie not one to another, seeing that ye have put off the old man with his deeds;10 And have put on the new man, which is renewed in knowledge after the image of him that created him:

BE HOLY WITHOUT SIN!!!!!!!!! Be Christ like. This is what putting off the old man means. To put on the new man (which is walking as Christ walked) is what you must do if you want to go to heaven in glory and reside with the Father.

1 Thessalonians 2:10 Ye are witnesses, and God also, how holy and justly and unblameably we behaved ourselves among you that believe:

Paul tells us that he was holy and without blame, and the people he is talking to saw that he lived by the example of Jesus. This is an example of walking sinless. If Paul, an ordinary man, can walk sinless so can you. Just choose not to sin! Or do you think Paul had some supernatural power to resist sin? Well He did! It's called the baptism of the Holy Spirit, which is the same thing you are commanded to receive in **Acts 1:4-5**. Just get sinless and accept it. It has already been given to us at Pentecost. It is a free gift from the Father to all of His children. Or don't you believe it? This is for all Christians, for all time. As God the Father is no respecter of persons, He loves all people the same as He loves His son.

1 Thessalonians 2:12 That ye would walk worthy of God, who hath called you unto his kingdom and glory.

Do you not think that walking worthy is the same as walking sinless and holy? Not walking holy is the opposite of walking holy, and if you're in the kingdom with one your out of the kingdom with the other. Ya think?

1 Thessalonians 3:8 For now we live, if ye stand fast in the Lord.

To live is to be spiritually alive and to stand fast is resist sin, thereby remaining holy. To sin is to die spiritually.

1 Thessalonians 4:7 For God hath not called us unto uncleanness, but unto holiness.

No comment is need here. I hope!

1 Thessalonians 5:19 Quench not the Spirit.

To quench the Holy Spirit is to be in sin. The command here is not to sin thereby quenching the Holy Spirit and causing Him to leave you to Satan. God does not share.

1 Thessalonians 5:22 Abstain from all appearance of evil.

This goes beyond just saying "don't sin". It says don't even look like you're in sin.

1 Timothy 1:19 Holding faith, and a good conscience; which some having put away concerning faith have made shipwreck:

Holding on to faith and having a "GOOD" conscience are the same as saying remain sinless and holy. Remember that Jesus' blood removes all the guilt of sin from your conscience. Paul is saying that you must resist temptation and don't sin. Ah! A shipwreck; do you think this means sin, a lack of faith, makes a wreck of your life and those around you? This also shows us it is possible to lose your salvation by sinning (<u>by being shipwrecked</u>). The doctrine of "once saved always saved is a lie of Satan. Can you see this??

1 Timothy 5:22 Lay hands suddenly on no man, neither be partaker of other men's sins: keep thyself pure.

Jesus never laid hands on anyone without the leading of the Holy Spirit and neither must you. Pray first and listen for the answer before doing anything. Remember God does not answer or even hear the prayers of sinners(**John 9:31 and Isaiah 1:15**), so keep yourself holy. It's simple, don't follow the example of other sinners and get yourself into sin also. We are commanded to remain sinless.

1 Timothy 6:14 That thou keep this commandment without spot, unrebukeable, until the appearing of our Lord Jesus Christ:

The commandment is to love your brother as you love yourself. "Without spot and unrebukeable" means that you must stay holy by staying sinless, and remaining that way until you see Jesus either at your physical death or at the second coming.

2 Timothy 2:11 It is a faithful saying: For if we be dead with him, we shall also live with him:12 If we suffer, we shall also reign with him: if we deny him, he also will deny us:

We die to sin in Jesus' name and live to Him sin free. The world hates us and will persecute us. To deny Christ can be done in many ways but mostly it is by being a sinner, not repenting, not witnessing, not loving your neighbor, not loving God. To deny Christ is to be anti-Christ, and to deny Jesus is to be a sinner.

2 Timothy 2:16 But shun profane and vain babblings: for they will increase unto more ungodliness.

I'll tell ya, James was right. The hardest thing to control is your tongue. If you can control it you've come a long way to walking in a sinless holy condition. Remember what comes out of your mouth can never go back in. It cannot be unsaid.

2 Timothy 2:20 But in a great house there are not only vessels of gold and of silver, but also of wood and of earth; and some to honour, and some to dishonour.21 If a man therefore purge himself from these, he shall be a vessel unto honour, sanctified, and meet for the master's use, and prepared unto every good work. 22 Flee also youthful lusts: but follow righteousness, faith, charity, peace, with them that call on the Lord out of a pure heart.

Vessels of dishonor and honor are the conditions of being a sinner and of being holy. See you can get rid of sin by repenting and asking forgiveness of God the Father through Jesus. By purging yourself you become holy and pure before God. The phrase is " if you purge yourself" right? This means that you have the free will choice to stay a sinner or to purge yourself of all sin in your life and become holy. Stay away from sin like it's the plague because it will kill you, but pursue righteousness through the blood of Jesus. A pure heart! What do you think this is? Sinlessness, YA think?

Titus 2:11 For the grace of God that bringeth salvation hath appeared to all men,12 Teaching us that, denying ungodliness and worldly lusts, we should live soberly, righteously, and godly, in this present world;

The grace talked about here is the gift of grace called Jesus the Christ who appeared to men as a simple man himself.

The teaching is the good news of the gospel as told to us by Jesus, which is a call to be holy is what we are here on the earth to learn to be. God even makes it as easy as just listening to, and obeying His commandments

Hebrews 10:23 Let us hold fast the profession of our faith without wavering; (for he is faithful that promised;)

What ! Do you not think that this is a call to and for Holiness? By the way, a lack of faith is a sin. Here's one! To sin is a sin in and of itself. It is also a sin not to be saved. What a wonderful God I serve!! God never breaks His word , it is impossible for Him to do so and remain the moral governor of the universe. For to sin would put Him on the same level as we were before salvation, IE. a sinner!!! And yes God has freewill, where do you think we got it?

Hebrews 10:31 It is a fearful thing to fall into the hands of the living God.

What do you think GOD WILL DO TO YOU IF YOU DISOBEY HIS COMMAND TO BE SAVED? Throw you into hell because of your choice to remain a sinner. Is this not a fearful thing? You can say that God loves you so much that He will allow you your choice of heaven or hell. What will it be? Where do you want to spend eternity? For me and mine I choose God the Father and Jesus this day and forevermore.

Hebrews 12:1 Wherefore seeing we also are compassed about with so great a cloud of witnesses, let us lay aside every weight, and the sin which doth so easily beset us, and let us run with patience the race that is set before us,

These witnesses are all the Old Testament saints that went to heaven with Jesus. They are our example along with all the holy people of the body of Christ. As they are holy so must we be, or we go to hell. You choose!

Hebrews 12:4 Ye have not yet resisted unto blood, striving against sin.

This is what Jesus did in the praying in the garden right before He was arrested. God loves Jesus. God is no respecter of persons. God loves all equally. So God expects you to obey as Jesus did, even to resisting to the extent of shedding your own blood. The really neat thing is that God will not allow you to be tempted beyond what you can resist. I was once complaining and groaning to God about some sin in my life that I thought I could not control. He answered me, in a voice that was unmistakable and said, "Have you shed blood yet"? I knew immediately what He meant and I quite complaining at that moment and have not yet complained again about sin not being under my control, and never will. PTL.

Hebrews 12:14 Follow peace with all men, and holiness, without which no man shall see the Lord:

Read what it says, believe what is says, do what it says and you will go to heaven. In essence it is saying love your neighbor, and all those you come into contact with. This is a Godly love not some kind of man's love. Get a Strong's concordance and look up the three forms of love in the new testament.

James 1:2 My brethren, count it all joy when ye fall into divers temptations; 3 Knowing this, that the trying of your faith worketh patience. 4 But let patience have her perfect work, that ye may be perfect and entire, wanting nothing.

Do not give in to temptation and fall into sin. The joy is in resisting the temptation. Temptation in and of itself is not sin. It is only sin when you dwell on or act on the temptation that comes to you by Satan or your own mind.

You have to learn patience, it comes by practice. This practice of you resisting sin in faith, that Jesus was not a sinner and that you are a person just as Jesus was and that

you are able to resit sin jsut as Jesus did. This will teach you to be sinless and patient. This patience is what will carry you to the end of your salvation, which is heaven in glory with God
.

James 1:12 Blessed is the man that endureth temptation: for when he is tried, he shall receive the crown of life, which the Lord hath promised to them that love him. 13 Let no man say when he is tempted, I am tempted of God: for God cannot be tempted with evil, neither tempteth he any man:

Here we see that the way for you to be holy and pure is by resisting temptation and not falling into sin. Also we see that, by implication, one sin will take you to hell. You can also see that God the Father has nothing to do with the temptation that comes your way. In fact He, God, controls and limits the amount of temptation that comes to you.

James 1: 14 But every man is tempted, when he is drawn away of his own lust, and enticed. 15 Then when lust hath conceived, it bringeth forth sin: and sin, when it is finished, bringeth forth death.

You can see the path of temptation to full blown sin and spiritual death. This is the result of just that one sin. Think how hardened you become after a lifetime of sin. So don't wait, come to Jesus now!

James 1:20 For the wrath of man worketh not the righteousness of God. 21 Wherefore lay apart all filthiness and superfluity of naughtiness, and receive with meekness the engrafted word, which is able to save your souls.

Man's wrath is sinfulness. We are commanded to stop sinning, to obey the word of God, and to have holiness in our lives with Christ. If you are a sinner you're not saved, if you're saved you're not a sinner. Simple EH! God is a one way God!

Do it God's way or don't even try, you'll lose. God's way is a one way highway, or a red light. If you break the law you get a ticket to hell on the fast train. The thing to remember is that God is not a cop who has to see you break the law. He, God, knows immediately when you sin (break the law).

James 4:17 Therefore to him that knoweth to do good, and doeth it not, to him it is sin.

The definition of sin. To know the good and to **not** do the good, but to do the bad instead. You can say right or wrong in place of good or bad. Can you see that this is a choice of doing the good or doing the bad. Nothing makes you sin but you. The devil did not make you do it! Here you see that babies or young children can NOT be sinners because they have no moral understanding of the moral consequences of their actions. Good or bad, right or wrong. They are not held accountable for their actions until they come to that age when they do understand moral right and wrong. They then they turn into sinners, and then they need Jesus for salvation.

1 Peter 1:15 But as he which hath called you is holy, so be ye holy in all manner of conversation;16 Because it is written, Be ye holy; for I am holy.

You can see by the many verses that say be Holy that God is really serious about this subject. To be Holy means to stop sinning. You can not have fellowship with God if you are a sinner, even if you where once saved. There is only one way to get back into God's grace and that is to ask forgiveness and repent of your sin.

There is no such thing as a sinning or carnal Christian.
You either is or you ain't!

No middle ground with God, He is a red light God. His way or hit the road Jack. CLEAR?

1 Peter 4:1 Forasmuch then as Christ hath suffered for us in the flesh, arm yourselves likewise with the same mind: for he that hath suffered in the flesh hath ceased from sin; 2 That he no longer should live the rest of his time in the flesh to the lusts of men, but to the will of God.

Live "to the will of God". Kinda says it all don't Ya think? And what is that will? I think it is "cease from sin". How much more clear can it be? To suffer in the flesh is to have withdrawal from your sins, be persecuted, trials and tribulations, ECT.

2 Peter 1:3 According as his divine power hath given unto us all things that pertain unto life and godliness, through the knowledge of him that hath called us to glory and virtue: 4 Whereby are given unto us exceeding great and precious promises: that by these ye might be partakers of the divine nature, having escaped the corruption that is in the world through lust.

There is not one book in the New Testament that does not call us to be sinless and holy before God the Father and Jesus. Peter does it here as part of his salutation to the church. How else can we be "partakers of the divine nature", but by holiness?

We have escaped corruption and worldly lust by being born again in the spirit, and to perfection and holiness through the removal of the sin from our conscience through Jesus' holy shed blood.

1 John 2:6 He that saith he abideth in him ought himself also so to walk, even as he walked.

Another command to walk sin free, be holy as Jesus is holy, walk in the same way Jesus walked, do all the things that Jesus did while on this earth and more. With God's kind of love in our lives for all mankind, how can we do any less? By the way, the 'more' we do is real simple: one: bring people to the knowledge of salvation through Jesus' shed blood , and two: bring people to the knowledge of and into the baptism of the Holy Spirit. These are the two things that were impossible for Jesus to do while He was on this earth. Think about it!!!

1 John 3:9 Whosoever is born of God doth not commit sin; for his seed remaineth in him: and he cannot sin, because he is born of God. 10 In this the children of God are manifest, and the children of the devil: whosoever doeth not righteousness is not of God, neither he that loveth not his brother.

Verse 9 is misunderstood. It does not say that your free will, to sin or not to sin, is taken away from you at salvation. What it does say is that if you want to remain in Jesus you will choose not sin. It is imposable to remain in Jesus and sin at the same time. To be reborn spiritually of God is a free will choice to stop sinning. This command (to stop sinning) of God is still in effect after you are born again. There are so many verses that say it is a choice to sin. See the study further on, "The lie of once saved, always saved". You can not sin and remain born again. Verse 10 tells us how to know who is and who ain't in the kingdom.

1 John 3:23 And this is his commandment, That we should believe on the name of his Son Jesus Christ, and love one another, as he gave us commandment. 24 And he that keepeth his commandments dwelleth in him, and he in him. And hereby we know that he abideth in us, by the Spirit which he hath given us.

Believe in Jesus and keep his commandments. Verse 23 gives us the commandments of God, this also means that we have the choice of not doing what we are commanded to do. Do we not have free will? If you disobey and break the commandments of God, you are then a sinner and out of the kingdom of God. Look at these verses, understand what they say! In verse 24 it says, if you obey you stay! Is not the opposite true also? It also says that we know that He is with us by the Holy Spirit. This is the sure and certain knowledge that we are saved and in His kingdom. So if we sin do we also not know that the Holy Spirit has left us? The answer is resounding YES if we are honest with ourselves.

1 John 5:18 We know that whosoever is born of God sinneth not; but he that is begotten of God keepeth himself, and that wicked one toucheth him not.

Be holy and sin not. That is our call to the born again life . If you sin you are no longer holy, you are spiritually dead, you are out of the kingdom, and Satan has the right to come against you. You have, by sinning, made to be of no avail your being born again. You must now repent and ask forgiveness and start again in your walk with Jesus. By 'keeping yourself' you're making the choice to stay sin free and in the kingdom of God, thus making sure that Satan can not attack you. God will protect you from Satan as long as you are holy by obeying and continuing in His commandments. Satan CANNOT attack or harm you as long as you remain in God's care. This means sin free in Jesus, which is being holy and pure.

2 John 1:9 Whosoever transgresseth, and abideth not in the doctrine of Christ, hath not God. He that abideth in the doctrine of Christ, he hath both the Father and the Son.

This verse tells us what happens if we are not walking in holiness, and what happens if we are walking holy without sin. With sin there is no fellowship with God, without sin you are in constant fellowship with Jesus the Father and the Holy Spirit.

3 John 1:11 Beloved, follow not that which is evil, but that which is good. He that doeth good is of God: but he that doeth evil hath not seen God.

Make no mistake this is a call to holiness. It confirms James 4:17 as a definition of sin. Which is "to know the good and do it not". So do good and thereby be holy.

Jude 1:21 Keep yourselves in the love of God, looking for the mercy of our Lord Jesus Christ unto eternal life.

To remain in the love of God is to be holy and without sin in your lives. Jesus is that "ONLY" way to eternal life with God the Father.

Revelation 1:7 He that hath an ear, let him hear what the Spirit saith unto the churches; To him that overcometh will I give to eat of the tree of life, which is in the midst of the paradise of God.

To overcome! What? SIN! Ya think? If you don't you will go to hell not heaven.

Revelation 2:10 Fear none of those things which thou shalt suffer: behold, the devil shall cast some of you into prison, that ye may be tried; and ye shall have tribulation ten days: be thou faithful unto death, and I will give thee a crown of life. 11 He that hath an ear, let him hear what the Spirit saith unto the churches; He that overcometh shall not be hurt of the second death.

To overcome is to remain sinless. By overcoming you remain in the kingdom of God and will be with Him for eternity. To be hurt by the second death is to be thrown into hell.

Revelation 3:12 Him that overcometh will I make a pillar in the temple of my God, and he shall go no more out: and I will write upon him the name of my God, and the name of the city of my God, which is new Jerusalem, which cometh down out of heaven from my God: and I will write upon him my new name.

The overcomer: is holy, remains in the kingdom, will be marked with the mark of God (the Holy Spirit baptism), and not with the mark (sin) of the beast who is mankind who's number is 666 (**see Rev.13:18**). Again this is not the number of Satan!

Revelation 3:19 As many as I love, I rebuke and chasten: be zealous therefore, and repent.

Do you want to be spanked (punished and disciplined) by God? If not repent and stay sinless. To be zealous about being sinless is to make the lack of sin very very important in your life.

Revelation 3:21 To him that overcometh will I grant to sit with me in my throne, even as I also overcame, and am set down with my Father in his throne.

A call to holiness! To be sinless as Jesus was sinless. Jesus set the example for us not to sin. He gave up all His Godly powers and became a man, just as you and I are, with NO special powers to resist temptation and sin. As He says "I overcame", and He expects us to do the same. Jesus is the example of how to live our lives if we want to stay in the Kingdom of God. To follow Jesus' example we must study the bible to learn what He did and how He did it while He was on this earth, and then do the same. If you don't answer this call to holiness you will not be in heaven with JESUS.

Herod Slaughters the Babies

Matthew 2:16 Then Herod, when he saw that he was mocked of the wise men, was exceeding wroth, and sent forth, and slew all the children that were in Bethlehem, and in all the coasts thereof, from two years old and under, according to the time which he had diligently enquired of the wise men.

Matthew 2:9-11 When they had heard the king, they departed; and, lo, the star, which they saw in the east, went before them, till it came and stood over where the young child was. When they saw the star, they rejoiced with exceeding great joy. And when they were come into the house, they saw the young child with Mary his mother, and fell down, and worshipped him: and when they had opened their treasures, they presented unto him gifts; gold, and frankincense, and myrrh.

It seems to me that Jesus was visited by the wise men (three kings) well after His birth. As much as two years. You can see in verse 11 that when the Wise Men showed up where Jesus was living it is called a house, and Jesus is called a young child. This should tell us Jesus, at the time of the of the wise men's visit, was not a baby and not in a manger. So much for the "three kings of the orient " visiting baby Jesus in a cave in a manger! Another of man's teaching that is not scriptural. The important thing about this short study is that it is one more example of wrongness in man's church. How many more are there that are just accepted and not checked out because 'Oh they are such small matters'. Here is the thing, if you accept a small lie it will be easier to get you to accept bigger, and bigger lies until the gospel you believe has no truth of the bible in it. Again this why you should study the bible, never stop, so you will know automatically when an untruth comes your way.

Faith not Fasting

Matthew 17:15 Lord, have mercy on my son: for he is lunatick, and sore vexed: for ofttimes he falleth into the fire, and oft into the water.16 And I brought him to thy disciples, and they could not cure him.17 Then Jesus answered and said, O faithless and perverse generation, how long shall I be with you? how long shall I suffer you? bring him hither to me.18 And Jesus rebuked the devil; and he departed out of him: and the child was cured from that very hour.19 Then came the disciples to Jesus apart, and said, Why could not we cast him out? 20 And Jesus said unto them, Because of your unbelief: for verily I say unto you, If ye have faith as a grain of mustard seed, ye shall say unto this mountain, Remove hence to yonder place; and it shall remove; and nothing shall be impossible unto you.21 Howbeit this kind goeth not out but by prayer and fasting.

Mark 9:19 He answereth him, and saith, O faithless generation, how long shall I be with you? how long shall I suffer you? bring him unto me.

Mark 9:29 And he said unto them, This kind can come forth by nothing, but by prayer and fasting.

Jesus tells the disciples that faith is what is needed to cast out demons, and to build up your faith it takes fasting and prayer. Did He not call them a faithless generation? Did He not say it did not go out because of their 'unbelief"? What is unbelief but a lack of faith! Why did it not go out? Lack of faith! Jesus never prayed and fasted before casting out demons. He just did it by the power of the Holy Spirit, the same baptism we as Christians have. Do not the scriptures say that we will do all that He did and more? We cast out demons in His name having our faith built up by being in His word and being in constant prayer, fasting, and prayer in the Spirit.

The only reasons, that I know of, that demons will not leave are:

1- Your lack of faith for the deliverance.

2- The person being delivered does not want the demons to leave.

Our faith is built up by Fasting, reading the word and hearing it, prayer and prayer in the Holy Spirit which comes as a result of the Baptism of the Holy Spirit.

This teaching of casting out demons by fasting is coming from misreading scripture; that to cast out demons, at least some of them but which ones, you must fast first and them go to casting out; that it is the fasting alone which make the demons leave. Sounds good doesn't it? It's not, it is leading you to failure, and by failure an even greater lack of faith. This is another lie of Satan to bring defeat to Christians trying to do the work they are called to do. Do you not think it possible that these defeats will cause unbelief and doubt of the word of God for some Christians? If it does, it is a victory for Satan, not you the Christian warrior.

Concerning divorce

Matthew 19:9 And I say unto you, Whosoever shall put away his wife, except it be for fornication, and shall marry another, committeth adultery: and whoso marrieth her which is put away doth commit adultery.

Divorce is legal in God's eyes for adultery, fornication outside of marriage, by either partner.

1 CO 7:14 For the unbelieving husband is sanctified by the wife, and the unbelieving wife is sanctified by the husband: else were your children unclean; but now are they holy. 15 But if the unbelieving depart, let him depart. A brother or a sister is not under bondage in such cases: but God hath called us to peace.

In the first place this was not a marriage sanctified by God, both were unbelievers. At best only one was saved, or one of the partners got saved after the marriage and by this the marriage is sanctified. It does not mean that the unsaved partner or the children will be saved by the saved partner. The only way to salvation is a personal choice to be saved by and through Jesus. The children in this marriage are sanctified by the saved parent. Otherwise they are cursed as are the unsaved parents. Now the children can break the curse of generations anytime they want to by becoming saved themselves.

The second reason to divorce. If the unsaved partner wants to leave you can let them go.

Jesus' prayer in the garden

Matthew 26:36 Then cometh Jesus with them unto a place called Gethsemane, and saith unto the disciples, Sit ye here, while I go and pray yonder. 37 And he took with him Peter and the two sons of Zebedee, and began to be sorrowful and very heavy. 38 Then saith he unto them, My soul is exceeding sorrowful, even unto death: tarry ye here, and watch with me. 39 And he went a little farther, and fell on his face, and prayed, saying, O my Father, if it be possible, let this cup pass from me: nevertheless not as I will, but as thou wilt.

Mark 14:36 And he said, Abba, Father, all things are possible unto thee; take away this cup from me: nevertheless not what I will, but what thou wilt.

Luke 22:42 Saying, Father, if thou be willing, remove this cup from me: nevertheless not my will, but thine, be done.

Jesus is praying that He be not killed by stoning before He goes to the cross. Not that he get out of going to the cross as most of man's churches teach.

The Jews and the religious leaders of the day tried to kill Him ten times before He went to the very public death on the cross that was prophesied. He was praying that the Father watch over Him until He went to the death on the cross. His death had to be public to show the world that He, a sinless man, did die for all the sins of the world. If this death was in secret how would the world have known of it? How could a secret death by stoning, or being thrown off a cliff be payment for the sins of that world if the world did not know of it. Legally it had to be a public death. Any other thought is ludicrous. Did He not tell His disciples He would go to the cross? Do you believe that Jesus, who came by His free will, is trying to get out of doing what He was commanded by the Father and agreed to do from the foundations of the world? Do you really think Jesus would chicken out and ask the Father to get Him out of the cross? Jesus proved His worthiness by His rejection of sin and by His obedience to the commands of the Father. This worthiness is what allowed Him to open the book of life as stated in the book of Revelation; to purge heaven of all the angels who rebelled against God as stated in the book of Revelation, and last, but by far not least, provide His shed Holy, sinless, blood for the salvation of all the people of the world who would come to Him in truth, and thereby be granted entrance into the kingdom of God.

What is tithing

Matthew 6:1 Take heed that ye do not your alms before men, to be seen of them: otherwise ye have no reward of your Father which is in heaven. 2 Therefore when thou doest thine alms, do not sound a trumpet before thee, as the hypocrites do in the synagogues and in the streets, that they may have glory of men. Verily I say unto you, They have their reward. 3 But when thou doest alms, let not thy left hand know what thy right hand doeth: 4 That thine alms may be in secret: and thy Father which seeth in secret himself shall reward thee openly. 5 And when thou prayest, thou shalt not be as the hypocrites are: for they love to pray standing in the synagogues and in the corners of the streets, that they may be seen of men. Verily I say unto you, They have their reward. 6 But thou, when thou prayest, enter into thy closet, and when thou hast shut thy door, pray to thy Father which is in secret; and thy Father which seeth in secret shall reward thee openly.

Tithing is not giving 10% of your income to the "church", it is "GIVING" as the Holy spirit leads you to give. This is called being led of the Holy Spirit. The Old Testament Saints did not have the Holy Spirit to guide them in their walk with God, so God made laws for them to follow. We have the Holy Spirit, they did not. We who have the Holy Spirit Baptism do not need the law to guide us. This is one reason the Holy Spirit Baptism in so important and a command of Jesus to all who would be Christian. See **Acts 1:4-5**. In New Testament giving we are guided by the Holy Spirit to give of our monetary blessings, material blessings, our time to the family in need down the street, or it may be a street preacher giving his heart to the unsaved; it may be time spent helping others in need, witnessing Jesus to the down trodden and sinners of the world or even in the place where you worship. This is true GIVING in the name of Jesus.

Mark 4:20 And these are they which are sown on good ground; such as hear the word, and receive it, and bring forth fruit, some thirtyfold, some sixty, and some an hundred.

Luke 8:15 But that on the good ground are they, which in an honest and good heart, having heard the word, keep it, and bring forth fruit with patience.

This these verses are NOT, as some teach, about tithing. It is witnessing the word of God to bring others into the body of Christ. This is giving of your time to, and for God. Your fruit is multiplied to the Father by the ones you bring to Him by Jesus.

Luke 6:38 Give, and it shall be given unto you; good measure, pressed down, and shaken together, and running over, shall men give into your bosom. For with the same measure that ye mete withal it shall be measured to you again.

This is not talking about money, but it is talking about giving love, compassion, and all that Jesus would have you do. Love your neighbor as you love yourself. This giving of our sustenance is all by the guidance of the Holy Spirit.

Mark 12:41 And Jesus sat over against the treasury, and beheld how the people cast money into the treasury: and many that were rich cast in much.

42 And there came a certain poor widow, and she threw in two mites, which make a farthing. 43 And he called unto him his disciples, and saith unto them, Verily I say unto you, That this poor widow hath cast more in, than all they which have cast into the treasury: 44 For all they did cast in of their abundance; but she of her want did cast in all that she had, even all her living.

Luke 21:3 And he said, Of a truth I say unto you, that this poor widow hath cast in more than they all: 4 For all these have of their abundance cast in unto the offerings of God: but she of her penury hath cast in all the living that she had.

What this woman did is an example of giving not tithing. You can see that Jesus approves of what she did and not what the rich people did. Shows 'ta go ya' you can't buy your way into heaven with anything, i.e. money, material things, favors, work, etc.

2 Corinthians 9:5 Therefore I thought it necessary to exhort the brethren, that they would go before unto you, and make up beforehand your bounty, whereof ye had notice before, that the same might be ready, as a matter of bounty, and not as of covetousness.6 But this I say, He which soweth sparingly shall reap also sparingly; and he which soweth bountifully shall reap also bountifully.7 Every man according as he purposeth in his heart, so let him give; not grudgingly, or of necessity: for God loveth a cheerful giver.

You can see here that it is giving, not tithing 10%. This giving is the rule for the Body of Christ. What a perfect place to have said "you must tithe 10% of what your increase is". It says "God loves a cheerful GIVER" not cheerful thither. You will receive blessings from God for giving of your money, time, goods, and words to Gods work. We as the born again, baptized in the Holy Spirit, children of God, are led of the Holy Spirit to give. Under the old covenant, the natural law of sin and death, the people of Israel did not have the Holy Spirit (only Kings and Priests had the Holy Spirit) to guide them so God made the natural law of tithing 10% to guide them in how much to pay the temple. We are not under this law of sin and death, but we are under the spiritual law of life, love, and Grace that Jesus came and confirmed to the world. There is no more worldly temple, we now are the temple of God. So how can you give 10% tithe to yourself as you are the temple of God.

The building, built by man on the corner is no longer the temple of God, or as some say His house. God destroyed the building, temple, where He lived in 70AD with the Roman army to show He no longer lived in a building built by man. Now He resides in the flesh and blood temple of His children that He is building into the once and forever finished bride of Christ. Remember we are all living stones in the temple walls. The up shot of all this is, give as you are led of the Holy Spirit to give, and not as the laws of man's church demand.

Incorrect translations

Matthew 6:13 And lead us not into temptation, but deliver us from evil: For thine is the kingdom, and the power, and the glory, for ever. Amen.

Luke 11:4 And forgive us our sins; for we also forgive every one that is indebted to us. And lead us not into temptation; but deliver us from evil.

This should read keep us from temptation. God does not tempt any one with evil!
(James 1:13 Let no man say when he is tempted, I am tempted of God: for God cannot be tempted with evil, <u>neither tempteth he any man:</u>)

Note: This is a new insight of the lord's prayer given to us by the Holy Spirit to a sister in Christ.

Our Father is in Heaven.
His name is
Hollowed and Holy.
Father come with heaven so your will
Will be done here on earth.
Thank you Father for the bread you
Give each day.
Father forgive us our debts and help
Us to walk in forgiveness
For those that trespass against us
Past, present , future.
You Father lead us and keep us
From temptation, so that evil
Can not abide in us.
You deliver us into freedom.
For your kingdom is power
And glory forever.
Thank you Father.
Amen!

Matthew 19:24 And again I say unto you, It is easier for a camel to go through the eye of a needle, than for a rich man to enter into the kingdom of God.

Mark 10:25 It is easier for a camel to go through the eye of a needle, than for a rich man to enter into the kingdom of God.

Luke 18:25 For it is easier for a camel to go through a needle's eye, than for a rich man to enter into the kingdom of God.

This should say "a rope " through the eye of a needle. This is from the Peshitta bible, which is from the eastern orthodox church. It is translated from the original Aramaic text——the language of Jesus . The difference between the Aramaic word for camel and the word for rope is just one little fly speck.

Luke 14:26 If any man come to me, and hate not his father, and mother, and wife, and children, and brethren, and sisters, yea, and his own life also, he cannot be my disciple.

The "Peshitta reads" "put aside his father and his mother.....". It does not mean literally hate your father and mother. This 'to put aside' makes more sense to me than the word "hate". You have to hold Jesus in and of more importance than anyone else in the world. In other words this means that Jesus must be of more importance in your life than anything else in this world!

Matthew 27:46 And about the ninth hour Jesus cried with a loud voice, saying, Eli, Eli, lama sabachthani? that is to say, My God, my God, why hast thou forsaken me?

Mark 15:34 And at the ninth hour Jesus cried with a loud voice, saying, Eloi, Eloi, lama sabachthani? which is, being interpreted, My God, my God, why hast thou forsaken me?

This should read " My God, my God, for this I was spared !" This is from the Eastern orthodox bible called the "Peshitta". The translators have used the incorrect translation of the Greek so as to go along with the idea that Jesus became full of sin or was literally made to be guilty of all of the sins of the world while on the cross, which is ludicrous, because His blood needed to be, had to be, holy without sin to provide salvation for the world full of sinners. His blood would not have been holy if He was a sinner.

Jesus was made (by His choice) to be a pure and holy, white, without spot or wrinkle, sacrificial lamb. A one time, in place of you, payment for the sins of the world, by His own free will choice to obey the command of the Father. Did the Father literally make His son a sinner? How would this be possible? Sin is a free will moral choice and the Father could not make that choice for His Son Jesus. Again, He was not made against His will to be sin. Did Jesus make Himself a sinner? If He did it would mean that He committed a sin. The bible says he obeyed all the commands of God the Father. It also says that sin is a CHOICE. So, which command did Jesus choose to disobey? If He did sin, His blood would not have been Holy and pure, with out blemish, and His sacrifice would have been useless and a waste of time. If He was made literally to be a sinner then how was His blood Pure and Holy, and by what process was HE made a sinner? Did the sin of the world just jump on Him, and stick to Him like peanut butter? He paid the price for your willful sin in the sinful world by His choice to be the perfect sacrificial lamb on the cross. His sacrifice was a one time payment for the sins of the world. Think of it in this way: You Know of somebody who is in real bad debt, your heart is Good and you feel a need to help this person. So you go down to the loan Co. and pay his debt. Now think. Does this payment you have just made for this other person make his debt your debt? No, you do not become the debtor nor does the debt become yours just because you payed it.

Jesus by making payment on the cross paid your debt for your sins NOT HIS as He had none, and your debt for sin did not become His debt, or your sins His sins. The only way God the Father could accept this one time payment was because Jesus was the perfect sinless man who assumed your debt and "made" the one time payment for all of us. Once again the question begs asking: How did the sins of the world become the responsibility of Jesus? Yes he chose to pay the debt, but He did not chose to accept the sin or the guilt of the sin in place of you. When he took the sin of the world He just made payment for it. He did not become it! How did Jesus become a sinner with your sins when, in fact, He never sinned in the first place? Did God the father make Jesus a sinner by making His son a sinner with your sins? The real question is **HOW**, and by what process did Jesus become a sinner ? Did God change the definition of sin just this once so Jesus could become a sinner for the cross? How unthinkable this would be! You tell me how Jesus was 'made a sinner'. A reminder: sin is a moral choice every time you sin. No one else can ever be guilty of your sins!

One more thought on this subject of did Jesus become sin or was He made sin on the cross. The following verse says "and in Him is no sin". I take this to mean that from the foundations of the world, though the cross & resurrection, and on into eternity Jesus was never a sinner in any way or form. This does show categorically that Jesus never even came close to being 'a sinner' or that He somehow, beyond His will, was made to be "sin"!!!! To think that he was made sin or that He became sin is not logical or even sane. The phrase " that He was manifested to take away our sin, and in Him is no sin" literally means that He was & is sinless - from the get go all the way to the end. Just where and when did sin come on Him, in what fashion, and by what process did He get sinful? The answer to these questions is: He did not!*

*1 John 3:5 And ye know that he was manifested to take away our sins; and in him is no sin.

Acts 12:4 And when he had apprehended him, he put him in prison, and delivered him to four quaternions of soldiers to keep him; intending after Easter to bring him forth to the people.

I believe this to be a true translation. It is talking about the Roman holiday of Easter celebrating the goddess of fertility. This is not talking about Passover.

Being born again (salvation)

John 3:3 Jesus answered and said unto him, Verily, verily, I say unto thee, Except a man be born again, he cannot see the kingdom of God.

Acts 2:38 Then Peter said unto them, Repent, and be baptized every one of you in the name of Jesus Christ for the remission of sins, and ye shall receive the gift of the Holy Ghost.

Acts 1:4-5 And, being assembled together with them, commanded them that they should not depart from Jerusalem, but wait for the promise of the Father, which, saith he, ye have heard of me. For John truly baptized with water; but ye shall be baptized with the Holy Ghost not many days hence.

A three-step process: 1- Repentance & asking forgiveness, 2- Full immersion water baptism, 3- Baptism of the Holy Spirit (with a prayer language).

Colossians 2:11 In whom also ye are circumcised with the circumcision made without hands, in putting off the body of the sins of the flesh by the circumcision of Christ: 12 Buried with him in baptism, wherein also ye are risen with him through the faith of the operation of God, who hath raised him from the dead. 13 And you, being dead in your sins and the uncircumcision of your flesh, hath he quickened together with him, having forgiven you all trespasses; 14 Blotting out the handwriting of ordinances that was against us, which was contrary to us, and took it out of the way, nailing it to his cross;

This is being born again, renewed in the spirit, walking with Jesus! One thing you must see here is that Jesus nailed your sins to His cross by His shed blood and your choice to use that Holy shed blood for forgiveness !!! There is a movement, in man's church, to have the congregation come forward and nail their sins, written on a piece of paper, to some wooden cross the Pastor has brought in to his building. To do this is to say that Jesus' work on the cross was ineffective, and is a slap in the face of Jesus! If you have done this you must repent of it . It's the same as doing penance for your sins all the while Jesus has already paid the price for your sins. You don't have the where-withal or the means to pay God for your sins. That is why Jesus had to die Holy and Pure on the cross.

Matthew 10:39 He that findeth his life shall lose it: and he that loseth his life for my sake shall find it.

Mark 8:35 For whosoever will save his life shall lose it; but whosoever shall lose his life for my sake and the gospel's, the same shall save it.

To give up the worldly pleasures and walk, with Gods kind of love, in repentance of sinfulness. This is to say that you give up one life for another life. You give up your life (lose it) of sinful rebellion towards God and take up your life (find it) of walking sinless before God .

Luke 8:18 Take heed therefore how ye hear: for whosoever hath, to him shall be given; and whosoever hath not, from him shall be taken even that which he seemeth to have.

If you have Jesus you shall be given the reward of heaven. If you do not have Jesus (salvation), at death or the second coming, you will lose even the "chance of salvation" and the reward of heaven, and be thrown into outer darkness with wailing and gnashing of teeth, or in other words thrown into hell. What you lost that you did not (seemeth) have is salvation, and the chance of ever having it.

Luke 14:26 If any man come to me, and hate not his father, and mother, and wife, and children, and brethren, and sisters, yea, and his own life also, he cannot be my disciple.

Hate means to put aside in favor of Jesus. This means that Jesus MUST be first, above all else in your life. To put Jesus first is to walk sinless. This is what it is to be a member of His body. See page 47, Luke 14:26.

Luke 17:33 Whosoever shall seek to save his life shall lose it; and whosoever shall lose his life shall preserve it.

John12:25 He that loveth his life shall lose it; and he that hateth his life in this world shall keep it unto life eternal. 26 If any man serve me, let him follow me; and where I am, there shall also my servant be: if any man serve me, him will my Father honour.

You must give up (lose) your life of sin in the world and save your life by being born again in the spirit to be in the spiritual kingdom of God with Jesus. To hate your life full of sin is to come to Jesus for salvation and eternal life with God in Heaven. To follow and serve Jesus is to remain, live, without sin in your Christian life.

Luke 18:10-14 Two men went up into the temple to pray; the one a Pharisee, and the other a publican. The Pharisee stood and prayed thus with himself, God, I thank thee, that I am not as other men are, extortioners, unjust, adulterers, or even as this publican. I fast twice in the week, I give tithes of all that I possess. And the publican, standing afar off, would not lift up so much as his eyes unto heaven, but smote upon his breast, saying, God be merciful to me a sinner. I tell you, this man went down to his house justified rather than the other: for every one that exalteth himself shall be abased; and he that humbleth himself shall be exalted.

A good example of how to approach Jesus and the Father for salvation. Have a broken and contrite heart, and be not prideful of all that you have done for God.

John 8:31 Then said Jesus to those Jews which believed on him, If ye continue in my word, then are ye my disciples indeed; 32 And ye shall know the truth, and the truth shall make you free.

This is being born again into the new covenant of Grace and love, and walking in the truth of the word of God. This is what believing on Him is. It shall set you free from the law of sin and death (old covenant), and as adopted sons & daughters of God you will reap / receive the reward of heaven. Health, spiritual rebirth, and all of your material needs (including physical protection) will be met. These are the three parts of the atonement given to us By Jesus' work on the cross.

John 15:10 If ye keep my commandments, ye shall abide in my love; even as I have kept my Father's commandments, and abide in his love. 11 These things have I spoken unto you, that my joy might remain in you, and that your joy might be full.

This is how the born again person lives his / her life, and the result of that pure and holy life. Only if you obey the commandments of Jesus. This fullness of Joy, beyond understanding of sinners, comes only through salvation by and through a personal choice to go through Jesus' shed blood for the remission of sins and entrance into the Kingdom of God.

John 15:19 If ye were of the world, the world would love his own: but because ye are not of the world, but I have chosen you out of the world, therefore the world hateth you.

This is what you get, when you are born again from the world of sin that you have given up as a bad deal. Life for death and death for life. Ain't it great!!

John 20:22 And when he had said this, he breathed on them, and saith unto them, Receive ye the Holy Ghost:

Ephesians 1:13-14 In whom ye also trusted, after that ye heard the word of truth, the gospel of your salvation: in whom also after that ye believed, ye were sealed with that holy Spirit of promise, Which is the earnest of our inheritance until the redemption of the purchased possession, unto the praise of his glory.

Revelation 13:15-18 And he had power to give life unto the image of the beast, that the image of the beast should both speak, and cause that as many as would not worship the image of the beast should be killed. And he causeth all, both small and great, rich and poor, free and bond, to receive a mark in their right hand, or in their foreheads: And that no man might buy or sell, save he that had the mark, or the name of the beast, or the number of his name. Here is wisdom. Let him that hath understanding count the number of the beast: for it is the number of a man; and his number *is* Six hundred threescore *and* six.

John 20:22 is giving the disciples the promise of the Holy Spirit, showing that they were now born again. This is not the baptism of the Holy Spirit. That happens at Pentecost which is still 40 some days in the future for these men and the women who will wait for it in the upper room for the comforter. Today it happens thousands of time a day all over the world. The verse in **Ephesians** is saying that at salvation you receive the Holy Spirit who is our proof and assurance of the work of salvation in our lives. Salvation is an action word that means : you were saved, you are being saved, and you will continue to be saved until the final judgment for the saints and the sinners when the work of salvation is finished.

Rev. 13:15-18 says 666 is the mark of the beast, the seal of sin, in the lives of all mankind who have not yet come to God the Father through Jesus.

The mark of the beast, who's number is 666, is given to you by sin in your life. This means your master is Satan. You receive this mark by your free will choice to sin. Without this 666 mark (sin) you will not be able to buy and sell in the natural or spiritual world of mankind, which is the anti-Christ religion and anti-Christ government.

Try and speak the truth of scripture in man's church and see what happens. See what happens when you break a man's law that goes against God's law. What we must understand is that there are two marks : sin and holiness. Which mark do you wear?

Romans 3:10 As it is written, There is none righteous, no, not one:

Romans 3:23 For all have sinned, and come short of the glory of God;

These verses are used, by man's church, to show that we are all just sinners no matter what we do, that we have a sin nature and that there is nothing we can do about it. This is Calvinistic teaching. What lie of Satan! All that these verses mean is that before you come to Jesus you are a sinner! Read the verses before and after, then figure out what Paul is talking about. Read further the scriptures in chapter three through verse 25 and you will see that the end result for those who come to Jesus is freedom from sin. See also **1Jh1:9.**

Romans 3:22-25 Even the righteousness of God which is by faith of Jesus Christ unto all and upon all them that believe: for there is no difference: For all have sinned, and come short of the glory of God; Being justified freely by his grace through the redemption that is in Christ Jesus: Whom God hath set forth to be a propitiation through faith in his blood, to declare his righteousness for the remission of sins that are past, through the forbearance of God;

There is no difference in that we who are saved were all sinners before salvation. We all have the same chance (justified freely) for salvation. The phrase "for all have sinned" is the spiritual condition before salvation. You will notice that the next line, "being justified freely by His grace", is saying that we, through Jesus, are no longer sinners. These verses put a lie to the idea that we are still sinners after salvation. "To be a propitiation" means that Jesus was a one time substitutionary sacrifice (payment) for the sins of all mankind. "Of sins that are past" means that only the sins that have already been committed can be forgiven. Once you commit a sin it is in the past. There is no such thing as future sins. How can there be ? They have not yet been committed, or you can say, come into existence YET. Yes there is a possibility of sins in your future, but they are only by your free will choice, and the possibility is that you may choose not to sin.

Romans 5:18 Therefore as by the offence of one judgment came upon all men to condemnation; even so by the righteousness of one the free gift came upon all men unto justification of life. 19 For as by one man's disobedience many were made sinners, so by the obedience of one shall many be made righteous.

By one man sin entered into the world and by one man forgiveness entered into the world.

Verse 19 says that <u>many were made</u> sinners and <u>many shall be made</u> righteous. The word "made" is the same word in the Greek in both places. Do you think that many means "all"? Ya it does ! But not "all" are saved, you can see that, just look around you in the world. So what does this verse mean by the word "made"? You must see what all other scriptures say about this being made a sinner or being made saved, and then come to a conclusion . What I believe it means is that you have to see that both words "made" mean the same thing. That many are made saved <u>by a free will choice</u> or many are made sinners<u> by a free will choice.</u> These are the choices we must all make. There are only two choices in this world —— to sin or not to sin!!!

Romans 7:14 For we know that the law is spiritual: but I am carnal, sold under sin.15 For that which I do I allow not: for what I would, that do I not; but what I hate, that do I.

Ephesians 2:2-3 Wherein in time past ye walked according to the course of this world, according to the prince of the power of the air, the spirit that now worketh in the children of disobedience: 3 Among whom also we all had our conversation in times past in the lusts of our flesh, fulfilling the desires of the flesh and of the mind; and were by nature the children of wrath, even as others.

This is the condition of all people BEFORE being Born Again into the sinless Holy Spiritual Kingdom of God. It's called habitable Sin, or learned sin. Verse 15 shows you what it is like to be in habitual sin of your making. This is also called your "sin nature". This "sin nature" is not put upon or given to you by some mysterious force in the universe. You develop this so called "sin nature" or sin habit for yourself, by yourself.

This "Sin Habit" is acquired by committing sins as a child. As a child you do not have this understanding of the morality of your actions (sins), so it is not held accountable to you. You will continue to turn to a sin when you reach the age of moral maturity because it has been your life long habit. This age is when you have an understanding of the morality of your actions whether good or bad. At this point you need Jesus to be born again! Again, we are not born guilty of sin or with a fallen nature. We learn it, develop it, and use it all by our lonesome. No one else is to blame for our learned habit of sin, not Adam, God, or your earthly family, NO ONE!!

Your salvation through Jesus is a decision that you make, learn, develop and use for the benefit of all that come in contact with you. The only difference is, after being born again, you are no longer led by Satan but by the Holy Spirit who is sent by Jesus to you and now leads you into all truth and knowledge.

The phrase " by nature we are children of wrath"(**EHP 2:3**) is used to show we are "born that way by man's teaching not scripture." This is a lie. In the Thayer's Greek lexicon the word nature means (as used in Eph. 3:2) a learned habit. Can you see this now? Again we are born with the ability to do good or to do bad!

Romans 7:19 For the good that I would I do not: but the evil which I would not, that I do.

This is what your learned "sin nature" or "learned habit" gets you, it's called habitual sin. This is before salvation. This word nature in the Greek means "a person who has become uncircumcised spiritually by his iniquity". It is something that you do by choice.

Romans 7:24 O wretched man that I am! who shall deliver me from the body of this death? 25 I thank God through Jesus Christ our Lord. So then with the mind I myself serve the law of God; but with the flesh the law of sin.

Romans 8:1 There is therefore now no condemnation to them which are in Christ Jesus, who walk not after the flesh, but after the Spirit.

Paul asks a question (verse 7: 24-25) and then answers it (verse8:1). Can you see and understand this? This is not a life long affliction, it is a before and after salvation question and the answer.

Romans 8:1 There is therefore now no condemnation to them which are in Christ Jesus, who walk not after the flesh, but after the Spirit. 2 For the law of the Spirit of life in Christ Jesus hath made me free from the law of sin and death.

This is where you come to when you are born again. It means that you don't have to continue in sin, you have the choice not to sin or to fall back into sinfulness. You have had all of your sin removed from your conscience by the shed blood of Christ . This could not be done under the law of sin and death - also called the old covenant. Only the holy, pure blood of Jesus has the power to remove the guilt of sin from your conscience and set you free from sin. It is your choice to remain sin free by not returning to sin.

Romans 8:5 For they that are after the flesh do mind the things of the flesh; but they that are after the Spirit the things of the Spirit.6 For to be carnally minded is death; but to be spiritually minded is life and peace. Romans 8:8 So then they that are in the flesh cannot please God.

We are spiritual beings, born again, no longer ruled by our flesh. The word flesh here does not mean your flesh body. It does mean your learned carnal nature of sinfulness. If your are in the flesh (sin) you are not in fellowship with God or Jesus and this does not please God the Father. Is this a position that you want to be in? Some teach that sin is in your flesh body. This is not true as I have shown sin in the conscience not the physical flesh.

Hebrews 9:14 How much more shall the blood of Christ, who through the eternal Spirit offered himself without spot to God, purge your conscience from dead works to serve the living God?

You can see here that verse 9:14 says that your sin or guilt of your sin is in your conscience not your flesh body. Can you understand that "dead works" is another name for sin?

Romans 8:10 And if Christ be in you, the body is dead because of sin; but the Spirit is life because of righteousness.11 But if the Spirit of him that raised up Jesus from the dead dwell in you, he that raised up Christ from the dead shall also quicken your mortal bodies by his Spirit that dwelleth in you.

This is what the born again experience will do for you. Your spirit is brought to life by renewed contact with the Father, and your body is dying physically because of sin, as we no longer have the tree of life to eat from. Remember we are all appointed once to die physically.

The phrase "quicken your mortal bodies" also means physical healing; which is part and parcel of the work on the cross by Jesus. You cannot separate healing from salvation. They both are part of the atonement along with material needs. Do you believe this?

Romans 8:14 For as many as are led by the Spirit of God, they are the sons of God. Romans 8:16 The Spirit itself beareth witness with our spirit, that we are the children of God:

When we are born again the Holy Spirit guides us and confirms to us that we are saved. We have the sure and certain knowledge that we are saved by the removal of all sin and the guilt of sin from our conscience by Jesus' shed blood (**Heb 9:14**) The witness of the Holy Spirit is in convincing of us of sin if we slip up, and that when we repent we are back in the Kingdom of God.

Romans 8:38 For I am persuaded, that neither death, nor life, nor angels, nor principalities, nor powers, nor things present, nor things to come, 39 Nor height, nor depth, nor any other creature, shall be able to separate us from the love of God, which is in Christ Jesus our Lord.

Nothing can take you out of God's hands. In fact God will not shut the door in your face, only you can do this! You are the only one who can chose not to stay with God or even come to Him in the first place. You can go back into sin any time you want to. God does not take away your free will after you are saved. That is why He tells us so many times to remain sinless and holy. We must learn to be holy if we are to be with the Father for eternity. Do you think you can be clean and dirty at the same time? Can they mix? I think not!!

Romans 10:9 That if thou shalt confess with thy mouth the Lord Jesus, and shalt believe in thine heart that God hath raised him from the dead, thou shalt be saved.10 For with the heart man believeth unto righteousness; and with the mouth confession is made unto salvation.

This is how you become born again. These verses put a lie to the concept of predestination of who will be saved. If predestination of who was true, why then do we have to chose to confess with our mouth to salvation? "That **if** thou shalt confess with your mouth" says it is a free will choice. So if salvation is a free will choice then to remain a sinner is also a free will choice. NOTHING makes you sin but you, and nothing can make you saved but your choice of Jesus! The Big 'IF' is what says that salvation is a choice.

1 Corinthians 6:17 But he that is joined unto the Lord is one spirit.

We are one body and one spirit with Jesus, and there is no division in our minds or spirit in the body of Christ. We all have the same truth that the holy Spirit delivers and confirms to everyone in the one true body of Christ.

2 Corinthians 1:22 Who hath also sealed us, and given the earnest of the Spirit in our hearts.

Ephesians 1:13 In whom ye also trusted, after that ye heard the word of truth, the gospel of your salvation: in whom also after that ye believed, ye were sealed with that holy Spirit of promise, 14 Which is the earnest of our inheritance until the redemption of the purchased possession, unto the praise of his glory.

Ephesians 4:30 And grieve not the holy Spirit of God, whereby ye are sealed unto the day of redemption.

This is the promise of the Holy Spirit that is given to us as an engagement ring, as we are the bride of Christ. It is the guarantee of our salvation. We are bought at a very high price, it's called "the Cross".

This is NOT the baptism of the Holy Spirit as some teach.

The wedding will not be until the second coming of Jesus. He is coming for two reasons : 1- for final judgment, 2- for His holy and pure bride. Just in case you don't understand Holy and Pure: they mean without sin! "Don't grieve the Holy Spirit" means DON'T SIN!

2 Corinthians 5:17 Therefore if any man be in Christ, he is a new creature: old things are passed away; behold, all things are become new.

All things are made new in the Spirit by the salvation experience. We are new creatures in Christ, sinless, our sin has been removed from us, and with the guidance of the Holy Spirit in our lives we will remain that way as we choose. This is what is new. We are the HOLY BRIDE. We have been born again with our spirit back in fellowship with the Father. Now you must understand that this is only a spiritual renewal not physical. Physical and material renewal are also in and part of the cross. But separate from the spiritual. This is called Healing and Providing.

2 Corinthians 7:10 For godly sorrow worketh repentance to salvation not to be repented of: but the sorrow of the world worketh death.

This is the start of the salvation walk. It is a heart full of Godly sorrow for your crimes against the Father. Worldly sorrow is that which you show when you hurt some one in the world before you are saved. This worldly sorrow will not and does not bring you to salvation; only the sorrow of your heart (spirit) towards God for all the evil things you did in your unsaved life. This Godly sorrow is also the same as being broken on the rock of Jesus.

Galatians 2:19 For I through the law am dead to the law, that I might live unto God.20 I am crucified with Christ: nevertheless I live; yet not I, but Christ liveth in me: and the life which I now live in the flesh I live by the faith of the Son of God, who loved me, and gave himself for me.

This is an example of what you become when you are born again. This is living as Christ lived ——Sinless! Sin is a choice, and we have the power to resist sin by using His name to take into captivity any and all stray thoughts of immorality and temptations, and rejecting them. Besides, the Father will not let us be tempted beyond what we can resist. The flesh life is our normal physical life in this world. This shows that sin is not in the flesh of our bodies. Faith is not something our bodies can have. Faith is in our spirit and that is where the guilt of sin resides not in our flesh bodies as some teach.

Galatians 6:15 For in Christ Jesus neither circumcision availeth anything, nor uncircumcision, but a new creature.

Nothing in the flesh is important to Christ, the only thing that is important is that you are born again in the spirit, a new sinless, spiritual creature in Jesus, and remain that way. This is called the spiritual circumcision of the heart, not of the flesh.

Ephesians 4:22 That ye put off concerning the former conversation the old man, which is corrupt according to the deceitful lusts; 23 And be renewed in the spirit of your mind;

Be born again. Give up sin for a holy and pure life in fellowship with the Father, Son, and Holy Spirit.

Philippians 2:12 Wherefore, my beloved, as ye have always obeyed, not as in my presence only, but now much more in my absence, work out your own salvation with fear and trembling.

You are responsible for your own salvation, not some pastor in the pulpit. Trembling and fear, you had better fear God, He can throw you into hell. If you don't come to Jesus in repentance God will allow Satan to have his way with you. More to the point, you are giving Satan permission to beat you up. How would you like sickness, hate, and discontent in your life? If it's there now, then come to Jesus and get delivered from it. When You call on the name of God, He is obligated to save you through Jesus Christ. "You" must do this. It is impossible for anyone else to do it for you no matter what church you go to or even if you don't go to church. God still loves you, and there is no sin that God will not forgive (except for blasphemy against the Holy Spirit–which you cannot commit unless you are already saved). You don't have to "get" better before you get saved, that is a lie of Satan to keep you from being saved. By the way baby baptism does not get you to heaven, all it does is get the baby wet and make the parents feel that they did something good. This baby baptism was never used in the early church. It did not show up until about 300AD. It is NOT in the bible.

2 Thessalonians 2:9 *Even him*, **whose coming is after the working of Satan with all power and signs and lying wonders,10 And with all deceivableness of unrighteousness in them that perish; because they received not the love of the truth, that they might be saved.11 And for this cause God shall send them strong delusion, that they should believe a lie:12 That they all might be damned who believed not the truth, but had pleasure in unrighteousness.**

This is what happens to all those people who do not come to Jesus or who are led astray by false doctrines. People who like their ears tickled, and do not want the truth of the complete word of God. God will let them have their delusions of false Christianity; that what they are doing is of God when really it is of Satan. God will send a deceiving spirit to them. Can you imagine how hard it would be the realize the truth, and come back to it, when God has allowed a deceiving spirit come upon you?

2 Timothy 3:15 And that from a child thou hast known the holy scriptures, which are able to make thee wise unto salvation through faith which is in Christ Jesus.

"From a child" means from when you first became born again. The scripture shows us the way to the salvation which is of faith in Jesus the Christ. You must believe by faith that Jesus is who He says he is.

Wise, what does it mean? Well to be smart enough to recognize the truth when you see it. The knowledge of scripture will help keep you on the straight and narrow path to your final salvation in heaven. Contrary to what some churches teach, you can lose your salvation by not repenting of any and all sins you 'might' fall into after your initial salvation. The word salvation means: you begin your salvation, you continue your salvation, and you finish your salvation. Salvation is a work in progress up to your death or the second coming of Christ were it will finally be set and finished for eternity in glory with the Father, Son, and Holy Spirit..

2 Timothy 3:16 All scripture is given by inspiration of God, and is profitable for doctrine, for reproof, for correction, for instruction in righteousness:17 That the man of God may be perfect, throughly furnished unto all good works.

The word is given to us to teach us how to be Christians, and what being a Christian really is all about. If you don't know the word, how can you know what a Christian is or what he/she is supposed to do? You can't trust the man in the pulpit to tell you. In fact he is most likely to be educated by man in man's doctrine, not God's. He is no better than you and does not have a lock on God. God loves you as much as He loves anybody else in this world, even His Son Jesus, who was an ordinary man on this Earth with no more power to resist sin than you and I have as a Christians. Trust your salvation to no one but yourself. Verse 17 tells us "that the man of God" must be sin free. You will only do "good works" when you are sin free.

Your works are held up to the light of your morality. Works can be a sin if done with the wrong attitude. So check out your morality (attitude) every time you do works, because it is your attitude that make them good or bad. Did you do a good thing for God or for yourself and the world? For God is where you want your "good works" to be, not for the world or yourself!

Also there is no sin so bad that you can not be saved. Did not Jesus die for all the sins of the world? Did not Jesus say "It is finished"? By that He meant all of His work on this earth. The bible does not say 'except for these sins' now does it? The only sin not forgivable is blasphemy against the Holy Spirit, and to commit this sin you must have been saved in the first place. See study number 11 on the Blasphemy for more info on this subject.

2 Timothy 4:2 Preach the word; be instant in season, out of season; reprove, rebuke, exhort with all longsuffering and doctrine.3 For the time will come when they will not endure sound doctrine; but after their own lusts shall they heap to themselves teachers, having itching ears;4 And they shall turn away their ears from the truth, and shall be turned unto fables.

Be ready at all times to answer when a sinner or brother Christian comes to you with a question about the word of God. To do this you must study, know, and understand the holy scriptures. How else can you preach and teach Jesus if you don't Know or understand Him? Are we not commanded to preach the gospel? Look around at all the harlot churches on the corners of our cities. We are in the end times, which started at the cross. There are more and more feel good, just love them into the kingdom, pay your tithe - the more you pay the better seat you will have in heaven, churches today than ever before. Just open your eyes and you will see them for what they are, they're everywhere. Check them against the bible. They are the abode of Satan. Do you not see that these churches are built by man for man and not for Jesus? Jesus asked "will I find any faith on the earth when I come back "? Where is your faith today, with God or with some man?

Titus 3:5 Not by works of righteousness which we have done, but according to his mercy he saved us, by the washing of regeneration, and renewing of the Holy Ghost;

This is being born again!
Saved by the blood of Jesus. Washing away, removing, cleansing all of our past sin from our conscience, by our free will choice to be saved, and walking in the statutes of God by the power of the Holy Spirit baptism.

Hebrews 12:2 Looking unto Jesus the author and finisher of our faith; who for the joy that was set before him endured the cross, despising the shame, and is set down at the right hand of the throne of God.

Jesus who was 'JOYIOUS' to be the one who has provided for our salvation by His horrible death on the cross. Rising from the grave to sit at the right hand of God to rule and reign until the second coming for the Judgment of the world and the saints. Jesus won the war with Satan at the cross and resurrection. All we're doing now is the mopping up of the sinful world which is led by Satan in a gorilla war. This is called spiritual warfare! This is the fight for any and all who will come to God the Father. Jesus now sits on the throne of the Kingdom until the second coming when He, Jesus, will turn the Kingdom back over to the Father for eternity in glory.

1 Peter 1:22 Seeing ye have purified your souls in obeying the truth through the Spirit unto unfeigned love of the brethren, see that ye love one another with a pure heart fervently:23 Being born again, not of corruptible seed, but of incorruptible, by the word of God, which liveth and abideth for ever.

Born again into holiness by the Blood of Jesus. Anything else is a lie! "Purified your souls in obeying the Truth"! Do you not think that this means that we are, by our choice, made sinless? Or are we MADE to obey, with no choice whatsoever? We are saved, purified by Jesus' blood and our choice to accept Him in our lives. We become born again by giving up the sin habit we learned from our youth, that rules our lives, with a Godly sorrow and a broken heart for Jesus. God never changes, this is why we can trust Him to do what He declares that he will do.

1 John 1:8 If we say that we have no sin, we deceive ourselves, and the truth is not in us. 9 If we confess our sins, he is faithful and just to forgive us our sins, and to cleanse us from all unrighteousness. 10 If we say that we have not sinned, we make him a liar, and his word is not in us.

The first verse is talking about how all men need Jesus. No matter what you say, before salvation you are a dirty rotten sinner. It is after salvation that verse 9 comes into play. That is, if you sin, as a Christian, God's mercy will let you repent as many times as necessary to get you to the point of saying NO to sin completely. This verse says that our sin is removed from us and that we are made righteous before God. So you see, the modern church teaches a contradiction; your sin is removed, but your still a sinner.

Verse 10 is saying again that the natural man is a sinner and it doesn't make any difference how much he protests, and says "I'm a good man". This is the only way to understand these verses. Otherwise they contradict themselves, and as there are no contradictions in the bible this is the correct way to understand what these verses say.

1 John 2:1 My little children, these things write I unto you, that ye sin not. And if any man sin, we have an advocate with the Father, Jesus Christ the righteous:

"That we sin not." Just what do you think this means? Stop sinning EH! Ah! What's this? "IF any man sin," don't you think that this means that sin is in your control, a choice? Big word 'If' . Eh? As sinners we have the free will choice to go Jesus to have His blood remove our sins from us to and to stop sinning . We then have NO sin in us. Right? "IF" after being born again we sin we then go to Jesus by way of 1 John 1:9, ask forgiveness, repent, and become sin free and righteous once more.

1 John 2:3 And hereby we do know that we know him, if we keep his commandments. 4 He that saith, I know him, and keepeth not his commandments, is a liar, and the truth is not in him.

1 John 5:10 He that believeth on the Son of God hath the witness in himself: he that believeth not God hath made him a liar; because he believeth not the record that God gave of his Son.

If you are obedient, stop sinning, obey all His other commands, then you will have the sure and certain knowledge of your salvation. Again the big word IF, a choice to obey or to disobey. If you're are a sinner and still claim to be saved you're a LIAR and are not saved. It doesn't matter if you don't believe this, it is what scripture says. Do you really want to point you finger in God's face and call Him a liar? You know maybe the world cannot tell if you're lying but God certainly can.

1 John 4:15 Whosoever shall confess that Jesus is the Son of God, God dwelleth in him, and he in God.

1 John 5:1 Whosoever believeth that Jesus is the Christ is born of God: and every one that loveth him that begat loveth him also that is begotten of him. 2 By this we know that we love the children of God, when we love God, and keep his commandments. 3 For this is the love of God, that we keep his commandments: and his commandments are not grievous.

To confess Jesus is the Son of God is called witnessing, and you must, have to, are commanded to do this witnessing. Being a member of the body of Christ is not a private, only for you to know, thing. This is the start of the salvation, born again, experience. From this point on you must walk sin free if you want to stay in the Kingdom of heaven. Your salvation is an ongoing process that teaches you to come to the point in your struggle against sin, of not continuing in sin. The more you refuse to fall into or commit sin, the easier it is to say no to any and all sin. The reason that God put **1 John 1:9** in the bible is He knew the possibility of our falling back into our old habit of sin. He will forgive you as many times as necessary to get you to that point where you say no to all sin and temptations. This is called God's Mercy.

To have the absolute certainty that we are saved we must first obey the commandments of God. The first and foremost commandant is to stop sinning. If this is not a requirement of our salvation, then why did Jesus come and die on the cross for the removal of our sin from our conscience? Just so we can continue in our sin filled happy little life in and of the world? By the way it is a sin not to be saved.

Are we, the born again of Christ, not called out of the world, to live separate from the lusts of the world? Do you really believe that you can have your cake and eat it too? To be a sinner or to be a saint, that is the question you must answer for yourself! To say that you are both is an oxymoron, it is being 'double minded', and 'blessing and cursing' from the same mouth. 'Yes and no' at the same time, 'bitter water and sweet water' from the same well. This is NOT possible!! Use the mind that God gave you, figure it out for yourself . Do you love Jesus? Are you still sinning?

If this is the case then you love your sin more than you love Jesus! Does not Jesus say that if you love me keep my commandments? Well? Check out all that is told to you by any and all expounders of the word in the word for yourself. This work included. Don't trust your salvation to someone else! Only to God!

1 John 5: 4 For whatsoever is born of God overcometh the world: and this is the victory that overcometh the world, even our faith.5 Who is he that overcometh the world, but he that believeth that Jesus is the Son of God?

Does this pertain to you? If it does, you have overcome the world of sin and stopped sinning by faith in and love for Jesus. Are you born again? This is what is says right? That we "HAVE" overcome the world "IF" we are believers in Jesus. This overcoming is by Faith. In other words we are the saved of Jesus if we have stopped sinning. The word If means that we have a free will choice.

These verses also put a lie to the teaching of who is saved by predestination. The word "whosoever" means any and all. Salvation is a free will choice, not God picking and choosing who will go to heaven and who will go to hell. Predestination really means the method of our salvation, which is by the holy and pure blood of Christ and our choosing to avail ourselves of it. In other words it means how we are saved not who is saved.

Exodus 32:33 And the LORD said unto Moses, Whosoever hath sinned against me, him will I blot out of my book.

Here is God's answer to just one sin. Your name is removed from the book of life in heaven and you are on the broad road to hell. Ask yourself how many sins does it take to make you a sinner? You see the word "sinned"? It does not mean more than one, it is a singular verb. You are made a sinner by your choice of committing just ONE sin. By that one sin you're out and on your way to the fire. You can also see here God really does have a holy eraser, and you are the only one who can 'make' God use it.

Blasphemy against the Holy Spirit

Romans 11:30 For as ye in times past have not believed God, yet have now obtained mercy through their unbelief: 31 Even so have these also now not believed, that through your mercy they also may obtain mercy.

"In times past" means before you came to salvation through Jesus' blood. Verse 31 means the same thing about salvation, and that God's mercy is available to all who accept it. These verses are talking about God's mercy, and salvation going to the all people of the world including the Jews. Before we see what the only unforgivable sin is we must see that God's mercy is for all people for all time–and this mercy means that no sin other than <u>Blasphemy against the Holy Spirit,</u> is unforgivable - for as many times as it takes to get you saved and to stay that way. This is called God's mercy. The word went to the gentiles to make the Jews jealous and thereby draw them back to God.

Matthew 12:31 Wherefore I say unto you, All manner of sin and blasphemy shall be forgiven unto men: but the blasphemy against the Holy Ghost shall not be forgiven unto men. 32 And whosoever speaketh a word against the Son of man, it shall be forgiven him: but whosoever speaketh against the Holy Ghost, it shall not be forgiven him, neither in this world, neither in the world to come.

Mark 3:28 Verily I say unto you, All sins shall be forgiven unto the sons of men, and blasphemies wherewith soever they shall blaspheme:29 But he that shall blaspheme against the Holy Ghost hath never forgiveness, but is in danger of eternal damnation.

Luke 12:10 And whosoever shall speak a word against the Son of man, it shall be forgiven him: but unto him that blasphemeth against the Holy Ghost it shall not be forgiven.

This is the ONLY sin that you can COMMIT and NOT be forgiven. You must be a Christian in the first place. Then by an act of your free will you reject and turn your back on God, Jesus, and the work of the Holy Spirit in your life to return to the worldly way of selfish sinfulness. You are then, with no chance of forgiveness, on the wide, worldly road to hell. Your course is set and cannot be changed!!

Hebrews 6:4 For it is impossible for those who were once enlightened, and have tasted of the heavenly gift, and were made partakers of the Holy Ghost, 5 And have tasted the good word of God, and the powers of the world to come, 6 If they shall fall away, to renew them again unto repentance; seeing they crucify to themselves the Son of God afresh, and put him to an open shame.

Here is a perfect description of blasphemy against the Holy Spirit. In simple terms it means that if you do not just fall back into sinfulness, but turn away from God and reject Him from all parts of your life, then you are GUILTY of BLASPHEMY against the HOLY SPIRIT. At this point you are lost forever with NO chance of repentance.

Hebrews 10:26 For if we sin wilfully after that we have received the knowledge of the truth, there remaineth no more sacrifice for sins, 27 But a certain fearful looking for of judgment and fiery indignation, which shall devour the adversaries.

Hebrews 10:29 Of how much sorer punishment, suppose ye, shall he be thought worthy, who hath trodden under foot the Son of God, and hath counted the blood of the covenant, wherewith he was sanctified, an unholy thing, and hath done despite unto the Spirit of grace?

This is also a description of blasphemy against the Holy Spirit. It is a quality decision in your life to turn away from God the Father, The Son, and the Holy Spirit in a conscious choice to return to a sinful life (not just the occasional sin), thereby rejecting all that you knew of God. You are now doomed forevermore, there is no forgiveness left for you. Just to make it clear, just falling back into sin is not the same as making a decision to reject God, and you must be saved in the first place for you to be able to blaspheme the Holy Spirit.

I believe salvation is a three step process: 1- Repentance and asking forgiveness from a heart broken on the Rock of Jesus 2-Full immersion water baptism 3- The baptism of the Holy Spirit with the evidence of a unknown tongue, also called a prayer language.

2 Thessalonians 3:6 Now we command you, brethren, in the name of our Lord Jesus Christ, that ye withdraw yourselves from every brother that walketh disorderly, and not after the tradition which he received of us.

This may not seem to be in the right study, but I believe that this is a case of Blasphemy against the Holy Spirit. The thing that made me decide is that we are commanded not to fellowship with this person or persons. This is different than what we are told to do with a fellow Christina who just slips up and falls back into sin. In one case we are told to try and guide the fallen person back into the fold. In the other case we are 'commanded' to have nothing to do with the sinner. Can you see this?

Titus 3:10 A man that is an heretick after the first and second admonition reject;11 Knowing that he that is such is subverted, and sinneth, being condemned of himself.

A sinner "by choice" is rejected from the body for refusing to repent. Again Blasphemy Against the Holy Spirit. You can see this one by the phrase "condemned of himself".

2 Peter 2:20 For if after they have escaped the pollutions of the world through the knowledge of the Lord and Saviour Jesus Christ, they are again entangled therein, and overcome, the latter end is worse with them than the beginning. 21 For it had been better for them not to have known the way of righteousness, than, after they have known it, to turn from the holy commandment delivered unto them.

"The latter end is worse". What is worse that not being saved? The answer is losing all chance of being saved. If they had not known of the way of righteousness, being born again, in the first place , then they would still have a chance at being born again.

As it is this person or persons have completely turned their backs on and rejected God by walking back into the world of sinfulness on purpose with full knowledge of what they were and are doing. They are lost forevermore. You might say that they spit on The Holy Spirit.

1 John 5:16 If any man see his brother sin a sin which is not unto death, he shall ask, and he shall give him life for them that sin not unto death. There is a sin unto death: I do not say that he shall pray for it. 17 All unrighteousness is sin: and there is a sin not unto death.

The sin unto death is the sin of a completely turning away from God with the full knowledge and complete understanding of God's work and love in your life. This is called Blasphemy against the Holy Spirit, and is a personal choice that you make. It is life changing, and there is no going back. Blasphemy against the Holy Spirit is the only sin that is not forgivable.

No matter what they were, <u>ALL other sins are forgivable</u>.

AGAIN the ONLY exception is Blasphemy against the Holy Spirit as explained above!

Do we Judge others

Matthew 15:18 But those things which proceed out of the mouth come forth from the heart; and they defile the man. 19 For out of the heart proceed evil thoughts, murders, adulteries, fornications, thefts, false witness, blasphemies: 20 These are the things which defile a man: but to eat with unwashen hands defileth not a man.

We have a mind with the ability to think and an intelligence that is given to us by God. With this mind and intelligence we cannot help but judge other Christian's words and actions. We do not judge their hearts, only God can judge your heart. But as we see above in the scripture, words come from the heart. So you decide just what we are to Judge. Whatever you decide, we must judge against and by the word of God, and in the love of God not some love that comes from the hearts of unsaved mankind, that says that we must never offend or make anyone feel bad about their sins or life in general. To quote a good and Godly man, " It is one thing to call a brother to repentance out of love and compassion for his soul and quite another to assign him to hell with contempt in our hearts."

Those sinners in the world who have not yet come to Jesus are not to be judged, we have no business doing so. That is what Jesus will do at the second coming. We can see that they are in sin. We can tell them how to get rid of sin and how to stop sinning, but we can not be holier than thou in our attitude toward them. We Must operate in God's kind of love only.

Luke 6:37 Judge not, and ye shall not be judged: condemn not, and ye shall not be condemned: forgive, and ye shall be forgiven:

Judge not as the world judges with hate and malice, but do judge in love with the word of God's love as your guide so as to be able to bring a wayward brother back into the fold. Not to condemn is to be in the love of Christ, to forgive is a command of the Jesus and the Father. Again we must judge, but without condemnation and in forgiveness. This is the love of Christ manifested in our lives.

What is the way in which we judge? How we judge is by our words of love, our actions of love, and our attitude of love. This love is called Agape* which is God's kind of love. This is the only love we must walk in, any other would be a lie.

* See **Romans 13:8-10.**

Luke 6:42 Either how canst thou say to thy brother, Brother, let me pull out the mote that is in thine eye, when thou thyself beholdest not the beam that is in thine own eye? Thou hypocrite, cast out first the beam out of thine own eye, and then shalt thou see clearly to pull out the mote that is in thy brother's eye

This is an example of judging as the world judges. This is hurtful, and not operating in the love of Jesus. If you have a beam in your eye then you are in as much sin, if not more than your brother. This makes you unqualified to be a judge of anything. Removing the beam by repenting allows us to react in the love of Christ to our brothers mote, thereby helping /guiding him to remove it in LOVE. We must also understand that by living by in Agape Love we will cause hurt that will bring a fallen brother or sister back to God. Do not be fearful of this.

Luke 6:45 A good man out of the good treasure of his heart bringeth forth that which is good; and an evil man out of the evil treasure of his heart bringeth forth that which is evil: for of the abundance of the heart his mouth speaketh.

We again see that we determine the condition of a brother's heart by the words that come out of his mouth and thereby know what is in his heart; for out of the heart comes your intent and words. This may not be a falling back into sin, but may only be a momentary slip up - so react in love. By this I mean we can not know the complete condition of our brother's heart just because he slipped up. We again, only judge outward words or actions not the heart. Only Christ can know and judge the heart completely.

John 7:24 Judge not according to the appearance, but judge righteous judgment.

This is judgment guided by the Holy Spirit. Just because someone doesn't look like what you think a Christian should look like does not mean that they are not saved. This is just an example. I'm positive you know what Jesus means here.

Romans 14:10 But why dost thou judge thy brother? or why dost thou set at nought thy brother? for we shall all stand before the judgment seat of Christ.

This means to not to judge your brother in unrighteousness. You could say "do not judge your brother by your own self righteousness". Do not reject a brother for your idea of what a Christian should be. We have an instruction manual that tells us who and what a brother in Christ is.

Romans 14:13 Let us not therefore judge one another any more: but judge this rather, that no man put a stumblingblock or an occasion to fall in his brother's way. 14 I know, and am persuaded by the Lord Jesus, that there is nothing unclean of itself: but to him that esteemeth any thing to be unclean, to him it is unclean. 15 But if thy brother be grieved with thy meat, now walkest thou not charitably. Destroy not him with thy meat, for whom Christ died. 16 Let not then your good be evil spoken of: 17 For the kingdom of God is not meat and drink; but righteousness, and peace, and joy in the Holy Ghost.

We must not look at other Christian's askew, we must see them as Jesus sees them. Do not do anything that will cause a brother to stumble - even if it is not sin in your life. Example: don't dance in front of your brothers who believe dancing is a sin, don't have that one cold beer on a really hot day in front of a brother who feels all drinking is a sin. I'm one of those brothers who don't drink alcohol or smoke and I do believe at least for me they are sins, but I can not know what the holy Spirit is working on in my brothers heart. So unless it is really an out and out sin, mentioned in the bible, it is no business on mine.

Romans 15:13 Now the God of hope fill you with all joy and peace in believing, that ye may abound in hope, through the power of the Holy Ghost.14 And I myself also am persuaded of you, my brethren, that ye also are full of goodness, filled with all knowledge, able also to admonish one another.

This tells us that when we admonish (judge) each other, we must do it with the full knowledge of the word of God and by the power of the Holy Spirit which leads to the end of sin in our lives. In other words we must not be in sin when we judge others of sin. If we don't help one another in love who will?

1 Corinthians 2:15 But he that is spiritual judgeth all things, yet he himself is judged of no man.

The key here is to understand that the sinless spiritual man of God operates as the Holy Spirit guides him. He cannot be judged because there is nothing in him that is not of Jesus and the Father in heaven. Again we as Christians do not judge the sinners of the world, Jesus will. We can see that they are sinners but all we are commanded to do is witness Jesus to them for their salvation.

1 Corinthians 5:12 For what have I to do to judge them also that are without? do not ye judge them that are within?13 But them that are without God judgeth. Therefore put away from among yourselves that wicked person.

Those "without" are the sinners of the world and those within are the saved of Jesus. Again we are to judge those who are our brothers and reject them if they will not repent (the wicked), and we are NOT to judge the sinners of the world that is God's job.

1 Corinthians 6:5 I speak to your shame. Is it so, that there is not a wise man among you? no, not one that shall be able to judge between his brethren?6 But brother goeth to law with brother, and that before the unbelievers.

Christians taking Christians to court, what an outrage. We as a community of Christians, in the Body of Christ are of one mind. The unholy world system of law can not judge us as long as we stay sinless. We must judge ourselves, or the world will - to our sorrow.
As a side light we, the saved in Christ, are not called to, and must not obey any law of the world that is contrary to God's law. In fact God does not have a sense of humor about putting man's law above His law. So don't do it!!

1 Corinthians 10:15 I speak as to wise men; judge ye what I say.

The world says "Judge not lest you be Judged" as 'finger pointing of their righteousness' against Christians not to judge them, and they are right. But we as Christians must judge the words of other Christians because words come from the heart. Again we only judge the words and actions of other Christens. There is no such thing as "I didn't mean it". If it comes out your mouth it came from your heart.
Paul says here that wise men will judge his words. Are we not also to judge all of our brothers words, and also have our words judged? Paul words are the gospel and they came from his heart. Other Christian men and women speak the gospel also, but some of them have not yet learned to control what they say. They don't think first, and they speak in anger. You know how it works. Their words, of the moment, come from the heart. It doesn't matter how much you say "I didn't mean it"! Be careful what you speak because it can never return to your mouth. This is why we must judge our words (best done before they come out your mouth) and the words of others.

As it says in **James 3:10 Out of the same mouth proceedeth blessing and cursing. My brethren, these things ought not so to be.**

James 4:11 Speak not evil one of another, brethren. He that speaketh evil of his brother, and judgeth his brother, speaketh evil of the law, and judgeth the law: but if thou judge the law, thou art not a doer of the law, but a judge.

Here is an example of judging wrongly. A judge of the law! Did not God write the law? So how can we judge some to be good or bad against the law that God wrote?? The answer is: we do not have the ability to judge God's law, no matter what your IQ is. Nor do we have the authority to judge God, because that is what you are doing if you judge the law given by God. We are not called to be above the law as a judge of the law.

1 Peter 4:17-18 For the time is come that judgment must begin at the house of God: and if it first begin at us, what shall the end be of them that obey not the gospel of God? And if the righteous scarcely be saved, where shall the ungodly and the sinner appear?

The time is now that we must "judge" ourselves, our brothers and sisters in Christ, the church that man built, and decide if they are truly of God. The judgment of those who do not obey the commandments of God will be judged by Jesus at the White Throne Judgment. What would you rather have; judgment in love by your fellow Christians that will help bring you back into the fold if you have sinned, or the judgment of Jesus at the end of time for sinners that will send you to hell?

The Rock of the church

Matthew 16:17 And Jesus answered and said unto him, Blessed art thou, Simon Barjona: for flesh and blood hath not revealed it unto thee, but my Father which is in heaven. 18 And I say also unto thee, That thou art Peter, and upon this rock I will build my church; and the gates of hell shall not prevail against it.

Jesus tells Peter that he is the stone (Greek for Peter) and that he Peter will help build the church of Christ, but you must see and understand that Jesus is the ROCK and FOUNDATION that the church is built on, not the stone of Peter. That the church is built on Peter is blasphemy against Jesus. You will see over and over in scripture that Jesus is the rock and foundation, not Peter. As a side light: There is no proof that Peter was even in Rome.

John 1:42 And he brought him to Jesus. And when Jesus beheld him, he said, Thou art Simon the son of Jona: thou shalt be called Cephas, which is by interpretation, A stone.

Peter the stone is not the rock / foundation of the body. Jesus is! The body is built on the foundation of the rock of Jesus. Peter was one of the builders of the body, but again Jesus laid the foundations, and is the Rock that the foundations sits on.

Matthew 21:42 Jesus saith unto them, Did ye never read in the scriptures, The stone which the builders rejected, the same is become the head of the corner: this is the Lord's doing, and it is marvellous in our eyes? 43 Therefore say I unto you, The kingdom of God shall be taken from you, and given to a nation bringing forth the fruits thereof. 44 And whosoever shall fall on this stone shall be broken: but on whomsoever it shall fall, it will grind him to powder.

Luke 20:17 And he beheld them, and said, What is this then that is written, The stone which the builders rejected, the same is become the head of the corner? 18 Whosoever shall fall upon that stone shall be broken; but on whomsoever it shall fall, it will grind him to powder.

These verses tells us that Jesus is the rock , the foundation. The corner stone of the body of the church of Christ. It is Jesus only that provides salvation not some man named Peter. If you reject Jesus, as the nation of Israel did, you will be destroyed and ground into powder as the nation of Israel was. If your are of Jesus you are broken and remade /renewed a new man in Christ. How would you like to shattered and ground into powder?

Notice in verse 43 that Jesus is telling the Jew of the day that if they don't accept Him as the Messiah that their kingdom on the earth and that the spiritual kingdom to come will be given to others. These others are the rest of the world. This is exactly what happened. The Jews from the cross up through today and beyond have to go through Jesus' shed blood just as everyone else in the world. There is no special salvation for anyone in the world other than through Jesus

John 14:30 Hereafter I will not talk much with you: for the prince of this world cometh, and hath nothing in me.

Jesus is sinless, He says so here, looking forward to the cross. If He <u>wasn't</u> sinless the work on the cross would have been null and void. If God the Father imputed sin onto Jesus on the cross, the work of the cross would have been a waste of time. Jesus HAD to REMAIN sinless for ALL of HIS WORK on the earth or it would have been a useless work. A waste of time. See the study on Mistranslation for a better explanation of whether or not Jesus was made a sinner.

John 15:4 Abide in me, and I in you. As the branch cannot bear fruit of itself, except it abide in the vine; no more can ye, except ye abide in me.5 I am the vine, ye are the branches: He that abideth in me, and I in him, the same bringeth forth much fruit: for without me ye can do nothing.

Jesus is the source of our salvation and the only way to get to heaven. It is only by Jesus and the Holy Spirit that we are able to witness effectively thereby garnering more fruit for the Kingdom of heaven.

John 16:33 These things I have spoken unto you, that in me ye might have peace. In the world ye shall have tribulation: but be of good cheer; I have overcome the world.

Jesus overcame the world by <u>remaining sinless</u> (even on the cross) and going to the cross, a one time substitutionary payment, a Perfect Holy sacrifice. By an act of His own free will he was the perfect Sacrificial Lamb. By this work He defeated Satan, sin, hell, and spiritual death. BUT to accept this work is decision you make. It is your free will choice to accept it, or reject it. Your life for or against God is conditional on your decision. Whether or not you stay sinless is a free will choice made by nobody but you. See **James 4:17.** You must remember that Jesus in the only way to change your life for the better.

John 17:15 I pray not that thou shouldest take them out of the world, but that thou shouldest keep them from the evil.

God will protect you from evil as long as you are sinless. Satan cannot harm you as long as you remain in God's sheepfold. The only thing that allows Satan to come against you is for you to take yourself out of God's protection by one un-repented sin. This verse puts a lie to the rapture being at any other time but at the second coming of Jesus, the last trump, by saying that God protects us through all trials, tribulations, and troubles. He does not take us out of it, but He does take us through it without harm . Ex. Noah and the flood , and a lot and his family.

John 19:30 When Jesus therefore had received the vinegar, he said, It is finished: and he bowed his head, and gave up the ghost.

All the work that Jesus came to do is finished, and all Old Testament prophecy is now fulfilled. The word of God is given, Satan is defeated and cast out of heaven (this was done at the cross) to the earth; no longer able to condemn the saints to God in heaven. See Rev. 11:15 through Rev. 12.

The removal of sin from your conscience is now made possible. The baptism of the Holy Spirit is given, and much more.

Acts 4:10-12 Be it known unto you all, and to all the people of Israel, that by the name of Jesus Christ of Nazareth, whom you crucified, whom God raised from the dead, even by him does this man stand here before you whole. This is the stone which was rejected by you builders, which has become the head of the corner. Neither is there salvation in any other: for there is no other name under heaven given among men, by which we must be saved.

The Stone, as you see here, is Jesus and it is by Him we are saved. Not man's church in Rome that claims it's authority is from some man named Peter. Now don't misunderstand, Peter was one of the greatest apostles, was loved of Jesus, and is a very great example to us in that he sinned and repented and was forgiven. He, Peter, went on to do many astounding and very great works for God by the Holy Spirit operating in his life. We should do as well. Peter was charged with helping build the body of Christ, but he is not the Rock that the body is built on. Jesus the Christ has that honor because of His sinless work on the earth, the cross, and the resurrection.

Peter and the other apostles built the church on the "foundation Rock of Jesus Christ", not on the 'little stone' of Peter.

Romans 9:32 Wherefore? Because they sought it not by faith, but as it were by the works of the law. For they stumbled at that stumbling stone;33 As it is written, Behold, I lay in Sion a stumbling stone and rock of offence: and whosoever believeth on him shall not be ashamed.

This stumbling stone is Jesus, you can be offended by Him and be crushed beneath him or you can fall on to Him with a broken heart and be part of His holy family. Your choice.

It was as true for the Jews in Jesus' time as it is today and on into the future. The only way to salvation is through Jesus. There is no other plan of salvation for the Jews or anyone else. Any other teaching is a LIE. I cannot say this strong enough. No other religion provides salvation by the removal of sin, or any salvation at all! How can there be salvation without the removal of sin? How can you pay for a lifetime worth of sin without Jesus' shed blood? These false religions includes Judaism, Buddhism, Hinduism, Mohammedanism, Mormonism or any of the other 'ISM's'.

1 Corinthians 3:11 For other foundation can no man lay than that is laid, which is Jesus Christ.

The foundation (Jesus) is what the church is built on, it's like a house built on bed rock. It will not fall down at the onset of storms as some, not built on the rock of Jesus, that will fold up and go away at the smallest of problems. The problems and contrariness of men cannot hurt the house that Jesus built. Is it not neat that Jesus is the bedrock that the foundation is laid and is also the cornerstone which all else is measured against. WOW, what a building we are.

The temple of God. Now remember if you slip off the rock of Jesus you are a ruined building that is falling down. You can not stand straight and tall (without sin in your life) without a foundation set on bed rock and the massive corner stone of Jesus Christ.

Ephesians 2:20 And are built upon the foundation of the apostles and prophets, Jesus Christ himself being the chief corner stone;

Jesus is the foundation (see above **1Cor 3:11**) , cornerstone of the body, and what the church of Christ is built on. The apostles built upon the foundation by continuing to spread the word of God to the world as it was given by Jesus The Christ. How could Peter be that foundation when scripture say that Jesus is the foundation? Peter and the other Apostles built on the foundation of Jesus.

1 Corinthians 10:4 And did all drink the same spiritual drink: for they drank of that spiritual Rock that followed them: and that Rock was Christ.

Jesus was the head of His body/church even way back then in the desert with Moses. This Rock (Jesus) did give them real water to drink. It is also an example (type) pointing to the Spiritual Water, Rivers of Living Water (the word), in the new covenant of Spirit and Grace which we have through Jesus' confirming work, and by our choice to go with Him as our master in our lives.

2 Corinthians 5:21 For he hath made him to be sin for us, who knew no sin; that we might be made the righteousness of God in him.

God did not impute sin onto or into Jesus! He was and still is absolutely sin free. Jesus was a sacrifice by His own free will. He was made, by His choice, to be a substitutionary payment for our sins. Another way to say it is that God the Father accepted Jesus' free will sacrifice made for the sins of the world in place of us, the creation, having to pay for them. Do you really think that if the sins of the world were put on and in Jesus that His blood would have remained Holy and pure? How could God the Father have accepted the sacrifice of a sinner? By the way, if Jesus was made to be a sinner guilty of the sins of the world How did He get rid of them to go to heaven where no sin can abide? What sacrifice was made for the sins on Jesus? Don't tell me when he died they just fell off Him. If he was made a sinner with the sins of the world how did He become the Head of the Church (see below) when you have to be sin free to get into His church (kingdom) in the first place? Kind of like a oxymoron? Eh!

Ephesians 1:22 And hath put all things under his feet, and gave him to be the head over all things to the church, 23 Which is his body, the fulness of him that filleth all in all.
Not only the "rock of the foundation", but also the Head, corner stone, in charge, number one, the boss, the director, the one and only, He's it. What else can you say?

Ephesians 2:21 In whom all the building fitly framed together groweth unto an holy temple in the Lord: 22 In whom ye also are builded together for an habitation of God through the Spirit.

We as individuals are the temple of God wherein the Holy Spirit resides. Together we make up the body of Christ, a holy work by Jesus. To be in this body you must be holy, that is sinless. To stay in the body you must stay sinless. For the Holy Spirit to stay with you, you have to remain in a holy condition. One sin and He leaves until you repent and ask forgiveness. God does not share with Satan, which is who you belong to every time you sin. The only way back to Jesus is to repent and ask forgiveness of the Father in Jesus' name. See **1 John 1: 9**.

Hebrews 1:8 But unto the Son he saith, Thy throne, O God, is for ever and ever: a sceptre of righteousness is the sceptre of thy kingdom.9 Thou hast loved righteousness, and hated iniquity; therefore God, even thy God, hath anointed thee with the oil of gladness above thy fellows.

God the Father calls Jesus "God", not "A" god as some of man's religions call Him. To call Jesus a god is to say that Jesus is one of many gods. This is another lie of Satan. In fact one particular church had their own bible written, changing the verses in the book of John to say that Jesus is "A" god, thereby reducing Him to second class status.

You can also see here that God, who is the Father, Son, and holy Spirit all in One, who hates sin and loves righteousness. The trinity is three separate personalities who are in 100% agreement 100% of the time held together by love, which is by their free will. The reason Jesus is anointed with the oil of gladness is because He is sinless. We also have this joy in our lives when we come to salvation through Jesus. This verse also says that Jesus in above everyone(with the exception of the Father), that He is the head.

John 1:1 In the beginning was the Word, and the Word was with God, and the Word was God.

Jesus is the second member of the Godhead, who are three distinct personalities who are in 100% agreement, in 100% love with each other 100% of the time. This makes up the one true God. By the way Jesus is also called the Word.

Hebrews 2:9 But we see Jesus, who was made a little lower than the angels for the suffering of death, crowned with glory and honour; that he by the grace of God should taste death for every man.

Hebrews 2:14 Forasmuch then as the children are partakers of flesh and blood, he also himself likewise took part of the same; that through death he might destroy him that had the power of death, that is, the devil;

Hebrews 2:16 For verily he took not on him the nature of angels; but he took on him the seed of Abraham.

Hebrews 2:17 Wherefore in all things it behoved him to be made like unto his brethren, that he might be a merciful and faithful high priest in things pertaining to God, to make reconciliation for the sins of the people.

18 For in that he himself hath suffered being tempted, he is able to succour them that are tempted.

Hebrews 4:15 For we have not an high priest which cannot be touched with the feeling of our infirmities; but was in all points tempted like as we are, yet without sin.

As you can see by these verses Jesus gave up all of His Godly powers and became a man just the same as you and I. He was baptized in the Holy Spirit when John the Baptist baptized Him in the Jordan river. The power to cast out demons, feed the 5000, raise the dead, heal the sick, and preach the Gospel was from the Holy Spirit working through Him. Just as he works through us. The power to resist sin came from within Him by His free will choice of doing the right or of doing the wrong thing. Is it not great that he chose to do the good in all things? You have this same choice to make. It is still the same for us in this day and age. Some churches and some people believe that Jesus came to the earth with all of His godly powers intact, and that is how He did all His great works and did not give in to temptation and then sin. This is a lie of Satan to deceive the body and to convince us that we cannot stop sinning, or do the works of Jesus. One reason Jesus gave up His Godly powers is so He would understand our trials and tribulations, and thereby help us in our need. Jesus said we will do all that He did and more. The "more" is bringing salvation to the people of the world and then getting them baptized in the Holy Spirit. Neither of which could Jesus do while on the earth.

Hebrews 5:8 Though he were a Son, yet learned he obedience by the things which he suffered; 9 And being made perfect, he became the author of eternal salvation unto all them that obey him; 10 Called of God an high priest after the order of Melchisedec.

This is Jesus! To learn obedience is what we must do if we want to go to heaven. We will suffer in this life just as Jesus suffered. He was, as we will be, made perfect by sufferings. Man's church says He was actually made a sinner, that God put all the sins of the world on Him like sticky tape, or God the father smeared Him with the sins of axel grease. <u>Read these verses again</u>. Jesus was made a PERFECT sacrifice by His free will CHOICE, or this verse is lying. Again How could Jesus be our head, the high Priest of Melchisedec, if He were made literally to be sin? We must also become perfect, as Jesus was, by being sin free. This is NOT sinless perfection, only Jesus can claim that as He never once sinned. One of the most important commands to obey is to "stop sinning". Jesus was "made perfect" by never sinning as a man. This means that He, Jesus, chose of His own free will not to give in to temptation and sin, and to die on the cross for a world full of undeserving sinful people such as you and I. We are made perfect by our choice to repent of sin and remain sin free. There is the difference between us and Jesus. By His choice, such a small thing "to choose", we have freely been given a very large thing. It's called salvation, freedom from sin! We must make this very small choice to get this very large reward

Hebrews 7:25 Wherefore he is able also to save them to the uttermost that come unto God by him, seeing he ever liveth to make intercession for them.

Jesus, by being obedient to the Father's will, is now our intercessor with the Father. He tells the Father who belongs to Him. "Come to God by Him" means that God calls all men and that they go through Jesus to get to the Father. THIS IS THE ONLY WAY TO THE FATHER!! No other religion, including most if not all of mans organized denominations or so called Christian churches, can get you to heaven! Again Jesus is our intercessor with the Father. Not Mary or any of the so called saints named by man can do anything for you. They're DEAD! They can not hear your prayers. The scripture

Verses that Say in the Kingdom of God 75

tells us to pray to the Father in only Jesus' name! By the way the bible calls all who are saved by Jesus' blood saints; they cannot be made saints by man's church. What a lie!

Hebrews 12:24 And to Jesus the mediator of the new covenant, and to the blood of sprinkling, that speaketh better things than that of Abel.

Jesus sits and rules at the right hand of God, our intercessor, and mediator to God the Father. The blood we are sprinkled with is the holy blood of Jesus, shed for our redemption under the new covenant brought and confirmed by Jesus, as foretold in— **Daniel 9:26 And after threescore and two weeks shall Messiah be cut off, but not for himself: and the people of the prince that shall come shall destroy the city and the sanctuary; and the end thereof shall be with a flood, and unto the end of the war desolations are determined. 27* <u>And he shall confirm the covenant with many for one week:</u> and in the midst of the week he shall cause the sacrifice and the oblation to cease, and for the overspreading of abominations he shall make it desolate, even until the consummation, and that determined shall be poured upon the desolate.**

As I've said before, Jesus is our intercessor and in who's name we pray to God the Father, not to Mary or church made saints. To pray in anyone's name other than Jesus is a sin, and is contrary to what the bible teaches.

God will not hear prayers in anyone's name but Jesus'. To do so would be to hear the prayers of sinners, which God chooses not to. See **John 9:31 & Isa 1:15** among others.

*The underline is mine. The confirmation of the covenant is by Jesus. This is not the anti-Christ coming to "make a covenant" with Israel (many). Read it and you will see the lie that is taught in this day and age that the anti-Christ will come and MAKE a covenant. These teachers are changing scriptures and are cursed for it.

1 Peter 2:4 To whom coming, as unto a living stone, disallowed indeed of men, but chosen of God, and precious, 5 Ye also, as lively stones, are built up a spiritual house, an holy priesthood, to offer up spiritual sacrifices, acceptable to God by Jesus Christ. 6 Wherefore also it is contained in the scripture, Behold, I lay in Sion a chief corner stone, elect, precious: and he that believeth on him shall not be confounded. 7 Unto you therefore which believe he is precious: but unto them which be disobedient, the stone which the builders disallowed, the same is made the head of the corner, 8 And a stone of stumbling, and a rock of offence, even to them which stumble at the word, being disobedient: whereunto also they were appointed.

Jesus is the Stone, the Rock, the Foundation, the Corner Stone, of the body. We are but small stones built into in the body. The disobedient stumble on Jesus and are crushed. They are appointed to their condition by their own free will choice to sin, by not repenting, and by not asking forgiveness of God the Father through Jesus the Christ, for their sin.

God gave me a **"Vision of the Stones"**: Imagine, if you will, a black velvet painting with a pure black sky and massive lighting strikes all around. In the middle of all this there is a up-thrust foundation of Granite Bed Rock from the barren ground. With a loose field stone wall being built on it with no mortar. One of the stones in the wall had my name on it.

The meaning of this vision is: The blackness of the sky and ground is the sinful world. The lightning strikes are God's wrath on the world of sinfulness. The up-thrust foundation of Granite Bed Rock is Jesus the Christ. The stones in the wall are born again, sinless, members of the body of Christ. No mortar means that you can be ejected from the wall at any time by falling back into sin and not repenting of it. <u>Is your name on a stone in this wall?</u>

1 Peter 2:24 who his own self bare our sins in his own body on the tree, that we, being dead to sins, should live unto righteousness: by whose stripes ye were healed.

"To bare our sin in His body", means that Jesus paid our debt, took our debt to God the Father for "our sins", of His own free will. He did not literally have our sin, nor was he made to be literally a sinner. Jesus was not made into sin, He just substituted Himself and 'made' payment for our sins. If He was made to be sin, then how could His blood have been holy and pure as it needed to be for a righteous, holy, substationary payment for the sins of the world to the Father? We now owe nothing to the Father for our sins against Him. It is a paid debt, but we have to avail our selves of the payment made by Jesus. The sinners of the world have NO way other than to go to Jesus for the "payment" of their sins that He made. We as the "born again", who are sinless, must continue to live a sinless life or we are slapping Jesus in the face and telling Him His work on the cross was a waste of time.

Some people actually feel that they were way to evil, or such a bad sinners that they never could forgiven unless they pay for it by some form of penance. What a lie of Satan to keep people out of the kingdom of God. Jesus' work on the cross and resurrection was and is for all sinners of the world. This salvation is for you. Accept it, go with God to glory.

"By His stripes we are healed" means that healing is in the atonement, and is part of the work of the cross. You cannot separate healing from the cross anymore than you can separate salvation from the cross.

Also in the atonement is the provision for all of our material needs to be met. Jesus showed this over and over, with examples like Feeding the 4000, the gold coin in the fish's mouth, etc. So if you believe in salvation by being born again of the spirit, then you must also believe that Jesus still heals as well as saves, and provides for all our material needs. The string is that we must meet His conditions, not what we think He wants. If we don't meet the conditions we don't receive. Does this answer your question as to why you don't have an answer to your prayers. God does not hear the prayers of sinners.* Praying amiss is praying in sin or for things you should not have or need.

As Jesus saves every time, so also does He heal every time, and provide every time. There are conditions you must adhere to for both salvation and healing, and having your needs met every time. These conditions are:

1- For salvation, you must first believe and then repent and ask forgiveness for your sins, this all by faith.

2-For healing, and material needs you must ask in faith, be sinless, and really want the healing and your needs met, not just mouth the words to show how much you believe the bible, and impress people.

1 John 2:2 And he is the propitiation for our sins: and not for ours only, but also for the sins of the whole world. * see The Study on Prayer.

1 John 4:10 Herein is love, not that we loved God, but that he loved us, and sent his Son to be the propitiation for our sins.

Jesus was a one time substitution for our sins. It was and is NOT a literal payment, if it was He would still be on the cross. He came to save us, the horrible sinners of the world, who had no right to even think of salvation, in unconditional love for us His creation.

1 John 2:22 Who is a liar but he that denieth that Jesus is the Christ? He is antichrist, that denieth the Father and the Son. :23 Whosoever denieth the Son, the same hath not the Father: he that acknowledgeth the Son hath the Father also.
1 John 4:2 Hereby know ye the Spirit of God: Every spirit that confesseth that Jesus Christ is come in the flesh is of God: 3 And every spirit that confesseth not that Jesus Christ is come in the flesh is not of God: and this is that spirit of antichrist, whereof ye have heard that it should come; and even now already is it in the world.

There is so much talk about who the "anti-Christ" is. The scripture tells us exactly who he is. The anti-Christ is any and all governmental, religious systems, or just plain people, such as the natural Jew, who deny that Jesus has come in the flesh as the Christ. This denial takes many forms, but most of all it is the willful sinning and blatant disregard for God's laws. Another way is the natural Jews saying that Jesus was not the Christ (messiah).

1 John 2:25 And this is the promise that he hath promised us, even eternal life.

The reward of being born again and remaining sin free is life in glory with the Father, Son, and Holy Spirit.

1 John 5:6 This is he that came by water and blood, even Jesus Christ; not by water only, but by water and blood. And it is the Spirit that beareth witness, because the Spirit is truth.

The water is the word. The blood is the Holy, Pure, Sinless Blood shed by Jesus on the cross. The Spirit is the Holy Spirit who is a witness for Jesus the Christ on the earth.

1 John 5:7 For there are three that bear record in heaven, the Father, the Word, and the Holy Ghost: and these three are one.

In heaven they are the Father, the Son, and the Holy Spirit. The 'Word' can mean word of God as given by Jesus or Jesus Himself. Knowing which one is meant is by context.

1 John 5:8 And there are three that bear witness in earth, the Spirit, and the water, and the blood: and these three agree in one.

On the earth, the Holy Spirit, the Word, Shed Blood (Son of God Jesus).

There is, in some circles, confusion about three being one God. Here is the way I see them: They are three distinct, different personalities who are in 100% agreement 100% of the time, and they make up the Godhead of ONE GOD in who all three are one GOD who are and act in complete love for each other by their free will choice to be that way.

Again the witnesses on the earth are the Holy Spirit, the Word of God as given by Jesus, and the Shed Blood of Jesus on the cross.

1 John 5:11 And this is the record, that God hath given to us eternal life, and this life is in his Son. 12 He that hath the Son hath life; and he that hath not the Son of God hath not life.

This Jesus is the one that makes available everlasting Spiritual life for and to us. If we don't go through Jesus to the Father in heaven, then we will continue to be dead spiritually and will be sent to hell by our own free will choice. We literally make God throw us into hell by not coming to Jesus and conforming to His commandments. You say that a God of love would not do this. I say to you that a God of love has no choice but to do this. He is a JUST GOD is He not? He loves you so much that He will allow you your choice of heaven or hell. He gave us the free will to choose good or bad, the right or the wrong. What's your choice?

Revelation 1:5 And from Jesus Christ, who is the faithful witness, and the first begotten of the dead, and the prince of the kings of the earth. Unto him that loved us, and washed us from our sins in his own blood,

It is Jesus' blood that has "washed us from our sins". This means that Jesus' work on the cross was 'perfect and holy'. Jesus is the first perfect (sinless) man to be raised from physical death in righteousness to an immortal body (as we will be at the final judgment). By Jesus' work of obedience on the earth God the Father has made Him King over all the universe, with the exception of the Father Himself.

We as the born again are perfect in our sinless walk with Jesus. This is not 'sinless perfection'! Only Jesus walked in 'sinless perfection' this is because He never sinned in the first place. We are made perfect and holy by our choice of having Jesus' shed Blood wash our sin from us thereby removing the guilt of our sins from our conscience. We remain this way as long as we stay sinless. If we sin then we go to '**1 John 1:9**' to get forgiveness and cleansed from all unrighteousness, in other word we are perfect and holy again.

His blood does what the old testament sacrifices of the blood of bulls and goats could not do, it actually removes our sin from our conscience. The blood of bulls and goats only provided forgiveness by covering sin. By the way, the teaching in modern man's church is that Jesus' blood covers your sin. This is a lie (check out **Hebrews**

chapter 9:14). You don't get under the blood, you are washed clean by the blood. Do you see the difference? The teaching of "under the blood" allows you to sin and still feel good about yourself. This teaching is as if Jesus' blood protects you from the consequences of sin. This is a lie of Satan, don't believe it.

Jesus is the plan of salvation which is called predestination from the foundations of the world. It is not who will and will not be saved. Jesus came to save all who would come to Him. It is "not who would be saved" by God's picking and choosing who would and would not be saved, but "how we are saved". This wonderful salvation is by the shed blood of Christ! Jesus the Christ is the plan of predestination from the foundations of the world.

Revelation 5:2 And I saw a strong angel proclaiming with a loud voice, Who is worthy to open the book, and to loose the seals thereof?

The answer to this question asked by Satan (the strong angel) is 'Jesus is worthy'. Again this strong angel is Satan. Remember Jesus said that you should bind the "strong man" before you plunder his house. Well Satan is the strong man as well as the strong angel. Satan was in the habit of condemning the saints to God the Father.

Asking who was worthy is saying that there was no one without sin on the earth. This was true before the work of the cross. Jesus' shed blood provides what the blood of bulls and goats could not, it removes your sin, or you can say the 'guilt of sin' from your conscience.

The old testament saints had all of their sins in their conscience. Jesus, in death, descended (while in the grave) into Abraham's bosom. He told all of the O. T. saints that He had come and fulfilled the prophecies of the Messiah which then allowed them to be "born again" thereby allowing them to ascend to heaven with Jesus as a cloud of witnesses. This is contrary to some who teach the lie that Jesus went to hell to wrestle with Satan for the keys. Why would Jesus do such a thing ? He made Satan! Satan was nowhere near powerful enough to even begin a fight with Jesus. Does it not say the Jesus defeated Satan on and by the cross? Look it up! If Satan had that kind of power why didn't he, Satan, just outright kill Jesus before He went to the cross? Satan did try to kill Jesus through his servants, the Jewish leadership, at least 10 times before Jesus went to the cross, where He, Jesus, defeated, made to be of no avail, made ineffective, and had him kicked out of heaven to never again accuse the saints of being sinners to God in heaven.

Revelation 5:6 And I beheld, and, lo, in the midst of the throne and of the four beasts, and in the midst of the elders, stood a Lamb as it had been slain, having seven horns and seven eyes, which are the seven Spirits of God sent forth into all the earth.
Revelation 5:7 And he came and took the book out of the right hand of him that sat upon the throne.

Revelation 5:9 And they sung a new song, saying, Thou art worthy to take the book, and to open the seals thereof: for thou wast slain, and hast redeemed us to God by thy blood out of every kindred, and tongue, and people, and nation;

This lamb is the risen Christ who is without sin. Jesus is able to open the book of life.

Revelation 12:7 And there was war in heaven: Michael and his angels fought against the dragon; and the dragon fought and his angels, 8 And prevailed not; neither was their place found any more in heaven. 9 And the great dragon was cast out, that old serpent, called the Devil, and Satan, which deceiveth the whole world: he was cast out into the earth, and his angels were cast out with him. 10 And I heard a loud voice saying in heaven, Now is come salvation, and strength, and the kingdom of our God, and the power of his Christ: for the accuser of our brethren is cast down, which accused them before our God day and night. 11 And they overcame him by the blood of the Lamb, and by the word of their testimony; and they loved not their lives unto the death.

He, Jesus, being a holy and sinless priest for all time to come, is the "worthy one" who rose to heaven and opened the book of life and sat on the Throne as the KING. It is at this point that Satan was thrown out of heaven to the earth never to return. God, at this point, will no longer stand for any sin in heaven. Are you sinless? This is what Jesus came to do. Provide a way to heaven for all who would come. The crowing of Jesus as King is beginning of the end for Satan and all who remain sinners.

This is the True Body

Matthew 18:20 For where two or three are gathered together in my name, there am I in the midst of them.

This is the way true members of the body of Christ should meet. Not in some man's building on the corner, one or two days a week, with hundreds or even thousands of people in the congregation! How can you, in these mega-churches, know who your brothers and sisters in Christ are? Or even know what they believe in? How can you be in accord with, of one mind with someone you don't even know? How can the leadership of these mega churches even come close to knowing who you are and what your needs from Jesus are?

The true scriptural gatherings are in homes, rented buildings, etc., and should be a common occurrence on any day or days of the week. Not any one man is in charge as Jesus is the head, but all have a part in the worship, prayer, teaching, prophecy, healings, and so on . Christ should be on our minds and out our mouths every day, constantly.

Matthew 12:8 For the Son of man is Lord even of the sabbath day.

Mark 2:27 And he said unto them, The sabbath was made for man, and not man for the sabbath: 28 Therefore the Son of man is Lord also of the sabbath.

Luke 6:5 And he said unto them, That the Son of man is Lord also of the sabbath.

Jesus is to be worshiped each and every day, man does not set the day of worship. What does your church do? Is Jesus lord of your "church", or is some man?

Romans 14:5 One man esteemeth one day above another: another esteemeth every day alike. Let every man be fully persuaded in his own mind.6 He that regardeth the day, regardeth it unto the Lord; and he that regardeth not the day, to the Lord he doth not regard it..............

Here we see that you can worship any day you like. Whatever day you choose you must still worship the Lord your God. God ordained one day a week as a rest day. You choose what day you want to rest. I believe that in your walk as a Christian you must worship God every day in some form or fashion. Whether it is prayer, witnessing for Jesus, or studying the word to show yourself approved of God. Most of all you must show your love for God by not sinning in word, thought, or deed .

Luke 9:50 And Jesus said unto him, Forbid him not: for he that is not against us is for us.

There are only two ways in the world .The first is living in and being part of the world, a sinner. The second is living in but not being part of the world, sinless in Jesus Christ. There is NO middle ground , either you is or you ain't saved.

Luke 11:17 But he, knowing their thoughts, said unto them, Every kingdom divided against itself is brought to desolation; and a house divided against a house falleth.

There is no division in the true body of Christ. It can not split and form a new body, or a new church. With over 2000 different, so called, Christian church denominations in the world, which one is the true Body of Christ? There is only one true head (Jesus) and there is only one true Body (the truly born again). There are only two kinds of religious bodies in the world :
1- Those owned and run by Satan.
2- Those owned and run by Jesus.
Is Jesus the head of your church or is it some pastor, governing board? Is it the new Christianity? The new emergent church? Does your church put more importance on entertainment, and new age ideas? Does your church teach just love them into the kingdom? You get the picture? Is this where your church is? If you answer 'yes' why are you still there?

Ephesians 4:3 Endeavouring to keep the unity of the Spirit in the bond of peace. 4 There is one body, and one Spirit, even as ye are called in one hope of your calling;

One body, one mind, one church, one Spirit, one Son, one Father, one God, with no division, all in agreement with the Holy Spirit, and Jesus as the head.

Luke 12:8 Also I say unto you, Whosoever shall confess me before men, him shall the Son of man also confess before the angels of God: 9 But he that denieth me before men shall be denied before the angels of God.

When you witness for Jesus He tells all of heaven that you are a good and faithful servant. One way to deny Jesus is to refuse to witness for and about Him, another way is not to come to Him in spirit and truth, THEN you are an anti-Christ! Witnessing is a command. You can see in verse 9 that there is a punishment for not witnessing. This should tell you that being a Christian is not your private religion.

John 14:12 Verily, verily, I say unto you, He that believeth on me, the works that I do shall he do also; and greater works than these shall he do; because I go unto my Father.

The two works that the body of Christ does that Jesus could not do, while on the earth, are get the saved baptized in the Holy Spirit, and bring people to salvation in the first place. These two works are what Jesus could not and did not do before the work of the cross and rising from the grave to heaven. To see what Jesus did do read **Mathew, Mark, Luke, and John.**

1 Corinthians 1:10 Now I beseech you, brethren, by the name of our Lord Jesus Christ, that ye all speak the same thing, and that there be no divisions among you; but that ye be perfectly joined together in the same mind and in the same judgment.

We are one body, one mind, and one God with Jesus as the Head of the body. So how can there be so many different opinions about what God's word says? Do you think that most if not all of teachings of the modern "man's church" are wrong or right?

I favor wrong! Read the bible for yourself, ask the Holy Spirit to guide you in understanding the word of God and you will do better than sitting in some church listening to a sermon on how beautiful the sunrise was, really great worldly music, or some really good motivational speaker.

1 Corinthians 3:16 Know ye not that ye are the temple of God, and that the Spirit of God dwelleth in you? 17 If any man defile the temple of God, him shall God destroy; for the temple of God is holy, which temple ye are.

The earthly temple in Jerusalem was destroyed by the Romans in 70A.D. never to be rebuilt. Oh! By the way, there is NO prophecy that a new temple will ever be built in Jerusalem or anywhere else period (all old testament prophecy was fulfilled by Jesus on the Cross). We as the followers of Christ are the "New Temple of God" being built by Jesus and the Holy Spirit on the 'ROCK of CHRIST' not Peter. Construction on the Holy Temple is God, through the Holy Spirit in our lives, teaching us how to obey His commands.

God resides within us, as He once did in the temple building in Jerusalem, unless we fall back into sin. If that happens the Holy Spirit will leave, and try to convince you to be repentant. He will return at your repentance, and the holy construction project of your life will begin again.

What do you think defiling the temple means? Two things: one is sin un-repented of, and second is doing deliberate physical harm to your body (the temple of God), such as smoking, drinking, doing drugs, gluttony, you get the idea. All these things I've named, and lots of others are a free will choice and are NOT sickness and disease. You have no excuse as no one makes you do the 'wrong' stuff, it is your free will choice every time!

1 Corinthians 10:17 For we being many are one bread, and one body: for we are all partakers of that one bread.

We are one in Jesus, no divisions, one truth, one mind, one body, one head, one gospel, one Jesus, one Father, one Spirit, one God. Does this describe your church ? Is your church in agreement with other churches? Are you one with Jesus, or do you play just a little in the world? The bread is Jesus. So are you a partaker?

1 Corinthians 10:21 Ye cannot drink the cup of the Lord, and the cup of devils: ye cannot be partakers of the Lord's table, and of the table of devils.

You cannot be a sinner and a Christian at the same time. Is this not clear? One sin puts you at the devil's table, and repentance brings you back to the table of the Lord God. You CANNOT eat at both tables at the same time. We are here on the earth to learn to stop sinning, and to come to Jesus and the Father by our free will love for them. It is said there will be no sin and no temptation in heaven. No sin is by our choice and no temptation is by God's command.

Yes you can sin in heaven, but you won't want to. I do not believe that God takes away our free will when we are saved or when we die and go to heaven. Did not Satan sin in heaven, and was he not kicked out for that sin?

1 Corinthians 11: 27 Wherefore whosoever shall eat this bread, and drink this cup of the Lord, unworthily, shall be guilty of the body and blood of the Lord. 28 But let a man examine himself, and so let him eat of that bread, and drink of that cup. 29 For he that eateth and drinketh unworthily, eateth and drinketh damnation to himself, not discerning the Lord's body. 30 For this cause many are weak and sickly among you, and many sleep.

Do not let your pastor ask forgiveness of your sins for you. He can't do it, **1 John 1:9** says that "you" must ask. You must be sin free to take the body and blood of Jesus, this is so you can honor Him in remembrance and renew the covenant you cut with Jesus at your salvation. You were sinless at salvation and you must be sinless at communion. To take communion with sin on your conscience is a slap in the face of Jesus, the work He came to do, and is a sin in and of itself. He provided a way for you to be sin free, and if you take the body and blood of Jesus in sin you are saying you don't need His shed Holy Blood to remove your sins from you. You might say it is a grievous insult to Jesus and the Father. I don't know about you, but I personally don't want to insult the most powerful being there is, creator of all that there is. Does it not say that taking communion in sin causes early death and sickness? Read verse 29 again.

Take the body and blood of Jesus often, not just once a month, to renew and confirm your covenant with Jesus. This covenant like all others given by God is confirmed by blood. Your drinking the spiritual blood at communion reconfirms your commitment to the covenant you entered into with Jesus when you became born again. You can do this at home as long as it is with the right moral attitude. Nowhere in scripture does it say you have to take communion in a church, on a given day, or that it be given by a pastor.

1 Corinthians 12:12 For as the body is one, and hath many members, and all the members of that one body, being many, are one body: so also is Christ.13 For by one Spirit are we all baptized into one body, whether we be Jews or Gentiles, whether we be bond or free; and have been all made* to drink into one Spirit.14 For the body is not one member, but many.

We are all equal in God's eyes and all members of ONE body. Not 2000 + man made, so called, Christian denominations. There is only ONE true body of Christ, and I believe it is spread through all Christian denominations. I would doubt that the denominations themselves are all of Christ for the most part.

We each have a job that is given to us by God, and no one job is of more authority than any other in God's eyes. Of course man sees it differently and puts an order of authority, top to bottom, to all the jobs in man's church. The only one in the body who is important and has the ultimate authority is Jesus. By the way, the word denomination is not in the bible.

*There is that word "made" (verse 13) again, in this case as well as in **Romans 5** (look it up), it means "made" by choice. Or do you think God takes our free will away at salvation?

Philippians 2:3 Let nothing be done through strife or vainglory; but in lowliness of mind let each esteem other better than themselves.

1 Peter 5:3 Neither as being lords over God's heritage, but being ensamples to the flock.

Again we are all equal in God's eyes. We must be humble in all that we do. No one man is in charge of the body. How many pastors do you know that think that they are of special importance to and for the church? Well here you see God's opinion of how we are to operate in the body of Christ.

1 Corinthians 12:25 That there should be no schism in the body; but that the members should have the same care one for another.

1 Corinthians 12:27 Now ye are the body of Christ, and members in particular.

Again we are all in the same body, and there will be no division in this body of Christ. No in-fighting in the body, no one is better than any one else, no one is higher than any one else. We are all equal in God's eyes. Do you get the idea? The only thing I could say about the members of the body is that there are different levels of maturity, such as : babies in Christ, young children, young people, fathers and mothers, elders, and so on.

2 Corinthians 10:12 For we dare not make ourselves of the number, or compare ourselves with some that commend themselves: but they measuring themselves by themselves, and comparing themselves among themselves, are not wise.

Don't compare yourselves against or with other Christians. This causes sinful pride, sinful jealousy, or both. Be satisfied in your walk with God growing as you can. Just be what God wants you to be. Study to show yourself approved of God.

2 Corinthians 10:17 But he that glorieth, let him glory in the Lord.18 For not he that commendeth himself is approved, but whom the Lord commendeth.

Here it says don't be proud of yourself, but be humble before the Lord. Is not pride a sin? Let the lord commend you, not man.

Ephesians 4:11 And he gave some, apostles; and some, prophets; and some, evangelists; and some, pastors and teachers;12 For the perfecting of the saints, for the work of the ministry, for the edifying of the body of Christ:13 Till we all come in the unity of the faith, and of the knowledge of the Son of God, unto a perfect man, unto the measure of the stature of the fulness of Christ:14 That we henceforth be no more children, tossed to and fro, and carried about with every wind of doctrine, by the sleight of men, and cunning craftiness, whereby they lie in wait to deceive; 15 But speaking the truth in love, may grow up into him in all things, which is the head, even Christ:

This is talking about being saved and coming to the full understanding of what it means to be in the body of Christ. God has given different people different jobs so that sinners of the world can be given the truth of the word of God, and be brought to salvation as a result of the preparation of the saints by the five fold ministry.

Once we are in the body we are sinless and in unity with all others in the body. This is called "in the fullness of Christ". We no longer are part of the world of sinners, we now look to Jesus with the Holy Spirit to guide us in our walk with Him.

Hebrews 5:12 For when for the time ye ought to be teachers, ye have need that one teach you again which be the first principles of the oracles of God; and are become such as have need of milk, and not of strong meat.13 For every one that useth milk is unskilful in the word of righteousness: for he is a babe.14 But strong meat belongeth to them that are of full age, even those who by reason of use have their senses exercised to discern both good and evil.

1 Corinthians 3:2-3 I have fed you with milk, and not with meat: for hitherto ye were not able to bear it, neither yet now are ye able. For ye are yet carnal: for whereas there is among you envying, and strife, and divisions, are ye not carnal, and walk as men?

Milk is for baby Christians. We must mature to the point that we eat the strong meat of the gospel. Strong meat can be defined as being sinless by choice, or as James says choosing the right thing to do. Milk is defined as healing, baptisms, raising the dead etc. These former Christians are called carnal because they fell back into sin and were not considered to be in a state of salvation. This is why they still needed milk of baby Christians, they need to start again from the beginning. The phrase "carnal Christians" is an oxymoron.

There is no such thing as, never has been, and never will be "Carnal Christians" period! Do you see the question Paul asks "… are you not carnal and walk as men"? What do you think this means? Could it mean that they walk as men (sinners) in the world and not as the saved of Christ?

Hebrews 6:1 Therefore leaving the principles of the doctrine of Christ, let us go on unto perfection; not laying again the foundation of repentance from dead works, and of faith toward God, 2 Of the doctrine of baptisms, and of laying on of hands, and of resurrection of the dead, and of eternal judgment.

We must continue to grow in Jesus and in the knowledge of the gospel. If we think that there is nothing beyond salvation we are deceived by Satan. If we don't study the word, get baptized in the Holy Spirit (which is a command of Jesus. See **Acts 1:4-5**.) we then remain babies in the body. We must grow to be mature adults in Christ. One of the most important things as we grow is to learn how to "stop sinning", as it is a command of God. You must first of all resist temptation. To do this you bind in Jesus name, you cast down in Jesus name, you take into captivity in Jesus' name all the wayward thoughts and temptations (from you or Satan) that come at you every day. You repent if you slip up.

Ephesians 5:20 Giving thanks always for all things unto God and the Father in the name of our Lord Jesus Christ; 21 Submitting yourselves one to another in the fear of God.

This is how the real body of Christ operates. All are equal, all are humble, there is no power structure, there is no head pastor, there is no one man in charge. It is all Jesus or not at all.

Philippians 1:27 Only let your conversation be as it becometh the gospel of Christ: that whether I come and see you, or else be absent, I may hear of your affairs, that ye stand fast in one spirit, with one mind striving together for the faith of the gospel;

A command to be of one body with no controversy or division in the body. To walk sinless by standing fast in the Holy Spirit, being of one mind, in unity working together to increase everybody's faith by the word of Jesus. This is the true body of Christ. Are you in it?

Philippians 2:1 If there be therefore any consolation in Christ, if any comfort of love, if any fellowship of the Spirit, if any bowels and mercies,2 Fulfil ye my joy, that ye be like minded, having the same love, being of one accord, of one mind.

Again, be of one body! Not one of the numerous Christian denominations that are without the same opinion of what the bible says. There is only one true meaning, and it is given by the Holy Spirit.

Colossians 3:15 And let the peace of God rule in your hearts, to the which also ye are called in one body; and be ye thankful.16 Let the word of Christ dwell in you richly in all wisdom; teaching and admonishing one another in psalms and hymns and spiritual songs, singing with grace in your hearts to the Lord.

This is what the body of Christ does. This is the true church and how it operates. Doing these things together makes it is a whole lot easier to remain sinless and focus on Christ.

1 Thessalonians 5:14 Now we exhort you, brethren, warn them that are unruly, comfort the feebleminded, support the weak, be patient toward all men.15 See that none render evil for evil unto any man; but ever follow that which is good, both among yourselves, and to all men.

These are instructions for the body of Christ. Now the phrase "that which is good" refers to not committing sin. **James 4:17 Therefore to him that knoweth to do good, and doeth it not, to him it is sin.** You see here that James defines sin as "not" doing the "good" that you know.
It tells us that sin is a choice to do the good or to do the bad.

2 Thessalonians 3:6 Now we command you, brethren, in the name of our Lord Jesus Christ, that ye withdraw yourselves from every brother that walketh disorderly, and not after the tradition which he received of us.

2 Thessalonians 3:14 And if any man obey not our word by this epistle, note that man, and have no company with him, that he may be ashamed. 15 Yet count him not as an enemy, but admonish him as a brother.

2 Th 3:6 is a different situation from verse 14. In Verse 3:6 this person has turned their back on God and walks in the world and doesn't want to come back to Jesus. This is blasphemy of the Holy Spirit. It is of no use to try and talk to this person. They are lost with no hope of redemption. Verse 14 says that this is a brother that has fallen back into sin and will not repent. The instructions are clear. Have nothing to do with a backslidden Christian as long as they refuse to repent. As you can see this is a "command". This is a Christian who returned to sin. You must not fellowship with this person, but you must tell him/her that he /she has stepped off of the narrow road of Christ so as to help him/her back into the fold. This person still has a chance to come to repentance.

1 Timothy 5:20 Them that sin rebuke before all, that others also may fear

Instructions, for the body, about brothers who refuse to repent of sin. So much for not naming names as modern man's church teaches.

1 Timothy 1:9 Knowing this, that the law is not made for a righteous man, but for the lawless and disobedient, for the ungodly and for sinners, for unholy and profane, for murderers of fathers and murderers of mothers, for manslayers,......

The Old testament law of sin and death is for sinners only. If you keep one law you MUST keep them all. We, the born again, are under the new covenant of grace and love bought and confirmed by Jesus. As long as we remain sinless we are above the law and have the grace of God in our lives. If we fall back into sin we are back under the law of sin and death and the grace that guided our lives will be gone. Our only chance at this point is to ask forgiveness and repent. It is the only way to get back the grace of God.

1 Timothy 3:8 Likewise must the deacons be grave, not doubletongued, not given to much wine, not greedy of filthy lucre;9 Holding the mystery of the faith in a pure conscience.

The office holders of the church are called to be sinless and holy. As we are all equal in God's eyes, then we must ALL be sinless and holy. This is what a pure conscience is, it has no guilt of sin in it.

1 Timothy 6:11 But thou, O man of God, flee these things; and follow after righteousness, godliness, faith, love, patience, meekness

This is for the office holders of the church, but is also for the rest of us. Obey the commandments of God, any of them you break will put you into sin and get you thrown out of the kingdom. The parable of the wedding feast tells of a man who came not dressed in wedding finery. The king, God, saw this man and asked him how he came there in ordinary cloths. The king had him thrown out.

The moral here is if you come to the wedding of Christ and are still in sin you will be thrown out. Now consider, this man who was thrown out was invited, but He did not avail himself of new robes (become sinless through Christ) without spot or wrinkle. This shows us that God does invite the whole world of sinners to take part in the wedding feast of Jesus, but we must have Jesus' approval, by being sinless, to be accepted. Read this parable for yourself

(**Mat 21 :1-14**). In the last verse it says many (means all) are called but few are chosen.

This means not all choose to be sin free. You are not picked by God to be saved. It is by your own free will that your are chosen. You can say you are chosen by your free will choice to obey Jesus' commands. The first and foremost commananment is to remain sinless.

2 Timothy 2:15 Study to shew thyself approved unto God, a workman that needeth not to be ashamed, rightly dividing the word of truth.

Study and learn what the word of God says and God will smile on you. If you don't the world will ridicule you for your lack of knowledge and your inability to defend your faith. How can you answer questions from a sinner, or even your Christian brothers, if you don't know and understand the scriptures in your mind and heart?

2 Timothy 3:12 Yea, and all that will live godly in Christ Jesus shall suffer persecution.

As long as you remain sinless with Christ the world will make you suffer in one way or another. If not outright killing you. This is also called trials and tribulations. Don't think that you can escape this tribulation / persecution, it will happen in one form or another to all members of the body of Christ. Find the Joy of the Lord in it and you will survive.

2 Timothy 4:18 And the Lord shall deliver me from every evil work, and will preserve me unto his heavenly kingdom: to whom be glory for ever and ever. Amen.

Revelation 3:10 Because thou hast kept the word of my patience, I also will keep thee from the hour of temptation, which shall come upon all the world, to try them that dwell upon the earth.

God protects us from all evil as long as we remain in His will by obeying all of His commandments. This does not mean we will not be persecuted.

God is no respecter of persons so as he did this for Paul and Jesus(the Jews of the day tried to kill Jesus 10 times before He went to the cross) He will do it for all Christian's. This is with the understanding that we remain sinless and holy.

Hebrews 4:15 For we have not an high priest which cannot be touched with the feeling of our infirmities; but was in all points tempted like as we are, yet without sin.16 Let us therefore come boldly unto the throne of grace, that we may obtain mercy, and find grace to help in time of need.

We don't need someone, pastor or priest, to go to God and pray for us. Jesus was tempted and killed as Christians are all over the world today. He understands all the troubles and trials that we go through. So he knows how to help us and he tells the Father that we are His.

We all, as the saved, are priests and kings and have the right and obligation to go directly to the Father through Jesus for all of our needs. In other words we don't need anyone else to pray for us, we can do it for ourselves. That is if we are sinless, because God does not hear the prayers of sinners (see the chapter on "Prayer").

Hebrews 10:19 Having therefore, brethren, boldness to enter into the holiest by the blood of Jesus, 20 By a new and living way, which he hath consecrated for us, through the veil, that is to say, his flesh; 21 And having an high priest over the house of God; 22 Let us draw near with a true heart in full assurance of faith, having our hearts sprinkled from an evil conscience, and our bodies washed with pure water.

As we of the body of Christ are sinless, we can go directly to God through Jesus. We don't have to go to a pastor or priest for prayer. We are all equal in God's eyes. Our hearts are 'sprinkled' with Jesus' blood for the clean up of our conscience, and our bodies 'washed' with the pure water of the word of Christ, also called the Holy Bible.

Hebrews 10:25 Not forsaking the assembling of ourselves together, as the manner of some is; but exhorting one another: and so much the more, as ye see the day approaching.

Man's church; they all are if they are in a "church" building, have a name, can split, have a man in charge, etc. They would have you believe that this verse means that you should come to the building on some corner every Sunday and Wednesday night. If you don't you will not be saved is what most teach. If you get together, no matter where, with other members of the body of Christ whether it is two, five, or fifty, it is not forsaking the gathering together. It does not have to be in a "man's church", or on any particular day. Jesus said "where two or more are gathered together there will I be".

Hebrews 12:5 And ye have forgotten the exhortation which speaketh unto you as unto children, My son, despise not thou the chastening of the Lord, nor faint when thou art rebuked of him:6 For whom the Lord loveth he chasteneth, and scourgeth every son whom he receiveth.7 If ye endure chastening, God dealeth with you as with sons; for what son is he whom the father chasteneth not?8 But if ye be without chastisement, whereof all are partakers, then are ye bastards, and not sons. 9 Furthermore we have had fathers of our flesh which corrected us, and we gave them reverence: shall we not much rather be in subjection unto the Father of spirits, and live?10 For they verily for a few days chastened us after their own pleasure; but he for our profit, that we might be partakers of his holiness.

When we sin God allows His big stick, it's called Satan, to correct us, along with the convincing of the Holy Spirit. So remain sinless and holy and you won't get a whipping. We who are the body are loved by God. If HE didn't love us why would he punish us for wrong doing? When God brings chastisement upon us, His Children, it is for correction, and teaching most of all.

James 1:22 But be ye doers of the word, and not hearers only, deceiving your own selves. 23 For if any be a hearer of the word, and not a doer, he is like unto a man beholding his natural face in a glass: 24 For he beholdeth himself, and goeth his way, and straightway forgetteth what manner of man he was. 25 But whoso

looketh into the perfect law of liberty, and continueth therein, he being not a forgetful hearer, but a doer of the work, this man shall be blessed in his deed.

This is what the body is called to. To be doers of the word is putting feet to your faith. As it is said "walk your talk". If we don't focus on and study the Word and it's commands we are lost, will not be able to defend our faith, tell others about Jesus, bring salvation to the world, baptize people into the Holy Spirit; in other words "be doers of the word".

James 3:5 Even so the tongue is a little member, and boasteth great things. Behold, how great a matter a little fire kindleth! 6 And the tongue is a fire, a world of iniquity: so is the tongue among our members, that it defileth the whole body, and setteth on fire the course of nature; and it is set on fire of hell.

James3:8 But the tongue can no man tame; it is an unruly evil, full of deadly poison. 9 Therewith bless we God, even the Father; and therewith curse we men, which are made after the similitude of God.10 Out of the same mouth proceedeth blessing and cursing. My brethren, these things ought not so to be. 11 Doth a fountain send forth at the same place sweet water and bitter?

One of the most important things we <u>must</u> learn is not to curse and bless from the same mouth. In all reality we must not curse at all. We must control our mouths. Without Jesus it's next to impossible, but with Him for strength and the Holy Spirit for guidance it is entirely doable. Try it you'll like it! Again it is a choice that we make every time we open our mouths.

You must remember one thing. The words that come out your mouth can NEVER be called back, and in most cases "I'm sorry" won't cut it. You will be truly sorry, but your words still have consequences, good or bad. In the name Of Jesus, please make all of your words GOOD!

James 3:13 Who is a wise man and endued with knowledge among you? let him shew out of a good conversation his works with meekness of wisdom.14 But if ye have bitter envying and strife in your hearts, glory not, and lie not against the truth. 15 This wisdom descendeth not from above, but is earthly, sensual, devilish.16 For where envying and strife is, there is confusion and every evil work.17 But the wisdom that is from above is first pure, then peaceable, gentle, and easy to be intreated, full of mercy and good fruits, without partiality, and without hypocrisy.

Good conversation equals being sinless, and meekness of wisdom means don't push your knowledge down other peoples throats. Be respectful of other peoples opinion. Don't beat them up because you think they are in error. Verse 14-16 says that only the wisdom from God is worth anything. The conventional wisdom of the world is a waste of time and can lead you into trouble if not outright sin. Example: The world says talk to your 5 year old child and he will understand and obey you. God says use some form of discipline and your child will respect you and obey. Now think about how this 5 year old will act at age 15 if you just talk to him. Do you think he will mind you any better than when he was 5? Which do you believe works? This is why we must rely (verse 17) on God and His wisdom, which is given to us in the bible and by the Holy Spirit. God's wisdom guides us into all truth and holiness.

So study it, learn, and you will be approved of by God the Father.

For being obedient the Father will reward you with the desires of your heart. I was walking in my store where we had paintings by local artist's, and I noticed one I liked and said to my self that I really would like to have it. But not having the money I just dismissed the thought. Next Sunday in church the woman who did the water color, that I admired, came up to me and said that the painting was mine, and that God told her to give it to me. I never said anything to anyone about liking or wanting that painting. God granted me the desire of my heart. God is truly GREAT! I am also sure, in my heart, that the Father rewarded the artist for being obedient.

James 4:7 Submit yourselves therefore to God. Resist the devil, and he will flee from you. 8 Draw nigh to God, and he will draw nigh to you. Cleanse your hands, ye sinners; and purify your hearts, ye double minded.

This is real clear! By resisting the devil (temptation), you remain sinless and Satan cannot harm you. God will protect you from all harm. Remember what the most important condition is: you must obey. Again to purify yourself is to be sinless and remain that way. A double minded man does not know even what direction he walks in. You cannot be in God's kingdom and Satan's kingdom at the same time. A double minded man will try this. It's called being a middle roader, a fence sitter, a sinner, and so on.

James 4:17 Therefore to him that knoweth to do good, and doeth it not, to him it is sin.

Here is the only definition of sin that you will ever need. It says that to sin or not to sin is a choice that you make every time you are tempted. The good or the bad, what do you choose? It also says that you know the 'good', but you are only held accountable for what you know. This should not be an excuse to stop gaining knowledge.

James 5:13 Is any among you afflicted? let him pray. Is any merry? let him sing psalms. 14 Is any sick among you? let him call for the elders of the church; and let them pray over him, anointing him with oil in the name of the Lord: 15 And the prayer of faith shall save the sick, and the Lord shall raise him up; and if he have committed sins, they shall be forgiven him.

This is the duty of the elders of the body. Need I say more? All healing is by your faith in Jesus to accomplish the healing, but, again, remember it is your FAITH. This is only the second place I've included any verses on healing, because there are so many good teachings already available. The best one I know of is from "faithtech@juno.com". See, also, The Study, Furlher on, in this book.

1 Peter 3:8 Finally, be ye all of one mind, having compassion one of another, love as brethren, be pitiful, be courteous:

The true body of Christ is of one opinion on the things of God. They reject all of man's teachings that do not agree with the Word of God. They are not of the many denominations that believe that their doctrine is the only correct one and all others are wrong. Is your doctrine of Jesus or of man?

1 Peter 2:9 But ye are a chosen generation, a royal priesthood, an holy nation, a peculiar people; that ye should shew forth the praises of him who hath called you out of darkness into his marvellous light;

Revelation 1:6 And hath made us kings and priests unto God and his Father; to him be glory and dominion for ever and ever. Amen.

We as the true body of Christ are called out of the world and live apart from the world of sin. By the baptism of the Holy Spirit we are guided and empowered in this walk of holiness. These and other verses say the we, as the body, are Priests and kings. It's kinda funny that in the Old Testament only Priests and Kings had the Holy Spirit upon them as a mantle, but now, after Jesus, we the truly saved of Christ have the Holy Spirit dwelling within us as we are all Priests and Kings. God didn't change the rules he just made us priests and kings so we could have the holy Spirit (among other reasons). The rule, again, is only Priests and Kings can have the Holy Spirit for guidance. We are Priests and Kings in the Spiritual kingdom of God, and by this we can approach God directly without any pastors or priests intervention. A "Holy Nation" says what it means. We must be holy to enter into this nation (the new Spiritual Israel), this means being and staying sinless.

1 Peter 3:9 Not rendering evil for evil, or railing for railing: but contrariwise blessing; knowing that ye are thereunto called, that ye should inherit a blessing.10 For he that will love life, and see good days, let him refrain his tongue from evil, and his lips that they speak no guile:11 Let him eschew evil, and do good; let him seek peace, and ensue it.

This describes your holy walk in the kingdom of God. It is a call to be sinless. <u>To "eschew evil" means to avoid it. Do you do this?</u>

1 Peter 3:15 But sanctify the Lord God in your hearts: and be ready always to give an answer to every man that asketh you a reason of the hope that is in you with meekness and fear: 16 Having a good conscience; that, whereas they speak evil of you, as of evildoers, they may be ashamed that falsely accuse your good conversation in Christ.

1 Peter 3:21 The like figure whereunto even baptism doth also now save us (not the putting away of the filth of the flesh, but the answer of a good conscience toward God,) by the resurrection of Jesus Christ:

1 Peter 4:8 And above all things have fervent charity among yourselves: for charity shall cover the multitude of sins. 9 Use hospitality one to another without grudging.

More instruction on how to walk in the kingdom of God . Having a "good conscience" is being sinless. Remember that Jesus' blood removes your confessed, repented of sin from your conscience to make you guilt free and sinless in God eyes. Read charity as God's kind of love.

1 Peter 4:17 For the time is come that judgment must begin at the house of God: and if it first begin at us, what shall the end be of them that obey not the gospel of God? 18 And if the righteous scarcely be saved, where shall the ungodly and the sinner appear?

We as the body of Christ must police ourselves. We have already seen instructions on how and what to do about members in the body who fall back into sin. Do you think that this says "judge not lest you be judged"? There is a marked difference between the righteous body of Christ and the sinners of the world. The righteous have the mark of the Holy Spirit (sinlessness). The sinners have the mark of the beast which is sin. Mankind's number is 666. IT IS NOT Satan's number. It is your number if your a sinner. See **Revelation 13:18.**

How many un-repented sins does it take to make you an ungodly sinner and have the mark of the beast? Ya think just ONE? The saved of Jesus have the mark of God which is called the baptism of the Holy Spirit. If you are not yet baptized in the Holy Spirit, seek it. It is a command of Jesus. See **Acts1:4-5**. The mark of God represents a sinless walk. Sin is a choice (**James 4:17**) as is everything from God. What this means is that you don't have to sin, and nothing makes you sin but "your choice". To think that you are made to sin is an excuse to sin which makes you say "OH well I was made this way so I had to do it, and I had no choice, so how can I be guilty of any thing". This kind of teaching is in a lot of man's churchs. It's called Calvinism, and it will send you to hell. This attitude goes along with "born a sinner, a natural sinner, fallen nature not by choice, guilty of Adam's sin and so on. These are lies of Satan. This born sinful teaching did not start in the church until 300AD. It was not taught before that time by Jesus or any of the Apostles.

1 Peter 5:5 Likewise, ye younger, submit yourselves unto the elder. Yea, all of you be subject one to another, and be clothed with humility: for God resisteth the proud, and giveth grace to the humble.

The elders are charged with instructing and helping the young in Christ grow into mature Christians. The younger must respect and follow their Elders. The first thing you need to do is figure out just who the elders are. One thing they are NOT is the elected of man's church. They are mature, sinless members of the body who have a very good understanding of what the word says and means. Age is not a factor here.

If you, as new Christians, refuse the help and don't listen to your Elders you are not holding them in respect. Nevertheless we all must love each other equally and not think we are better than the others in the body. Only Jesus is the head, and all power and authority stems from Jesus through the Holy Spirit, not man.

Pride is a sin! To be humble shows that you are not prideful. Just don't fall into the sin of false humility; it's just as bad as pride. Grace is given to the humble, the sinless members of the body of Christ. Remember what God's Grace is: <u>'Gods continuing influence in your life and it's resulting reflection therein'</u>. In the New Testament it does not mean an unmerited gift of favor. Look it up in the Greek. The Strong's concordance is a good place to start.

2 Peter 1:5 And beside this, giving all diligence, add to your faith virtue; and to virtue knowledge; 6 And to knowledge temperance; and to temperance patience; and to patience godliness; 7 And to godliness brotherly kindness; and to brotherly kindness charity. 8 For if these things be in you, and abound, they make you that ye shall neither be barren nor unfruitful in the knowledge of our Lord Jesus Christ.

More instructions on how the body of Christ MUST operate! This is also a good description of God's kind of love. If you fail in this God will let you repent (**1John 1: 9**) as many times as necessary for you to figure out that it is against God's will that you sin. Logic says that to sin is a sin in and of itself. This is to say that as a sinner you are made, by your first sin, guilty of two sins. A two for one, what a deal. To have the understanding and knowledge of the Lord Jesus Christ you must be sinless (born again). This condition will result in you being given Grace (Grace comes by righteousness, see **Romans 5:21**) by the Father and the baptism of the Holy Spirit, which will lead you into all truth and wisdom.

1 John 2:5 But whoso keepeth his word, in him verily is the love of God perfected: hereby know we that we are in him.

To keep the word of God means to be sinless among other commands. We, as born again, sin free Christians, have the sure and certain knowledge that we are saved (in Him) and going to heaven as long as we remain sin free. Or "IF", our choice,(**1 John 2:1**) we sin, we then ask forgiveness and repent and get on with our walk in the light of Jesus.

1 John 2:15 Love not the world, neither the things that are in the world. If any man love the world, the love of the Father is not in him. 16 For all that is in the world, the lust of the flesh, and the lust of the eyes, and the pride of life, is not of the Father, but is of the world.

We who are in the body of Christ have no business being part and parcel with the world in any form or fashion . It is full of sin. If you claim to be born again and take part of anything of the world that becomes more important than God the Father and Jesus in your life, then you are a sinner and you really have become part of the world. We live in this physical world but are commanded not to be part of it. We are to live Spiritually in the Spiritual kingdom of God. We are a holy, spiritual, called out, set aside people that belong to the Father God. God must be FIRST in your life or you die spiritually (become a sinner), and are separated from God, and that leads to hell.

1 John 3:2 Beloved, now are we the sons of God, and it doth not yet appear what we shall be: but we know that, when he shall appear, we shall be like him; for we shall see him as he is. 3 And every man that hath this hope in him purifieth himself, even as he is pure.

If you are in the body this is your hope; To see Jesus when he comes as your savior and not to judge you for the sins you did. They have been removed from you by Jesus' blood (**1 John 1:7**). You will be judged for the good that you did for your reward in heaven. Have you made yourself pure, without sin, as is Jesus? The meaning in verse 3 is that purifying yourself is a choice that you make. Also the words "every man" says that it is up to us, not God, to decide to be saved. It also puts a lie to the teaching of 'who' is predestined.

Does it not say that "God calls all men"? But here again not all men chose to follow that calling.

As verse 3 says: it is a choice by faith and future hope to remain sinless. This puts a lie 'once saved always saved'. We can chose to be saved, and we can also chose to undo that salvation. As I've said before 'Predestination' is not who is saved but how we are saved, and that is by Jesus' shed blood.

1 John 3:5 And ye know that he was manifested to take away our sins; and in him is no sin. 6 Whosoever abideth in him sinneth not: whosoever sinneth hath not seen him, neither known him.

Jesus is the example that we must live by. As Jesus was, and stll is sinless so must we be. If you're not sin free then you are in no way an adopted brother of Jesus (by your free will choice). This means even one sin will put you into that place (the world of sin) of not knowing Jesus. Do you believe this? It's what scripture says. Right?

1 John 3:8 He that committeth sin is of the devil; for the devil sinneth from the beginning. For this purpose the Son of God was manifested, that he might destroy the works of the devil.

Here it is! If you sin you belong to Satan. That is one sin! Is not the word sin in this case singular?

1 John 3:18 My little children, let us not love in word, neither in tongue; but in deed and in truth.

I guess you could say that "actions speak louder than words".

1 John 3:24 And he that keepeth his commandments dwelleth in him, and he in him. And hereby we know that he abideth in us, by the Spirit which he hath given us.

Remain sin free and stay saved. We know we are walking with God as long as the Holy Spirit resides in us. The Holy Spirit will leave if you get into even one sin. God doesn't share! The big question is: How many sins does it take you to get kicked out of the Kingdom of God? Do you know?

Figure it out. How many sins did Satan commit to get kicked out of heaven? One ya think? The other question is: why would a God of Love put up with anyone breaking even one command? You say a God of love will just ignore the 'few little sins in your life". Right? Wrong? Jesus (a person on this earth) was required to be sinless. Can our JUST God, who is no respecter of persons, let any other person get away with just a few little sins? I think not! It is love, Godly love, not brotherly love, that God operates in. This Godly love will allow you your choice to go to heaven or hell. Do you think God enjoys or likes your choice to go to hell by rejecting him? He loves you enough to allow you your free will choice to do what you want with your life no matter what He, God, wants. I believe that our actions outside of what God would have us do grieves God greatly.

1 John 4:7 Beloved, let us love one another: for love is of God; and every one that loveth is born of God, and knoweth God

1 John 4:19 We love him, because he first loved us.

1 John 5:3 For this is the love of God, that we keep his commandments: and his commandments are not grievous.

If you are born again you will not sin against your fellow man or God. You will also witness to the lost. These are some of the ways you must act in love.

Now there are three kinds of love talked about in the bible . The love talked about here is Agape or God's kind of love. It is not brotherly love or sexual love. Which do you think that God would have you live your life in? There is nothing wrong with brotherly love to our friends and family, or sexual love in a husband and wife relationship. These loves of worldly things, not of God, must be subjected to love for God, and be of least importance in your life compared with God's kind of love in your life. All things of God MUST be FIRST in your moral life and attitude. This includes your job, family, entertainment, and the rest of the worldly things that impinge on you.

1 John 5:19 And we know that we are of God, and the whole world lieth in wickedness.

I've been telling you how wicked the world is, here's the verse that tells you this. This is why we are called out of the world to be a set aside people not part of anything in the world filled with sin.

2 John 1:10 If there come any unto you, and bring not this doctrine, receive him not into your house, neither bid him God speed: 11 For he that biddeth him God speed is partaker of his evil deeds.

Here are instructions concerning all who come to you with false doctrines. This is why you MUST study the word. If you don't study how will you know what is a true doctrine or a false doctrine? This is important; look and see the result of welcoming false teaching into your heart, mind, life, and house as given by verse 11.

Revelation 3:5 He that overcometh, the same shall be clothed in white raiment; and I will not blot out his name out of the book of life, but I will confess his name before my Father, and before his angels.

Remain sinless by overcoming the temptations that are from Satan and from within you. Think now, if you don't remain sinless the contra-positive logic says that Jesus will not confess you as one of His before God the Father, and that your name will stay in the book of life. This verse puts a lie to "once saved always saved". The person that overcomes is saved, but he who stops overcoming will have his name removed from the book of life. Do you see this?

Revelation 13:17 And that no man might buy or sell, save he that had the mark, or the name of the beast, or the number of his name. 18 Here is wisdom. Let

him that hath understanding count the number of the beast: for it is the number of a man; and his number is Six hundred threescore and six.

Without the mark of the beast, which is sin, you cannot buy or sell in the anti-Christ religious or anti-Christ governmental systems. It has nothing to do with buying food, clothes, or such. It is a spiritual buying and selling.

To have the mark of the beast, which is the number of mankind, means your are a sinner. All the mark of the beast has to do with Satan is that you, as a sinner, belong to him. The number of mankind is 666 it is NOT Satan's number.

If you are in the true body of Christ the spiritual mark you will have is the promise of the Holy Spirit in your salvation walk. This marks you as belonging to God, and not to the world of sin and Satan. In other words, the mark of God is holiness, purity, and living for Jesus without sin. With this mark you will not be able to buy and sell in the Satanic religious, or Governmental systems of the world. Look at the Gov. of the U.S.A. and tell me it's operated and controlled by Christians! The same is true of all the different church denominations. Do you really think that Christians run things in this country or in the churches on the corners of our cities, or anywhere else in thw world?

Revelation 14:9 And the third angel followed them, saying with a loud voice, If any man worship the beast and his image, and receive his mark in his forehead, or in his hand, 10 The same shall drink of the wine of the wrath of God, which is poured out without mixture into the cup of his indignation; and he shall be tormented with fire and brimstone in the presence of the holy angels, and in the presence of the Lamb:

This mark is un-repented sinfulness. Here is the reward of sinners. You can remove the mark of the beast by repenting and asking forgiveness of your sins, and thereby become holy and sinless, baptized in the Holy Spirit with the mark of God.

The "wine of the wrath of God" I think is not something you want to taste.

Revelation 20:4 And I saw thrones, and they sat upon them, and judgment was given unto them: and I saw the souls of them that were beheaded for the witness of Jesus, and for the word of God, and which had not worshipped the beast, neither his image, neither had received his mark upon their foreheads, or in their hands; and they lived and reigned with Christ a thousand years.

The saints who witnessed for Jesus had no sin in their conscience. They did not take the mark of the beast, but stayed pure, holy, and righteous before God.

This thousand years is not the natural kingdom of God on the earth. There will be no such thing. See the study on the kingdom of God. The term "a thousand years" in the Greek means an unending number, many thousands of years.

Revelation 14:12 Here is the patience of the saints: here are they that keep the commandments of God, and the faith of Jesus.

Read James about patience. Through your patience and obedience to God's commands you are saved. This is patience: learning to stop sinning.

Prayer

Psalms 103:10 He hath not dealt with us after our sins; nor rewarded us according to our iniquities.

Isaiah 1:15 And when ye spread forth your hands, I will hide mine eyes from you: yea, when ye make many prayers, I will not hear: your hands are full of blood.

Isaiah 59:2 But your iniquities have separated between you and your God, and your sins have hid his face from you, that he will not hear. 3 For your hands are defiled with blood, and your fingers with iniquity; your lips have spoken lies, your tongue hath muttered perverseness.

John 9:31 Now we know that God heareth not sinners: but if any man be a worshipper of God, and doeth his will, him he heareth.

See also **Isaiah 29:13, Micah 3:1-4, and Psalm 66:16-19.**
To put it bluntly God does NOT, by His choice, hear the prayers of sinners! In fact there is no such thing as the 'sinners prayer' in the bible, and nowhere does it say to say a prayer for forgiveness to become born again. It does say believe in Jesus, Repent, and you will be saved.

Matthew 21:22 And all things, whatsoever ye shall ask in prayer, believing, ye shall receive.

Without faith (believing before receiving) you will receive nothing from God. No matter how hard or how long you pray. A lack of faith is also a sin.

Mark 11:24 Therefore I say unto you, What things soever ye desire, when ye pray, believe that ye receive them, and ye shall have them.25 And when ye stand praying, forgive, if ye have ought against any: that your Father also which is in heaven may forgive you your trespasses.26 But if ye do not forgive, neither will your Father which is in heaven forgive your trespasses.

James 4: 2 Ye lust, and have not: ye kill, and desire to have, and cannot obtain: ye fight and war, yet ye have not, because ye ask not. 3 Ye ask, and receive not, because ye ask amiss, that ye may consume it upon your lusts. 4 Ye adulterers and adulteresses, know ye not that the friendship of the world is enmity with God? whosoever therefore will be a friend of the world is the enemy of God.

1 John 3:22 And whatsoever we ask, we receive of him, because we keep his commandments, and do those things that are pleasing in his sight.

You must pray as God would have you pray, without sin and in faith that you will receive what you are praying for. You must be sin free so examine yourself before you pray.

By the way, as a Christian you must walk as Jesus walked, a sin free life. Remember you must pray in all seriousness and not for useless wants. God will supply all your, key word, NEEDS?

As a sidelight, there is no such thing as the "sinners Prayer".

It is not in the bible. By the time this so called "sinners prayer" comes out of your mouth you are already saved and forgiven. God sees your heart first, and the decision to repent comes from your mind to your heart before it comes out your mouth. You must ask for forgiveness and tell God that you repent out loud with your mouth.

This is not a sinners prayer. It is telling God the you are sorry from your heart that you sinned. Now some would have you confess to God all of the sins you have ever committed. This is next to impossible, and is not what God wants, a blanket confession of sin and repentance is sufficient to start of the process of your salvation walk. However, I will say if you have ever been involved in any kind of occult practices; oh say, Ouija boards, Horoscopes, having your future told, palm reading, role playing games such as "dungeons and Dragons, Wicca, white or black magic, any new age teachings, Yoga and mystic arts, plus so many other things that I can't even begin to name them all. You really HAVE to name and reject, ask forgiveness for, repent of, each and every one you 'remember'. This is so you will be set free of any influence they have on you that keeps you from the really great things of God the Father. This will also block demons from continuously coming against you, as you, a sinner, once belonged to them.

John 14:13 And whatsoever ye shall ask in my name, that will I do, that the Father may be glorified in the Son.14 If ye shall ask any thing in my name, I will do it.

To receive anything from Christ, after salvation, you must be sin free and ask in faith. God always answers all prayers spoken in the truth and in the spirit. God's answers are always YES as long as you meet the conditions He has laid down. By the way you ALWAYS ask in Jesus' name of the Father. There is no other name by which we ask anything of God, NOT Mary or some dead people declared to be saints by some man's organization. Man's church that declares some men /women to be saints is not of God in this aspect. The bible says we all are saints, see if you can find this statement, it's in more than one place. We, the saved of Christ, are all priests and kings with the right to go to God directly through Jesus. We don't have to go through some dead person and ask that they influence Jesus to ask the Father for us. To do this is against the word of God and people who do this are deceived by the lying teachings they have received.

John 15:7 If ye abide in me, and my words abide in you, ye shall ask what ye will, and it shall be done unto you.

The conditions of having your prayers answered. Stay in Jesus and abide by His words. Remain sinless and ask in faith believing you will receive what you ask for. God will supply all your "needs" not necessarily just what you want. Do you really need that pink Cadillac?

John 16:23 And in that day ye shall ask me nothing. Verily, verily, I say unto you, Whatsoever ye shall ask the Father in my name, He will give it you.

You must ask in Jesus' name 'only,' not Mary or any of the so called man made saints. Ask in faith, with no sin on your conscience, and you will have your answer from the Father.

John 16:24 Hitherto have ye asked nothing in my name: ask, and ye shall receive, that your joy may be full.

Before Jesus rose to heaven prayer went through the temple priests not Jesus. Now that Jesus is ruling and reigning in heaven you ask only in His name, in faith, and you will receive from the Father in heaven.

1 Timothy 2:5 For there is one God, and one mediator between God and men, the man Christ Jesus;

Jesus says ask (pray) in My name and the Father will answer your prayer. You are not told to pray in anyone else's name at all. In fact I believe that if you pray in any name other than Jesus Christ you will be praying to false gods, and that folks is a major sin. Notice ! It says Jesus is the ONLY MEDIATOER between us and God the Father.

1 Timothy 2:8 I will therefore that men pray every where, lifting up holy hands, without wrath and doubting.

You can see by this verse that God really wants all men and women, who are born again Christians, to pray in faith for all things, not in anger or thinking they won't receive.

James 1:5 If any of you lack wisdom, let him ask of God, that giveth to all men liberally, and upbraideth not; and it shall be given him. 6 But let him ask in faith, nothing wavering. For he that wavereth is like a wave of the sea driven with the wind and tossed. 7 For let not that man think that he shall receive any thing of the Lord.

Ask in faith! All that you do with the Lord God in heaven is done in and by faith. A lack of faith is a sin, and God does not hear the prayers of a sinners. Why would you pray not expecting (with no faith) to receive what you are praying for? This is called a exercise in uselessness. Or is it a public demonstration so others will know how close you are to God??

James 1:8 A double minded man is unstable in all his ways.

This is a man that does not even know what direction his life is going; in prayer he is unsure God hears let alone that God will answer; he's not positive about much of anything especially God in his life. He makes excuses for everything that does not go right. He says 'I'll try' while not doing his best to accomplish his task. He uses the word try as an excuse for failure. Do you?

James 4:3 Ye ask, and receive not, because ye ask amiss, that ye may consume it upon your lusts.

You must ask in faith believing that you will receive what you ask for. You must be holy, sin free, and pure before God to have Him even hear your prayers let alone answer them. As I've said before, God will supply all your needs, whether they are for healing, spirituality, or material things, <u>if you meet His conditions.</u>

This does not include the "I wants just because". This is asking 'amiss'. Again this is want (lusts) not need.

1 Peter 3:12 For the eyes of the Lord are over the righteous, and his ears are open unto their prayers: but the face of the Lord is against them that do evil.

Here are the conditions you must abide by for God to hear your prayers. Again God does NOT hear the prayers of sinners ("them that do evil"). Or don't you think that you as a "sinning Christian" are not in the category of evil doers? Think again!! There is no such thing as a sinning Christian! It took only ONE sin to get Satan kicked out of heaven, and only one sin to get Adam & Eve kicked out into the big, bad, cold world. Do you think God, as no respecter of persons, will treat you any differently?

1 John 3:22 And whatsoever we ask, we receive of him, because we keep his commandments, and do those things that are pleasing in his sight.

God chooses to only hear the prayers of the righteous 'His Kids'. So get yourself right and God will hear you and answer your prayers with a resounding YES. It's a waste of time to pray if you're your doing things that <u>are not</u> pleasing to His sight.

1 John 5:14-15 And this is that we have in Him, that, if we ask anything according to His will, He heareth us: And if we know that he hear us, whatsoever we ask we know that we have the petitions that we desired of Him.

This the final statement in this study on prayer, says it all. To put it very simply; if we ask according to What God's Will is, we will receive what we are asking for.

Not asking according to God's will is one of the answers to the question of "why didn't God answer my prayers?" Other reasons are aslo spelled out in this study on prayer.

Predestination

Ephesians 1:4 According as he hath chosen us in him before the foundation of the world, that we should be holy and without blame before him in love: 5 Having predestinated us unto the adoption of children by Jesus Christ to himself, according to the good pleasure of his will,

We see here that we are chosen in Jesus the Christ from the beginning of the world. This is on the odd chance that Adam and Eve used their free will and disobeyed God's command. Which they did. This is God's plan to save humanity from sin, to give everybody a chance. Jesus was the predestined One, not we who come to Jesus for salvation. God predestined a family of holy people for Himself without knowing who they would be. He just knew that there would be a loving family for Him. Loving is a key word here. Without the free will to chose to love God how can God know we love Him for Himself? Did He not test Abraham by telling him to sacrifice his son? God wanted to know for sure that Abraham loved and would obey Him. Did God not say "Now I know"(**Ge 22:12**)? If we were predestined without any choice in the matter how would God know that we really did love Him?

Ephesians 1:11 In whom also we have obtained an inheritance, being predestinated according to the purpose of him who worketh all things after the counsel of his own will:

We are the predestined family of God through Jesus. The "purpose of Him" means that God the Father chose to have an alternate plan, if Adam and Eve did not work out, for a loving family (the inheritors) and that this family should come through Jesus who died on the cross for this family. This plan was predestined from before the world was formed. Again it is through Jesus by our free will choice, and not God picking and choosing who would go to heaven and who would go to hell. Adam And Eve were plan "A" and Jesus was Plan "B" if Adam and Eve did not live up to expectations.

Matthew 22:14 For many are called, but few are chosen.

We are chosen by OUR FREE WILL choice to believe in Christ. Is our gateway into the fellowhip of the chosen of God. Does not God call all men?

1 Corinthians 7:17 But as God hath distributed to every man, as the Lord hath called every one, so let him walk. And so ordain I in all churches.

That all men are called puts a lie to the concept of a God that picks and chooses who will and who won't be saved. This picking is also mistakenly called Predestination and is a lie of Satan.

1 Corinthians 7:24 Brethren, let every man, wherein he is called, therein abide with God.

All men are called of God, but not all men are saved. It is a free will choice that every man must make. This verse is telling men that the best thing that they can do in their lives is to walk with Jesus. This is what God the Father would have all men do.

Acts 2:21 And it shall come to pass, that whosoever shall call on the name of the Lord shall be saved.

How can some be chosen by God to be saved to glory and some to damnation when here it says "whosoever," which means any and all who chose to be saved? You can say anyone who calls on the name of God will be saved.
Predestination is not who will be saved, but how we are to be saved. By the cross! By the way, whosoever means all or anyone who chooses, not just a select few.

Romans 10:13 For whosoever shall call upon the name of the Lord shall be saved.

Kinda puts the lie to who is predestined to be saved. Eh! Anyone can call on the name of the Lord as we all have free will.

Romans 8:29 For whom he did foreknow, he also did predestinate to be conformed to the image of his Son, that he might be the firstborn among many brethren. 30 Moreover whom he did predestinate, them he also called: and whom he called, them he also justified: and whom he justified, them he also glorified.

Jesus was the one predestined to provide salvation. It is how we are saved not who will be saved. God wants a family of holy people who chose to come to Him, in Spirit and Truth, by their free will choice. God predestined a holy family through forgiveness and the removal of sin from our conscience. All this by the work that Jesus did by the cross and the resurrection. "Them He also called: and whom he called" means everyone in the world. See above : God calls all men.

Romans 11: 32 For God hath concluded them all in unbelief, that he might have mercy upon all.

That word "all" kinda puts a lie to the belief that predestination is who will be saved.

1 Corinthians 15:21 For since by man came death, by man came also the resurrection of the dead. 22 For as in Adam all die, even so in Christ shall all be made alive.

Calvinists, and most of man's churches will say that this is predestination of who will be saved. But it really means that it is a free will choice to sin or to be saved. The word "all" is the key to understanding verse 22. Do you really think that "all" men are saved? If so, are there any who go to hell? The words "all be made alive", or born again in and of the Spirit, must be understood that "made" means alive by our free will choice. This then means the idea that God picks and chooses who will and will not be saved is a "lie". We have the free will to chose to go to heaven or to hell.

Ephesians 3:11 According to the eternal purpose which he purposed in Christ Jesus our Lord:

"The eternal purpose" is the plan of salvation from the foundations of the world. It is called predestination. "Purposed in" means Jesus was planned to be the savior of mankind. Again Jesus was and is the plan of How we are saved not who is saved!

2 Timothy 1:9 Who hath saved us, and called us with an holy calling, not according to our works, but according to his own purpose and grace, which was given us in Christ Jesus before the world began,

"In Christ Jesus before the world began", this is predestination : how we are saved not who is saved. Salvation is a personal choice we make, how else can God know we come to him because we love Him for Himself. If God chose us as individuals, to be saved, without our free will, then it would not be a loving choice on our part now would it?

Titus 1:2 In hope of eternal life, which God, that cannot lie, promised before the world began;

The plan of salvation, which is Jesus, was from before God created the world. This is called the plan of predestination. The plan of HOW the people of the world would have a free will choice for salvation, NOT who of the people of the world would be saved by God's arbitrary choice .

Hebrews 4:3 For we which have believed do enter into rest, as he said, As I have sworn in my wrath, if they shall enter into my rest: although the works were finished from the foundation of the world.

The plan of salvation (God's rest) was finished from the foundation of the world or you can say before time began for us. This plan is called predestination, it was that Jesus would come at the right time, by the Fathers command, and provide a way of salvation that allows us to be sin free, and in loving (Agape) fellowship with God.

James 1:17 Every good gift and every perfect gift is from above, and cometh down from the Father of lights, with whom is no variableness, neither shadow of turning. 18 Of his own will begat he us with the word of truth, that we should be a kind of first fruits of his creatures.

The perfect gift is Jesus. The word of truth is Jesus. You can see this from verse 17. God the Father is the one who begot us through Jesus. Again this is the plan of salvation from the foundations of the world and Jesus is that plan . We are saved by Jesus' work on the earth not by God the Father picking and choosing who will be saved and who will go to hell.

1 Peter 1:2 Elect according to the foreknowledge of God the Father, through sanctification of the Spirit, unto obedience and sprinkling of the blood of Jesus Christ: Grace unto you, and peace, be multiplied.

There are so many different elements here, but this is where I decided to put it. The foreknowledge of God means that he knew that there would be a body of people that would be saved by Jesus' work on the earth. God knew HOW the salvation process would work , but NOT who would be saved. See what Peter says: it is through the Spirit, by obedience , by the blood of Jesus that we are saved. All this means is that we are saved by OUR CHOICE to come to the blood, obey His commands, and follow the leading of the HOLY SPIRIT to salvation. To say that God makes us do this is to say we are the same as robots with no free will. This scripture puts a lie to the concept of predestination, of who will be saved or that God picks and chooses who will go to hell and who will go to heaven, which is one of the major tenants of Calvinism.

1 Peter 1:18 Forasmuch as ye know that ye were not redeemed with corruptible things, as silver and gold, from your vain conversation received by tradition from your fathers; 19 But with the precious blood of Christ, as of a lamb without blemish and without spot: 20 Who verily was foreordained before the foundation of the world, but was manifest in these last times for you,

Here you see it, Jesus was the one foreordained, the how of salvation not the who.
If God really does pick and choose, why do we need Jesus? Picking and choosing, if you believe it, means that it does not matter what you do or who you are, you are chosen to go hell or heaven arbitrarily. In other words you have no free will in this matter. This is just not thinking right or you might say it's unintelligent.

1 John 3: 3 And every man that hath this hope in him purifieth himself, even as he is pure.

The phrase "every man" means that all men who come to God come of their own free will. It does not mean that God picks and chooses who will be saved. This decision is yours not God's. This verse also says we have free will by saying every man 'purifieth himself.' This is Jesus as it says 'even as He is pure.'

Revelation 3:20 Behold, I stand at the door, and knock: if any man hear my voice, and open the door, I will come in to him, and will sup with him, and he with me.

The phrase "any Man" means just what it says. The choice of salvation is open for all men as stated by the phrase "any man". If God meant predestination to mean who will be saved then why would He say "any man" will be saved by his choice? You know it is your choice because you have to open the door for Christ.

Revelation 13:8 And all that dwell upon the earth shall worship him, whose names are not written in the book of life of the Lamb slain from the foundation of the world.

All whose names are not in the book of life will worship Jesus at the final judgment, they will have no choice in this, and will have to admit that they were wrong about Jesus.

The plan of salvation from the foundations of the world is the Slain Lamb. Jesus on the cross, three days in the grave, risen to rule and reign at the right hand of the Father. This plan is how we are saved, not who God picks and chooses to be saved. Is your name written in the book of life? Mine is, thank God for Jesus.

Divorce of the nation of Israel

Matthew 23:37 O Jerusalem, Jerusalem, thou that killest the prophets, and stonest them which are sent unto thee, how often would I have gathered thy children together, even as a hen gathereth her chickens under her wings, and ye would not!38 Behold, your house is left unto you desolate.39 For I say unto you, Ye shall not see me henceforth, till ye shall say, Blessed is he that cometh in the name of the Lord.

Luke 13:34 O Jerusalem, Jerusalem, which killest the prophets, and stonest them that are sent unto thee; how often would I have gathered thy children together, as a hen doth gather her brood under her wings, and ye would not!35 Behold, your house is left unto you desolate: and verily I say unto you, Ye shall not see me, until the time come when ye shall say, Blessed is he that cometh in the name of the Lord.

"Your house is left to you desolate"! This is the pronouncement of divorce to Israel for adultery to false gods.

Luke 13:28 There shall be weeping and gnashing of teeth, when ye shall see Abraham, and Isaac, and Jacob, and all the prophets, in the kingdom of God, and you yourselves thrust out.29 And they shall come from the east, and from the west, and from the north, and from the south, and shall sit down in the kingdom of God. 30 And, behold, there are last which shall be first, and there are first which shall be last.

This is the divorce of the nation of Israel. Seeing the prophets is at the second coming and to be thrust out means that they, the Jews who did not accept Jesus, are there for the judgment of sin and will be sent to outer darkness where there will be weeping and gnashing of teeth. Their candlestick was taken away from them for adultery to false Gods, and not following God's commandment to bring God to the world. This is their sin. The kingdom of God is now given to "ALL" who will come through Jesus to the Father. The nation of Israel was first and they rejected Jesus as the Christ. The gentiles of the world who come to Jesus were last and now are first. The people of the nation of Israel, the Jews of today, still have a chance at heaven, it is the same one we have as the gentiles of the world. It's called Jesus!

John 1:11 He came unto his own, and his own received him not.

This is one of the reasons that Israel was divorced . They, the nation of Israel, took themselves out of God's hands. It was their CHOICE to reject Jesus as the son o God even though in their heart of hearts they knew who He was. They, the leadership, did not want to lose the power they had through the authority of Rome.

John 19:15 But they cried out, Away with him, away with him, crucify him. Pilate saith unto them, Shall I crucify your King? The chief priests answered, We have no king but Caesar.

The words out of the mouths of the religious leadership of the nation of Israel, of Jesus' day and still to this day, condemns them. They claim Caesar instead of God as their ruler. Why would God keep and respect a people that rejected HIM for a mere man.

Acts 7:55 But he, being full of the Holy Ghost, looked up stedfastly into heaven, and saw the glory of God, and Jesus standing on the right hand of God, 56 And said, Behold, I see the heavens opened, and the Son of man standing on the right hand of God. 57 Then they cried out with a loud voice, and stopped their ears, and ran upon him with one accord,

The vision Stephen had, while being grilled before the religious leaders, of Jesus "standing" literally meant that Jesus had dismissed and rejected the Jewish nation and they knew it. When a king stands up he is signifying that he is DONE with you. They killed Stephen because of this. They could not bear to hear the truth of Jesus being the Christ, and that they had not accepted Him (Jesus) for who He was.

Acts 13:46 Then Paul and Barnabas grew bold, and said, It was necessary that the word of God should first have been spoken to you: but seeing you put it from you, and judge yourselves unworthy of everlasting life, lo, we turn to the Gentiles.

The Jews received the word of God first and rejected it, as you can see by Luke's testimony in this verse about what Paul and Barnabas told the Jews in Antioch. This is a rejection of eternal life with Jesus, by the Jews own free will choice, and by disbelief that Jesus was the Christ. It is, for all practical purposes, a rejection of God by the Jews. This turning to the Gentiles is, in reality, a divorce for the turning away from God to false gods, i.e. Caesar. Since God is a fair and just God the Jews, to this day, have the same chance for salvation as we the gentiles of the world have. Please note here that these Jews were the common people and not just the leadership of the day.

Romans 2:28 For he is not a Jew, which is one outwardly; neither is that circumcision, which is outward in the flesh: 29 But he is a Jew, which is one inwardly; and circumcision is that of the heart, in the spirit, and not in the letter; whose praise is not of men, but of God.

This shows that all who are in the Spiritual Kingdom of Jesus are the true Jews. Being "in the spirit" shows that we are circumcised of the heart not the flesh, and that our praise is from God not man. We are above the law in the new covenant of love and Grace, and no longer under the law of sin and death. This also tells us that the Kingdom of God is a spiritual kingdom, not a natural kingdom of the flesh (the sin filled world).

Romans 9:27 Esaias also crieth concerning Israel, Though the number of the children of Israel be as the sand of the sea, a remnant shall be saved:

Romans 11:23 And they also, if they abide not still in unbelief, shall be graffed in: for God is able to graff them in again.

The nation of Israel is rejected by God for the rejection of Jesus. But the individual Jew can be saved, grafted in, anytime he or she decides to give it up for Jesus.

Romans 9:30 What shall we say then? That the Gentiles, which followed not after righteousness, have attained to righteousness, even the righteousness which is of faith. 31 But Israel, which followed after the law of righteousness, hath not attained to the law of righteousness. 32 Wherefore? Because they sought it not by faith, but as it were by the works of the law. For they stumbled at that stumblingstone; 33 As it is written, Behold, I lay in Sion a stumblingstone and rock of offence: and whosoever believeth on him shall not be ashamed.

The nation of Israel refused the new covenant that Jesus came to confirm with them. He, Jesus, became a road block to them and they were broken (Jerusalem destroyed by the Romans in 70 A. D.) and rejected by God; no longer a nation under His care.

God no longer works with nations, only with individuals. Is not salvation for the individual? To say that any country is Christian is wrong. There are NO Christian countries. Question: what percentage of people in any given nation must be truly Christian before it can be called a Christian nation? 10% 51% 99% ! I think a 100%, this includes the government! This is not to say that some countries were not formed under and by Christian principles.

Romans 10:21 But to Israel he saith, All day long I have stretched forth my hands unto a disobedient and gainsaying people.

These are the reasons God rejected Israel. For 1500 years Israel did it their way and not God's. The straw that broke the camel's back was their rejection of Jesus as the Christ, and claiming that Caesar was their king. Then came 70AD and the Roman army. Do you think that God used the Roman army for His purpose? I Do!

Romans 11:2 God hath not cast away his people which he foreknew. Wot ye not what the scripture saith of Elias? how he maketh intercession to God against Israel saying,

God rejected the nation of Israel but not the individual Jew who accepted Jesus as the Christ. God planned and knew He would have a "people". What He did not know was who they would be. These people now, the new spiritual nation of Israel, is anyone who comes to God the Father through Jesus, Jew or Gentile.

Romans 11:20 Well; because of unbelief they were broken off, and thou standest by faith. Be not highminded, but fear:21 For if God spared not the natural branches, take heed lest he also spare not thee. 22 Behold therefore the goodness and severity of God: on them which fell, severity; but toward thee, goodness, if thou continue in his goodness: otherwise thou also shalt be cut off.

The natural branch is the Jew and he was broken off of the vine (Jesus) and thrown out of God's family. Be careful that you, of God's family, do not fall into unbelief or pride (sin) or you too will be cast out. Be holy or be out. Can you see? God does cut off sinners?

Romans 11:26 And so all Israel shall be saved: as it is written, There shall come out of Sion the Deliverer, and shall turn away ungodliness from Jacob:27 For this is my covenant unto them, when I shall take away their sins.

There is a teaching in man's church that uses these verses to say that God has a special plan of salvation for the nation of Israel when Jesus comes for the second time. This is not what this verse says. It is telling of the "first coming" of Jesus and the chance that the Jews had to accept Jesus as the Christ. "All Israel" means all who choose to come to Jesus. Are not the all of the born again, saved of Christ, called spiritual Israel? Did not the Jews then and now and have free will, and the choice to come to the Father through Jesus the Christ?

1Corinthians 5 But with many of them God was not well pleased: for they were overthrown in the wilderness.

Even back then the Jews rejected the will of God they constantly rebelled against God, and were punished. As God says, they are a stiff necked, and brass browed people. Look it up. A hint it's in the Old Testament.

Jesus in the grave

Matthew 27:52 And the graves were opened; and many bodies of the saints which slept arose,53 And came out of the graves after his resurrection, and went into the holy city, and appeared unto many.

1 Peter 3:19 By which also he went and preached unto the spirits in prison;

1 Peter 4:6 For this cause was the gospel preached also to them that are dead, that they might be judged according to men in the flesh, but live according to God in the spirit.

When Jesus descended into the earth He went to Upper Sheol, paradise, also called, Abraham's bosom, where all the righteous Old Testament saints were. These were those who could not go to heaven because of the sin in their conscience. That is their sins that could not be removed by the blood of bulls and goats; it only covered their sins. But by the shed blood of Jesus they were able to be freed from the guilt of sin and have it removed from their conscience. See **Hebrews chapter 9:14**.

As No sinner can go to heaven God cannot abide any sin! Jesus descended and told them (the Old TestamentSaints) 'I Am the one you have been waiting for.' The Christ. This is why Jesus had to descend to Abraham's bosom, to free the Saints of sin so they would be able to choose and go to heaven with Jesus when he rose to rule and reign. This was their long awaited reward.

We, the born again, can go to heaven because Jesus' Holy and Pure Shed Blood removes all of our <u>past</u> sins from our conscience this is only by our free will choice, thereby making us no longer sinners. Unless we choose to continue in sin after being delivered of sinfulness, and again become sinners and lose our salvation.

The phrase "judged according to men in the flesh" tells us that " those that are dead" are not men in the world dead spiritually, but that it means that they are the physically dead old testament saints in Abraham's bosom.

John 3:13 And no man hath ascended up to heaven, but he that came down from heaven, *even* **the Son of man which is in heaven.**

We see here that no one, not one man or woman went to heaven before Christ died and resurrected and rose to heaven with the cloud of Old Testament Saints.

Acts 1:9 when he had spoken these things, while they beheld, he was taken up; and a cloud received him out of their sight. 10 And while they looked stedfastly toward heaven as he went up, behold, two men stood by them in white apparel; 11 Which also said, Ye men of Galilee, why stand ye gazing up into heaven? this same Jesus, which is taken up from you into heaven, shall so come in like manner as ye have seen him go into heaven.

Revelation 1:7 Behold, he cometh with clouds; and every eye shall see him, and they also which pierced him: and all kindreds of the earth shall wail because of him. Even so, Amen.

Jesus rose to heaven with and in a cloud of Old Testament Saints. The same ones he talked to in "Upper Sheol, Paradise, also called Abraham's Bosom." They were seen coming out of their graves and walking around Jerusalem. See above. This is the same way He will come back, in a cloud of all the Saints from heaven.

Colossians 2:15 And having spoiled principalities and powers, he made a shew of them openly, triumphing over them in it.

1 John 3:8 He that committeth sin is of the devil; for the devil sinneth from the beginning. For this purpose the Son of God was manifested, that he might destroy the works of the devil.

Jesus did not go to <u>Lower Sheol</u> (the hell of torment) and fight with Satan. He defeated and destroyed (made to be as of no effect) the works of Satan by His work on the cross. Jesus created Satan and all of the angels, why would He fight him. Satan is just not powerful enough to fight Jesus. Ya think? As a side light you will notice the statement that "He that committeth sin is of the devil". This says the word "sin" this does not mean more than one sin it means Just "ONE SIN" makes you a child of the devil. It does not matter who or what you were before you sinned but it is the fact that you choose to sin that puts you on the road to hell..

Luke 23:42 And he said unto Jesus, Lord, remember me when thou comest into thy kingdom.43 And Jesus said unto him, Verily I say unto thee, To day shalt thou be with me in paradise.

This is the thief that went to Abraham's Bosom (also called upper Sheol, or Paradise) with Jesus. This also says that the kingdom started after the cross and is a spiritual kingdom. One last thing it says is that Jesus did not go to hell for punishment or to wrestle with Satan. There is "NO" scripture anywhere in the bible that even comes close to saying the Jesus fought Satan in hell. The work of defeating Satan was all done once and for all time on the cross.

Just for your information; The door of hell will not be open until the Final Judgement.

Acts 2:31 He seeing this before spake of the resurrection of Christ, that his soul was not left in hell, neither his flesh did see corruption.

This hell referred to here is Upper Sheol, also called Paradise ,or Abraham Bosom. Not the Lower Sheol, a place of torment. Jesus' body did not rot while in the grave.

Hebrews 9:23 It was therefore necessary that the patterns of things in the heavens should be purified with these; but the heavenly things themselves with better sacrifices than these.24 For Christ is not entered into the holy places made

with hands, which are the figures of the true; but into heaven itself, now to appear in the presence of God for us:

After Jesus rose to heaven He sprinkled His shed blood on the Holy Tabernacle in the temple of heaven thereby purifying it forever. This is why sin can no longer be in heaven, and why God was, legally, able to order Satan thrown out of heaven, at that point in time, down to the earth never to return to heaven and accuse the saints of sin. Read **Rev chapter 5, see also Rev 12:4-6-12.** You will see that Jesus was the one pure and holy man able to open the book of life. Also notice that the strong angel with the big mouth was Satan who was also called the strong man by Jesus.

At the point of Jesus opening the book of life Satan was ordered out of heaven never to return. He was cast down to the earth and was bound from influencing the nations of the earth for all time. I believe that satan has been loosed now into the world, and that time is short as man measures time.

The Lie of Mary Remaining a Life Long Virgin or Without Sin.

Matthew 12:47 Then one said unto him, Behold, thy mother and thy brethren stand without, desiring to speak with thee.

Mark 6:3 Is not this the carpenter, the son of Mary, the brother of James, and Joses, and of Juda, and Simon? and are not his sisters here with us? And they were offended at him.

Galatians 1:19 But other of the apostles saw I none, save James the Lord's brother.

Luke 8:20 And it was told him by certain which said, Thy mother and thy brethren stand without, desiring to see thee.

Mary did not remain a virgin after Jesus birth, she had other children. A major church venerates and teaches that Mary remained a virgin, is sinless, and did not die but rose straight to heaven where she is now the 'queen of heaven', and intercedes with Jesus for us. This is an unholy lie of Satan! See the study on prayer. Mary is blessed of all women but she was just as human as the rest of us and she died like we all will. She went to heaven because she was sinless, if she wasn't she didn't. I believe that she did go to heaven, just as we will as long as we walk as Jesus walked.

Luke 2:22 And when the days of her purification according to the law of Moses were accomplished, they brought him to Jerusalem, to present him to the Lord; 24 And to offer a sacrifice according to that which is said in the law of the Lord, A pair of turtledoves, or two young pigeons.

If Mary remained sinless after Jesus birth, as a major mans' church teaches, why then did she need to sacrifice for her purification according to the law. She became sinless the same way we do, by Jesus' shed blood and our choice to remain that way. She was born again just as we are.

Saved by faith and Grace

Romans 10:17 So then faith cometh by hearing, and hearing by the word of God.

Romans 12:3 For I say, through the grace given unto me, to every man that is among you, not to think of himself more highly than he ought to think; but to think soberly, according as God hath dealt to every man the measure of faith.

This faith is what God has built into us to believe with and be saved by. Without faith we can not accept that Jesus really existed, that He was sinless, or that He died on the cross and rose from the dead. It is unreserved belief in these things that allows us to know Jesus as our savoir. If we choose to use it (faith). All men have the faith to believe and be saved, but not all men choose to use their God given faith to find salvation through Jesus.

Romans 14:23 And he that doubteth is damned if he eat, because he eateth not of faith: for whatsoever is not of faith is sin.

If you doubt (lack of Faith) you will not be saved, healed, or have material prosperity from God. It is your choice to use the faith that God has instilled in ALL men for the ability to believe in Christ for all the perks that are given freely to us from God the Father.

Luke 7:50 And he said to the woman, Thy faith hath saved thee; go in peace.
Romans 1:17 For therein is the righteousness of God revealed from faith to faith: as it is written, The just shall live by faith.

To be Just you must first be saved and sin free. This is all done by FAITH in Jesus. To live by faith is to live sinless, and the belief (faith) that God will honor all of His promises .

Romans 4:16 Therefore it is of faith, that it might be by grace; to the end the promise might be sure to all the seed; not to that only which is of the law, but to that also which is of the faith of Abraham; who is the father of us all,

Romans 5:1 Therefore being justified by faith, we have peace with God through our Lord Jesus Christ: 2 By whom also we have access by faith into this grace wherein we stand, and rejoice in hope of the glory of God.

By Faith we are saved through Grace. Grace comes from Jesus and we receive it by being righteous. The definition of the Greek word for Grace is in the New Test. is *"Gods continuing influence in your life and the example you put forward to the world."*

So yes, we are saved by Grace, but it is not an unmerited gift of favor as most of man's churches teach. The saying that they use is "I'm just a sinner saved by grace". The really sad thing is that they don't even try to understand what the word grace means. Or much else of the word of God. They twist it to fit what they believe. They do not take their belief from what the bible says, but what they want it to say. The end of the promise means to the second coming of Jesus where our walk of salvation will be finished and made permanent.

Romans 5:21 That as sin hath reigned unto death, even so might grace reign through righteousness unto eternal life by Jesus Christ our Lord.

This verse tells us how and under what conditions we receive Grace. Notice that grace reigns (is given) through righteousness. Again this verse is saying spiritual death through sin, and Grace through righteousness.

Romans 8:24 For we are saved by hope: but hope that is seen is not hope: for what a man seeth, why doth he yet hope for? 25 But if we hope for that we see not, then do we with patience wait for it.

This is faith for things in the future that Paul is talking about. "Saved by hope" means that we will continue in the future in our salvation walk with Jesus. As we can fall back into sin and lose all that we had gained by first coming to Jesus. The word saved means, you were saved, you are saved, and you will continue to be saved. This tells us that our personal salvation is not set in granite but is conditional of our remaining sinless. It will not be set in granite until we get to heaven, or at the second coming.

Galatians 3:11 But that no man is justified by the law in the sight of God, it is evident: for, The just shall live by faith.

We live by faith in Christ and not under the law of sin and death, but rather under the new covenant of Grace. This faith is that Jesus really was killed on the cross and resurrected to life. We have Faith to be saved and then receive Grace by having our sin removed from our conscience. This removal of sin means, literally, that we are righteous before God the Father.

Grace: God's continuing influence in your life and it's resulting change for the better.
This works only if you listen to the Holy Spirit who delivers Grace to us.

Galatians 3:14 That the blessing of Abraham might come on the Gentiles through Jesus Christ; that we might receive the promise of the Spirit through faith.

Galatians 3:26 For ye are all the children of God by faith in Christ Jesus.

Again through FAITH, always faith, for without it you can not please God.

Ephesians 2:5 Even when we were dead in sins, hath quickened us together with Christ, (by grace ye are saved;)

Ephesians 2:8 For by grace are ye saved through faith; and that not of yourselves: it is the gift of God:

Yes we are saved by grace, but first we must be born again by repentance and asking forgiveness of God by Jesus' shed holy and pure blood. This is by faith that Jesus really was a person on the earth and did what the bible says He did. The only way you can receive Grace is by becoming righteous, and this is through "FAITH". Remember faith comes before Grace.

You must understand that salvation is an ongoing process. So yes, with God's grace in our lives (as long as we remain sinless), we will be saved. So you can say we are saved by grace, but it is not (as some say) an unmerited gift of favor. Again faith, righteousness, and then Grace.

Ephesians 3:2 If ye have heard of the dispensation of the grace of God which is given me to you-ward:

Ephesians 3:7 Whereof I was made a minister, according to the gift of the grace of God given unto me by the effectual working of his power.

The result of grace in your life can be the same as it was for Paul. Who knows what God has for you. Remember the definition of Grace. It will work in your life as it did in Paul's.

2 Timothy 3:15 And that from a child thou hast known the holy scriptures, which are able to make thee wise unto salvation through faith which is in Christ Jesus.

Again we see that we must have faith in Jesus, that He is who He says he is, to be saved. We are not just picked and saved by grace without faith. Faith comes first and then when we are righteous before God, through repentance of and asking forgiveness of sin, we then receive grace and it's works (God suggestions) in our lives. This all depends on our choice to follow God's suggestions given to us by the Holy Spirit.

Titus 2:11 For the grace of God that bringeth salvation hath appeared to all men, 12 Teaching us that, denying ungodliness and worldly lusts, we should live soberly, righteously, and godly, in this present world;

Yes, again, grace does bring salvation, but you must be saved first.

Salvation is an ongoing process by that the grace you receive from the Father. Grace allows and helps you learn to stop sinning and obey the commands of God. Without this grace I don't believe that you will be able to complete your salvation walk. Grace is for all who become sinless and is given without asking.

Titus 3:7 That being justified by his grace, we should be made heirs according to the hope of eternal life.

This grace, that is given to us, teaches us to be holy and brings justification (legally not guilty of sin) to us as we walk in Jesus' foot steps. A godly man once told me that being justified was the same as "just as if you never sinned".

Hebrews 3:18 And to whom sware he that they should not enter into his rest, but to them that believed not? 19 So we see that they could not enter in because of unbelief.

Hebrews 4:3 For we which have believed do enter into rest, as he said, As I have sworn in my wrath, if they shall enter into my rest: although the works were finished from the foundation of the world.

Unbelief is a lack of faith. Without using your God given faith you cannot please God or be saved. These, who were in unbelief, were the Jews who God brought out of Egypt, the same is true for us today as it was for them. Read the curses in **Due. 28: 15-45**. Do you want them on your head? The phrase "works were finished from the foundation of the world" means that the plan of salvation (predestination of Jesus' work on this earth) was made from before the earth was created. God, being who He is, can see all possibilities and plan for them. This does not mean that God knows beyond a doubt all that will happen in the future. He knows what He will do in the future (hence the "plan"), but does not know our future choices only the probability of the many choices that we make every day.

Hebrews 10:38 Now the just shall live by faith: but if any man draw back, my soul shall have no pleasure in him.

The just live by faith ! Does this not mean trust in God and walk sinless? A lack of faith, choosing not to use your God given faith, is a sin. If you "draw back" God has no pleasure in you. Is this what you want? It is what you will get by sinning, because drawing back is choosing to walk away from the commands of God by sinning. Just one sin will do it for you.

Hebrews 11:1 Now faith is the substance of things hoped for, the evidence of things not seen.

Believing a thing before there is any evidence whatsoever of a thing. Example: Believing, with out seeing, that there was and is a Jesus and that He did die on the cross for your sins, and did rise from the grave to live and sit at the right hand of the Father in heaven ruling and reigning .
See Hebrews chapter 11 for a study of the faith of the old test. saints. It's quite Good.

James 2:14 What doth it profit, my brethren, though a man say he hath faith, and have not works? can faith save him?

James 2:17 Even so faith, if it hath not works, is dead, being alone. 18 Yea, a man may say, Thou hast faith, and I have works: shew me thy faith without thy works, and I will shew thee my faith by my works.

James 2:20 But wilt thou know, O vain man, that faith without works is dead?

This defines how to use your faith. You must step out in faith believing what your faith tells you is already done for you. This is putting works to faith, or you might say 'walking your talk'. Jesus put works to His faith. Which are the works He would do on the earth that would bring salvation by providing the chance for the removal of sin for all the people of the world. What were His works. Do you know? Well! They were the giving of the gospel, the death on the cross, and the resurrection to name some of them.

James 2:26 For as the body without the spirit is dead, so faith without works is dead also.

Your spirit is dead because of your sins. Without believing in Jesus your faith is dead. Your work of believing is to come to Jesus for salvation. Jesus brought us a way to be born again in the spirit, He also brought us a way to put works to our faith and make it alive. He gave us a choice!

James 4:6 But he giveth more grace. Wherefore he saith, God resisteth the proud, but giveth grace unto the humble.

James 4:10 Humble yourselves in the sight of the Lord, and he shall lift you up.

Here again we see that grace is given to the humble (say righteous), which is another name for those of us who are and remain sinless and holy. Remember that "pride," as well as false humility, is a sin in God's eyes. "To lift you" up means that God will continue to provide His influence in your life, which is grace. To be held up also means to be declared a citizen of the kingdom of God for all to see.

1 Peter 1:13 Wherefore gird up the loins of your mind, be sober, and hope to the end for the grace that is to be brought unto you at the revelation of Jesus Christ;

As I have said grace comes after salvation from God the Father. It will influence our lives to the end result of sinlessness, salvation and an eternity with Jesus in heaven.

1 Peter 1:13-16 Wherefore gird up the loins of your mind, be sober, and hope to the end for the grace that is to be brought unto you at the revelation of Jesus Christ; As obedient children, not fashioning yourselves according to the former lusts in your ignorance: But as he which hath called you is holy, so be ye holy in all manner of conversation; Because it is written, Be ye holy; for I am holy.

Here we see that Grace comes at salvation when you have repented and are sin free. "The grace that is brought to you at the revelation of Jesus Christ" means at salvation. Remember you are saved "by grace through FAITH". Believing by faith comes first then the Grace of God is given to help you remain saved and to work out your salvation with trembling and fear. This grace comes from God by your being righteous (without sin in your life). Verses 14, 15, & 16 tell us we must be holy and shows that the grace in verse 13 is given and remains only as long as your are holy and sinless. Can you see this?

1 John 5:4 For whatsoever is born of God overcometh the world: and this is the victory that overcometh the world, even our faith.

The way to victory is to live in holiness by faith in Jesus. This faith tells us that Jesus did come to save us from our sins, did die on the cross, and did rise from the grave to life in heaven in glory along side the Father. That His commandments are not to hard to obey. That the belief that He will come and take us, who have remained sinless, to heaven for eternal glory is also by our faith in Him.

The Baptism of the Holy Spirit and His work in your life

Comments:

The modern man's church has relegated the Holy Spirit and His work to a second class position in the God head. We must understand that although the Holy Spirit is not mentioned in our worship of Jesus and the Father, He still guides us. He is, and always will be GOD, as the Father is GOD, as the Son is GOD. You can think of the Father as the prime designer of Creation, Jesus as the prime contractor, and the Holy Spirit as the prime facilitator of the actual physical work of the creation of the universe. This does not mean that Jesus and the Holy Spirit are any less God than the Father. They are three separate personalities who make up one God, and who are in 100% agreement 100% of the time, and are 100% equal.

The purposes of this teaching is to show how the Holy Spirit works, what He does, what He is responsible for, and who He helps. First of all, the Holy Spirit's job is to convince all sinners that they are in fact sinners. He does this by bringing to your mind (conscience) the sins you are doing, and have done. At this point the only answer to your problems is that you need Jesus' forgiveness for all of your past sins. By the way, there is no such thing as future sins. The bible even says "past sins." Look it up in **Romans 3:25**.

When you are born again (through Jesus) and baptized in water the Holy Spirit is given to you as the promise of your rebirth into the spiritual kingdom of God. What He does at salvation is to renew, regenerate, and make new (born again) your spirit which brings you back into contact with the Father. This work of salvation involves convincing you that you're dead in you're sins, and then for you to come to repentance, and ask forgiveness (by Jesus' blood). Then, and only then, can the Holy Spirit (at the Father's command) remove of all guilt of "past sins" from your conscience. At this point you are absolutely pure and Holy. This is just the start of your walk with God, and the Holy Spirit's influence in your life. After water baptism you must be baptized in the Holy Spirit by Jesus. This is a command (**Acts 1:4-5**), and is a separate experience from the promise of the Spirit in your life..

The Holy Spirit baptism involves your willingness to trust God by accepting the Holy Spirit's further work of helping you grow in Christ. The first physical evidence of this special (for the born again only) baptism of the Holy Spirit is a prayer language. A language you have never learned, also called an unknown tongue.

The Holy Spirit will not come and reside with you if you're still in sin! If you slip up and sin after you are saved and baptized in the Holy Spirit the Holy Spirit will leave you until you repent and ask forgiveness. At this point of repentance He will return and you will pick up your Christian walk from where you left off (sinned). You can not serve two masters at the same time! In other words, if you're in sin your master is Satan, if you are sinless your master is Jesus.

God the father will not 'SHARE' you with Satan . It's only one way or the other. You choose! The Greek word for prayer language is defined as a "Language that you have never learned". This is for you and only you and is to be used in private. It is not the "gift of tongues" which is one of the nine gifts of the Holy Spirit.

It is voluntary, God does not make you speak it. It is of the Holy Spirit (with your permission) using your throat, vocal cords, tongue, and lips to pray a perfect prayer back to God the Father from God the Holy Spirit in you. Again, it is with your permission. You can not do this without the baptism of the Holy Spirit, and He can not pray through you unless YOU decide to let Him do so.

After you are baptized in the Holy Spirit it gets real interesting to see how God will use you. One of the primary jobs of the Holy Spirit after you are born again is the same as when you were a sinner (by the way, you don't have to sin), and that is to convince you that you screwed up and sinned, and that you must now repent. You will learn to stop sinning if you listen to the Holy Spirit. It takes awhile to unlearn your sin habit, but you will get there as long as you stick to it. It is by the power of God the Holy Spirit that you are able to do anything effectively in "Truth & Spirit". This includes witnessing Jesus to others, worshiping God, living sin free (although this is a choice you make to stay saved), operating in the gifts of the Holy Spirit, having and showing to the world the fruits of the Spirit. If you, and it's a big IF, sin the only thing the Holy Spirit can do for you is to convince you of the sin you just committed until you repent. Then it's as if you never committed that last sin. You just pick up where you left off.

The gifts of the Holy Spirit are only given to those who trust God to the point of accepting the gift of the Baptism of the Holy Spirit in their lives. I would also say that to be effective in any of the five fold ministries you must also be Baptized in the Holy Spirit. Remember, without the evidence of a prayer langue you are not baptized in the Holy Spirit.

<u>Now on to the study of the Baptism of the Holy Spirit.</u>

Ephesians 1:13-14 In whom ye also trusted, after that ye heard the word of truth, the gospel of your salvation: in whom also after that ye believed, ye were sealed with that holy Spirit of promise, Which is the earnest of our inheritance until the redemption of the purchased possession, unto the praise of his glory.

Ephesians 1:17-18 That the God of our Lord Jesus Christ, the Father of glory, may give unto you the spirit of wisdom and revelation in the knowledge of him: The eyes of your understanding being enlightened; that ye may know what is the hope of his calling, and what the riches of the glory of his inheritance in the saints,

In verses 13 &14 the Holy Spirit is given at salvation for the renewal of your spirit. You are born again, into a spiritual relationship with the Father in heaven. This is not the baptism of the Holy Spirit. It is, you might say, an engagement ring of promise for the ultimate wedding of the bride of Christ to Jesus.

The word salvation is a progression: you were saved, you are saved, and you will be saved. This is all conditional on you remaining sinless. This is why God says work out your salvation with trembling and fear. Again, it is an on going work in your life preformed by you with the guidance of the holy Spirit.

This guidance is shown to us by verses 17&18. This is the second act of the Holy Spirit in our lives. It is called "The Baptism of the Holy Spirit which is a command of Jesus (see below **Acts 1 :4-5**). This second work brings us knowledge, wisdom, understanding, and availability of the nine spiritual gifts as given in **1 Co 12**. The first evidence that you are baptized in the Spirit is a prayer language. This language is from the Holy Spirit through you by your giving your free will permission to the Holy Spirit to use your vocal cords to pray a perfect prayer to God the Father in a language you have never learned. It is, by some, called God praying to God. Once more, you must see that these are TWO separate experiences that we receive From God by our free will choices.

Luke 24:49 And, behold, I send the promise of my Father upon you: but tarry ye in the city of Jerusalem, until ye be endued with power from on high.

Acts 1:4 And, being assembled together with them, commanded them that they should not depart from Jerusalem, but wait for the promise of the Father, which, saith he, ye have heard of me. 5 For John truly baptized with water; but ye shall be baptized with the Holy Ghost not many days hence.

To be "endued with power from on high" is the baptism of the Holy Spirit by Jesus.

This is a command! To disobey and not be baptized in the Spirit is to be in sin. It does not matter that 85%+ of modern man's churches do not believe in the B. H. S. Their non-belief does not change the facts of the bible. You must choose who you will believe, the Bible or some man who just wants your money every Sunday.

John 1:33 And I knew him not: but he that sent me to baptize with water, the same said unto me, Upon whom thou shalt see the Spirit descending, and remaining on him, the same is he which baptizeth with the Holy Ghost. 34 And I saw, and bare record that this is the Son of God.

This is the prophecy of the baptism in the Holy Spirit by Jesus. It was given by John the Baptist, the one who baptized Jesus the in the Jordan river. When He, Jesus, was given the Holy Spirit empowerment by God the Father, the spirit was seen as a dove descending onto Him.

Acts 2: 16 But this is that which was spoken by the prophet Joel; 17 And it shall come to pass in the last days, saith God, I will pour out of my Spirit upon all flesh: and your sons and your daughters shall prophesy, and your young men shall see visions, and your old men shall dream dreams:18 And on my servants and on my handmaidens I will pour out in those days of my Spirit; and they shall prophesy:

This is the explanation, by Peter, of the fulfillment of prophecy in Joel of the Baptism of the Holy Spirit, and the last days which started at the cross .

Acts 2:1 And when the day of Pentecost was fully come, they were all with one accord in one place. 2 And suddenly there came a sound from heaven as of a rushing mighty wind, and it filled all the house where they were sitting. 3 And there appeared unto them cloven tongues like as of fire, and it sat upon each of them. 4 And they were all filled with the Holy Ghost, and began to speak with other tongues, as the Spirit gave them utterance. 5 And there were dwelling at Jerusalem Jews, devout men, out of every nation under heaven.6 Now when this was noised abroad, the multitude came together, and were confounded, because that every man heard them speak in his own language.

This is the fulfillment of John the Baptist's prophecy about the baptism of the Holy Spirit, where more than 120 people including the Apostles obeyed the command of Jesus given in **Acts 1:4-5**. I believe the 'cloven tongues like as of fire' was the physical proof of the cares of the world being burned out of these Disciples and Apostles. How else could they have done the works of Jesus as well as and as wonderfully as they did?

John 14:16 And I will pray the Father, and he shall give you another Comforter, that he may abide with you forever; 17 Even the Spirit of truth; whom the world cannot receive, because it seeth him not, neither knoweth him: but ye know him; for he dwelleth with you, and shall be in you. 18 I will not leave you comfortless: I will come to you.

This is the BAPTISM OF THE HOLY SPIRIT, which is different than the promise of the Holy Spirit you receive at salvation. The first promise is the same as an engagement ring for a bride; which we are. The second promise of the Holy Spirit comes at the rising of Jesus to heaven and the command of the Father. This command was given at Pentecost. It comes to you by your deciding to accept Him, the Holy Spirit, through the prayer of Jesus (verse 16). Just accept the gift of the Baptism of the Holy Spirit it's already given. He will reside with you as long as you remain sin free. Again, you don't have to ask for it as it is already given, just accept it in your spirit and heart.

The Spirit leaves when you sin, and comes back when you repent. As I've said before, 'God does not share"! One of the most important works we will do is learn to stop sinning.

One of the jobs of the Holy Spirit is to comfort us in our troubles, another is to teach us about God and what He wants in our lives, and one of the most important is to <u>convince</u> us of our sins. We convict ourselves of sin by our own conscience.

John 14:26 But the Comforter, which is the Holy Ghost, whom the Father will send in my name, he shall teach you all things, and bring all things to your remembrance, whatsoever I have said unto you.

This is only one of the jobs of the Holy Spirit, another is to pray through you, using your mouth, a perfect prayer back to the Father in heaven. This teaching is, again, needed badly by the body of Christ so we can all stand together and be in unity with the mind of Christ.

John 15:26 But when the Comforter is come, whom I will send unto you from the Father, even the Spirit of truth, which proceedeth from the Father, he shall

testify of me: 27 And ye also shall bear witness, because ye have been with me from the beginning.

Acts 1:8 But ye shall receive power, after that the Holy Ghost is come upon you: and ye shall be witnesses unto me both in Jerusalem, and in all Judaea, and in Samaria, and unto the uttermost part of the earth.

Another job of the Holy Spirit in your life, to testify of the truth of Jesus and His words to the world. This is called letting the Holy Spirit give you the words to witness for Christ, which is a command. This power we receive is beyond any power man can give you. It is literally the power of God in your life.

John 16:7 Nevertheless I tell you the truth; It is expedient for you that I go away: for if I go not away, the Comforter will not come unto you; but if I depart, I will send him unto you.8 And when he is come, he will reprove the world of sin, and of righteousness, and of judgment:9 Of sin, because they believe not on me;10 Of righteousness, because I go to my Father, and ye see me no more;11 Of judgment, because the prince of this world is judged.

The Holy Spirit was sent on the day of Pentecost, 40 days after Passover. You can see that the work of the Holy Spirit is the only way that Christianity can survive and flourish.
Verse 11 is talking about the defeat of Satan by Jesus on the cross.

One of the two things Jesus could not do while on the earth was baptize people in the Holy Spirit. The second thing Jesus could not do that we can and must do is bring people to salvation through His shed Blood.

John 16:13 Howbeit when he, the Spirit of truth, is come, he will guide you into all truth: for he shall not speak of himself; but whatsoever he shall hear, that shall he speak: and he will shew you things to come.14 He shall glorify me: for he shall receive of mine, and shall shew it unto you.15 All things that the Father hath are mine: therefore said I, that he shall take of mine, and shall shew it unto you.

1 Corinthians 2:10 But God hath revealed them unto us by his Spirit: for the Spirit searcheth all things, yea, the deep things of God. 11 For what man knoweth the things of a man, save the spirit of man which is in him? even so the things of God knoweth no man, but the Spirit of God.

1 Corinthians 2:13 Which things also we speak, not in the words which man's wisdom teacheth, but which the Holy Ghost teacheth; comparing spiritual things with spiritual.

Again ! What the Holy Spirit does for you as long as you are baptized in Him. I know that you have heard people say that we cannot understand or really know God because He is so much higher than we are. Well here it says that the Holy Spirit will show us all the depths of God that we need to know. See, we can know and understand God! For the Holy Spirit to work in your life to this extent you must be baptized into the Holy Spirit of God.

Acts 2:33 Therefore being by the right hand of God exalted, and having received of the Father the promise of the Holy Ghost, he hath shed forth this, which ye now see and hear.

What you see here is that the gift of the Holy Spirit can be seen and heard.

What you see and hear is the joyous worship and the praising of God in an unknown language, a language that you have never learned. This is called a prayer language, which is the first physical evidence of the baptism of the Holy Spirit. It is also a manifestation of the Gifts of the Holy Spirit in operation in your life. You must also understand that this 'prayer language' is only to be used in private!

Acts 8:17 Then laid they their hands on them, and they received the Holy Ghost.18 And when Simon saw that through laying on of the apostles' hands the Holy Ghost was given, he offered them money,

It was obvious that the Baptism of the Holy Spirit was given and accepted because the evidence of it was seen. To paraphrase Jesus: what is easier, to say you are baptized in the Spirit or to see physical evidence of the baptism of the Holy Spirit, such as an unknown language.

Acts 10:44 While Peter yet spake these words, the Holy Ghost fell on all them which heard the word.45 And they of the circumcision which believed were astonished, as many as came with Peter, because that on the Gentiles also was poured out the gift of the Holy Ghost. 46 For they heard them speak with tongues, and magnify God. Then answered Peter,

Again the physical evidence of the baptism of the Holy Spirit was seen, heard, and even named. By hearing this unknown language; Ya think? How else did they become astonished at what happened?

Acts 19:6 And when Paul had laid his hands upon them, the Holy Ghost came on them; and they spake with tongues, and prophesied.

Here it is ! It actually says that they spoke in TONGUES after receiving the baptism of The Holy Spirit. Tongues, in the Greek, means a language you have never learned. The phrase "and Prophesied" means that they also received one of the nine spiritual gifts called prophecy. You know that this is a prayer language because there is no gift of interpretation mentioned, which is required when the gift of tongues is used.

Romans 8:26 Likewise the Spirit also helpeth our infirmities: for we know not what we should pray for as we ought: but the Spirit itself maketh intercession for us with groanings which cannot be uttered.

This is the unknown language, also called the prayer language, that you receive at your baptism into the Holy Spirit. This verse gives us one of the reasons we need it.

Romans 8:27 And he that searcheth the hearts knoweth what is the mind of the Spirit, because he maketh intercession for the saints according to the will of God.

This is what the prayer language does for you.
Another reason for the prayer language.

1 Corinthians 2:14 But the natural man receiveth not the things of the Spirit of God: for they are foolishness unto him: neither can he know them, because they are spiritually discerned.

This natural man is of the world. Also a Christian not baptized into the Holy Spirit of God is not complete, and is without the guidance of the Holy Spirit in their life. This is why you have so much argument about scriptures. The baptism of the Holy Spirit is a command of Jesus. To refuse to be so baptized is a sin, and by this to commit this sin of refusal, or any other sin, you are no longer a Christian. This is another reason for the baptism of the Holy Spirit! It is a command! Without the Baptism of the Holy Spirit we can not understand the spiritual things of God the Father.

1 Corinthians 12:1-11 Now concerning spiritual gifts, brethren, I would not have you ignorant. Ye know that ye were Gentiles, carried away unto these dumb idols, even as ye were led. Wherefore I give you to understand, that no man speaking by the Spirit of God calleth Jesus accursed: and that no man can say that Jesus is the Lord, but by the Holy Ghost. Now there are diversities of gifts, but the same Spirit. And there are differences of administrations, but the same Lord. And there are diversities of operations, but it is the same God which worketh all in all. But the manifestation of the Spirit is given to every man to profit withal. For to one is given by the Spirit the word of wisdom; to another the word of knowledge by the same Spirit; To another faith by the same Spirit; to another the gifts of healing by the same Spirit; To another the working of miracles; to another prophecy; to another discerning of spirits; to another divers kinds of tongues; to another the interpretation of tongues: But all these worketh that one and the selfsame Spirit, dividing to every man severally as he will.

These are the nine spiritual gifts that the Holy Spirit gives us to use as we need. You can ask for a particular gift, but it is still up to the Holy Spirit which one, if any, He will let you use. For the most part it is a matter of FAITH on your part, and which particular gift you need at that particular time. I do not believe that these are "Ministry Gifts". They are given to any and all, who are Baptized in the Spirit and a member of the body of Christ, to use when needed for the continuing work of Jesus in the body and in the world.

1 Corinthians 14:14 For if I pray in an unknown tongue, my spirit prayeth, but my understanding is unfruitful.15 What is it then? I will pray with the spirit, and I will pray with the understanding also: I will sing with the spirit, and I will sing with the understanding also.

Paul, here, tells us just what the prayer language is, and where is comes from. It is a spiritual prayer given to your spirit by the Holy Spirit.
You know this because it is in a language that you do not know. This is the result of the baptism into the Holy Spirit.

1Corinthians 14:18 I thank my God, I speak with tongues more than ye all:

Contrary to most of what man's church says, Paul is saying it is a good thing to pray in tongues. Oh! by the way the prayer language is not the same as tongues and interpretation, which are two of the nine Spiritual Gifts found in **1Co12:7-12**. They travel in two different directions. One to God and one from God.

1 Corinthians 14:39 Wherefore, brethren, covet to prophesy, and forbid not to speak with tongues.

The tongues spoken of here is one of the nine gifts of the Holy Spirit. You can see that we are ordered not to forbid the operation of this gift, or the other eight gifts, of the Holy Spirit in the body of Christ. If your church forbids or does not believe in these gifts of the Holy Spirit, then I must say that your church is controlled by Satan!!! The really sad thing is that 85+ % of man's modern church denies or forbids the Baptism of the Holy Spirit as a separate experience from salvation. This is another lie of Satan.

2 Corinthians 10:3 For though we walk in the flesh, we do not war after the flesh:4 (For the weapons of our warfare are not carnal, but mighty through God to the pulling down of strong holds;

We war in the spirit! The Holy Spirit guides us in this spiritual war we fight for God. We use the gifts of the Holy Spirit and the Prayer tongue (language) as our weapons. One must be baptized in the Holy Spirit to be able to use these weapons. Two spiritual weapons that are given to us are prayer in the Spirit, and the sword of the word, these are the first and foremost of many . See **Ephesians 6: 17&18,**

2 Corinthians 13:14 The grace of the Lord Jesus Christ, and the love of God, and the communion of the Holy Ghost, be with you all. Amen.

To have communion (fellowship) with the Holy Spirit you must be baptized into the Holy Spirit.

Ephesians 6:18 Praying always with all prayer and supplication in the Spirit, and watching thereunto with all perseverance and supplication for all saints;

Prayer in the Spirit is to pray without understanding, in the unknown language you were given when you were baptized into the Holy Spirit. This is an example of how to fight the devil, win souls for Jesus, and protect the saints. This is one of your weapons of spiritual warfare, use it. It really is effective. How can it not be? It comes from God!

1 Thessalonians 1:5 For our gospel came not unto you in word only, but also in power, and in the Holy Ghost, and in much assurance; as ye know what manner of men we were among you for your sake. 6 And ye became followers of us, and of the Lord, having received the word in much affliction, with joy of the Holy Ghost.

Here are examples of what the Holy Spirit brings to you who are baptized into Him. Power, assurance, joy, knowledge, the true word.

2 Timothy 1:14 That good thing which was committed unto thee keep by the Holy Ghost which dwelleth in us.

The good thing talked about here is the love of Christ and your salvation through Jesus' work on the cross and His resurrection. The Holy Spirit's job is to convince us of sin, if we sin, and to bring us into remembrance of the things of God. This, in your life, is the baptism of the Holy Spirit.

Titus 3:5 Not by works of righteousness which we have done, but according to his mercy he saved us, by the washing of regeneration, and renewing of the Holy Ghost;

The first thing the Holy Spirit does for you when you repent is to wash you of all sin and regenerate your Spirit back to life. The second thing the Holy Spirit does, by Jesus, is for you to be baptized into Him. This again is by your choice to accept the gift of the Holy Spirit baptism given by Jesus, sent by the Father, to all who would walk with Jesus. The baptism of the Holy Spirit is part and parcel of your salvation. It is the third step in your walk of ongoing salvation. The three steps of salvation are repentance and asking forgiveness, water baptism, and the Holy Spirit baptism. The reason I say this over and over is because it is so very important in your Christian walk, and IT IS A COMMAND OF JESUS!

1 John 2:27 But the anointing which ye have received of him abideth in you, and ye need not that any man teach you: but as the same anointing teacheth you of all things, and is truth, and is no lie, and even as it hath taught you, ye shall abide in him.

The anointing here is the baptism of the Holy Spirit . You can see that we are taught by Him in all things that pertain to God. Without the Holy Spirit active in your sinless life how can you know and understand the scriptures to the depth that is so very important and needed in our walk on the narrow road of Jesus? This Baptism empowers us to fight the good fight as warriors for God the Father.

1 John 3:24 And he that keepeth his commandments dwelleth in him, and he in him. And hereby we know that he abideth in us, by the Spirit which he hath given us.

God dwells in us as long as we keep His commandments. The Spirit that is given to us by the Father is the Holy Spirit that was prayed for by Jesus and sent by the Father at Pentecost for all who would be followers Christ. This is called the baptism into the Holy Spirit. One of the Holy Spirit's jobs is to convince us of sin in our lives.

One way he does this is to leave if we get into sin and He does not come back until we repent. By the way, it is convince not convict of sin. Our own conscience convicts us of sin . The Holy Spirit convinces us that our actions are sin then our conscience takes over and makes us feel guilty until we repent. Again, it is by, and a result of the Baptism of the Holy Spirit that we have the sure and certain knowledge of our salvation, because the Holy Spirit dwells in us. The job of the Holy Spirit is convincing Christians of sin if they fall back into sin. Also this job of convincing of sin by the Holy Spirit is for the whole world of sinners who have yet to come to Jesus. The Holy Spirit has a two part job, one is to convince sinners of their sin, and the second is His work in christians after the Baptism if the Holy Spirit.

Jude 1:20 But ye, beloved, building up yourselves on your most holy faith, praying in the Holy Ghost,

This prayer in the Holy Spirit is the prayer tongue that you received when you were baptized into the Holy Spirit. It is also the second way to build your faith, the first is to hear and or read the word of God. The third way to build your faith is by fasting.

Now the Gifts of the Holy Spirit are what most new Christians really want, and most want only the gifts that they think that they will like. There is a problem with this kind of thinking. It, to be blunt, is sin! It is putting your needs and wants over and in front of what God knows and wants for you. These gifts are not ministries, they are gifts that are given when you need that particular gift. Does not the bible say "desire" the gift of most importance? This is the Gift that is needed at any one particular time or situation .

You must be willing to work in any and all of the nine gifts of the Holy Spirit. This will happen automatically as long as you are sinless and submitted to God's will. You will be surprised at how often this will happen to you. It is the normal Christian walk. Are you walking it? Again, this will happen only if you trust Jesus to baptize you in the Holy Spirit. It is a free gift already given. All you have to do is receive it. It's kinda like a birthday present you get but never open. You have it but can't use it! So, open it an use it!

The nine gifts of the Spirit are:

1-The word of wisdom means God telling you of a future event that He will make or wants to come to pass, or what the person you are ministering to plans to do in the future.
2-The word of knowledge means God telling you information about someone so you can witness to them and convince them about Jesus. It is never embarrassing.
3-Faith, this is a special occasion where an overabundance of faith is Needed; Such as raising the dead, or replacing missing limbs.
4-Gifts of healing, this is so all sickness and disease can be dealt with. God does not want His people sick. This is for your Christian brothers and sisters.
5-The working of miracles, such as raising the dead, replacing missing limbs, etc. This almost always works along with the gift of faith.
This is for the healing of the unsaved as well as God's people.
6-Prophecy, this is the gift, not the office of the prophet. This is used for edification, teaching, comfort, and telling what God will do in the future of the person or Body of Christ you are prophesying to.
7-Discerning of spirits, is the ability to see into the spirit world. To see and know the spirits (good or bad) of the people you are witnessing to, or that you come into contact with. This is needed if you are casting out demons.
8-Tongues, is a spiritual language given to you to speak (as long as there is a willing interpreter present) in church as an example of God's power to the unsaved. You, as the deliver of the message, might also have to give the interpretation if no one else will. If there is no one who will interpret your message you must either give the message and interpret it yourself, or do not give the message at all. This is your choice.
9- Interpretation, is a translation of a message from Tongues into a known language given for the unbeliever in the church that day. It is not for the saved in church. This is an error made by many churches today.

Many of the gifts are use together in different combinations, such as: tongues and-interpretation, faith and healing, faith and miracles—-you get the point.

Most born again, baptized in the Holy Spirit, children of God are willing to use the gifts, but again we must be open to and willing for the Holy Spirit to use us with the gift that He knows to be the one that is most needed at any one particular time. We must have the faith to do as the Holy Spirit wills.

The Holy Spirit is also responsible for picking and anointing men/ women for the five fold ministry and other offices in the body of Christ. He gave some, apostles', and some prophets; and some evangelists, and some pastors, and teachers; For the perfecting of the saints, for the work of the ministry, for the edifying of the Body of Christ (**Eph. 4:11**).

1-<u>Apostles</u> are sent ones. They are church starters. They have signs and wonders in their ministry

2-<u>Prophets</u> the office, not the Holy Spirit gift, is one who gives God's Word (messages) to the Body of Christ. Signs and wonders also.

3-<u>Evangelists</u> are traveling men who speak the word of God with signs and wonders following, for the Body and for the sinners of the world.

4-<u>Pastors</u> are the under Shepherds of Christ to the body to protect and guide in spirit and truth. Also can have signs and wonders.

5-<u>Teachers</u> are the ones who, by the guidance of the Holy Spirit, bring the truth of God to the Body. Note: It is your responsibility to make sure that it is the truth by checking everything against the bible.

<u>Exhorter</u> is also an office of the body of Christ. They are the same as Evangelist, but without signs and wonders following. They call people to Christ. There is also the office of the <u>Bishop</u>, an elder in the body who oversees, for Christ, the pastors in his area of responsibility. Also there are <u>Deacons</u> who help the Pastor.

There are <u>Elders</u>, who are mature Christians, who also help oversee and bring the office of <u>Helps</u> to the Body. Plus there is <u>Administrations</u> which helps to oversee the details of running of the body. These are all chosen and anointed by the Holy Spirit for their work in the body.

Now I believe that these jobs are not listed in order of authority, but in order of importance to the body of Christ. Jesus is the only one in authority over the Body. The authority of Christ is delegated to the different offices so they, the body, can operate with efficiency under Christ. They do not have ultimate authority over anyone in the body. They are not responsible for you or your decisions. You are only responsible to Christ for what you decide. It is the same for ALL others in the Body. The officials in the Body can only suggest avenues of actions to you, and show you how to live by example. THEY DO NOT and are not empowered by the Holy Spirit to COMMAND the Body of Christ.

Most born again, baptized by the Holy Spirit Christians think that the baptism of the Holy Spirit is it. That they have all that God has to give them. They are wrong! This is just the beginning of their walk with God.

Do you think that Paul, John, Peter, and the rest of the Apostles and great men of God through history stopped at the point of the Baptism of the Holy Spirit? I don't! They continued to grow in Christ. This growth is a continuing maturity and strength in Jesus, and a complete burning out of the world and its concerns from within you.

We must also continue to grow in the Spirit so it becomes so commonplace that God is in our lives 100% of the time. At this point there is no doubt about that small voice (of the Father) that we hear. This leaves no room for worldly pursuits. He, the Holy Spirit, guides, teaches, gives gifts, leads us, comforts us, tells us the deep things of the Father, heals us, saves us, provides all our earthly needs, calls us His children, tells us to call the Father DADDY, and He, Jesus, intercedes for us. We hear His voice to the extent that we will miss it and ask what's wrong if we don't hear it. I am talking about the Father, Son, and Holy Spirit as the one God. This is what it takes to be in and stay in the big, happy, family of God. This is the sinless mature Christian walk, and it is what we must always strive for. If we are guided by the Holy Spirit we will be in the perfect will of God the Father. We must continue to grow in maturity and strength to get to the point where we trust God above all else, especially ourselves. All this guidance from the Holy Spirit is preparing us to be able to withstand any and all trials, tribulations, and persecutions that impinge upon us from the world.

You must remember that sinners of the world hate us. They hate us because they know the truth of God in their heart of hearts, and choose not to come to the truth of God by the blood of Jesus. They see us the body of Christ and know that they can't have what we have unless they surrender to Christ, and that they don't want to do so. They will say "what give up my independence?"

Our walk with God the Father, Jesus, and the Holy Spirit is a spiritual walk. Remember we are to have no part or parcel with worldly pursuits and pleasures. We are a called out peculiar people who are not of the world. We are being prepared for life eternal with the Father, Jesus, and the Holy Spirit, whereas the sinners of the world, for the most part, have no clue. Again, we live in the world but are not part of it.

The end of the world (the second coming of Jesus for judgment) or your death is coming fast. Have you allowed the Holy Spirit to guide you into all truth? Are you ready for Jesus to come back, or your life to end? The Holy Spirit is the preparer, do you listen to Him? This is a life style that we must hold on to with all of our strength. We stand firm with the help of Jesus, and the Holy Spirit. Are you a member of the body of Christ? I must warn you, you don't have all the time in the world. Your life can end in the next second. So give it up for God if you haven't, repent and ask forgiveness (**1 John 1:9**) if you are a former Christian who has fallen back into sin (even if it's only one). Remember, it only takes one sin and you're out. It's not three strikes and your out.

All this comes by obeying the commands that Jesus gave us and that the Holy Spirit reminds us about. Most important we must remain sinless. Most of man's church does not teach this. They say "don't sin", but teach you are born in sin (that it is your 'nature' to sin) and that you can't stop. What? How can this be? Is it not surprising that the world says that the bible has contradictions with this kind of teaching in the church? You must stop, but you can't. Another lie of Satan.

This is not the place to discuses the sin problem. You can find out about it for yourself. To do this you must study to see what the bible says about sin, and then live as the bible commands. My book called "Sin and Life in the Kingdom of God" explains sin as taught in the bible, and how God feels about it. Read it, it's eye opening.

Try and prove by scripture that you are born fallen in sin. Check the whole bible, not just one or two verses. Find out all of what God has to say about it. Check out the meanings of the words in the Greek and Hebrew dictionaries. The Strong's concordance is a good place to start. All the scripture on any one subject must be in 100% agreement. If your conclusion is not in 100% agreement with all the verses on the subject, then your conclusion is wrong, even if only one verse says something different than what you believe the other verses are saying. See the study on " the lie of being born in sin".

Remember all scripture must agree on any one subject. This is the only correct way to study the bible. Pray for the Holy Spirit to guide you in your studies. For this guidance to happen you must be Baptized in the Holy Spirit. You must decide for yourself that you want (choose) to be saved, and baptized in the Holy Spirit. You are not saved because you were baptized as a baby. All that did is get you wet and make your parents feel good. To be saved is a moral decision, and you can not make that decision as a baby. Again you are not baptized in the Holy Spirit at Salvation, it is a separate experience.

The Father calls all men

John 6:44 No man can come to me, except the Father which hath sent me draw him: and I will raise him up at the last day.

Acts 2:21 And it shall come to pass, that whosoever shall call on the name of the Lord shall be saved.

Acts 2:39 For the promise is unto you, and to your children, and to all that are afar off, even as many as the Lord our God shall call.

The Father will save anyone who calls on Him. By extension God calls all men.

Romans 1:19 Because that which may be known of God is manifest in them; for God hath shewed it unto them.20 For the invisible things of him from the creation of the world are clearly seen, being understood by the things that are made, even his eternal power and Godhead; so that they are without excuse:

All men, by God, are made with the knowledge of God through His creation and power. This shows also that God cares for all men and wants them to be part of His family in Christ. Why else would a loving God go to this much trouble?

Romans 2:11 For there is no respect of persons with God.

I had a problem deciding what subject to put this verse under, it fits in so many categories. But here it is. This says that God loves all men equally. He sent His son to provide a salvation that must be for all men–which was His purpose from the beginning. By the way, Jesus was a person on the earth and God loves you no less than He does Jesus. The catch is you must be obedient as Jesus was and is.

Romans 9:24 Even us, whom he hath called, not of the Jews only, but also of the Gentiles?

God calls "all" men & women to be part of His holy family, no mater who they are.

1 Corinthians 7:17 But as God hath distributed to every man, as the Lord hath called every one, so let him walk. And so ordain I in all churches.

Ephesians 4:4 There is one body, and one Spirit, even as ye are called in one hope of your calling;

As you are called of God and now have made the free will choice to be saved, now you must walk as God commands. That not all choose to be saved is evident in the world. So does God get His desire that all men be saved?

"One hope of your calling" means that Jesus is the only hope and way to be saved from your sin and thereby get to the Father in heaven. This also says that there is only one God. There is NO other road to heaven, but through Jesus the Christ. All others who say there is more than one plan of salvation or that all the gods of men are the same god, are liars of Satan whether or not they a claim to be Christian.

1 Timothy 2:3 For this is good and acceptable in the sight of God our Saviour; 4 Who will have all men to be saved, and to come unto the knowledge of the truth.

God really wants all men to come to Him, but we see in the world many examples of the unsaved refusing to repent and ask forgiveness of God. They prefer to believe a lie or just don't want any part of God. They have accepted and live in the lies of Satan. All other religions of the world are of Satan. Again there is salvation in none but Jesus the Christ.

1 Peter 5:10 But the God of all grace, who hath called us unto his eternal glory by Christ Jesus, after that ye have suffered a while, make you perfect, stablish, strengthen, settle you.

Every one who is in the Kingdom was called to be there. That being said: God calls all men to come to Him, but not all men answer that call. To be made perfect is a choice that we make to remain sinless and thereby reside in the Kingdom of God. To "Establish, strengthen, settle" us is to be guided by God's grace in our lives. This only comes to us if we remain sinless. Remember it is a choice to sin or to remain holy. So by logic we receive God's grace by our free will choice. If you can not point to these attributes in your life and you claim to be Christian then you need to do a reality check on what you've been taught and what you believe. The truth is in the bible, so seek out the Holy Spirit and let Him guide you in and by the word of Christ.

The lie of born in sin, guilty of sin, or with a fallen nature

Genesis 3:8 And they heard the voice of the LORD God walking in the garden in the cool of the day: and Adam and his wife hid themselves from the presence of the LORD God amongst the trees of the garden. 9 And the LORD God called unto Adam, and said unto him, Where art thou? 10 And he said, I heard thy voice in the garden, and I was afraid, because I was naked; and I hid myself. 11 And he said, Who told thee that thou wast naked? Hast thou eaten of the tree, whereof I commanded thee that thou shouldest not eat? 12 And the man said, The woman whom thou gavest to be with me, she gave me of the tree, and I did eat. 13 And the LORD God said unto the woman, What is this that thou hast done? And the woman said, The serpent beguiled me, and I did eat. 14 And the LORD God said unto the serpent, Because thou hast done this, thou art cursed above all cattle, and above every beast of the field; upon thy belly shalt thou go, and dust shalt thou eat all the days of thy life: 15 And I will put enmity between thee and the woman, and between thy seed and her seed; it shall bruise thy head, and thou shalt bruise his heel. 16 Unto the woman he said, I will greatly multiply thy sorrow and thy conception; in sorrow thou shalt bring forth children; and thy desire shall be to thy husband, and he shall rule over thee. 17 And unto Adam he said, Because thou hast hearkened unto the voice of thy wife, and hast eaten of the tree, of which I commanded thee, saying, Thou shalt not eat of it: cursed is the ground for thy sake; in sorrow shalt thou eat of it all the days of thy life; 18 Thorns also and thistles shall it bring forth to thee; and thou shalt eat the herb of the field; 19 In the sweat of thy face shalt thou eat bread, till thou return unto the ground; for out of it wast thou taken: for dust thou art, and unto dust shalt thou return.

Here are the curses that God laid on Adam and Eve along with being kicked out of the Garden of Eden. You can see that they are hard and to the point. My point is that this would be the perfect place for God say " Also as a result of your disobedience to my command of do not eat from the tree of the knowledge of good and evil, your children from this point on will forever be cursed with being born guilty of your sin, and have your fallen nature". Well God did not say that. Why not, because it's not true.

The other question here is how is this so called "sin nature" passed to unborn babies? By genes, by the blood, or by the spirit given by God? You decide. By the way, none of these answers are correct. If you think about it you will see this. Ok, let's see. By the blood, not possible since no blood passes from the parents to the baby. By genes, if this were so then it would be in our physical make up (nature) and we would have no control at all with regards to sinning or not sinning. By the spirit is the easiest to show. Our spirit is given by God to us, and do you really think that God would give us a spirit contaminated by sin? Also God giving us a defective spirit, that makes us sin, would make God responsible for all the sins we commit. Can you see the light at the end of the tunnel yet? Oh by the way sin, is not in the natural flesh of our bodies, it is in our spirit (conscience), and we sin because we choose to by our free will. See **Hebrews chapter 9:14**. One more thing you must consider, Jesus was born of a human woman and if sin is passed by the blood or by genes then Jesus would have been born a sinner. This obviously is wrong, so are we really born little sinners?

Ezekiel 18: 20 The soul that sinneth, it shall die. The son shall not bear the iniquity of the father, neither shall the father bear the iniquity of the son:…..

Genesis 4:6 And the LORD said unto Cain, Why art thou wroth? and why is thy countenance fallen? 7If thou doest well, shalt thou not be accepted? and if thou doest not well, sin lieth at the door. And unto thee shall be his desire, and thou shalt rule over him.

Here we see Cain and his anger over God's refusal to accept his offering, and God's explanation of sin. We see that sin is not in us but that it comes to us by our choice. God says that sin desires to get you, but that you have <u>rule (the choice) over sin if you so desire.</u> Again it's up to you whether you sin or not. Yes, mankind is fallen, but it is by choice and not inheritance. Sin is a learned habit, not something you are born with.(see Thayer's lexicon for the word nature in **Eph 2:3**. It means a learned habit.) Just think, if you are born with sin as part of your "<u>nature"</u>, how could you ever stop from sinning? There is some argument about where sin is in you. Some believe that it is in your flesh, not true. It is, however, in your conscience as the book of **Hebrews points out in chapter 9: 14 How much more shall the blood of Christ, who through the eternal Spirit offered himself without spot to God, <u>purge your conscience from dead works*</u> to serve the living God?** Your conscience is part of your spirit and God gives our spirit to us; so if we are truly born sinners then it is God's fault and we cannot be held accountable. "Dead works" are sin.
  * My under line.

Psalms 51:5 Behold, I was shapen in iniquity; and in sin did my mother conceive me.

This verse is the most used to prove that we are born in sin. That is NOT what it says. Who do you think the subject of the first part of the verse is? David ? I think not, it is his mother. The second part separated by a semicolon refers you back to the first part in which the subject is David's mother, and says that David's mother conceived him while she was in sin.

Job 31:13 If I did despise the cause of my manservant or of my maidservant, when they contended with me; 14 What then shall I do when God riseth up? and when he visiteth, what shall I answer him? 15 Did not he that made me in the womb make him? and did not one fashion us in the womb?

Job is saying that he and his servant where both made by God in the womb. If God made us sinners from the womb then He would be responsible for our sins, because how could we act differently than He made us. We are made neither holy or sinful, but neutral . We have the ability to CHOOSE the good or the bad (**see James 4:17**), to be holy or to be sinners. We learn to be sinful, and then we learn to be Holy after we come to Jesus.

Deuteronomy 24:16 The fathers shall not be put to death for the children, neither shall the children be put to death for the fathers: every man shall be put to death for his own sin.

Ezekiel 18:18 As for his father, because he cruelly oppressed, spoiled his brother by violence, and did that which is not good among his people, lo, even he shall die in his iniquity.19 Yet say ye, Why? doth not the son bear the iniquity of the father? When the son hath done that which is lawful and right, and hath kept all my statutes, and hath done them, he shall surely live. 20 The soul that sinneth, it shall die. The son shall not bear the iniquity of the father, neither shall the father bear the iniquity of the son: the righteousness of the righteous shall be upon him, and the wickedness of the wicked shall be upon him.

These verses say that you will die for your sins only, not someone else's such as Adam's. These verses also tell us that sin is a choice, and not something we are born with.

What a perfect place to say that we are responsible for Adam's sin, or that we have a sin nature inherited from Adam. Again, you die for your sins and only your sins! You really do have a sin nature, but it is a learned habit from birth. It is not inherited. It is learned by your free will choice to sin and continue in sin. As with any habit you can change it. Nobody or nothing other than <u>' your mind'</u> can or will make you sin.

Psalms 127:3-5 Lo, children are an heritage of the LORD: and the fruit of the womb is his reward. As arrows are in the hand of a mighty man; so are children of the youth. Happy is the man that hath his quiver full of them: they shall not be ashamed, but they shall speak with the enemies in the gate.

As God says that children are a reward, do you think that God would reward you with children that are less than perfect, who are no more than little, born that way, sinners! You will be happy with a whole bunch of children as the man of war is happy with a full quiver of arrows. Your children will also protect you from the enemies of God. They are your heritage from God to carry on your line through time. Again do you think or believe that God would /will give you a broken arrow, a little sinner?

Proverbs 5:21-23 For the ways of man are before the eyes of the LORD, and he pondereth all his goings. His own iniquities shall take the wicked himself, and he shall be holden with the cords of his sins. He shall die without instruction; and in the greatness of his folly he shall go astray.

God is saying here that, as in Ez 18: 20, we are responsible and will die for the sins that "we" commit. Again, how is sin passed from our parents? There are only three ways that I can think of: 1- By the blood, 2- By genes made imperfect by sin, 3- By a corrupt spirit imputed to us. All three of these are wrong! First there is NO blood passed between the parents and the baby. Second if the genes were corrupted by sin then our true physical nature would be changed and we would have no way to ever stop sinning. Did not Jesus tell us to stop sinning? Why would He command us to do something we were not able to do? The third way is impossible as our spirit is given to us by God. Do you believe that God would give you a damaged, imperfect, spirit? If you don't believe this then please explain to me how sin is passed to babies from their parents. Use scripture for your proof.

Also show me where in scripture it proves that we are born with a fallen nature, guilty of Adam's sin, a dirty, rotten, little sinner or whatever you want to call it. I'll save you some time, there are no scriptures that say we are born little sinners and that we are made to sin by the corrupt birth. You now will take me to **John 9:34**, and I will take you to **John 9:2-34**. The question here is who you believe the Pharisees or Jesus?

Mark 1:1 The beginning of the gospel of Jesus Christ, the Son of God; 2 As it is written in the prophets, Behold, I send my messenger before thy face, which shall prepare thy way before thee. 3 The voice of one crying in the wilderness, Prepare ye the way of the Lord, make his paths straight. 4 John did baptize in the wilderness, and preach the baptism of repentance for the remission of sins.

John the Baptist was planned from the beginning to go before Jesus and "prepare the way". To be a messenger of God he had to have the Holy Spirit in his life. In fact he was born with the Holy Spirit. When John was put into prison the Holy Spirit left him so he could make a free will choice for Jesus as the Christ. We know this because John sent his disciples to ask Jesus if He was the Christ. To have the Holy Spirit he, John, had to be sinless from the womb (see below). Now you can say God made special provision for John the Baptist, but my answer to you is "God is no respecter of persons" which means what He does for one He 'has to' do for all.

Luke 1:13 But the angel said unto him, Fear not, Zacharias: for thy prayer is heard; and thy wife Elisabeth shall bear thee a son, and thou shalt call his name John. 14 And thou shalt have joy and gladness; and many shall rejoice at his birth. 15 For he shall be great in the sight of the Lord, and shall drink neither wine nor strong drink; and he shall be filled with the Holy Ghost, even from his mother's womb.

John the Baptist was sinless from the womb, otherwise the Holy Spirit could not have been with him in the womb.

Luke 1:67 And his father Zacharias was filled with the Holy Ghost, and prophesied, saying, Luke 1:76 And thou, child, shalt be called the prophet of the Highest: for thou shalt go before the face of the Lord to prepare his ways;

All the old testament prophets had the Holy Spirit on them as a mantel. Not residing in them.

Luke 1:39 And Mary arose in those days, and went into the hill country with haste, into a city of Judea; 40 And entered into the house of Zacharias, and saluted Elisabeth. 41 And it came to pass, that, when Elisabeth heard the salutation of Mary, the babe leaped in her womb; and Elisabeth was filled with the Holy Ghost:

The baby, John the Baptist, jumped for joy in his mothers womb, by the leading of the Holy Spirit. How else? The Holy Spirit controlled John's life up until he was put into prison. If John was born a sinner by inheritance, or with a "sinful nature" received from Adam, how could the Holy Spirit be with him in the womb?

The answer is he, and "every" other baby born, is not born a sinner or with a fallen nature. A person is not born guilty of someone else's sin, or with a fallen nature. What is a fallen nature but sin in your life? You are born neutral and must eventually make a choice for good or evil. It's called free will. As a side light: When John the Baptist was put into prison, by King Herod, the Holy Spirit left John so He could choose Jesus of his free will.

Matthew 18:3 And said, Verily I say unto you, Except ye be converted, and become as little children, ye shall not enter into the kingdom of heaven.

Mark 10:15 Verily I say unto you, Whosoever shall not receive the kingdom of God as a little child, he shall not enter therein.

Luke 18:17 Verily I say unto you, Whosoever shall not receive the kingdom of God as a little child shall in no wise enter therein.

These three verses say the same thing. You must be as a child to enter into the kingdom of heaven. This is also called being born again. What is it about being a child that will get you into heaven?

1-It's not a lack of knowledge, or being of a young age. It is, however, being sinless.

To be sinless as a child you must have been born that way! As a child you have no concept of good or evil morally. So how can you be a sinner if you have no understanding of what sin is? To be guilty of sin you must have an understanding of the morality of your actions, and then commit a sin. See **Romans chapter 4:15** below.

2-To have the unquestioning faith of a child to believe in Jesus; faith is pleasing to God, and the only way to Jesus

Sin is defined in James 4:17 as **"Therefore to him that knoweth to do good, and doeth it not, to him it is sin".** By any reasoning this describes a free will choice.

John 9:2 And his disciples asked him, saying, Master, who did sin, this man, or his parents, that he was born blind? 3 Jesus answered, Neither hath this man sinned, nor his parents: but that the works of God should be made manifest in him.

As Jesus is no respecter of persons, and that He said that this man born blind was NOT born in sin, I believe that neither man nor his parents are born in sin. We learn to sin as we grow up and develop a sin nature (habit) by our own actions.
Look up the word 'Nature' as used in **Eph. 2:3** in the Thayer's Greek lexicon. It literally means a habit that you have learned while growing up in this sin filled world.

Romans 7:9 For I was alive without the law once: but when the commandment came, sin revived, and I died.

Romans 4:15 Because the law worketh wrath: for where no law is, there is no transgression.

Romans 5:13 (For until the law sin was in the world: but sin is not imputed when there is no law.

As little children, before we understand the right and wrong of a thing, we are not held to be guilty of committing sin by wrong actions that would be sin for a person who does understand right and wrong. Little children are without the understanding the morel meaning of the law. When you come to the age of understanding the moral consequences of your sin you then become guilty of sin, no matter what that moral age is for you. Knowing that you will be punished for certain actions, as a child, does not mean that the child understands the wrongness (morality) of his actions. They only know that they will be punished for it, and it will probably hurt.

We learn to sin from birth and when we come to the age of morality, understanding the ramifications of our right or wrong actions, we will turn to our learned habitual sin. At this point in our lives we now need Jesus to become sin free and forgiven. Before we come to the age of morality we are not held accountable for our sins; as Paul says, where there is no law (moral understanding of the law) there is no guilt for breaking the law.

Romans 7:9 For I was alive without the law once: but when the commandment came, sin revived, and I died.

Paul is telling us here that as a child he did not know or understand the law; therefore he was not guilty of his acts of breaking the law. He is also telling us that he was spiritually alive before he came to that age where he understood the ramifications of breaking the law (sinning). After he was of the age of moral understanding and sinned he was then guilty of sin, and he died spiritually because of that one sin. That he continued in sin is because it was his learned habit from his early youth.

As children we are not guilty of any sins, neither are we holy. We come to this choice, to sin or not to sin, when we finally do understand the morality of our actions–whatever age that is or was for you. We learned to sin as we matured into adulthood, and when reaching adulthood we automatically turned to our learned habit of sin and continued in this habit. At this point we are sinners and need Jesus to be made free of sin and thereby saved. Yes, we all have sinned and have come short of the glory of God. We all need to repent and ask forgiveness, of our past sins, of the Father in Jesus' name to become spiritually alive. This is what is called 'being born again', and if you want to spend eternity with the Father, Son, and Holy Spirit you will do this and remain sinless. If you slip up and sin God will convince and allow you go to **1 John 1:9** and get holy once again! This is called 'God's mercy'.

Romans 9:10 And not only this; but when Rebecca also had conceived by one, even by our father Isaac; 11 (For the children being not yet born, neither having done any good or evil, that the purpose of God according to election might stand, not of works, but of him that calleth;)

Verse 11 says that the babies, in the womb of Rebecca, had done no wrong, had not committed any kind of sin. So where did their fallen nature come from? Not from sin, not from God, and not from their parents. So where does your so called 'sin nature' come from? Try to find out in and from the bible, then give me book, chapter, and verse! As sin or holiness is a moral choice.

Do you really think that we are born with an understanding of morality? How could we be born guilty of sin? The questions that begs asking: how do we inherit sin? How is sin passed to us? By God to our spirit? By the blood? By sin having changed our genes? To these questions you can answer a resounding NO. By the Spirit would make God responsible, He gives the spirit. By the blood, no blood passes to the baby in the womb. By the genes, if this were true you would never be able to stop sinning. Also see the "kingdom of God" study for all the verses that say you must be innocent as a child to enter into the kingdom.

Innocent = sinless.

<u>The definitions of Sin</u>

James 4:17 Therefore to him that knoweth to do good, and doeth it not, to him it is sin.

1 John 5:17 All unrighteousness is sin: and there is a sin not unto death.

1 John 3:4 Whosoever committeth sin transgresseth also the law: for sin is the transgression of the law.

Romans 14:23 And he that doubteth is damned if he eat, because he eateth not of faith: for whatsoever is not of faith is sin.

These are not all of the definitions of sin, but they will do. You can see that doing the bad instead of the good is a sin; transgression of the law, and a lack of faith are sin and they will separate you spiritually from God. This is called spiritual death. It only takes one sin to kill you spiritually, and keep you out of heaven.

Now the question is, how can a baby commit any of the descriptions of sin? Since a definition of sin is an act committed by your free will with the moral understanding of the consequences, how could a baby do such acts while still in the womb? How could it make such choices? How could a baby in the womb have a lack of faith, and so on?

Ephesians 2:2-3 Wherein in time past ye walked according to the course of this world, according to the prince of the power of the air, the spirit that now worketh in the children of disobedience: Among whom also we all had our conversation in times past in the lusts of our flesh, fulfilling the desires of the flesh and of the mind; and were by <u>nature</u> the children of wrath, even as others. (Strong's # for nature is 5449)

The word here that I want you to see is nature. In the Thayer's Greek lexicon it says the word nature, in this verse, is a learned habit. You are not born with it you, do not inherit it, and it is not given to you by God. So how do you get a sin nature? By learning it, through your actions and choices, as you grow from a baby to adulthood, until it becomes such a habit that you don't even think about doing it any more.

John 9:2-3 And his disciples asked him, saying, Master, who did sin, this man, or his parents, that he was born blind? Jesus answered, Neither hath this man sinned, nor his parents: but that the works of God should be made manifest in him.

Now I would think that this verse would settle the born in sin or fallen nature issue once and for all since Jesus says that the man born blind did no sin. This had to be from the womb since he was born already blind. So was he a sinner from the womb or birth? Again what did Jesus say? As God is no respecter of persons, if one baby is not born sinful then all babies are sin free.

The Flesh

The word flesh is used in more than one application and in the Greek (SARX, Strong's number 4561) has more than one meaning. For example : (a)- The substance of the body, whether of beasts or men, 1Cor15;39;

(b)- The human body2Cor10:3, gal 2 :20 , Phil 1: 22.

(c)- Of mankind, in the totality of all that is essential to manhood, i.e. , spirit, soul, and body, Matt.24:22, John 1:13, Rom 3:20 ;

(d)- Of the holy humanity of the Lord Jesus, in the totality of all that is essential to manhood, i.e., spirit, soul and, body, John 1:14, 1Tim 3:16; 1 john4:2; 2 John 7, in Heb 5:7 'the days of his flesh' , i.e., His past life on earth in distinction from His present life in resurrection;

(e)- Or the complete person, John 6: 51-57, 2Cor. 7:5, Jam 5:3;

(f)- The weaker element in human nature, Matt. 26:41, Rom. 6:19, 8:3a ;

(g)- The unregenerate state of men, Rom.7: 5, 8: 8-9;

(h)- The seat of sin in man (but this is not the same thing as in the body), 2Peter 2:18, 1John 2:16;

(i)- The lower and temporary element in the Christian, Gal.3:3, 6:8, and in religious ordinances, Heb. 9:10;

(j)- the natural attainments of men, 1Cor. 1:26, 2Cor. 10:2,3b;

(k)- Circumstances, 1Cor.7:28; the externals of life, 2Cor.7:1, Eph. 6:5, Heb. 9:13;

(l)- The outward and seeming, as contrasted with the spirit, the inward and real, John6: 63, 2Cor. 5:16;

(m)- Natural relationship, 1Cor. 10:18,Gal.4:23, or marital, Matt. 19:5;

In Matt.26:41, Rom. 8:4,13, 1Cor. 5:5, Gal. 6:8 (not the holy Spirit, here), flesh is contrasted with spirit; in Rom. 2:28, 29, with heart and spirit, in Rom.7:25 with the mind, Col. 2:1, 5.

It is coupled with the mind in Eph. 2:3, and with the spirit in 2 Cor. 7:1.

Note: In Col.2:18 the Noun "SARX" is used in the phrase "(by his)
Fleshly mind", literally, 'by the mind of his flesh' [see (h) above], whereas the mind ought to be dominated by the spirit.

As you can see that the word "flesh" is used for the actual flesh only a few times and in that respect not for sin at all.

You can see, that the word "flesh" has many meanings, and the one that means literal flesh is not the one used in the book of Romans or anywhere else that talks about sin. See above.

Let's look at where the guilt of sin really does reside in us. We'll go to **Hebrews 9:12-14 Neither by the blood of goats and calves, but by his own blood he entered in once into the holy place, having obtained eternal redemption for us. For if the blood of bulls and of goats, and the ashes of an heifer sprinkling the unclean, sanctifieth to the purifying of the flesh: How much more shall the blood of Christ, who through the eternal Spirit offered himself without spot to God, *<u>purge your conscience</u> from dead works to serve the living God?** *Underlining is mine.

These verses say that Christ's blood (Holy and Pure) was better than the blood of bulls and goats. Good enough to purge "dead works" (sin) from our "CONSCIENCE".

At this point we are holy and pure before God the Father, unless, "if" we sin again. **(1 John 2:1 My little children, these things write I unto you, that ye sin not. And if (choice*) any man sin, we have an advocate with the Father, Jesus Christ the righteous)**. * My note.

Note: the blood of bulls and goats did not remove the guilt of sin from your conscience it only covered it, but the blood of Jesus removed it from your conscience. This verse shows that the guilt of sin resides in your "conscience" not in your flesh. Bulls and goats provided a "purifying of the flesh" by covering the sin and providing salvation, forgiveness, and righteousness to the Old Testament Saints. They were still considered sinners because they still had the guilt of sin in their conscience - as a side light the Old test saints could not go to heaven because of the sin in their conscience. Look up the story of the woman caught in adultery and see that Jesus said " any who are without sin throw the first stone", and they dropped their stones and left one by one. This is because they knew that they still had sin is their conscience even though they were righteous before God by their animal sacrifices in the temple. Oh! by the way this is the first time Jesus told someone to "stop sinning". Have you stopped yet? He, Jesus, told two people "to go forth and sin no more", do you know who the other person was? It's in the gospels, look it up. Think about this, why would Jesus command us to do something we were not able to do? I.e. stop sinning!!

Jesus provided His shed blood that removes your guilt from you totally and you are made, by Your Choice to go to Jesus, pure, holy, and righteous before God the Father.

He, Jesus, went to Abraham's bosom while in the grave, and told the O .T. saints He was the one they had been waiting for. They could not go to heaven because of the sin still in their conscience, which Jesus' blood removed by their accepting Jesus as the messiah. They then were born again and rose to heaven as a cloud of witnesses with Him as He rose from the mount of olives. See the study on "Jesus in the Grave."

Hebrews 9:22 And almost all things are by the law purged with blood; and without shedding of blood is no remission.

The Old Testament saints had the remission of sin, but not the removal of sin. We who are under grace have no guilt of sin in us, if you sin just once you are out in the cold. This is where **1Jo 1:9** comes in for forgiveness, and removal of sin from your conscience. It's called God's mercy.

Sidelight: **Hebrews 9:28 So Christ was once offered to bear the sins of many; and unto them that look for him shall he appear the second time without sin unto salvation.**

Jesus did bear the sins of the world (many).What this means is that He took the guilt* of those sins upon Him and by taking them he was responsible for their payment which He made on the cross. This is the same as if you took the guilt of a bank robber upon yourself and went to jail in his place. Your paying the penalty for him now makes him guilt free and no longer a bank robber, it does not mean that you turned into a bank robber. Just as sin is a choice, it is also a choice for the former bank robber not to rob any more banks.

Christ was not made a sinner. If He was how could He have been Holy and Pure on the cross? If he wasn't Holy and Pure how could His blood be a sinless payment for our sins? He was made by CHOICE a sacrifice for sin.

*This does not mean that He became literally guilty any more than He became literally a sinner. All this means is that he was a (and made a) substitutionary payment for the past sins of all in the world.

Romans 5:18-19 Therefore as by the offence of one judgment came upon all men to condemnation; even so by the righteousness of one the free gift came upon all men unto justification of life. For as by one man's disobedience many were made sinners, so by the obedience of one shall many be made righteous.

Here it says that judgment came on all men by the actions of one man and righteousness came on all men by the actions of one man. Also it says that by one many (all) were "made" sinners and by one many (all) were "made" righteous. The Greek word for made is: *'kathistemi', Strong's number 2525. It means to make, be, conduct, ordain, and set.* Now the word make here, in verse 19, is used twice and it means the same thing both times. To understand this usage we must understand that all men are not made sinners or made saved. We must see, that for this verse not to be contradictory, the words "by choice made" are understood to be the true meaning by context. We know that all men are sinners, but are they made that way without their choice? I think not, and no place in the bible can I find such a statement.

Sin is the breaking of God's moral law, and is defined as a free will choice. See definitions of sin above.

We also know that all men are not saved, we can see this with our own eyes, and we know that to be saved we must make a moral choice for Jesus. So as the word "made" is used for the sinner and the saved what other conclusion can we come to, but to be a sinner is a choice and to be saved is a choice. This way of looking at this verse is the only one that makes any sense at all.

The words "were made", are past tense. Before Jesus came all men had sin in their conscience and could not have it removed.

The words "shall be made", are future tense showing that to receive forgiveness and removal of sin from our conscience is a future choice (after committing sin) that all men must make. Or you can say that unless you choose salvation from Jesus you will not be made saved.

Once again, to be made a sinner is a moral choice, and to be made saved is a moral choice.

Nature and Natural

The Greek words are *Phusis*, Strong's number 5449, and *Phusikos*, **Strong's** number 5446.

Phusis: the nature (i.e. the natural powers or constitution) of a person or thing. Native disposition, constitution i.e. man.

Phusikos: physical i.e.(by impl.)instinctive:-natural.
In the **Thayer's** lexicon the word nature (5449) is defined as " a mode of feeling and acting which by long habit has become nature"

To say we are natural born sinners or are born with a fallen nature is to misuse the meanings of these words, or you must say that our nature has been changed by Adam's and Eve's sin. If this is so and it is our "nature" to sin, and as we can not change our nature we would never be able to stop sinning unless salvation changes our natural born native, constitution. Which it does not. Only our spirit is changed (reborn). While the born again experience make us new creatures in Christ it is our spirit that is renewed not our physical nature. The question is: If we are born with a sin nature, how do we relate the definition of word nature in Thayer's Greek Lexicon, a Learned Habit. With that belief that we are born sinners? How do we reconcile these two statements? One from the born sinful camp, and one from what the Thayers says. To me the Thayer's Greeks lexicon has the higher authority.

As I have said elsewhere it is the spirit that is made new, reborn by the removal of the guilt of un-repented sin from our conscience. Yes, all things are made new by salvation through Jesus. Here again we must ask just what has been changed by our becoming "saved". What has been born again? Our physical bodies? Or is it our Spirit? Or both? Scripture tells us it is our spirit which is renewed by the rebirth and the regeneration of our spirit by the Holy Spirit, back into fellowship with the Father. Is this not so? The healing in the work of the cross by Jesus is for all who are saved, but this healing does not change our nature. It just removes sickness and disease.

John 3:3 Jesus answered and said unto him, Verily, verily, I say unto thee, Except a man be born again, he cannot see the kingdom of God.

John 3:5-6 Jesus answered, Verily, verily, I say unto thee, Except a man be born of water and of the Spirit, he cannot enter into the kingdom of God. That which is born of the flesh is flesh; and that which is born of the Spirit is spirit.

The flesh is our natural body, or natural nature, and our spirit is what is reborn by the Holy Spirit. As a sidelight; our conscience is in our spirit. Where else but in the spirit can the guilt of sin reside?

Is it not our Spirit that is killed, separated from God the Father by sin, and not our physical natural flesh bodies which do not sin? It is our Spirit, killed by sin, that must be reborn to life through Christ to renew our relationship with the Father. As it is sin that kills the spirit, how is it that man teaches babies are born with a defective sinful spirit - before they even have had a chance to commit a sin? If it is a defective (sinful) spirit that babies are born with, and since God gives the spirit, then God is at fault for that defective spirit, and responsible for all acts of good and evil. The only way to spiritual death is by sin. You are not born with a defective spirit. Only by your free will choices can you 'kill' your spirit.

If our "nature" has been changed by Adam and Eve's sin then it has to be by something passed to us by our parents. Now you must figure out how that horrible 'something' is passed to you. Is it by the Blood? I think not since no blood is passed to the baby at all. Is it the genes? If so; this means that Adam's sin changed our physical bodies and it (sin) was in the natural genes, flesh of our bodies. Now this opens up a whole can of worms. Did not God give us our genes? Were they not perfect? How then can anything but the guilt of sin be in us? There is no sin in our physical flesh! Is sin a physical thing or just an action that starts in the mind and is accepted and dwelled on, and then carried out by the physical body? The sin starts with the acceptance of temptation to sin. See the book of James on sin. To answer the former question: Sin is the result of an action, or accepting the thoughts of temptation to do wrong. How then can sin be a physical thing in our bodies? The result of our sin can and does cause sickness, addictions to drugs, alcohol, but the physical things you sin with are not in and of themselves sin. Is packet of Illegal drugs, or a can of beer sin? NO!

The corruption of our bodies is a result of sin but not sin itself. Since the guilt of sin resides in the spirit (conscience). I would say that our genes were not changed. However, continued sin for thousands + of years by our ancestors I believe could change our physical bodies. This is seen as inherited diseases. This cannot be seen as inherited sin. Since no blood is passed to the baby from the parents, and the spirit comes from God, we are not then born with a fallen nature nor are we born filthy rotten little sinners. See if you can prove, by the bible, that we are fallen and sinners at birth. Remember that you must use the Greek definitions for the words you use to prove your point, and **all** scriptures on this subject must say and mean the same thing.

The Blood

Romans 4:7 Saying, Blessed are they whose iniquities are forgiven, and whose sins are covered.

This is the verse that is used to say that the blood of Jesus covers your sin. What a lie! This is not what Paul is talking about . He is talking about the Old Testament Saints that had their sin covered by the blood of bulls and goats. Yes, they were forgiven and had righteousness by the Old testament sacrifices, but they still had the guilt of their sins in their conscience. This is why they went to Upper Sheol, Abraham's bosom, Paradise, different names for the same place, instead of heaven to be with God the Father. Because of the sin in their conscience they could NOT go to heaven. This is why Jesus went to Upper Sheol, while He was in the grave, to tell them that He had come and they could now be born again (have their sin removed from their conscience). See the study "Jesus in the grave"

Hebrews 9:12 Neither by the blood of goats and calves, but by his own blood he entered in once into the holy place, having obtained eternal redemption for us. 13 For if the blood of bulls and of goats, and the ashes of an heifer sprinkling the unclean, sanctifieth to the purifying of the flesh: 14 How much more shall the blood of Christ, who through the eternal Spirit offered himself without spot to God, purge your conscience from dead works to serve the living God?

Hebrews 10:10 By the which will we are sanctified through the offering of the body of Jesus Christ once for all.

"By His own blood", which was sinless, Jesus entered the Holy of Holies in heaven and sprinkled His blood thereby proving to God the Father that all the work for salvation was done by His shed blood.

What does the phrase "without spot" means to you? To me it means that Jesus went and died on the cross sinless, without spot or wrinkle, holy and pure.

The blood of bulls and goats could only cover sin, it could not remove the sin from the conscience. Only Jesus' perfect sacrifice and shed blood could provide for salvation and holiness. Jesus, as our Perfect Priest, by His prefect blood, has no need to sacrifice over and over every year as the priest's of the temple in Jerusalem did. He did it just once for all time. His perfect one time blood sacrifice is all that is needed to purge our sin from our conscience.

Hebrews 10:3 But in those sacrifices there is a remembrance again made of sins every year. 4 For it is not possible that the blood of bulls and of goats should take away sins.

Hebrews 10:11 And every priest standeth daily ministering and offering oftentimes the same sacrifices, which can never take away sins:

Hebrews 9:25 Nor yet that he should offer himself often, as the high priest entereth into the holy place every year with blood of others;

Hebrews 9:28 So Christ was once offered to bear the sins of many; and unto them that look for him shall he appear the second time without sin unto salvation.

Hebrews 10:14 For by one offering he hath perfected for ever them that are sanctified.

Hebrews 10:17 And their sins and iniquities will I remember no more.

The blood of bull and goats only covered sin, it did not remove it. Jesus' "holy and sinless blood" is the reason that we have the salvation that the nation of Israel did not have. They were forgiven and righteous before God, but they could not go to heaven because of the sin in their conscience. They needed forgiveness every year on the Day of Atonement.

By the perfect blood of Jesus the Christ we have a one time forgiveness for all of our "past sins (see **RO. 3: 25**). You only need to go to the blood of the cross again "IF" (**1John 2:1**) you sin again after salvation.

After forgiveness God the Father will not remember your sin, the only ones who do are you and Satan. Satan will try to remind you of your forgiven sins. You must remember that you are forgiven and your sins have been removed from your conscience, and you must get on with your sinless life. Remember sinning is defined as "knowing the good, but not doing it" (**James 4:17**). So it is a choice you make every time you are tempted. By the way, God says that He will NOT allow you to be tempted beyond what you can resist. Any different beliefs such as a sin in ignorance, born in sin, a sin nature that makes you sin, the devil made me do it, and I just can't stop are all LIES of Satan. Don't listen! Make the choice to break your sin habit!

Hebrews 9:22 And almost all things are by the law purged with blood; and without shedding of blood is no remission.

God demands the shedding of blood for the forgiveness and removal of sin from us. Jesus' blood is holy, pure, and without sin. This is why the Father commanded Jesus to shed His blood on the cross (Jesus obeyed by His free will). It was the only legal way to provide a perfect salvation to an undeserving mankind. This holy blood did what the blood of bulls and goats could not do. It removed our sin and this makes us holy and pure.

Hebrews 10:22 Let us draw near with a true heart in full assurance of faith, having our hearts sprinkled from an evil conscience, and our bodies washed with pure water.

Our sin has been removed from us by the sprinkling of Jesus' Holy Blood, and we are washed by the water of the word of God. Being washed by the word is what gives us the strength to walk in the Spirit on the road to complete salvation in a sinless walk. This is the first witness to our salvation.

1 John 1:7 But if we walk in the light, as he is in the light, we have fellowship one with another, and the blood of Jesus Christ his Son cleanseth us from all sin.

Here we see the second witness to the removal of the guilt of sin in our conscience by the blood of Jesus shed on the cross, also called our salvation.

The blood! Again it removes all our "PAST" (**Romans 3:25**) sins from us thereby making us sin free and holy, by our free will choice. You can see it says that "IF" we walk in the light we walk sin free as Jesus did. This use of the word "IF" means it is a choice to walk in the light of Jesus. Or don't you believe in free will? This word "IF" literally means that sin is always a choice you make. No one can make it for you or make you do it.

2 Peter 1:9 But he that lacketh these things is blind, and cannot see afar off, and hath forgotten that he was purged from his old sins.

This verse is the third witness that your sins are removed from you. At that point you are no longer a sinner, unless you chose to sin again. This is why **1John 1: 9** is in the bible. God in His never ending mercy allows us to ask forgiveness as many times as necessary to come to the point in our lives that we have stopped sinning.

Some final thoughts:

1-As sin is a free will choice made by moral beings, how can anyone who is incapable of moral decisions be held accountable for those decisions that they make - whatever they are? Ex. How can a retarded person make a moral choice? This person will go to heaven no matter what he/she has done because they have no moral understanding and thereby are not guilty of sin.

2-As the guilt of sin resides in your conscience, and only moral beings have a conscience, how could babies be sinners? Babes develop their conscience by learning as they grow up into moral beings.

3-As it can not be proven by scripture (and scripture is our bench mark) that sin is passed from the parents to their children we know beyond a doubt that babes have not received a fallen nature nor are they born guilty of Adams sin. It's not in scripture? It's just that simple.

4- There is no place in scripture that can, by the definition of the words, show us that babes are made dirty, rotten, little sinners by someone else's sin.

5- As " sin nature" is defined as a "learned habit" how can it be inherited, imputed, or passed on?

6- As Ezekiel says: **Ezekiel 18:8-9 He that hath not given forth upon usury, neither hath taken any increase, that hath withdrawn his hand from iniquity, hath executed true judgment between man and man, Hath walked in my statutes, and hath kept my judgments, to deal truly; he is just,* <u>he shall surely live,</u> saith the Lord GOD.**

Ezekiel 18:17 That hath taken off his hand from the poor, that hath not received usury nor increase, hath executed my judgments, hath walked in my statutes; he *<u>shall not die for the iniquity of his father, he shall surely live.</u>

Ezekiel 18:19-20 Yet say ye, Why? Doth not the son bear the iniquity of the father? When the son hath done that which is lawful and right, and hath kept all my statutes, and hath done them, *<u>he shall surely live</u>. <u>The soul that sinneth, it shall die.</u> <u>The son shall not bear the iniquity of the father, neither shall the father bear the iniquity of the son:</u> the righteousness of the righteous shall be upon him, and the wickedness of the wicked shall be upon him.

This needs no explanation. It is real clear to me, and as God is no respecter of persons, and is the same forever, and does not change. These verses are as valid today as they were in Ezekiel's time.

7-As Thayer's defines nature as a "learned Habit," you cannot change the meaning of the word nature to say that nature means a fallen condition of your natural being, or that you are naturally born a sinner, as long as you are talking about nature as a sinning condition and not about a our natural body.

* All underlines are mine.

Obeying natural government

Romans 13:1 Let every soul be subject unto the higher powers. For there is no power but of God: the powers that be are ordained of God. 2 Whosoever therefore resisteth the power, resisteth the ordinance of God: and they that resist shall receive to themselves damnation. 3 For rulers are not a terror to good works, but to the evil. Wilt thou then not be afraid of the power? do that which is good, and thou shalt have praise of the same:4 For he is the minister of God to thee for good. But if thou do that which is evil, be afraid; for he beareth not the sword in vain: for he is the minister of God, a revenger to execute wrath upon him that doeth evil.5 Wherefore ye must needs be subject, not only for wrath, but also for conscience sake.6 For for this cause pay ye tribute also: for they are God's ministers, attending continually upon this very thing.7 Render therefore to all their dues: tribute to whom tribute is due; custom to whom custom; fear to whom fear; honour to whom honour.

There is a lot of confusion about what these verses mean. Yes they do command us to obey the government God has given us (the one we want and deserve). BUT we also MUST put God's laws FIRST, in FRONT of any laws made by man to govern us. Do you think that there is ANY government (church or secular) that conforms itself to God? Taxes or tithes? Pro abortion, anti- abortion ? Do you see ? We are commanded not to break God's laws. When man's law is contrary to God's law we must obey God's law first and not obey man's. Again what comes first in your life, Jesus or your carnal, secular, governing body?

1 Timothy 2:1 I exhort therefore, that, first of all, supplications, prayers, intercessions, and giving of thanks, be made for all men;2 For kings, and for all that are in authority; that we may lead a quiet and peaceable life in all godliness and honesty.

We, as Christians, are called and commanded to pray for the leaders of our government, local, state, and federal. They need it! All you really need to pray is for their salvation, and all else will fall into place, as for the most part, they are carnal leaders. You might also pray that the corrupt leaders in our Government are replaced or removed, and yes this is praying for them (my opinion).

1 Timothy 2:3 For this is good and acceptable in the sight of God our Saviour;4 Who will have all men to be saved, and to come unto the knowledge of the truth.

This is one way you pray for leaders and why.

1 Peter 2:13 Submit yourselves to every ordinance of man for the Lord's sake: whether it be to the king, as supreme; 14 Or unto governors, as unto them that are sent by him for the punishment of evildoers, and for the praise of them that do well. 15 For so is the will of God, that with well doing ye may put to silence the ignorance of foolish men: 16 As free, and not using your liberty for a cloke of maliciousness, but as the servants of God.

Again this is with the understanding that you only obey the laws of man as long as they don't contradict the laws of God. The rest is easy to understand.

1 Peter 2:19 For this is thank worthy, if a man for conscience toward God endure grief, suffering wrongfully. 20 For what glory is it, if, when ye be buffeted for your faults, ye shall take it patiently? but if, when ye do well, and suffer for it, ye take it patiently, this is acceptable with God.

God will not be disappointed with you if you refuse to obey a law of man that goes against God's law and you suffer and die for it. You must obey the laws of God over the laws of man. Who would you rather have mad at you God or man's government?

Matthew 22:20 And he saith unto them, Whose is this image and superscription? 21 They say unto him, Caesar's. Then saith he unto them, Render therefore unto Caesar the things which are Caesar's; and unto God the things that are God's.

This is Jesus' instruction about the natural government of men and the Moral government of God. Do you see the difference? What will you do if these two governments come into conflict? Which one will you obey? God's I hope.

Acts 5:27-29 And when they had brought them, they set *them* before the council: and the high priest asked them, Saying, Did not we straitly command you that ye should not teach in this name? and, behold, ye have filled Jerusalem with your doctrine, and intend to bring this man's blood upon us. Then Peter and the *other* apostles answered and said, We ought to obey God rather than men.

This is an excellent example of who we should obey in our walk with Jesus. You can see that even with terrible threats of physical harm (read the rest of the story) Peter and the rest of the Apostles bluntly told the temple council that no matter what they ordered them to do they would only obey God. This is our example in how to walk with Jesus and the Father in this sin filled world.

The lie of "Once Saved, Always Saved"

1 Corinthians 10:12 Wherefore let him that thinketh he standeth take heed lest he fall.

This says that it is possible to fall back into sin even after being sinless in Jesus.
" Once Saved Always Saved" (O.S.A.S.) goes hand in hand with predestination of who is saved, being picked by God no matter what you want. This O.S.A.S. also means who will go to hell no matter who they are or what they did, good or bad!

This also means that you have no free will. What a lie of Satan!

1 Corinthians 15:1 Moreover, brethren, I declare unto you the gospel which I preached unto you, which also ye have received, and wherein ye stand; 2 By which also ye are saved, if ye keep in memory what I preached unto you, unless ye have believed in vain.

We heard the gospel, we received the gospel, we understand the gospel, we accept the gospel, we are washed by the gospel. Now as long as we stay in the gospel we remain saved. If you have not accepted the gospel in truth then you are not saved. 100% of the gospel must be accepted, not just what your church teaches or what only you believe of the gospel. These verses show and say that it is possible to lose your salvation. Can you see it? Believed in vain means to believe wrongly or not to see the truth of the scriptures.

2 Corinthians 12:21 And lest, when I come again, my God will humble me among you, and that I shall bewail many which have sinned already, and have not repented of the uncleanness and fornication and lasciviousness which they have committed.

Paul is worried that when he goes again to the Corinthian church that he will find sinners that have not repented of their sinfulness after salvation. This allows the possibility of losing your salvation by falling back into sin and not repenting. Does not Jesus say two times go forth and sin no more before He went to the cross? Do you take this to mean that you are COMMANDED to stop sinning? You better, or you will lose everything you have from God by returning to sin. The question is : would Jesus command us to do something we are unable to do? What do you think? I dare you to answer this question!

2 Corinthians 13:5 Examine yourselves, whether ye be in the faith; prove your own selves. Know ye not your own selves, how that Jesus Christ is in you, except ye be reprobates?

It says if you are a reprobate (sinner) you don't have Jesus. Paul is talking to members of the Body of Christ. This shows that you can, by your free will choice, give up Jesus in your life by being a reprobate (sinner). This is how to lose your salvation. You can get it back by repenting and asking forgiveness. How many unrepented sins do you think it takes to be called a 'reprobate'? Maybe just one? Ya think?

Galatians 1:6 I marvel that ye are so soon removed from him that called you into the grace of Christ unto another gospel:

Here's another way to lose your salvation. Reject the teachings of Jesus and accept the teachings of man. These Galatians were saved by the true gospel and then turned to a false gospel, thereby losing their salvation.

Galatians 3:1 O foolish Galatians, who hath bewitched you, that ye should not obey the truth, before whose eyes Jesus Christ hath been evidently set forth, crucified among you?

Galatians 3:3 Are ye so foolish? having begun in the Spirit, are ye now made perfect by the flesh?

Again here the Galatians are drawn away from the truth of Jesus to the teachings of man and have now lost their salvation. Paul is exhorting them to come back to Christ. They were going back to the ceremonial laws of the Jews, or you can say living under the law of sin and death instead of the new covenant of faith and grace.

Galatians 4:9 But now, after that ye have known God, or rather are known of God, how turn ye again to the weak and beggarly elements, whereunto ye desire again to be in bondage?

With verses such as these how can you even begin to believe in "Once saved, Always saved"? In bondage literally means in sin. You were saved and then you lost it by your actions, and changing your beliefs thereby putting yourself back into bondage.

Galatians 4:19 My little children, of whom I travail in birth again until Christ be formed in you,

Paul is praying that the Galatians will come back to Jesus in repentance. Which means that they where saved but lost their salvation to sin. The key word here is AGAIN! Why would they need Christ a second time if they had not lost Him the first time?

Galatians 5:1 Stand fast therefore in the liberty wherewith Christ hath made us free, and be not entangled again with the yoke of bondage.

This verse allows for the fact that you CAN fall back into sin and thereby lose your salvation. It is a call to holiness also. To be told to stand fast means if you don't (which is a choice) you will lose what you were standing for. Do you see this?

Ephesians 5:15 See then that ye walk circumspectly, not as fools, but as wise,

Ephesians 5:17 Wherefore be ye not unwise, but understanding what the will of the Lord is.

These verses say don't sin. Right? If you look at the other side of what they say, it is "If you sin you lose". Right?

Do you think God will blink His eyes if you don't do what He commands? So what happens to your salvation if you sin and God doesn't blink?

Colossians 1:21 And you, that were sometime alienated and enemies in your mind by wicked works, yet now hath he reconciled 22 In the body of his flesh through death, to present you holy and unblameable and unreproveable in his sight: 23 If ye continue in the faith grounded and settled, and be not moved away from the hope of the gospel, which ye have heard, and which was preached to every creature which is under heaven; whereof I Paul am made a minister;

Paul is writing to the so called saved of the city of Colossus. He is telling them to refrain from sinfulness. The operative word here is "IF". It means that there is a possibility of not remaining in faith thereby losing your salvation. It says "IF" you remain sinless you will remain in faith and in the gospel, this implies a choice, and a chance to lose what you have, i.e. salvation.

Colossians 2:18 Let no man beguile you of your reward in a voluntary humility and worshipping of angels, intruding into those things which he hath not seen, vainly puffed up by his fleshly mind, 19 And not holding the Head, from which all the body by joints and bands having nourishment ministered, and knit together, increaseth with the increase of God.

If it's not possible to lose your salvation, then why is this warning given? The word "voluntary" means that it is your choice to remain with Jesus and the salvation He has provided to you. It also puts a lie to predestination, of who is saved. Not holding the head who is Jesus; by doing this you have rejected Jesus. You have now lost your salvation by turning to other doctrines and gods.

1 Timothy 1:19 Holding faith, and a good conscience; which some having put away concerning faith have made shipwreck:

Some have put away faith. This says that: First, they had faith (salvation) at one time; Second: That they gave it up and fell back into sin (shipwreck). They lost their salvation. O.S.A.S. Is a lie of Satan. Do you see this yet?

1 Timothy 4:1 Now the Spirit speaketh expressly, that in the latter times some shall depart from the faith, giving heed to seducing spirits, and doctrines of devils;

See! It says over and over that you can lose your salvation. Some churches, to prove their point of O.S.A.S., say that these people that fall away were never saved in the first place. This is another lie of Satan. It's not in the bible. What do these verses say? "Some shall depart from the faith", do you not think that this statement means that they were once Of the faith? How can you depart from something if you never had it in the first place? The real horror of 'Once Saved, Always Saved' is that it lets you believe in your salvation, but also lets you continue in your sin. You are then on the road to hell and as happy as a lark in the lie you have accepted.

That you cannot lose your salvation no matter what you do, because God has chosen you to be saved and just loves you into the kingdom, is one of Satan's biggest lies! Do you believe it?

1 Timothy 5:14 I will therefore that the younger women marry, bear children, guide the house, give none occasion to the adversary to speak reproachfully.15 For some are already turned aside after Satan.

"Turned aside after Satan", again this means that they where once saved but fell back into sin, and LOST their salvation. Turning aside is a free will choice. What does this say about OSAS? Do you think a lie? I Do!

Titus 3:10 A man that is an heretic after the first and second admonition reject; 11 Knowing that he that is such is subverted, and sinneth, being condemned of himself.

Some would say that this man was not saved in the first place, but they would be wrong. See where it says "a man that is a heretic after the first and second admonition". This means that he was once not a "heretic", but became that way after he started sinning again. This man came back to the Lord at least 2 times. Paul is telling us what to do if this brother falls back into sin (the 3rd time) and does not repent and ask forgiveness by Jesus from the Father, that is REJECT him! Do you think he was O.S.A.S.?

Hebrews 10:38 Now the just shall live by faith: but if any man draw back, my soul shall have no pleasure in him.

To draw back from being just and walking in faith means to fall back into sin and LOSE your salvation until you repent. Again a verse that puts a lie to 'Once Saved, Always Saved'. God will not throw you out of the kingdom. You to do that yourself when you choose to sin after you are saved. Remember; one sin and your out, but God's mercy says you will have as many chances to get it right as it takes to get you to heaven.

Heberws 12:14 Follow peace with all men, and holiness, without which no man shall see the Lord:15 Looking diligently lest any man fail of the grace of God; lest any root of bitterness springing up trouble you, and thereby many be defiled;16 Lest there be any fornicator, or profane person, as Esau, who for one morsel of meat sold his birthright.

These verses allow the possibility of, by choice, losing your ticket on the train to heaven. The only way to lose your salvation is for you to give it up by falling back into sinfulness, but God is just and merciful to allow you to repent as many times as it takes for you to get to the point of walking in a sinless condition. See **1John 1:9.**

James 5:19 Brethren, if any of you do err from the truth, and one convert him; 20 Let him know, that he which converteth the sinner from the error of his way shall save a soul from death, and shall hide a multitude of sins.

I was going to put these verses under " This is the true Body", but I thought that they fit here better. They, again, allow and show that you can lose your salvation by falling back into sinfulness. It says "brethren if any of you do err", this is a saved person who has fallen back into sin. You know this because he is called a brethren, and you know he fell because it says he did err. It also says 'if,' which a choice.

1 Peter 1:5 Who are kept by the power of God through faith unto salvation ready to be revealed in the last time.

1 Peter 1:9 Receiving the end of your faith, even the salvation of your souls.

" Kept by the power of God through faith" does not mean that salvation is against our free will, or that we cannot lose our salvation. It does mean that YOUR faith in God is what keeps you in the Kingdom. Do you remember what you get by being saved by Faith? Is it not Grace, and is not this Grace God's power for your continued salvation? We can get out of the kingdom of God any time we so desire. All we have to do is commit one sin and then Not repent, then you are on the fast train to hell. This is a lack of faith in the power of God to keep you.

Do you see the word "FAITH"? It tells us that we are responsible for our continuing salvation by remaining sinless. A lack of faith for anything from God is a sin. So be careful about what you believe and don't believe.

2 Peter 1:5 And beside this, giving all diligence, add to your faith virtue; and to virtue knowledge; 6 And to knowledge temperance; and to temperance patience; and to patience godliness; 7 And to godliness brotherly kindness; and to brotherly kindness charity. 8 For if these things be in you, and abound, they make you that ye shall neither be barren nor unfruitful in the knowledge of our Lord Jesus Christ. But he that lacketh these things is blind, and cannot see afar off, and hath forgotten that he was purged from his old sins.

You can see that a brother who lacks the things, described in verses 5-8, has fallen away from Christ. You can see (in verse 9) that he was once saved because he had his sin purged (removed) and then he fell back into sinfulness, because he lacks the attributes of the Christian life and walk. Verse 9 also tells us that not to have these attributes is a sign of a sinner who was saved and has turned his back on God.

Once again the lie of O.S.A.S. is proven by Holy scripture.

Note: also read the preceding verses 3-4.

2 Peter 1:10 Wherefore the rather, brethren, give diligence to make your calling and election sure: for if ye do these things, ye shall never fall:

We see here that there is a possibility of falling away from Jesus. This is proven by the statement saying that we must be diligent to our calling. Not to be so implies that sin has taken us over. As always, sin is a choice-as is being diligent. See **verse 1:15.**

2 Peter 2:20 For if after they have escaped the pollutions of the world through the knowledge of the Lord and Saviour Jesus Christ, they are again entangled therein, and overcome, the latter end is worse with them than the beginning. 21 For it had been better for them not to have known the way of righteousness, than, after they have known it, to turn from the holy commandment delivered unto them.

Again, a Christian who has fallen back into sin and lost their salvation. What does Peter say? It would have been better if that former Christian had never been saved.

This means that this man committed blasphemy against the Holy Spirit, for which there is no forgiveness, and so has even lost his chance for forgiveness. If he had not yet been saved he at least then would have had a chance at salvation.

1 John 3: 24 And he that keepeth his commandments dwelleth in him, and he in him. And hereby we know that he abideth in us, by the Spirit which he hath given us.

The opposite of "abiding in" is being removed from your place of dwelling. The one who does not keep the commands of God, after being born again, will lose their place in the Kingdom. Is this not clear? If you sin, break His commands, then you have lost your salvation.

2 John 1:8 Look to yourselves, that we lose not those things which we have wrought, but that we receive a full reward.

This is a warning to stay sinless. It allows the fact that we CAN fall back into sin and thereby lose our salvation. You know that the denominations that teach O.S.A.S will tell you that a person that returns to sin was never saved in the first place. That is not what this and so many other verses say. So who do you believe, the bible or some man's teaching ??

2 John 1:9 Whosoever transgresseth, and abideth not in the doctrine of Christ, hath not God. He that abideth in the doctrine of Christ, he hath both the Father and the Son.

This is a verse calling us to holiness, and telling us what will happen if we sin. Lose our salvation! It is also telling the worldly people that they cannot be with and of God without being sinless.

The word "Whosoever" means all people, saved or not. There are only two choices in this evil world, and they are to abide in Christ or the sinful world. There are no fence sitters! You either is or you ain't.

3 John 1:3 For I rejoiced greatly, when the brethren came and testified of the truth that is in thee, even as thou walkest in the truth. 4 I have no greater joy than to hear that my children walk in truth.

Think of what John is saying here. There are always two sides to the same coin. If you can stay with God, you can leave God. It's a free will thing. You have choices to make. The first is to come to Jesus or remain a sinner. If you come to Jesus you have the choice of staying with Him or returning to sin. That's it, the two most important choices that you can make in your life.

These choices, by the free will that we have from God the Father, put a lie to the doctrine of O.S.A.S. This lying doctrine says you do not have a choice and do not have free will. That you are a robot created by God for His pleasure of running you around.

Jude 1:3 Beloved, when I gave all diligence to write unto you of the common salvation, it was needful for me to write unto you, and exhort you that ye should earnestly contend for the faith which was once delivered unto the saints.

"Contend for the faith", in other words fight to keep your faith so you will not fall back into sin and lose your salvation. This is not witnessing. You can see that the faith was "delivered unto the saints" already. If you have to contend and fight to remain a Christian then it is possible to lose your salvation by not fighting hard enough. Have you sweat blood yet?

Revelation 2:4 Nevertheless I have somewhat against thee, because thou hast left thy first love.5 Remember therefore from whence thou art fallen, and repent, and do the first works; or else I will come unto thee quickly, and will remove thy candlestick out of his place, except thou repent.

"Left your first love". Do you think this is walking away from Jesus? So you can leave the Kingdom, it is done by sinning, but you can come back by repenting.

Revelation 3:5 He that overcometh, the same shall be clothed in white raiment; and I will not blot out his name out of the book of life, but I will confess his name before my Father, and before his angels.

Blot your name out of the book of life. Does this sound like you can lose your salvation? The way to keep this from happening is to remain sinless by overcoming the temptations to sin. See, God really does have a big eraser!

Revelation 3:15 I know thy works, that thou art neither cold nor hot: I would thou wert cold or hot. 16 So then because thou art lukewarm, and neither cold nor hot, I will spue thee out of my mouth.

Are you hot or cold? If you're cold God will reject you. These two verses are to the saved in the body. Some are hot for God and others are indifferent, or cold to God and His commands. It shows you that even if you were once on fire for God but now the cares of the world have you deceived into indifference, you are in danger of losing it all. I don't know about you but I don't want God to spit me out.

Think about being lukewarm and having God spit you out of His mouth. If you're cold then God can do something with you to bring you back into the fold, but being lukewarm means you think you have it all. At this point there is nothing God can do. It seems to me that most of man's churches are lukewarm.

Final statement:

All this being said 'Once Saved Always Saved' can be true IF, and it's a real big IF, you meet and follow the conditions laid down by Jesus and the Father. Those conditions being that you must pickup your cross daily and walk as Jesus walked, which is in a sinless condition. If you remain sinless you will remain in the kingdom of God. Again this is accomplished only by obeying the commands of God the Father totally in your life, and by putting all other things of this world last, in your life after the Father and Jesus.

If you truly are a born again Christian this is what you will do. You will let NOTHING come between you and God. Not your family, your Job, the TV, sports, car racing, food, or anything else you can do and like in this sin filled world.

Your Moto should be 'GOD FIRST'.
It is Mine!

The true Prophet of God

The Qualifications of a Prophet

1 - He must he Called of God

Isa.6:8 Also I heard the voice of the Lord saying, whom shall I send, and who will go for us? Then said I, Here am I; send me.

Ezek.1:28 As the appearance of the bow that is in the cloud in the day of rain, so was the appearance of brightness round about. This was the appearance of the likeness of the glory of the lord. And When I saw it, I fell upon my face, and I heard a voice of one that spake. 3:4 And he said unto me, son of man, go, get thee unto the house of Israel, and speak with my words to them. 11:4 Therefore prophesy against them, prophesy, O son of man.

Amos7:14 Then answered Amos, and said to Amaziah, I was no prophet, neither was I a prophets son, but I was a herdsman, and a gatherer of sycamore fruit: 15- And the Lord said unto me, Go, prophesy unto my people Israel.

2 Sam. 24:11 For when David was up in the morning, the word of the Lord came unto the prophet Gad, David's seer, saying,

Rev. 10:11 And he said unto me, Thou must prophesy again before many peoples, and nations, and tongues, and Kings.

This is what it takes, a willing man or woman to go and do what the Lord God in Heaven wills His prophets to do. Whatever God has said must be delivered as God has told you to. God picks you, you do not decide you want to be a prophet. As you can see prophesy is not just for Old Testament times, but is also for Christians now and for all time to come.

All prophets of the lord Most High must confess Jesus, be sinless, and be bold enough to speak in Jesus' name no matter the cost.

2 - The prophet must be inspired of God

Num.11:25 And the lord came down in a cloud and spake unto him, and took of the Spirit that was upon him ,and gave it unto the seventy elders: and it came to pass, that, when the Spirit rested upon them, they prophesied, and did not cease. 12:6 And He said, Hear now My words: If there be a prophet among you, I the Lord will make myself known unto him in a vision, and will speak unto him in a dream.

I Sam.3:10 And the Lord came, and stood, and called as at other times, Samuel, Samuel. Then Samuel answered, Speak; for thy servant heareth.

1 Kings 13:20 Now it happened, as they sat at the table, that the word of the LORD came to the prophet who had brought him back;

Acts 3: 21..whom heaven must receive until the times of restoration of all things, which God has spoken by the mouth of all His holy prophets since the world began.

Acts 19:6 And when Paul had laid hands on them, the Holy Spirit came upon them, and they spoke with tongues and prophesied.

Romans 16:26 but now has been made manifest, and by the prophetic Scriptures has been made known to all nations, according to the commandment of the everlasting God, for obedience to the faith –

Heb. l:1 God, who at sundry times and in divers manners spake in times past unto the fathers by the prophets,

James 5:10 My brethren, take the prophets, who spoke in the name of the Lord, as an example of suffering and patience.

Rev.4:1 After this I looked, and, behold, a door was opened in heaven: and the first voice which I heard was as it were of a trumpet talking with me; which said, come hither, and i will shew thee things which must be hereafter.

Rev.11:3 "And I will give power to my two witnesses, and they will prophesy one thousand two hundred and sixty days, clothed in sackcloth."

Rev.22:6 Then he said to me, "These words are faithful and true." And the Lord God of the holy prophets sent His angel to show His servants the things which must shortly take place.

God is the one who tells the prophets what to say. Prophesy does not come from within you! No matter how much you think you know of God's word, or what you think God wants you to say. It will be evident when God tells you to Prophesy, and it will never be outside of scripture. Most often it will be confirmation of what God has already told the person or people God has sent you to. Don't be a false prophet no matter how much good you think what you say will do. Be very careful, you hold other peoples lives in your hands. Do not continue to prophesy after you have soken the words God gave you.

3 - The prophet must have wisdom and understanding

Dan.1:17 As for these four children, God gave them knowledge and skill in all learning and wisdom: and Daniel had understanding in all visions and dreams.

Daniel 5:13 Then was Daniel brought in before the king. And the king spake and said unto Daniel, Art thou that Daniel, which art of the children of the captivity of Judah, whom the king my father brought out of Jewry? 14 I have even heard of thee, that the spirit of the gods is in thee, and that light and understanding and excellent wisdom is found in thee.
and
All wisdom, knowledge, and understanding are from God. Do not even think that this wisdom and understanding comes from within you. This is not the same as learning

from books, or life experiences. To have this "God's kind of Knowledge and wisdom" you must be in the will of God in the first place. That means that you must be obedient to all of God's commands. Can I say sinless? How else can God work with you ?

4 - Prophets must have the power to work Miracles.

1 Kings 13:11 Now there dwelt an old prophet in Bethel, and his sons came and told him of <u>all the works that a man of god had done</u> that day in Bethel; the words which he had spoken unto the King, them they told also to their father.(underline mine)

Dan.4:2 I thought it good to shew the signs and wonders that the High God hath wrought toward me.

The power to work miracles is from God not from within the prophet. It comes from the Holy Spirit. This is still valid today. In Old Testament times the Spirit was as a mantel resting on the prophets. In New Testament times we are filled with the Spirit through the baptism of the Holy Spirit. God the same yesterday, today, and tomorrow. Also God is no respecter of persons. What He did with and for Old Testament prophets He will also do for the New testament prophets. Again this is ALL by God's will and timing.

5 - A prophet is the protected of God

Jer. l:6 Then said I, Ah, Lord God! Behold ,1 cannot speak: for I am a child. 7 But the Lord said unto me, Say not, I am a child: for thou shalt go to all that I shall send thee, and whatsoever I command thee thou shalt speak. 8 Be not afraid of their faces: for I am with thee to deliver thee, saith the Lord.

Ezek. 2:6 And thou, son of man, be not afraid of them, neither be afraid of their words, though briers and thorns be with thee, and thou dost dwell among scorpions: be not afraid of their words, nor be dismayed at their looks though they be a rebellious house.

1 Chronicles 16:22 saying "..Do not touch My anointed ones and do My prophets no harm..."

Psalms 105:15 Saying, Touch not mine anointed, and do my prophets no harm.

Rev. 18:20 "Rejoice over her, O heaven, and you holy apostles and prophets, for God has avenged you on her!"

You as a prophet are supported and protected by God as long as you remain in His will. Or you can say "remain Sinless" and obedient .

The duties of the Prophet

1 - He must speak what God has told him to.

Num. 22:8 And he said unto them, Lodge here this night, and I will bring you word again, as the lord shall speak unto me:

1 Sam.3:16-17 Then Eli called Samuel, and said, Samuel, my son. And he answered ,here am I. 17-And he said, What is the thing that the Lord hath said unto thee? I pray thee hide it not from me: God do so to thee, and more also, if thou hide anything from me of all the things that He said unto thee.

1 Kings22:14 And Miciah said. As the lord liveth, what the lord saith unto me, that will I speak.

Jer.23:28 The prophet that hath a dream, let him tell a dream; and he that hath My word, let him speak My word faithfully.

Ezek.2:7 And thou shalt speak My words unto them, whether they will hear, or whether they will forbear: for they are most rebelious.

Acts 21:10 And as we stayed many days, a certain prophet named Agabus came down from Judea. 11 When he had come to us, he took Paul's belt, bound his own hands and feet, and said, ..Thus says the Holy Spirit, "So shall the Jews at Jerusalem bind the man who owns this belt, and deliver him into the hands of the Gentiles.."

Rev. 10:11 And he said unto me, Thou must prophesy again before many peoples, and nations, and tongues, and kings.

When God gives you a word, dream, or vision as a prophet of God you must deliver it to whom God tells you to, no matter the content or whether the prophesy is for reward or punishment. It may be for a single person or for the body in general.

The prophets predictions

1 - The predictions fulfilled.

Jos. 23:15 therefore it shall come to pass, that all good things are come upon you, which the lord your God promised you; so shall the lord bring upon you all evil things, until He has destroyed you from off this good land which the Lord your god hath given you.

2 Kings 10:10 Know now that there shall fall unto the earth nothing of the word of the Lord, which the Lord spake concerning the house of Ahab: for the Lord hath done that which He spake by His servant Elijah.

Hab. 2:3 for the vision is yet for an appointed time, but at the end it shall speak, and not lie: though it tarry, wait for it; because it surely come, it will not tarry.

Rev.22:6 And He said unto me, These sayings are faithful and true: and the Lord God of the holy prophets sent His angel to shew unto His servants the things which must shortly come be done.

God's word does not return to Him void, it will accomplish what He has sent it to do. This word given by God's prophets must be listened to and obeyed, as long as it is confirmed by the word of God. It will come to pass. If a warning, take heed. If a blessing, rejoice. We are to test the spirits of all who come to us in the body of Christ with a word from God. This is so that we will not be led astray by false prophets.

A Prophets honor

1 - A Prophet is accorded no honor in his own country.

Mark6:4 But Jesus said unto them, A prophet is not without honor, but in his own country, and among his own kind, and in his own house.

Luke4:24 And He said, Verily I say unto you, No prophet is accepted in his own country.
John4:44 For Jesus testified, that a prophet hath no honor in his own country.

We see this to this day, people remember who you were before you were saved and became a prophet. The dirty rotten sinner that you were is remembered and the sinless saint that you are now is ridiculed.

2 - How a prophet brings dishonor to Himself

I Corinthians 11:4 Every man praying or prophesying, having his head covered, dishonors his head.

I Corinthians 11:5 But every woman who prays or prophesies with her head uncovered dishonors her head, for that is one and the same as if her head were shaved.

For some reason the covering rule is not followed today. One reason is that Paul is giving his opinion. It is not a command of God.

Prophesy disbelieved

1 - Disbelief foretold and an example of disbelief.

Jer.7:27 Therefore thou shalt speak all these words unto them; but they will not hearken to thee; thou shalt also call unto them but they will not answer thee.

Jer.25:4 And the lord hath sent unto you all His servants the prophets, rising early and sending them; but ye have not hearkened, nor inclined your ear to hear.

The reason is that most people don't want to hear from God. They are happy with the way things are and don't want to change who, what, and why they are the way they are. Their attitude is "Just who does God think He is"!

2 - The penalty of disbelief.

Neh. 9:30 Yet many years didst thou forebear them, and testified against them by thy Spirit in thy prophets: yet would they not give ear: therefore gavest thou them into the hand of the people of the land.

Jer. 5:12 They have belied the Lord, and said ,It is not He, neither shall evil come upon us; neither shall we see sword or famine; 13 And the prophets shall become wind, and the word is not in them. 14 Wherefore thus saith the lord God of hosts, Because ye speak this word, behold, I will make my word in my mouth fire, and this people wood ,and it shall devour them.

Acts 3:23 "And it shall come to pass that every soul who will not hear that Prophet shall be utterly destroyed from among the people."

You can see by these verses that God has no respect for His people that deny His word, and what the result of God's anger at them is. You must consider that God's word comes two ways: one by the Holy Spirit, whether to you from God or from a prophet; the other way is by the bible.

3 - Gods feelings about prophet

1Thessalonians 5:20 Do not despise prophecies.

Need I say more.

False Prophets

1 - Described

Jer. 23:14 I have seen also in the prophets of Jerusalem a horrible thing: they commit adultery, and walk in lies: they strengthen also the hands of evil doers, that none doth return from his wickedness; they are all of them unto Me as Sodom ,and the inhabitants thereof as Gomorrah.

Jer. 29:9 For they prophesy falsely unto you in My Name; I have not sent them, saith the Lord.

Matthew 7:15 "Beware of false prophets, who come to you in sheep's clothing, but inwardly they are ravenous wolves.

Matthew 24:11 "Then many false prophets will rise up and deceive many.

Matthew 24:24 "For false Christ's and false prophets will arise and show great signs and wonders} so as to deceive} if possible} even the elect.

Mark 13:22..For false Christ's and false prophets will rise and show signs and wonders to deceive} if possible} even the elect.

Luke 6:26 "Woe to you when all men speak well of you, For so did their fathers to the false prophets....

1 John 4:1 Beloved, do not believe every spirit, but test the spirits, whether they are of God; because many false prophets have gone out into the world. Acts 13:6 Now when they had gone through the island to Paphos, they found a certain sorcerer, a false prophet, a Jew whose name was Bar-Jesus,

2 Peter 2:1 But there were false prophets also among the people, even as there shall be false teachers among you, who privily shall bring in damnable heresies, even denying the Lord that bought them, and bring upon themselves swift destruction. 2 And many shall follow their pernicious ways; by reason of whom the way of truth shall be evil spoken of. 3 And through covetousness shall they with feigned words make merchandise of you: whose judgment now of a long time lingereth not, and their damnation slumbereth not.

Rev.16:13 And I saw three unclean spirits like frogs coming out of the mouth of the dragon out of the mouth of the beast and out of the mouth of the false prophet.

Rev. 19:20 Then the beast was captured, and with him the false prophet who worked signs in his presence, by which he deceived those who received the mark of the beast and those who worshiped his image. These two were cast alive into the lake of fire buming with brimstone .

Rev.20:10 And the devil, who deceived them, was cast into the lake of fire and brimstone where the beast and the false prophet are. And they will be tormented day and night forever and ever.

False prophets tell lies to get you to do what they want or to make you feel good about getting into sin. The definition of a true prophet of God is: 100% truth from God 100% of the time. If the prophet is ever wrong, even once, He is not a prophet. In the O.T. they stoned prophets that were not 100% correct. You can see by these verses that true prophets of God are Not sinners and only say what God has told them to say.

2 - How to know a false prophet from a true prophet

Deut.18:21 And if thou say in thine heart, How shall we know the word which the Lord hath not spoken? 22 When a prophet speaketh in the name of the Lord, if the thing follow not ,nor come to pass, that is the thing which the Lord hath not spoken, but the prophet hath spoken it presumptuously: thou shalt not be afraid of him.

Jer. 28:9 The prophet which prophesieth of peace, when the word of the prophet shall come to pass, then shall the prophet be known, that the Lord has truly sent him.

1 Corinthians 14:3 But he who prophesies speaks edification and exhortation and comfort to men. 4 He who speaks in a tongue edifies himself, but he who prophesies edifies the church.

1 Corinthians 15:33 Be not deceived: evil communications corrupt good manners.

1 Thessalonians 5: 21 Test all things; hold fast what is good.

A false prophet lies and a true prophet of God tells the truth of God. Simple Eh! If the prophecy is not in the bounds of scripture then it's not of God. The real test is 100% accuracy. Also you must test by the Spirit of God and if it is not scriptural it is not from God. If you find this to be so you MUST reject it in its entirety. This so called prophecy that was given to you is most likely from Satan. The prophet must not speak in and of himself, ONLY THE WORDS GIVEN BY GOD CAN BE BELIEVED, no matter how good it sounds. You must test every prophecy against scripture. Even then you must be careful and let God confirm it as a true prophecy. If it is personal to you , I believe that it would already be known to you, or it will be confirmed to you in the near future. Believe nothing unless it is confirmed in your heart by God!

The definitions given below are for the Greek words edification, exhortation, and comfort that are found in 1 Cor. 14: 3, these words describe prophecy today.

__Edification:__ Oikodome (3619) denotes (a) **"the act of building"** *(oikos" "a home" " and demo" "to build": this is used only figuratively in the NT' in the sense of edification,* **the promotion of spiritual growth** *(lit., "the things of building up") Rom14:19, 15:2* **1Co 14:3**,*5,12,26" e.g.". (b) "a building, edifice, " whether material, Mat 24:1" e.g." **or figurative, church, "the body of Christ**, Eph. 2:21. See BUILDING.*

__Exhortation:__ Paraklesis (3874), akin to A, No.1, **primarily "a calling to one's side " and so "to one's aid," hence denotes(a)an appeal, entreaty,"(E "2Co 8:4; (h) encouragement"** *"exhortation," e.g.,Rom 12:8;in Act 4:36, RV,"exhortation," for KJV,"consolation" (c)"consolation and comfort" e.g. , Rom 15:4. See COMFORT Cf. Parakletos, l"an advocate/comforter."*

__Comfort:__ .Qaramuthja (3889), primarily **"a speaking closely to anyone"** (para,"near" muthos, "speech"),hence denotes **"consolation, comfort,"** with a greater degree of tenderness than No.1,1 CO. 14:3.

3 - The punishment of false prophets

Deut.18:20 But the prophet, which shall presume to speak in my name, which I have not commanded him to speak, or that shall speak in the name of other gods, even that prophet shall die.

Jer.14:15 Therefore thus saith the lord concerning prophets that prophesy in my name, and sent them not, yet they say, Sword and famine shall not be in this land; By sword and famine shall those prophets be consumed.

Jer.23:30-32 Therefore, behold, I am against the prophets, saith the Lord, that steal my words every one from his neighbor. 31 behold, I am against the prophets, saith the Lord, that use their tongues, and say, He saith.

32 Behold I am against them that prophesy false dreams, saith the lord, and do tell them, and cause my people to err by their lies, and by their lightness; yet I sent them not, nor commanded them: therefore they shall not profit this people at all, saith the Lord

I do not think that this is a position you would want to be in. To have the Lord God against you is a terrible thing. You may not be stoned to death in this day and age, but the punishment is just as great. It just may take longer to come to pass. I would think that sickness, ill health, disaster, and other horrible things happening in your life would get you to notice what is going on and to ask yourself " What am I doing wrong?".

Prophets are Persecuted

Acts 7:52 "Which of the prophets did your fathers not persecute? And they killed those who foretold the coming of the just One, of whom you now have become the betrayers and murderers,

I Thessalonians 2: 15 who killed both the Lord Jesus and their own prophets, and have persecuted us; and they do not please God and are contrary to all men,

Revelation 18:24 "And in her was found the blood of prophets and saints, and of all who were slain on the earth."

This is now happening all over the world every day. Consider yourself lucky that you live in the U.S.A., where at least we are not killed wholesale.

The prophet today

Acts 21:9 Now this man had four virgin daughters who prophesied.

Acts 10:43 ..To Him all the prophets witness that, through His name, whoever believes in Him will receive remission of sins...

Romans 12:4 For as we have many members in one body, and all members have not the same office: 5 So we, being many, are one body in Christ, and every one members one of another. 6 Having then gifts differing according to the grace that is given to us, let us use them: if prophecy, let us prophesy in proportion to our faith;

1 Corinthians 12:28 And God has appointed these in the church: first apostles, second prophets, third teachers, after that miracles, then gifts of healings, helps, administrations, varieties of tongues. 29 Are all apostles? Are all prophets? Are all teachers? Are all workers of miracles? 30 Do all have gifts of healings? Do all speakwith tongues? Do all interpret?

1 Corinthians 14:1 Pursue love, and desire spiritual gifts, but especially that you may prophesy.

1 Corinthians 14:5 I wish you all spoke with tongues, but even more that you prophesied; for he who prophesies is greater than he who speaks with tongues,

unless indeed he interprets, that the church may receive edification. 6 But now, brethren, if I come to you speaking with tongues, what shall I profit you unless I speak to you either by revelation, by knowledge, by prophesying, or by teaching?

1 Corinthians 14:22 Therefore tongues are for a sign, not to those who believe but to unbelievers; but prophesying is not for unbelievers but for those who believe.

1 Corinthians 14:29 Let the prophets speak two or three, and let the other judge. 30 If any thing be revealed to another that sitteth by, let the first hold his peace. 31 For ye may all prophesy one by one, that all may learn, and all may be comforted. 32 And the spirits of the prophets are subject to the prophets.

1 Corinthians 14:37 If any man think himself to be a prophet, or spiritual, let him acknowledge that the things that I write unto you are the commandments of the Lord.

1 Corinthians 14:39 Therefore, brethren, desire earnestly to prophesy, and do not forbid to speak with tongues.

Ephesians 2:20 having been built on the foundation of the apostles and prophets, Jesus Christ Himself being the chief cornerstone,

Ephesians 3:5 which in other ages was not made known to the sons of men, as it has now been revealed by the Spirit to His holy apostles and prophets:

Ephesians 4:11 And He Himself gave some to be apostles, some prophets, some evangelists, and some pastors and teachers,

1 Corinthians 12:7 But the manifestation of the Spirit is given to every man to profit withal. 8 For to one is given by the Spirit the word of wisdom; to another the word of knowledge by the same Spirit; 9 To another faith by the same Spirit; to another the gifts of healing by the same Spirit; 10 To another the working of miracles; to another prophecy; to another discerning of spirits; to another divers kinds of tongues; to another the interpretation of tongues:

2 Peter 1:19 We have also a more sure word of prophecy; where unto ye do well that ye take heed, as unto a light that shineth in a dark place, until the day dawn, and the day star arise in your hearts: 20 Knowing this first, that no prophecy of the scripture is of any private interpretation. 21 For the prophecy came not in old time by the will of man: but holy men of God spake as they were moved by the Holy Ghost.

Rev. 19:10 And I fell at his feet to worship him. And he said unto me, See thou do it not: I am thy fellow servant, and of thy brethren that have the testimony of Jesus: worship God: for the testimony of Jesus is the spirit of prophecy.

Prophets can be men or women! Prophets glorify Christ! Prophets only speak the word of God! Prophets must be sinless to prophesy!

It really hasn't changed from the old testament to the new testament! You will notice that prophecy is very important in the body of Christ. In fact it is the 2nd most important office (not of authority) of all those offices listed. You can see this by the two witnesses of **1 Cor.12:28 and Eph.4:11**. Now having said that let me explain what important means: in a word VALUE. These offices, all five, are of equal importance. These five offices are listed in order of value to the body, not in order of authority. I am talking about the office as given by the Holy Spirit. All offices are given only by the Holy Spirit. You do not get to pick the one you want just because you feel it's for you, and you are the best one for it, or so you can be the "important"(prideful) one in other peoples eyes. All in the body are equal in Jesus' eyes. You only have different jobs, and these are the jobs that the Holy Spirit picks you for. He knows what you are the best at. They all need doing.

You will see **in 1 Cor.12:10** that prophecy is also a gift of the Holy Spirit as well as one of the five fold ministries. These gifts are for any and all in the body of Christ who have been baptized in the Holy Spirit with the evidence of a prayer language given to you by the Holy Spirit. Jesus is the Spirit of prophecy in the body of Christ.

Prophecy

Acts 21:10 And as we stayed many days, a certain prophet named Agabus came down from Judea. 11 When he had come to us, he took Paul's belt, bound his own hands and feet, and said, "Thus says the Holy Spirit, 'So shall the Jews at Jerusalem bind the man who owns this belt, and deliver him into the hands of the Gentiles.' "

Romans 12:6 Having then gifts differing according to the grace that is given to us, let us use them: if prophecy, let us prophesy in proportion to our faith;

1 Corinthians 13:9 For we know in part and we prophesy in part.10 But when that which is perfect has come, then that which is in part will be done away.

1 Corinthians 14:1 Pursue love, and desire spiritual gifts, but especially that you may prophesy.

1 Corinthians 14:24 But if all prophesy, and an unbeliever or an uninformed person comes in, he is convinced by all, he is judged by all.

1 Corinthians 14:31 For you can all prophesy one by one, that all may learn and all may be encouraged.

1 Corinthians 14:39 Therefore, brethren, desire earnestly to prophesy, and do not forbid to speak with tongues.

Revelation 10:11 And he said to me, "You must prophesy again about many peoples, nations, tongues, and kings."

Revelation 11:3 "And I will give power to my two witnesses, and they will prophesy one thousand two hundred and sixty days, clothed in sackcloth."

Prophesied

Acts 19:6 And when Paul had laid hands on them, the Holy Spirit came upon them, and they spoke with tongues and prophesied.

Acts 21:9 Now this man had four virgin daughters who prophesied.

1 Corinthians 14:5 I wish you all spoke with tongues, but even more that you prophesied; for he who prophesies is greater than he who speaks with tongues, unless indeed he interprets, that the church may receive edification.

Prophesieth

1 Corinthians 11:5 But every woman who prays or prophesies with her head uncovered dishonors her head, for that is one and the same as if her head were shaved.

1 Corinthians 14:3 But he who prophesies speaks edification and exhortation and comfort to men. 4 He who speaks in a tongue edifies himself, but he who prophesies edifies the church.

Prophesyings

1 Corinthians 11:4 Every man praying or prophesying, having his head covered, dishonors his head.

1 Corinthians 14:6 But now, brethren, if I come to you speaking with tongues, what shall I profit you unless I speak to you either by revelation, by knowledge, by prophesying, or by teaching?

1 Corinthians 14:22 Therefore tongues are for a sign, not to those who believe but to unbelievers; but prophesying is not for unbelievers but for those who believe.

1 Thessalonians 5:20 Do not despise prophecies.

The False Prophet

Matthew 7:15 "Beware of false prophets, who come to you in sheep's clothing, but inwardly they are ravenous wolves.

Matthew 24:11 "Then many false prophets will rise up and deceive many.

Matthew 24:24 "For false christs and false prophets will arise and show great signs and wonders, so as to deceive, if possible, even the elect.

Mark 13:22 "For false christs and false prophets will rise and show signs and wonders to deceive, if possible, even the elect.

Luke 6:26 "Woe to you when all men speak well of you, For so did their fathers to the false prophets.

2 Peter 2:1 But there were also false prophets among the people, even as there will be false teachers among you, who will secretly bring in destructive heresies, even denying the Lord who bought them, and bring on themselves swift destruction.

1 John 4:1 Beloved, do not believe every spirit, but test the spirits, whether they are of God; because many false prophets have gone out into the world.

Acts 13:6 Now when they had gone through the island to Paphos, they found a certain sorcerer, a false prophet, a Jew whose name was Bar-Jesus,

Revelation 16:13 And I saw three unclean spirits like frogs coming out of the mouth of the dragon, out of the mouth of the beast, and out of the mouth of the false prophet.

Revelation 19:20 Then the beast was captured, and with him the false prophet who worked signs in his presence, by which he deceived those who received the mark of the beast and those who worshiped his image. These two were cast alive into the lake of fire burning with brimstone.

Revelation 20:10 And the devil, who deceived them, was cast into the lake of fire and brimstone where the beast and the false prophet are. And they will be tormented day and night forever and ever.

That Prophet

Acts 3:20 "and that He may send Jesus Christ, who was preached to you before, 21 "whom heaven must receive until the times of restoration of all things, which God has spoken by the mouth of all His holy prophets since the world began. 22 "For Moses truly said to the fathers, 'The Lord your God will raise up for you a Prophet like me from your brethren. Him you shall hear in all things, whatever He says to you 23 'And it shall come to pass that every soul who will not hear that Prophet shall be utterly destroyed from among the people.' 24 "Yes, and all the prophets, from Samuel and those who follow, as many as have spoken, have also foretold these days. 25 "You are sons of the prophets, and of the covenant which God made with our fathers, saying to Abraham, 'And in your seed all the families of the earth shall be blessed.'

Prophets

Acts 7:52 "Which of the prophets did your fathers not persecute? And they killed those who foretold the coming of the Just One, of whom you now have become the betrayers and murderers,

Acts 13:15 And after the reading of the Law and the Prophets, the rulers of the synagogue sent to them, saying, "Men and brethren, if you have any word of exhortation for the people, say on."

Acts 13:27 "For those who dwell in Jerusalem, and their rulers, because they did not know Him, nor even the voices of the Prophets which are read every Sabbath, have fulfilled them in condemning Him.

Acts 15:14-15 "Simon has declared how God at the first visited the Gentiles to take out of them a people for His name. 15 "And with this the words of the prophets agree, just as it is written:

Acts 10:43 "To Him all the prophets witness that, through His name, whoever believes in Him will receive remission of sins."

1 Cor12: 27-30 Now you are the body of Christ, and members individually. 28 And God has appointed these in the church: first apostles, second prophets, third teachers, after that miracles, then gifts of healings, helps, administrations, varieties of tongues. 29 Are all apostles? Are all prophets? Are all teachers? Are all workers of miracles? 30 Do all have gifts of healings? Do all speak with tongues? Do all interpret?

Ephesians 2:20 having been built on the foundation of the apostles and prophets, Jesus Christ Himself being the chief cornerstone,

Ephesians 3:5 which in other ages was not made known to the sons of men, as it has now been revealed by the Spirit to His holy apostles and prophets:

Ephesians 4:11 And He Himself gave some to be apostles, some prophets, some evangelists, and some pastors and teachers,

1 Thessalonians 2:15 who killed both the Lord Jesus and their own prophets, and have persecuted us; and they do not please God and are contrary to all men,

Hebrews 1:1 God, who at various times and in different ways spoke in time past to the fathers by the prophets.

Hebrews 11:32-34 And what more shall I say? For the time would fail me to tell of Gideon and Barak and Samson and Jephthah, also of David and Samuel and the prophets: 33 who through faith subdued kingdoms, worked righteousness, obtained promises, stopped the mouths of lions, 34 quenched the violence of fire, escaped the edge of the sword, out of weakness were made strong, became valiant in battle, turned to flight the armies of the aliens.

James 5:10 My brethren, take the prophets, who spoke in the name of the Lord, as an example of suffering and patience.

Revelation 11:10 And those who dwell on the earth will rejoice over them, make merry, and send gifts to one another, because these two prophets tormented those who dwell on the earth.

Revelation 18:20 "Rejoice over her, O heaven, and you holy apostles and prophets, for God has avenged you on her!"

Revelation 18:24 "And in her was found the blood of prophets and saints, and of all who were slain on the earth."

Revelation 22:9 Then he said to me, "See that you do not do that. For I am your fellow servant, and of your brethren the prophets, and of those who keep the words of this book. Worship God."

Protecting Prophets

1 Chronicles 16:22 saying, "Do not touch My anointed ones, and do My prophets no harm."

Psalms 105:15 Saying, "Do not touch My anointed ones, And do My prophets no harm." **16:6** For they have shed the blood of saints and prophets, and You have given them blood to drink. for it is their just due."

Prophetic Scripture

Romans 16:26 but now has been made manifest, and by the prophetic Scriptures has been made known to all nations, according to the commandment of the everlasting God, for obedience to the faith —

Revelation 22:6 Then he said to me, "These words are faithful and true." And the Lord God of the holy prophets sent His angel to show His servants the things which must shortly take place.

Divine Healing

What God says about it and how to be healed!

Note: All underlining in mine.

Exodus 15:26 And said, If thou wilt <u>diligently hearken to the voice of the LORD thy God,</u> and wilt <u>do that which is right in his sight,</u> and <u>wilt give ear to his commandments, and keep all his statutes,</u> I will put none of these diseases upon thee, which I have brought upon the Egyptians: <u>for I am the LORD that healeth thee.</u>

Exodus 23:25 And ye <u>shall serve the LORD your God,</u> and he shall bless thy bread, and thy water; and <u>I will take sickness away from the midst of thee.</u>

<u>**Deuteronomy 7:15** And the LORD will take away from thee all sickness, and will put none of the evil diseases of Egypt, which thou knowest, upon thee; but will lay them upon all them that hate thee.</u>

Psalms 103:2 Bless the LORD, O my soul, and forget not all his benefits: 3 Who <u>forgiveth all thine iniquities;</u> who <u>healeth all thy diseases;</u>

Psalms 107:20 He sent his <u>word,</u> and <u>healed them</u>, and delivered them from their destructions.

Isaiah 53:5 But He (Christ) was wounded for our transgressions, he was bruised for our iniquities: the chastisement of our peace was upon him; and <u>with his stripes we are healed.</u>

Malachi 4:2 But unto you that <u>fear my name</u> shall the Sun of righteousness arise with <u>healing</u> in his wings;......

Matthew 4:23 And Jesus went about all Galilee, teaching in their synagogues, and preaching the gospel of the kingdom, and <u>healing all manner of sickness and all manner of disease among the people.</u>

Matthew 8:16 When the even was come, they brought unto Him many that were <u>possessed with devils: and He cast out the spirits with his word, and healed all that were sick:</u> 17 That it might be fulfilled which was spoken by Esaias the prophet, saying, <u>Himself (Christ) took our infirmities, and bare our sicknesses.</u>

Proverbs 4:20 My son,<u> attend to my words</u>; incline thine ear unto my sayings. 21 Let them not depart from thine eyes; keep them in the midst of thine heart. 22 <u>For they are life</u> unto those that find them, and <u>health to all their flesh.</u>

James 5:15 And the<u> prayer of faith</u> shall <u>save the sick</u>, and the Lord shall <u>raise him up</u>; and if he have <u>committed sins,</u> they shall be<u> forgiven him.</u>

1 Peter 2:24 Who his own self (Christ) bare our sins in his own body on the tree, that we, being dead to sins, should live unto righteousness: by whose stripes ye were healed.

Mark 16:15 And he said unto them, Go ye into all the world, and preach the gospel to every creature. 16 He that believeth and is baptized shall be saved; but he that believeth not shall be damned. 17 And these signs shall follow them that believe; In my name shall they cast out devils; they shall speak with new tongues; 18 They shall take up serpents; and if they drink any deadly thing, it shall not hurt them; they shall lay hands on the sick, and they shall recover.

Ephesians 1:18-20 The eyes of your understanding being enlightened; that ye may know what is the hope of his calling, and what the riches of the glory of his inheritance in the saints, And what is the exceeding greatness of his power to usward who believe, according to the working of his mighty power, Which he wrought in Christ, when he raised him from the dead, and set him at his own right hand in the heavenly places,.....

These verses are very strong, think about them, study them, get them into your heart. These are healing verses.(**Eph :18-20**) Do you see this? It says that the power that God the Father used to raise Jesus from the dead is also "to us-ward:" Given to us so we can be brought to a perfect physical life (by our choice) as and when we are saved, and that we can and will know about this power for healing and salvation. This is only for the born again saved of God who are in the body of Christ.

2 Peter 1:3-4 According as his divine power hath given unto us all things that pertain unto life and godliness, through the knowledge of him that hath called us to glory and virtue: Whereby are given unto us exceeding great and precious promises: that by these ye might be partakers of the divine nature, having escaped the corruption that is in the world through lust.

God has given us all that we need for " all things that pertain to life". I believe that this includes HEALING, don't you? Also what about "great and precious promises"? Are these not promises for our benefit and welfare? Well, Ya!

New Testament examples of healing

Matthew 8:2 And, behold, there came a leper and worshipped Him, saying, Lord, if thou wilt, thou canst make me clean. 3 And Jesus put forth his hand, and touched him, saying, I will; be thou clean. And immediately his leprosy was cleansed.

Matthew 8:13 And Jesus said unto the centurion, Go thy way; and as thou hast believed, so be it done unto thee. And his servant was healed in the selfsame hour.

Matthew 8:14 And when Jesus was come into Peter's house, he saw his wife's mother laid, and sick of a fever.15 And he touched her hand, and the fever left her: and she arose, and ministered unto them.

Matthew 9:6 But that ye may know that the Son of man hath power on earth to forgive sins, (then saith he to the sick of the palsy,) Arise, take up thy bed, and go unto thine house. 7 And he arose, and departed to his house.

Matthew 9:20 And, behold, a woman, which was diseased with an issue of blood twelve years, came behind him, and touched the hem of his garment: 21 For she said within herself, If I may but touch His garment, I shall be whole. 22 But Jesus turned him about, and when he saw her, he said, Daughter, be of good comfort; <u>thy faith hath made thee whole</u>. And the woman was made whole from that hour.

Matthew 9:27 And when Jesus departed thence, two blind men followed Him, crying, and saying, Thou son of David, have mercy on us. 28 And when he was come into the house, the blind men came to him: and Jesus saith unto them, <u>Believe ye</u> that I am able to do this? They said unto Him, Yea, Lord. 29 Then touched he their eyes, saying, <u>According to your faith</u> be it unto you. 30 And their eyes were opened; and Jesus straitly charged them, saying, See that no man know it.

Matthew 12:10 And, behold, there was a man which had his hand withered. And they asked Him, saying, Is it lawful to heal on the sabbath days? that they might accuse him. 13 Then saith he to the man, Stretch forth thine hand. And <u>he stretched it forth</u>; and it was restored whole, like as the other.

Matthew 12:22 Then was brought unto him one possessed with a devil, blind, and dumb: and He healed him, insomuch that the blind and dumb both spake and saw.

Matthew 14:14 And Jesus went forth, and saw a great multitude, and was moved with compassion toward them, and He healed their sick.

Matthew 14:35 And when the men of that place had knowledge of Him, they sent out into all that country round about, and brought unto him all that were diseased; 36 And <u>besought him that they might only touch the hem</u> of His garment: and as many as touched were made perfectly whole.

Matthew 15:30 And great multitudes came unto Him, having with them those that were lame, blind, dumb, maimed, and many others, and cast them down at Jesus' feet; and He healed them:

Matthew 20:32 And Jesus stood still, and called them, and said, <u>What will ye that I shall do unto you? 33 They say unto Him, Lord, that our eyes may be opened. 34</u> So Jesus had compassion on them, and touched their eyes: and immediately their eyes received sight, and they followed Him.

Matthew 21:14 And the <u>blind and the lame came to Him</u> in the temple; and He healed them.

Mark 1:40 And there came a leper to Him, beseeching him, and kneeling down to Him, and saying unto Him, <u>If thou wilt, thou canst make me clean</u>.

Verses that Say in the Kingdom of God 179

41 And Jesus, moved with compassion, put forth his hand, and touched him, and saith unto him, <u>I will;</u> be thou clean. 42 And as soon as He had spoken, immediately the leprosy departed from him, and he was cleansed.

Mark 3:14 And he ordained twelve, that they should be with Him, and that He might send them forth to preach, 15 And to have power to heal sicknesses, and to cast out devils:

Mark 6:12 And they went out, and preached that men should repent. 13 And they cast out many devils, and anointed with oil many that were sick, and healed them.

Mark 6:56 And whithersoever He entered, into villages, or cities, or country, they laid the sick in the streets, <u>and besought Him</u> that they might touch if it were but the border of his garment: and as many as touched Him were made whole

Mark 7:32 And they bring unto Him one that was deaf, and had an impediment in his speech; and they beseech Him to put his hand upon him. 33 And He took him aside from the multitude, and put His fingers into his ears, and He spit, and touched his tongue; 34 And looking up to heaven, He sighed, and saith unto him, Ephphatha, that is, Be opened. 35 And straightway his ears were opened, and the string of his tongue was loosed, and he spake plain.

Mark 10:46 And they came to Jericho: and as he went out of Jericho with His disciples and a great number of people, blind Bartimaeus, the son of Timaeus, sat by the highway side begging. 47 And when he heard that it was Jesus of Nazareth, <u>he began to cry out, and say, Jesus, thou son of David, have mercy on me.</u> 51 And Jesus answered and said unto him, What wilt thou that I should do unto thee? The blind man said unto Him, Lord, <u>that I might receive my sight.</u> 52 And Jesus said unto Him, Go thy way; <u>thy faith hath made thee whole.</u> And immediately he received his sight, and followed Jesus in the way.

Luke 5:12 And it came to pass, when he was in a certain city, behold a man full of leprosy: who seeing Jesus fell on his face, <u>and besought Him, saying, Lord, if thou wilt, thou canst make me clean.</u> 13 And He put forth his hand, and touched him, saying, <u>I will</u>: be thou clean. And immediately the leprosy departed from him.

Luke 6:17 And He came down with them, and stood in the plain, and the company of His disciples, and a great multitude of people out of all Judaea and Jerusalem, and from the sea coast of Tyre and Sidon, which came to hear Him, and to be healed of their diseases; 18 And they that were vexed with unclean spirits: and they were healed. 19 And the whole multitude <u>sought to touch him</u>: for there went virtue out of Him, and <u>healed them all.</u>

Luke 10:8 And into whatsoever city ye enter, and they receive you, eat such things as are set before you: 9 And <u>heal the sick </u>that are therein, and say unto them, The kingdom of God is come nigh unto you(the words of Jesus to the disciples).

Luke 13:11 And, behold, there was a woman which had a spirit of infirmity eighteen years, and was bowed together, and could in no wise lift up herself. **12 And when Jesus saw her, He called her to him, and said unto her, Woman, thou art loosed from thine infirmity. 13 And He laid his hands on her: and immediately she was made straight, and glorified God.**(This woman was not demon possessed. Jesus never laid His hands on demon possessed men or women, my note.)

John 5:5 And a certain man was there, which had an infirmity thirty and eight years. 6 When Jesus saw him lie, and knew that he had been now a long time in that case, He saith unto him, Wilt thou be made whole? 7 The impotent man answered him, <u>Sir, I have no man, when the water is troubled, to put me into the pool: but while I am coming, another steppeth down before me</u>. 8 Jesus saith unto him, Rise, take up thy bed, and walk. 9 And immediately the man was made whole, and took up his bed, and walked: and on the same day was the sabbath. 14 Afterward Jesus findeth Him in the temple, and said unto him, Behold, thou art made whole: <u>sin no more</u>, lest a worse thing come unto thee.

John 9:6-7 When he had thus spoken, he spat on the ground, and made clay of the spittle, and he anointed the eyes of the blind man with the clay, And said unto him, Go, wash in the pool of Siloam, (which is by interpretation, Sent.) He went his way therefore, and washed, and came seeing.

John 11:41 Then they took away the stone from the place where the dead was laid. And Jesus lifted up his eyes, and said, Father, I thank thee that thou hast heard me. 42 And I knew that thou hearest me always: but because of the people which stand by I said it, that they may believe that thou hast sent me. 43 And when He thus had spoken, he cried with a loud voice, Lazarus, come forth. 44 And he that was dead came forth, bound hand and foot with grave clothes: and his face was bound about with a napkin. Jesus saith unto them, Loose him, and let him go.

Acts 3:6 Then Peter said, Silver and gold have I none; but such as I have give I thee: In the name of Jesus Christ of Nazareth rise up and walk. 7 And he <u>took him by the right hand, and lifted him up</u>: and immediately his feet and ancle bones received strength. 8 And he leaping up stood, and walked, and entered with them into the temple, walking, and leaping, and praising God.

(By the man rising up he made a profession of faith, or you can say put works to his faith for his healing. This is a requirement for any healing to be effective, my note.)

Acts 5:15 Insomuch that they brought forth the sick into the streets, and laid them on beds and couches, that at the least the shadow of Peter passing by might overshadow some of them. 16 There came also a multitude out of the cities round about unto Jerusalem, bringing sick folks, and them which were vexed with unclean spirits: and they were healed every one.

Acts 8:5 Then Philip went down to the city of Samaria, and preached Christ unto them. 6 And the people with one accord gave heed unto those things which Philip spake, hearing and seeing the miracles which he did.

7 For unclean spirits, crying with loud voice, came out of many that were possessed with them: and many taken with palsies, and that were lame, were healed. (Philip was not an apostle, he was the same as you and me, my note.)

Acts 9:33 And there he found a certain man named Aeneas, which had kept his bed eight years, and was sick of the palsy. **34** And Peter said unto him, Aeneas, Jesus Christ maketh thee whole: arise, and make thy bed. And he arose immediately.

Acts 9:40 But Peter put them all forth, and kneeled down, and prayed; and turning him to the body said, Tabitha, arise. And she opened her eyes: and when she saw Peter, she sat up. **41** And he gave her his hand, and lifted her up, and when he had called the saints and widows, presented her alive.

Acts 10:38 How God anointed Jesus of Nazareth with the Holy Ghost and with power: who went about doing good, and healing all that were oppressed of the devil; for God was with him.

Acts 14:8 And there sat a certain man at Lystra, impotent in his feet, being a cripple from his mother's womb, who never had walked: **9** The same heard Paul speak: who stedfastly beholding him, and <u>perceiving that he had faith to be healed,</u> **10** Said with a loud voice, Stand upright on thy feet. And he leaped and walked.

Acts 20:9 And there sat in a window a certain young man named Eutychus, being fallen into a deep sleep: and as Paul was long preaching, he sunk down with sleep, and fell down from the third loft, and was taken up dead. **10** And Paul went down, and fell on him, and embracing him said, Trouble not yourselves; for his life is in him.

Acts 28:8 And it came to pass, that the father of Publius lay sick of a fever and of a bloody flux: to whom Paul entered in, and prayed, and laid his hands on him, and healed him. **9** So when this was done, others also, which had diseases in the island, came, and were healed:

Hebrews 12:12 Wherefore lift up the hands which hang down, and the feeble knees; **13** And make straight paths for your feet, lest that which is lame be turned out of the way; but let it rather be healed.

James 5:14 Is any sick among you? let him call for the elders of the church; and let them pray over him, anointing him with oil in the name of the Lord: **15** <u>And the prayer of faith</u> shall save the sick, and the Lord shall raise him up; and if he have committed sins, they shall be forgiven him.

The underlined scripture above, points to the faith that the sick and maimed used to receive their healings. There are a few things I must say about healing. The first is that healing is a part of the atonement of the cross of Jesus the Christ. You cannot separate Salvation, Healing, and Material needs from each other. They are, all three, part and parcel of the work by Jesus on the cross. See **Isa : 53** the whole chapter.

Isaiah 53:5 But he was wounded for our transgressions, he was bruised for our iniquities: the chastisement of our peace was upon him; and with his stripes we are healed.

Psalms 103:2 Bless the LORD, O my soul, and forget not all his benefits: 3 Who forgiveth all thine iniquities; *who healeth all thy diseases*;

If you approach Jesus and the Father with repentance, asking forgiveness, believing in faith, and, as James says, putting work to your faith, you will be saved. This is so every time someone does this in this manner. Now if you go to Jesus to be healed with faith, in a sinless condition, putting work to your faith, and truly wanting to be healed you will be healed every time. It is the same with healing as it is with salvation, and is the same for material prosperity. You must meet God's conditions to receive anything from Him, this includes prayer (God chooses not to hear the prayers of a sinner).
(see **John 9:31** about prayer).

Here are the major reasons that people are not healed that I know of:

1- You have un-repented sin in your conscience . See 1 **Cor: 11:29-31**. God does not hear the prayers of sinners (see **John 9: 31, Isa. 1:15,** and the study on prayer), so why would He heal you if you're in sin? There are special circumstances where God will heal a pagan as a sign for them to come to repentance, this is called a miracle.

2- You don't have the faith for that particular healing. Remember, a lack of faith is also a sin.

3- You really don't want to be healed, or you will not accept healing from God. You're just going through the motions to show people that you believe in healing. You want to stay in your condition/sickness for sympathy, fear of what you will have to do if you're healed, or that you'll lose money when you are healed. In other words your life will change, by being healed, to something you don't want any more, or that you never wanted in the first place. You're comfortable in your disability /sickness. Or you feel that your not good enough for God to heal you, you have done so many bad things in your life that God could not possibly want to heal you. Which is a lie that you have accepted from Satan.
This problem of not being good enough is very prevalent in the body of Christ. For some reason you cannot believe that Christ's work on the cross really did remove your sin, because it was/is so horrible that you want to be punished for it. You just don't think that Jesus' work was good enough for your sins. Again this is a LIE of Satan. Do not believe it. What you're saying to God is that Jesus' work on the cross was ineffective. What a lie!!

4- You have not because you ask not.

To continue : There are three general classes of sickness. The first is that you have a genetically inherited sickness. The second one is sickness that you bring on yourself by your actions, you can say sins, such as smoking gives you lung cancer, drinking gives you a destroyed liver, eating as a glutton gives you colon cancer. These are general examples, but I think you get the idea. The third is that you accept a sickness that you hear is going around, or you are tempted / told about by Satan. That you are really getting sick is a lie that you do not have to accept, even if there are physical symptoms of sickness. Rebuke any and all symptoms of sickness in Jesus name, and refuse to let them convince you that you are becoming sick. Claim the perfect health that God has for you in the name of Jesus.

The more you do this the stronger you will become in fighting sickness. Healing, like salvation and material needs, is a part of Jesus' work on the cross. So if you believe in faith for Jesus' blood to remove your sins why don't you believe in faith for His stripes to heal you, and provide for you?

It seems to me that most Christians give lip service to healing from God. Why is that? Well what would your answer be if no one in your church was ever healed? Would it be easier to say "well it seems to us that God does not heal any more", or to say "we need to study the word and learn all that God has to say on faith and healing". What does your church say and do? What do you do? To me the answer is real clear, we must study the word of God instead of making excuses for failure. The biggest excuse is saying "I tried". Don't use the word "Try", because it is just an excuse to fail. If you only try to do something you will never do it, you'll just try and to try is to fail. Just do it. Another way to say it is "to try is a lack of faith", because you are just trying and not putting works to your faith (see the book of James).

Jesus told the man that He healed by the pool not to sin any more lest a worse thing come upon him. This verse says that his sickness was caused by sin, that if he sinned again he would not only lose the healing he received but that he would be worse off in the end. This shows that one of the ways we get sick is through sin.

Inherited sickness, flawed genes, is the result of sin back through the generations of your family line, this form of sickness we have no choice of receiving, but we do have a choice for healing by faith in Jesus and His work on the cross.

The last way of receiving sickness is always a choice. We are bombarded constantly with the news of all the sickness that is going around the world, and how dangerous it is.

It is a choice that we make as to whether we believe what the world tells us of all the horrible sicknesses that can and will kill us, or whether we have the faith in Jesus to walk in divine health, thereby refusing, in Jesus' name, to get sick by accepting and acting on the lies of the world. Again we must have faith in and act on the words of Jesus. To do this you must know scripture; and study holy scriptures constantly.

We as born again children, who are in the Spiritual kingdom of God, are required to walk holy and righteous (without sin) to stay in this Spiritual kingdom of truth. As long as we continue to resist and reject any and all temptation (such as sickness) from Satan we will walk in Holiness, in perfect health, and in the material prosperity that God has for us. In God's perfect Kingdom there is no sickness, no starvation, no sin, no bills past due, no fear, no lack of love, no poor in spirit, no lost children, no other gods, you get the idea. Again it is a perfect kingdom, and it is the ONLY true kingdom. All else is false! Now there is one thing you must understand, and it is that there is evil in the world. This evil will attack you every chance it can. The way this attack comes is by your acceptance of the temptation to sin, become sick or live without your material need met.

If you're not in the kingdom of God Satan will run you ragged. One other thing, this evil does not come or originate with God. It comes by the free will choice of Satan to rebel against God.

As we are in the kingdom of God, do you not think that God the Father wants to give us all the benefits that He has for us (such as perfect Divine health)? So search out God's face and plead your case in Spirit and truth and God WILL answer with a resounding YES. Remember Jesus said ask in faith and you SHALL receive. Remember that a lack of FAITH is a sin. If we don't have Divine health we must not look to God the Father and say, "Why haven't you healed me?" The problem is with us for not receiving from God . This is so every time, the answer to the problem is always with us on our end.

It takes a concentrated effort to stay in the Kingdom, to obey all of God's commands. Do you make this effort? If not why then should God bless you with any of His benefits? The Father loves you beyond measure, and desires to shower you with all of His gifts. Will you not accept them? All you have to do is obey! Is that so hard?

I cannot say this enough, my brothers and sisters, if you are in sin you will NOT receive ANY BENNIES from God until you repent and ask forgiveness (**1John 1:9**). There is a lot of confusion in regards to whether or not God heals every time. One set of scriptures that is used   to prove this is about Paul and the 'thorn in his side'. Since Paul healed all manner of sickness and diseases, do you really think he did not have the Faith to get himself healed? Paul tell us that the 'thorn in his side' was all of his trials and tribulations, which were pressures of the Jewish community , beatings, shipwrecks, etc. None of which was any kind of sickness.

2 Corinthians 11:24-30 Of the Jews five times received I forty stripes save one. Thrice was I beaten with rods, once was I stoned, thrice I suffered shipwreck, a night and a day I have been in the deep; In journeyings often, in perils of waters, in perils of robbers, in perils by mine own countrymen, in perils by the heathen, in perils in the city, in perils in the wilderness, in perils in the sea, in perils among false brethren In weariness and painfulness, in watchings often, in hunger and thirst, in fastings often, in cold and nakedness. Beside those things that are without, that which cometh upon me daily, the care of all the churches. Who is weak, and I am not weak? who is offended, and I burn not? If I must needs glory, I will glory of the things which concern mine infirmities.

2 Corinthians 12:7-10 And lest I should be exalted above measure through the abundance of the revelations, there was given to me a thorn in the flesh, the messenger of Satan to buffet me, lest I should be exalted above measure. For this thing I besought the Lord thrice, that it might depart from me. And he said unto me, My grace is sufficient for thee: for my strength is made perfect in weakness. Most gladly therefore will I rather glory in my infirmities, that the power of Christ may rest upon me. Therefore I take pleasure in infirmities, in reproaches, in necessities,

in persecutions, in distresses for Christ's sake: for when I am weak, then am I strong.

2 Corinthians 13:3-4 Since ye seek a proof of Christ speaking in me, which to you-ward is not weak, but is mighty in you. For though he was crucified through weakness, yet he liveth by the power of God. For we also are weak in him, but we shall live with him by the power of God toward you.

2 Corinthians 12:12 Truly the signs of an apostle were wrought among you in all patience, in signs, and wonders, and mighty deeds.

First you must understand that you have to meet God's conditions to receive anything from Him, this includes: Answered Prayer, Salvation, baptism of the Holy Spirit, material needs, protection, and not least of all Healing. Do you think that Paul was a sinner, or that he did not meet the conditions set forth by God?

One of the reasons some people give when they are not healed is that "Paul was sick and God did not heal him". That God's grace was good enough. This comes from misunderstanding the atonement (work of the cross) and God's "Grace", and from not understanding what Paul was talking about.

Paul's "Thorn in his side" was NOT sickness and diseases . The word he uses is "Infirmities". In the Vines Expository Dictionary and Strong's Concordance it is defined as: want of strength, weakness, indicating inability to produce results. In **2Cor. 11:30** it is weakness, in **2 Cor. 12:5,9- 10** it is weaknesses. We must also look at the context as well. **In 2Cor. 11:24-30** Paul tells us what befell him. Go to **2Cor. 12** and you will see what Paul considered to be "weakness". He considered the trials and tribulations that he suffered (**2Cor. 11:24-30**) for Christ to be to his advantage (**2Cor. 12:10**).

God's Grace is defined as "God's influence in your life (heart) and its corresponding result in your life". You receive Grace by being righteous (sinless) before God. See the study on faith and grace. How can you see this as a refusal to heal. What was God trying to teach/show Paul, that it is better to be sick and get God's grace (a lie of Satan)? If this is so then we should all be sick so we can get an overabundance of God's grace. What God was really telling Paul is that His grace was the strength that Paul needed, in his weaknesses, to continue in the work of an Apostle.

Paul's weakness was caused by continual trials, persecutions, and in distresses for Christ. He says by this weakness he is made "strong in Christ". The strength comes from God's continual influence in his life. You can see that Paul states that he is made strong when he is weak. This weakness is the result of time and again being beat up, stoned, whipped. Can you see that this is not sickness? Notice in **2 Cor. 13:3-4** that Paul considered himself made strong in Christ and that he was weak without Christ. Can you see and understand this?

There is one last thing we must look at, and understand. Paul was a worker of signs and wonders which included healing. Do you think that God refused to heal him when he, himself, was walking so close to Jesus that he was healing all manner of sickness and disease every time he was asked? I don't!

The Lords Supper, Communion

Matthew 26:26 And as they were eating, Jesus took bread, and blessed it, and brake it, and gave it to the disciples, and said, Take, eat; this is my body. 27 And he took the cup, and gave thanks, and gave it to them, saying, Drink ye all of it; 28 For this is my blood of the new testament, which is shed for many for the remission of sins.

Mark 14:22 And as they did eat, Jesus took bread, and blessed, and brake it, and gave to them, and said, Take, eat: this is my body.23 And he took the cup, and when he had given thanks, he gave it to them: and they all drank of it. 24 And he said unto them, This is my blood of the new testament, which is shed for many.

Luke 22:19 And he took bread, and gave thanks, and brake it, and gave unto them, saying, This is my body which is given for you: this do in remembrance of me. 20 Likewise also the cup after supper, saying, This cup is the new testament in my blood, which is shed for you.

1 Corinthians 11:23 For I have received of the Lord that which also I delivered unto you, That the Lord Jesus the same night in which he was betrayed took bread: 24 And when he had given thanks, he brake it, and said, Take, eat: this is my body, which is broken for you: this do in remembrance of me. 25 After the same manner also he took the cup, when he had supped, saying, This cup is the new testament in my blood: this do ye, as oft as ye drink it, in remembrance of me. 26 For as often as ye eat this bread, and drink this cup, ye do shew the Lord's death till he come. 27 Wherefore whosoever shall eat this bread, and drink this cup of the Lord, unworthily, shall be guilty of the body and blood of the Lord.and drink of that cup. . 28 But let a man examine himself, and so let him eat of that bread, 29 For he that eateth and drinketh unworthily, eateth and drinketh damnation to himself, not discerning the Lord's body 30 For this cause many are weak and sickly among you, and many sleep. 31 For if we would judge ourselves, we should not be judged.

These verses are a true description of how to take communion. It first took place at the "last supper", also called Passover (To read about the First Passover see Exodus chapter 12.) of Christ. The first church, or early church before 300A.D., took communion in the setting of a home with a meal, worship, prayer, teachings and fellowship. The Church at that time was, and should still be, a group of friends and visiting Christians meeting in homes as Jesus did. The modern church has bastardized this sacrament into a once a month event when a very small piece of cracker and a very small drink of grape juice is given by a priest or pastor who gives a corporate prayer of repentance.

You can see by the verses in 1 Corinthians (11:27-31) that taking the wine and bread of communion in sin has consequences. It is your place to repent. The pastor can not do this for you.

If you look at the context of Jesus' last Passover, when the first communion took place, you will see that communion was given by Jesus as part of the Passover "supper" in the upper room of a house. It was not done in the temple or any other religious buildings. Nor is it required to have a priest or pastor hand out the bread and wine or to pray about it. It is required that you personally repent and ask forgiveness of any sins not yet repented of. It is required that you do this often, which can be once a week or even once a day. You decide! Don't let some man, no matter what his title, tell you how to worship Jesus. You have the bible to tell you how, so read and know it. It's your salvation that's in question, not the pastors. He can't get you to heaven, only you can make the moral decision to come to Christ and be saved. AGAIN, no one can do this for you, and baby baptism will not give you fire insurance. By the way, baby baptism in NOT in the bible.

Just a short word on covenant. Taking communion is a outward symbol of the covenant that you cut with Jesus when you came to Him in repentance and asking forgiveness of your sins. Christ said do this often in remembrance of me. This keeps Jesus and His work for you on the cross fresh in your mind. All true covenants are sealed by the shedding of blood just as this covenant was sealed by the shedding of the blood of Jesus.

The Passover supper is held on what the modern church calls "Easter". This is incorrect as the name "Easter" comes from the name for a fertility goddess. Do you really think that God the Father will honor you for honoring a false goddess? Oh by the way! When you read about Passover in the bible you will not find anything about eggs or bunny rabbits either. They are also symbols of the false goddess of fertility.

The modern, or you can also say "man's", church holds to traditions which were brought about by a man, and believed to be sacred by those men, even though they are not in the New Testament. The pulpit, the robes of a priest, pastors or priests as a higher class, the so called laity as a lower class, pews, the church building, the sermon, tithing, Easter, Christmas, various other ceremonies, and man made church laws, are examples of these man made traditions. As this is so, can you really call the building on the corner a Christian "CHURCH"? We, as Christians, are the temple of God. What makes you think you have to go to some building controlled by some man to worship God? Did not Jesus say where two or more are gathered there will I be?

Do you read the bible? Do you go to man's church building on the corner? Are you a sinless Christian? Is there any other kind?

To take Communion you must be sinless, and you should do this in conjunction with other Christians in the setting of a meal.

"The words of Jesus as they relate to the natural Nation of Israel, and the natural Jew"

Note: All underlining mine

Before we start this study I would like to explain something. Most people who read Jesus' words in the New Testament do not consider just who Jesus was talking to. Yes His words are for all who read them, but they were also spoken to the Jews of His time. You must see that the meaning of His statements and parables were for those He spoke to directly and for us today. This study is only on what Jesus meant for those of His day, the Jews in the nation of Israel before 70 A.D. when Jerusalem was destroyed.

Matthew 5:
3 Blessed are the poor in spirit: for theirs is the kingdom of heaven.
4 Blessed are they that mourn: for they shall be comforted.
5 Blessed are the meek: for they shall inherit the earth.
6 Blessed are they which do hunger and thirst after righteousness: for they shall be filled.
7 Blessed are the merciful: for they shall obtain mercy.
8 Blessed are the pure in heart: for they shall see God.
9 Blessed are the peacemakers: for they shall be called the children of God.
10 Blessed are they which are persecuted for righteousness' sake: for theirs is the kingdom of heaven.
11 Blessed are ye, when men shall revile you, and persecute you, and shall say all manner of evil against you falsely, for my sake.
12 Rejoice, and be exceeding glad: for great is your reward in heaven: for so persecuted they the prophets which were before you.

Luke 6:20 And he lifted up his eyes on his disciples, and said, Blessed be ye poor: for yours is the kingdom of God. 21 Blessed are ye that hunger now: for ye shall be filled. Blessed are ye that weep now: for ye shall laugh. 22 Blessed are ye, when men shall hate you, and when they shall separate you from their company, and shall reproach you, and cast out your name as evil, for the Son of man's sake. 23 Rejoice ye in that day, and leap for joy: for, behold, your reward is great in heaven: for in the like manner did their fathers unto the prophets.

You will notice that Jesus shows us by these verses, that for the most part, the leadership of the nation of Israel is not in the description of who is in, and who will come into the kingdom of heaven. Did Jesus come for the righteous. *

*****Matthew 9:13 but go ye and learn what that meaneth, I will have mercy, and not sacrifice: for <u>I am not come to call the righteous, but sinners to repentance.</u>**

Matthew 18:11 For the Son of man is come to save that which was lost. Mark 2:17 When Jesus heard it, he saith unto them, They that are whole have no need of the physician, but they that are sick: I came not to call the righteous, but sinners to repentance.

Matthew 5:20 For I say unto you, That except your righteousness shall exceed the righteousness of the scribes and Pharisees, ye shall in no case enter into the kingdom of heaven.

The leadership and other devout Jews of the day were "made" forgiven and righteous by the law of sacrifices given to them by God. This was done by the covering of blood from the animal sacrifices in the Temple. These sacrifices could not make them pure, or you could say sinless, because only Jesus' blood shed on the cross can remove your sin from your conscience and make you holy and pure**.** See **Hebrews 9:11-14**. These righteous Jews still had to be born again after the cross and resurrection to enter into the kingdom of God.

The Temple was destroyed in 70A D. With it's destruction the Jews had no where to have animal sacrifices anymore. From that point on God will never again accept these kind of sacrifices. Jesus was the one holy, pure, sinless, and last sacrifice needed for all time. The Jews have this available to them just as we do. There is no salvation in animal sacrifice anymore, ever. Jesus is the "ONLY" way now. We, the born again, are the new temple of God in the new covenant confirmed by Jesus.

<u>They that mourn:</u> Those that mourn are those that will be comforted by the Holy Spirit. This is only for believers of Christ.
<u>The meek:</u> This word means being teachable, accepting the teaching of Jesus without argument. The leadership of Israel, to say the least, was not teachable.
<u>A hunger for Righteousness:</u> This is the desire for a sinless life through Jesus. Do you really think the Scribes and Pharisees wanted this?
<u>The merciful:</u> Here we see the command to love your neighbor as you love yourself. **Not** something the leadership of Israel did.
<u>The pure in heart:</u> The sinless people of the kingdom of God. How could the nation of Israel be this? They rejected Jesus, and Jesus is the only way to become sinless.
<u>The peacemakers:</u> Another example of loving your neighbor as yourself. This is a condition of salvation; you must be a peacemaker.
.<u>The persecuted:</u> Ah! Was not Jesus persecuted by the natural leadership of Israel? So then we as people in the kingdom, the righteous of Jesus, also will be persecuted.
<u>When men revile and persecute you:</u> They did this to Jesus! Can we expect any less? You must understand that this is only for the followers of Jesus. How could the nation of Israel be included in this statement? They rejected Jesus.
<u>Rejoice:</u> Be happy, you're in good company.

Matthew 5:13 Ye are the salt of the earth: but if the salt have lost his savour, wherewith shall it be salted? it is thenceforth good for nothing, but to be cast out, and to be trodden under foot of men

The 'salt of the earth' refers to the sinless. The only way to get rid of sin is through the shed blood of Jesus. This was a message to the nation of Israel, as it is to all people today, who then promptly rejected it as a whole. Yes, there were saved Jews in Jesus' time as well as in the Old Testament times (called the Old Testament saints), as there are today (called messianic Jews). But as a group of people they rejected Jesus in favor of the rule of Rome. You see the warning "to be cast out," the leadership of Israel did not heed it, so they as a nation were cast out and rejected.

You can say the God divorced them for adultery to false gods. What are false gods? The answer is anything that you hold in more importance in your life than God the Father and Jesus. The Pharisees' false God and religion was Caesar (he was their source of power).

Matthew 5:14 Ye are the light of the world. A city that is set on an hill cannot be hid.15 Neither do men light a candle, and put it under a bushel, but on a candlestick; and it giveth light unto all that are in the house. 16 Let your light so shine before men, that they may see your good works, and glorify your Father which is in heaven.

Mark 4:21 And he said unto them, Is a candle brought to be put under a bushel, or under a bed? and not to be set on a candlestick?22 For there is nothing hid, which shall not be manifested; neither was any thing kept secret, but that it should come abroad.

Luke 8:16 No man, when he hath lighted a candle, covereth it with a vessel, or putteth it under a bed; but setteth it on a candlestick, that they which enter in may see the light.17 For nothing is secret, that shall not be made manifest; neither any thing hid, that shall not be known and come abroad.

The light of the world means that you have the law, are covenant partners with God and that your part of the covenant is to spread the good news of God to the world. This is true today just as it was for the nation of Israel for 1500 years. You can see the good news of God is not a private thing to be kept to yourself. The nation of Israel did not spread the word, but kept it to itself for 1500 years. Do you think God was happy about this? Jesus says that nothing will be hidden or remain hidden. The Jews keep hidden, so to speak, the word of God. They did not do as God wished them to do.

Matthew 6:24 No man can serve two masters: for either he will hate the one, and love the other; or else he will hold to the one, and despise the other. Ye cannot serve God and mammon.

This is what the leadership, and the nation of Israel on a whole, tried to do. They wanted the rule of Rome with whom they had all the power they wanted, and they wanted God to rule the people with. The problem is that God will allow no other authority to share power with Him. He is Jealous of this sharing of power. Israel had to choose. They chose Rome and rejected God the Father and Jesus.

Matthew 7:15 Beware of false prophets, which come to you in sheep's clothing, but inwardly they are ravening wolves.16 Ye shall know them by their fruits. Do men gather grapes of thorns, or figs of thistles? 17 Even so every good tree brings forth good fruit; but a corrupt tree brings forth evil fruit.18 A good tree cannot bring forth evil fruit, neither can a corrupt tree brings forth good fruit. Every tree that bring not forth good fruit is hewn downs, and cast into fire. 19 Wherefore by their fruits ye shall know them.

The leaders of national Israel were, and are today, false prophets. They had 1500 years to spread the covenant of God the Father but as Jesus said they made anyone who came to Israel for the one true God twice dammed.* This means that they were dammed before, and dammed again after they came to worship the one true God by the rules of man's leadership in Israel. The leaders of Israel did not worship God in the manner that God decreed. They quite commonly worshiped false gods, whoever, and whatever they were. This being so, they as a nation were cut down and thrown into the fire. This is represented by the ripping of the temple veil and the destruction of Jerusalem in 70 AD. The nation and its leaders rejected Jesus even knowing who He was. Is it not fair that God the Father also rejected them and continues to reject them to this day for their continued rejection of Jesus? These verses also have a very important meaning for todays modern church. So be on guard, and check out every thing against the bible.

*Matthew 23:15 Woe unto you, scribes and Pharisees, hypocrites! for ye compass sea and land to make one proselyte, and when he is made, ye make him twofold more the child of hell than yourselves.

Matthew 7:21 Not every one that saith unto me, Lord, Lord, shall enter into the kingdom of heaven; but he that doeth the will of my Father which is in heaven. 22 Many will say to me in that day, Lord, Lord, have we not prophesied in thy name? and in thy name have cast out devils? and in thy name done many wonderful works? 23 And then will I profess unto them, I never knew you: depart from me, ye that work iniquity.

Here again we see that all who would worship God must do it His way or not at all. There are consequences for disobedience. The Jews of Jesus time, and all the way to the beginnings of the nation of Israel, were disobedient. God Himself called them stiff necked and brass browed. Here are Jesus' words warning Israel to give up works for true worship, or they would be rejected, and destroyed. Remember 70AD? This is still valid today. Are you trying to work your way to heaven?

It's like the old joke about Jones the self professed Christian. One day at work he got a call and was told his house burned down and his wife and kids were killed. While running home his dog was run over in front of him. As he started to cross the street to his burned down house a car ran over him. Getting up he saw a church on the corner, and struggled over to it. He went inside and cried out why me Lord, why me, why me? A big voice out of heaven said "because Jones, you made me mad!!"

Matthew 8:5 And when Jesus was entered into Capernaum, there came unto him a centurion, beseeching him, 6 And saying, Lord, my servant lieth at home sick of the palsy, grievously tormented. 7 And Jesus saith unto him, I will come and heal him. 8 The centurion answered and said, Lord, I am not worthy that thou shouldest come under my roof: but speak the word only, and my servant shall be healed. 9 For I am a man under authority, having soldiers under me: and I say to this man, Go, and he goeth; and to another, Come, and he cometh; and to my servant, Do this, and he doeth it. 10 When Jesus heard it, he marvelled, and said to them that followed, Verily I say unto you, I have not found so great faith, no, not in Israel.

11 And I say unto you, That many shall come from the east and west, and shall sit down with Abraham, and Isaac, and Jacob, in the kingdom of heaven. 12 But the children of the kingdom shall be cast out into outer darkness: there shall be weeping and gnashing of teeth.

The verses 11 & 12 are what we need to look at, the others are background. Jesus is saying that Israel has a lack of faith, that the Gentiles will inherit the kingdom of God, and that Israel will be cast out and destroyed. Now! The natural Jew has the same chance at salvation through Jesus as anyone else in the world.

Matthew 10:5 These twelve Jesus sent forth, and commanded them, saying, Go not into the way of the Gentiles, and into any city of the Samaritans enter ye not: 6 But go rather to the lost sheep of the house of Israel. 7And as ye go, preach, saying, The kingdom of heaven is at hand.

You can see here that Jesus gave the nation of Israel all the chances in the world, and they still rejected Him. He told them that He was the Christ. I believe that the Jews knew who He was then and still today, but continue to reject Jesus as the Christ.

Matthew 10:14 And whosoever shall not receive you, nor hear your words, when ye depart out of that house or city, shake off the dust of your feet. 15 Verily I say unto you, It shall be more tolerable for the land of Sodom and Gomorrha in the day of judgment, than for that city.

Jesus is telling them that if His gospel is rejected, they who reject it will be destroyed. This is what Israel did on a whole, this is not to say that many were not saved.

It is with these saved Jews (Messianic Jews) the modern church has its beginnings, the Messianic Jew.

Matthew 10:32 Whosoever therefore shall confess me before men, him will I confess also before my Father which is in heaven.33 But whosoever shall deny me before men, him will I also deny before my Father which is in heaven.

Here is what happened to the natural Jew who denied Jesus. He was and is, just as is anyone who refuses to come to Jesus, rejected by the Father. Just what does this mean? Well does "outer darkness and gnashing of teeth" ring a bell? Maybe hell for eternity

Matthew 10:38 And he that taketh not his cross, and followeth after me, is not worthy of me.

Matthew 10:40 He that receiveth you receiveth me, and he that receiveth me receiveth him that sent me.

Luke 9:23 And he said to them all, If any man will come after me, let him deny himself, and take up his cross daily, and follow me.24 For whosoever will save his life shall lose it: but whosoever will lose his life for my sake, the same shall save it.25 For what is a man advantaged, if he gain the whole world, and lose himself, or be cast away?

If you don't accept or receive the new covenant brought and confirmed by Jesus you will be cast out and burned up. By not receiving Jesus you reject God the Father. This is what the nation of Israel did!

The Jews did not "take up the cross", thereby showing their contempt for God the Father and His glorious Son. Is it any wonder that God had Jerusalem destroyed, and the nation disbanded? If you don't believe that God had it done, you must ask why He, God, did not protect the Jews?

Matthew 11:21 Woe unto thee, Chorazin! woe unto thee, Bethsaida! for if the mighty works, which were done in you, had been done in Tyre and Sidon, they would have repented long ago in sackcloth and ashes.22 But I say unto you, It shall be more tolerable for Tyre and Sidon at the day of judgment, than for you.23And thou, Capernaum, which art exalted unto heaven, shalt be brought down to hell: for if the mighty works, which have been done in thee, had been done in Sodom, it would have remained until this day.24 But I say unto you, That it shall be more tolerable for the land of Sodom in the day of judgment, than for thee.

Repent or go to hell is the warning here. As he is talking to the Jews, this message is for todays Jews as well as for us 2000 + years later. Since Israel did not repent, but instead rejected Jesus they where destroyed in 70 AD. The only chance of salvation today for the Jews is to accept Jesus as the Messiah. By not doing so they condemned themselves. Is it possible that we in the USA and the rest of the world are in that same position in this day and age?

Matthew 12:33 Either make the tree good, and his fruit good; or else make the tree corrupt, and his fruit corrupt: for the tree is known by his fruit.34 O generation of vipers, how can ye, being evil, speak good things? for out of the abundance of the heart the mouth speaketh. 35 A good man out of the good treasure of the heart bringeth forth good things: and an evil man out of the evil treasure bringeth forth evil things.36 But I say unto you, That every idle word that men shall speak, they shall give account thereof in the day of judgment.37 For by thy words thou shalt be justified, and by thy words thou shalt be condemned.

Jesus here is talking to the religious leadership of Israel. He is warning them and telling them that they had better change their ways or else. The leadership of Israel spoke against Jesus to the extent that they called Caesar their king. This showed that their hearts were selfish, hateful, and fearful. They hated Him for the truth that he told them. They perceived Him as a threat to the power they had granted to them by Rome. They were fearful. Since Jesus had no army, his power was spiritual, while Rome's was a physical army, they chose Rome. This fear was not that Jesus personally would overthrow them, but that if He became the new king of Israel Rome would see this new king as a threat and wipe out Israel.

Matthew 12:43 When the unclean spirit is gone out of a man, he walketh through dry places, seeking rest, and findeth none.44 Then he saith, I will return into my house from whence I came out; and when he is come, he findeth it empty, swept, and garnished.45 Then goeth he, and taketh with himself seven other spirits more wicked than himself, and they enter in and dwell there: and the last state of that man is worse than the first. Even so shall it be also unto this wicked generation.

At first glance you will say what relevance do these verses have? Read on!

Verses 43 through 44 show the condition of the nation of Isreal that Jesus is talking about. The worship of false gods i.e. demons was a major problem. Anything not of or from God is of and from Satan. Look in the Old Testament and you will see that Israel worshiped so many false gods that it is hard to count them. They came back and left God many, many times. Do you see now? Is it any wonder that God destroyed them?

They had the chance to avoid all the pain and suffering that they went through and still are going through. Jesus came to renew the Jews to God by providing them with a way to have their sin removed from them, and to fill them with the Holy Spirit: In essence cleaning their house. They could been purified and filled with the Holy Spirit making their house holy before God. They chose a different path which led to destruction. Think 70AD and the Roman army.

Matthew 15:10 And he called the multitude, and said unto them, Hear, and understand:11 Not that which goeth into the mouth defileth a man; but that which cometh out of the mouth, this defileth a man.12 Then came his disciples, and said unto him, Knowest thou that the Pharisees were offended, after they heard this saying?13 But he answered and said, Every plant, which my heavenly Father hath not planted, shall be rooted up.14 Let them alone: they be blind leaders of the blind. And if the blind lead the blind, both shall fall into the ditch.

Verse's 10-12 are background for what Jesus is saying in verses 13- 14. The Pharisees where so set in their ways that they refused to hear and accept the truth that Jesus was telling them. "Up rooted" and thrown into the fire of torment, Ya think? Verse 14 says that they are blind to the truth and only lead others who will also reject the truth; they both will be destroyed. These are the leaders of Israel, they rejected Jesus and His one and only truth.

Do you think that God is pleased with the natural Jew even today? They still reject Jesus, they are still brass browed and stiff necked. Do you really think that God blessed such a rebellious people with a new nation in 1948, and continues to bless them into this new century?

Matthew 16:6 Then Jesus said unto them, Take heed and beware of the leaven of the Pharisees and of the Sadducees.

Jesus knew, even in the early to middle years of His ministry, that the leadership of Israel was anti-Jehovah and would become anti-Christ. This "attitude" of the leadership and the regular* citizens of Israel all through Jesus' walk on the earth (and the 1500 years pervious to Jesus' coming) was, and still is, nails in their coffin.

*regular citizen refers to the temple going Jews, not to the sinners and publicans that Jesus came for.

Matthew 16:13 When Jesus came into the coasts of Caesarea Philippi,he asked his disciples, saying, Whom do men say that I the Son of man am?14 And they said, Some say that thou art John the Baptist: some, Elias; and others, Jeremias, or one of the prophets.15 He saith unto them, But whom say ye that I am?16 And Simon Peter answered and said, Thou art the Christ, the Son of the living God.

17 And Jesus answered and said unto him, Blessed art thou, Simon Barjona: for flesh and blood hath not revealed it unto thee, but my Father which is in heaven.

Mark 8:27 And Jesus went out, and his disciples, into the towns of Caesarea Philippi: and by the way he asked his disciples, saying unto them, Whom do men

say that I am?28 And they answered, John the Baptist; but some say, Elias; and others, One of the prophets.29 And he saith unto them, But whom say ye that I am? And Peter answereth and saith unto him, Thou art the Christ.30 And he charged them that they should tell no man of him.**

Here we see the opposite attitude, or belief from what Israel on a whole believed. There were some who believed, but for the most part the leadership of Israel did not want to believe that Jesus was the Christ. I think in their heart of hearts they did know the truth of Jesus as the messiah.

Matthew 17:22 And while they abode in Galilee, Jesus said unto them, The Son of man shall be betrayed into the hands of men:23 And they shall kill him, and the third day he shall be raised again. And they were exceeding sorry.

The Jews rejected and hated Jesus for his threat to their natural power granted to them by Rome. They had no understanding of what Jesus came to do. They knew He was the Christ, they could count the years to His promised coming (**Daniel 9**, 7-70's or 490 years from the Babylonian captivity. So they were looking for Him *, but He brought a Kingdom they did not want. He brought and confirmed a "Spiritual Kingdom" not a "natural, physical" kingdom where He would sit on a throne and rule as king. The thought of this physical Kingdom is what the national leadership was fearful of. They had no concept of a spiritual kingdom.

*Luke 2:25 And, behold, there was a man in Jerusalem, whose name was Simeon; and the same man was just and devout, waiting for the consolation of Israel: and the Holy Ghost was upon him. He would not see death, before he had seen the Lord's Christ 27 And he came by the Spirit into the temple: and when the parents brought in the child Jesus, to do for him after the custom of the law, 28 Then took he him up in his arms, and blessed God, and said,29 Lord, now lettest thou thy servant depart in peace, according to thy word:30 For mine eyes have seen thy salvation,

Luke 2:36 And there was one Anna, a prophetess, the daughter of Phanuel, of the tribe of Aser: she was of a great age, and had lived with an husband seven years from her virginity; 37And she was a widow of about fourscore and four years, which departed not from the temple, but severed God with fastings and prayers, night and day.38 And she coming in that instant gave thanks likewise unto the Lord, and39 spake of him to all them that looked for redemption in Jerusalem.

These verses confirm that the Jews in Jesus' day knew the time span to the coming of Jesus and were looking for Him. Again, they could count the years prophesied for the coming of the Christ Jesus.

Matthew 18:1 At the same time came the disciples unto Jesus, saying, Who is the greatest in the kingdom of heaven?2 And Jesus called a little child unto him, and set him in the midst of them,3 And said, Verily I say unto you, Except ye be converted, and become as little children, ye shall not enter into the kingdom of heaven.4 Whosoever therefore shall humble himself as this little child, the same is greatest in the kingdom of heaven. 5 And whoso shall receive one such little child in my name receiveth me. 6 But whoso shall offend one of these little ones which

believe in me, it were better for him that a millstone were hanged about his neck, and that he were drowned in the depth of the sea.

To enter into the Kingdom of heaven you must be a follower of Jesus, and to be a follower you must have repented and been made sin free, even as children are free of the guilt of sin and have a pure faith. If you reject anyone who belongs to Jesus you will be rejected. If you attack, persecute, or in any way harm a Christian, your end will be worse than your beginning. Now you must ask yourself: have the Pharisees, the leadership, and the nation of Israel done this by rejecting and then having Jesus killed? Can they enter into the kingdom of Heaven without believing in Jesus? Have they been thrown into the sea with a millstone around their necks? Or you might say: "destroyed as a nation"? Yes they Have by God destroying the nation of Israel in 70 A.D. The really sad thing is they are still in a state of denial of Jesus as the Son of God. So do you really think that God is blessing them in this day and age?

Matthew 21:12 And Jesus went into the temple of God, and cast out all them that sold and bought in the temple, and overthrew the tables of the moneychangers, and the seats of them that sold doves,13 And said unto them, It is written, My house shall be called the house of prayer; but ye have made it a den of thieves.

Mark 11:15 And they come to Jerusalem: and Jesus went into the temple, and began to cast out them that sold and bought in the temple, and overthrew the tables of the moneychangers, and the seats of them that sold doves;16 And would not suffer that any man should carry any vessel through the temple.17 And he taught, saying unto them, Is it not written, My house shall be called of all nations the house of prayer? but ye have made it a den of thieves.

Luke 19:45 And he went into the temple, and began to cast out them that sold therein, and them that bought; 46 Saying unto them, It is written, My house is the house of prayer: but ye have made it a den of thieves.

John 2:13 And the Jews' passover was at hand, and Jesus went up to Jerusalem. 14 And found in the temple those that sold oxen and sheep and doves, and the changers of money sitting:15 And when he had made a scourge of small cords, he drove them all out of the temple, and the sheep, and the oxen; and poured out the changers' money, and overthrew the tables;16 And said unto them that sold doves, Take these things hence; make not my Father's house an house of merchandise.

This is one of the ways Jesus came against the power of the religious leadership of Israel. They made money, lots of it, from the people selling and exchanging money in the temple. By challenging the leadership in this way Jesus caused them to hate, and conspire against Him. Jesus also clamed to be the Son of God which made those in high positions gnash their teeth against Him. To them it was just one more reason to hate.

Do you think that these people who had so much hate for the Son of God would be respected and brought into the Kingdom of heaven by God the Father unless they repented, asked forgiveness, and accepted Jesus as the Christ? Or do you think that maybe God the Father would reject and destroy such a hateful people if they did not give up their hate?

Matthew 21:18 Now in the morning as he returned into the city, he hungered. 19 And when he saw a fig tree in the way, he came to it, and found nothing thereon, but leaves only, and said unto it, Let no fruit grow on thee henceforward for ever. And presently the fig tree withered away.

Here you see an example of what did happen to Israel. Israel had the law of God for 1500 years and the commission to spread the word of God to the rest of the world. Which they did not do, but kept it to themselves. They grew no fruit! Hence their commission was taken from them and given to the gentiles. Their tree withered and died and was thrown into the all consuming fire in 70 AD with the destruction of Jerusalem.

Matthew 21:28 But what think ye? A certain man had two sons; and he came to the first, and said, Son, go work to day in my vineyard.29 He answered and said, I will not: but afterward he repented, and went.30 And he came to the second, and said likewise. And he answered and said, I go, sir: and went not. 31 Whether of them twain did the will of his father? They say unto him, The first. Jesus saith unto them, Verily I say unto you, That the publicans and the harlots go into the kingdom of God before you.32 For John came unto you in the way of righteousness, and ye believed him not: but the publicans and the harlots believed him: and ye, when ye had seen it, repented not afterward, that ye might believe him.

The first son is everyone in the world that accepts, and believes in Jesus. They were sinners first and saved second. The second son is Israel. Is this not real clear? They accepted the law of God and then proceeded to break it constantly. The Nation of Israel did not do what God ordained them to do. God then turned to the unwashed sinners who believed, of the world and said, 'will you do as I command?' Do you believe that the Nation of Israel 2000+ years ago rejected Jesus and still does today? If so, what do you think God has done and will yet do?
    Heaven or Hell that is the question!!

Matthew 21:33 Hear another parable: There was a certain householder, which planted a vineyard, and hedged it round about, and digged a winepress in it, and built a tower, and let it out to husbandmen, and went into a far country: 34 And when the time of the fruit drew near, he sent his servants to the husbandmen, that they might receive the fruits of it. 35 And the husbandmen took his servants, and beat one, and killed another, and stoned another. 36 Again, he sent other servants more than the first: and they did unto them likewise. 37 But last of all he sent unto them his son, saying, They will reverence my son. 38 But when the husbandmen saw the son, they said among themselves, This is the heir; come, let us kill him, and let us seize on his inheritance.39 And they caught him, and cast him out of the vineyard, and slew him.40 When the lord therefore of the vineyard cometh, what will he do unto those husbandmen? 41 they say unto him, He will miserably destroy those wicked men, and will let out his vineyard unto other husbandmen, which shall render him the fruits in their seasons.

Luke 20:9 Then began he to speak to the people this parable; A certain man planted a vineyard, and let it forth to husbandmen, and went into a far country for a long time.10 And at the season he sent a servant to the husbandmen, that they should give him of the fruit of the vineyard: but the husbandmen beat him, and

sent him away empty.11 And again he sent another servant: and they beat him also, and entreated him shamefully, and sent him away empty. 12 And again he sent a third: and they wounded him also, and cast him out.13 Then said the lord of the vineyard, What shall I do? I will send my beloved son: it may be they will reverence him when they see him.14 But when the husbandmen saw him, they reasoned among themselves, saying, This is the heir: come, let us kill him, that the inheritance may be ours.15 So they cast him out of the vineyard, and killed him. What therefore shall the lord of the vineyard do unto them?16 He shall come and destroy these husbandmen, and shall give the vineyard to others. And when they heard it, they said, God forbid.

The householder / man is God the Father, the Husbandmen is Israel. God sent many many prophets and servants to Israel over the 1500 years of their existence, and they killed most if not all of them. The son of the householder is Jesus the Christ. Israel killed the Christ knowing who He was. Verse 41 in Matthew and verse 16 in Luke tells it all. Destruction! The "other Husbandmen" in verse 41 of Matthew is the Gentiles. Verse 16 in Luke shows us that the king / Lord (Jesus after the resurrection) came as the prince, as given in **Daniel chapter 9:27**, and destroyed Jerusalem in 70 AD for killing the Son (Jesus on the cross).

Matthew 21:42 Jesus saith unto them, Did ye never read in the scriptures, The stone which the builders rejected, the same is become the head of the corner: this is the Lord's doing, and it is marvellous in our eyes? 43 Therefore say I unto you, The kingdom of God shall be taken from you, and given to a nation bringing forth the fruits thereof. 44 And whosoever shall fall on this stone shall be broken: but on whomsoever it shall fall, it will grind him to powder.45 And when the chief priests and Pharisees had heard his parables, they perceived that he spake of them.

Mark 12:10 And have ye not read this scripture; The stone which the builders rejected is become the head of the corner:11 This was the Lord's doing, and it is marvellous in our eyes?

This is real simple. Reject Jesus and you will be rejected! The builders are the Jews and by them rejecting the corner stone, Jesus, they will be destroyed. To be ground into powder sounds a lot like being destroyed, does it not?

The kingdom of God was then given to all that would, and still will, come to Jesus; this includes all natural Jews to this day, and to the Second Coming. After which there will be no more chances for anyone!!!! In verse 45 you can see exactly who Jesus is talking to and about.

Matthew 22:1 And Jesus answered and spake unto them again by parables, and said,2 The kingdom of heaven is like unto a certain king, which made a marriage for his son,3 And sent forth his servants to call them that were bidden to the wedding: and they would not come.4 Again, he sent forth other servants, saying, Tell them which are bidden, Behold, I have prepared my dinner: my oxen and my fatlings are killed, and all things are ready: come unto the marriage.5 But they made light of it, and went their ways, one to his farm, another to his merchandise:6 And the remnant took his servants, and entreated them spitefully, and slew them.7 But when the king

heard thereof, he was wroth: and he sent forth his armies, and destroyed those murderers, and burned up their city.8 Then saith he to his servants, The wedding is ready, but they which were bidden were not worthy.9 Go ye therefore into the highways, and as many as ye shall find, bid to the marriage. 10 So those servants went out into the highways, and gathered together all as many as they found, both bad and good: and the wedding was furnished with guests.11 And when the king came in to see the guests, he saw there a man which had not on a wedding garment:12 And he saith unto him, Friend, how camest thou in hither not having a wedding garment? And he was speechless.13 Then said the king to the servants, Bind him hand and foot, and take him away, and cast him into outer darkness, there shall be weeping and gnashing of teeth.14 For many are called, but few are chosen.

This is the marriage feast of Jesus. All men are invited, but first the Jews. You can see in verse 3-5 they had better things to do and money to make. In verse 6 you will see that Israel killed the prophets, servants, of God. Verses 7-8 describe the result of Israel's refusal to accept the Christ, which is the absolute destruction of their country, never to be formed again. The modern nation of Israel is not of God, but was put into place by man and Satan.

Verses 9-10 reveals who will receive the kingdom of God. Verses 11-14 tell us that we must be clothed in white robes, pure, without spot, and sinless, to get into the Kingdom. This is also called being holy and righteous, which we must be if we are to stay in the kingdom of God. This man without wedding clothes was kicked out because he was not sinless and by that we know that he did not come through the shed blood of Jesus to the wedding feast. In other words he was a gate crasher without the invitation given to all those saved by Jesus' blood. This man without wedding clothing was thrown into outer darkness, because he was an unrepentant sinner. We know this because he did not have on the wedding clothes of a white robe without spot or wrinkle.

Verse 14 is misunderstood in the fact that all are called but few MAKE THE FREE WIIL CHOICE FOR JESUS. To be chosen means that we must chose. This is what free will means. To be chosen means the we have the opportunity, have chosen, and we are approved of by God. I will not serve a God that picks and chooses who will and will not be saved no matter what you do or say.

Matthew 23:1 Then spake Jesus to the multitude, and to his disciples, 2 Saying, The scribes and the Pharisees sit in Moses' seat:3 All therefore whatsoever they bid you observe, that observe and do; but do not ye after their works: for they say, and do not.4 For they bind heavy burdens and grievous to be borne, and lay them on men's shoulders; but they themselves will not move them with one of their fingers.5 But all their works they do for to be seen of men: they make broad their phylacteries, and enlarge the borders of their garments,6 And love the uppermost rooms at feasts, and the chief seats in the synagogues,7 And greetings in the markets, and to be called of men, Rabbi, Rabbi.

Here is the example of who and what the Pharisees are. They believed in the saying "don't do as I do, do as I say". They were more concerned about building their reputations before men than what God wanted them to do as leaders of Israel. This is one of the reasons that they were cast out into outer darkness. The really sad thing is that they took the nation of Israel with them.

Matthew 23:13 But woe unto you, scribes and Pharisees, hypocrites! for ye shut up the kingdom of heaven against men: for ye neither go in yourselves, neither suffer ye them that are entering to go in. **14** Woe unto you, scribes and Pharisees, hypocrites! for ye devour widows' houses, and for a pretence make long prayer: therefore ye shall receive the greater damnation. **15** Woe unto you, scribes and Pharisees, hypocrites! for ye compass sea and land to make one proselyte, and when he is made, ye make him twofold more the child of hell than yourselves. **16** Woe unto you, ye blind guides, which say, Whosoever shall swear by the temple, it is nothing; but whosoever shall swear by the gold of the temple, he is a debtor! **17** Ye fools and blind: for whether is greater, the gold, or the temple that sanctifieth the gold? **18** And, Whosoever shall swear by the altar, it is nothing; but whosoever sweareth by the gift that is upon it, he is guilty. **19** Ye fools and blind: for whether is greater, the gift, or the altar that sanctifieth the gift? **20** Whoso therefore shall swear by the altar, sweareth by it, and by all things thereon. **21** And whoso shall swear by the temple, sweareth by it, and by him that dwelleth therein. **22** And he that shall swear by heaven, sweareth by the throne of God, and by him that sitteth thereon. **23** Woe unto you, scribes and Pharisees, hypocrites! for ye pay tithe of mint and anise and cummin, and have omitted the weightier matters of the law, judgment, mercy, and faith: these ought ye to have done, and not to leave the other undone. **24** Ye blind guides, which strain at a gnat, and swallow a camel. **25** Woe unto you, scribes and Pharisees, hypocrites! for ye make clean the outside of the cup and of the platter, but within they are full of extortion and excess. **26** Thou blind Pharisee, cleanse first that which is within the cup and platter, that the outside of them may be clean also. **27** Woe unto you, scribes and Pharisees, hypocrites! for ye are like unto whited sepulchres, which indeed appear beautiful outward, but are within full of dead men's bones, and of all uncleanness. **28** Even so ye also outwardly appear righteous unto men, but within ye are full of hypocrisy and iniquity. **29** Woe unto you, scribes and Pharisees, hypocrites! because ye build the tombs of the prophets, and garnish the sepulchres of the righteous, **30** And say, If we had been in the days of our fathers, we would not have been partakers with them in the blood of the prophets. **31** Wherefore ye be witnesses unto yourselves, that ye are the children of them which killed the prophets. **32** Fill ye up then the measure of your fathers. **33** Ye serpents, ye generation of vipers, how can ye escape the damnation of hell? **34** Wherefore, behold, I send unto you prophets, and wise men, and scribes: and some of them ye shall kill and crucify; and some of them shall ye scourge in your synagogues, and persecute them from city to city: **35** That upon you may come all the righteous blood shed upon the earth, from the blood of righteous Abel unto the blood of Zacharias son of Barachias, whom ye slew between the temple and the altar. **36** Verily I say unto you, All these things shall come upon this generation.

You can see that Jesus was completely disgusted with the leadership of Israel. They are guilty of shedding righteous blood and various other crimes against God and the people of Israel, so Jesus pronounces judgment (verse 35-36) upon them. They were so concerned about what people thought and how rich they could become that they made up their own laws contrary to what God's law says. This alone was cause enough to reject them, but they went even farther by rejecting the Christ they were supposed to be waiting for. In verse 36 Jesus is prophesying of the coming destruction of Jerusalem in 70 AD.

Matthew 23:37 O Jerusalem, Jerusalem, thou that killest the prophets, and stonest them which are sent unto thee, how often would I have gathered thy children together, even as a hen gathereth her chickens under her wings, and ye would not! 38 Behold, your house is left unto you desolate. 39 For I say unto you, Ye shall not see me henceforth, till ye shall say, Blessed is he that cometh in the name of the Lord.

Jesus mourns the fact that the nation of Israel has and will continue to reject Him. Notice that Jesus said that their, the Jew's, house is left "desolate" to them. This is the pronouncement of the divorce on the nation of Israel given by Jesus. To this day Israel is in this state of divorce, never to be a nation favored over others by God again. Do you really think that the modern nation of Israel was ordained into existence by God? Are not the natural Jews in the natural nation of Israel still rejecting Jesus? Do they not teach that the Christ has not yet come? As this is all true, why would God honor them and call them His chosen people? Paul tells us that the true Jew is a spiritual person not a natural one. You must know by now that the kingdom of God is SPIRITUAL not natural. The individual Jew can come back to God any time he/she wants to. All they have to do is accept Jesus as the Christ and believe.

A side light: God does not work through nations since the advent of the cross; salvation is now for individuals not nations. In fact; any individual, Jew or Gentile, hasthe same chance at salvation, but this salvation is only through Jesus the Christ (the Messiah). Jesus is the way. Praise the Lord!!

Matthew 25:1 Then shall the kingdom of heaven be likened unto ten virgins, which took their lamps, and went forth to meet the bridegroom. 2 And five of them were wise, and five were foolish. 3 They that were foolish took their lamps, and took no oil with them: 4 But the wise took oil in their vessels with their lamps. 5 While the bridegroom tarried, they all slumbered and slept. 6 And at midnight there was a cry made, Behold, the bridegroom cometh; go ye out to meet him. 7 Then all those virgins arose, and trimmed their lamps. 8 And the foolish said unto the wise, Give us of your oil; for our lamps are gone out. 9 But the wise answered, saying, Not so; lest there be not enough for us and you: but go ye rather to them that sell, and buy for yourselves. 10 And while they went to buy, the bridegroom came; and they that were ready went in with him to the marriage: and the door was shut. 11 Afterward came also the other virgins, saying, Lord, Lord, open to us. 12 But he answered and said, Verily I say unto you, I know you not. 13 Watch therefore, for ye know neither the day nor the hour wherein the Son of man cometh.

There are many teachings about this parable. What I want you to see is that the 5 foolish virgins represent the nation of Israel who did not come to Jesus for salvation, but relied on the old covenant of the law by which you could not be saved, plus they had the Holy Spirit residing with them only through the temple priests. The veil of the temple was torn beyond repair at the death of Jesus on the cross signifying that God no longer was with them and that animal sacrifice was no longer accepted. Their lamp no longer had the Spirit of God in it. The lamp was their temple which was destroyed in 70 AD. At this point they were left desolate, without God. After the act of the veil being torn, the only way to have the Holy Spirit in your lamp was to be born again to Jesus the Christ. This is the only way the natural Jew can fellowship with God from the cross to the second coming of Jesus. There are other valid meanings here but it is not in the scope of this study. These not so smart virgins, the unrepentant Jews, are rejected by God. Did they not reject Jesus first??

Bring this parable into todays meaning and the 5 stupid virgins are former Christians who have fallen back into sin and thereby have lost the Holy Spirit (Oil) in their lives. They are relying on past performance (which means nothing if you are in sin).

Matthew 25:14 For the kingdom of heaven is as a man travelling into a far country, who called his own servants, and delivered unto them his goods. 15 And unto one he gave five talents, to another two, and to another one; to every man according to his several ability; and straightway took his journey. 16 Then he that had received the five talents went and traded with the same, and made them other five talents. 17 And likewise he that had received two, he also gained other two. 18 But he that had received one went and digged in the earth, and hid his lord's money. 19 After a long time the lord of those servants cometh, and reckoneth with them. 20 And so he that had received five talents came and brought other five talents, saying, Lord, thou deliveredst unto me five talents: behold, I have gained beside them five talents more. 21 His lord said unto him, Well done, thou good and faithful servant: thou hast been faithful over a few things, I will make thee ruler over many things: enter thou into the joy of thy lord. 22 He also that had received two talents came and said, Lord, thou deliveredst unto me two talents: behold, I have gained two other talents beside them. 23 His lord said unto him, Well done, good and faithful servant; thou hast been faithful over a few things, I will make thee ruler over many things: enter thou into the joy of thy lord.

24 Then he which had received the one talent came and said, Lord, I knew thee that thou art an hard man, reaping where thou hast not sown, and gathering where thou hast not strawed: 25 And I was afraid, and went and hid thy talent in the earth: lo, there thou hast that is thine. 26 His lord answered and said unto him, Thou wicked and slothful servant, thou knewest that I reap where I sowed not, and gather where I have not strawed: 27 Thou oughtest therefore to have put my money to the exchangers, and then at my coming I should have received mine own with usury. 28 Take therefore the talent from him, and give it unto him which hath ten talents. 29 For unto every one that hath shall be given, and he shall have abundance: but from him that hath not shall be taken away even that which he hath. 30 And cast ye the unprofitable servant into outer darkness: there shall be weeping and gnashing of teeth.

Luke 19:12 He said therefore, A certain nobleman went into a far country to receive for himself a kingdom, and to return. 13 And he called his ten servants, and delivered them ten pounds, and said unto them, Occupy till I come. 14 But his citizens hated him, and sent a message after him, saying, We will not have this man to reign over us. 15 And it came to pass, that when he was returned, having received the kingdom, then he commanded these servants to be called unto him, to whom he had given the money, that he might know how much every man had gained by trading. 16 Then came the first, saying, Lord, thy pound hath gained ten pounds. 17 And he said unto him, Well, thou good servant: because thou hast been faithful in a very little, have thou authority over ten cities.18 And the second came, saying, Lord, thy pound hath gained five pounds.19 And he said likewise to him, Be thou also over five

cities. 20 And another came, saying, Lord, behold, here is thy pound, which I have kept laid up in a napkin: 21 For I feared thee, because thou art an austere man: thou takest up that thou layedst not down, and reapest that thou didst not sow. 22 And he saith unto him, Out of thine own mouth will I judge thee, thou wicked servant. Thou knewest that I was an austere man, taking up that I laid not down, and reaping that I did not sow: 23 Wherefore then gavest not thou my money into the bank, that at my coming I might have required mine own with usury? 24 And he said unto them that stood by, Take from him the pound, and give it to him that hath ten pounds. 25 (And they said unto him, Lord, he hath ten pounds.) 26 For I say unto you, That unto every one which hath shall be given; and from him that hath not, even that he hath shall be taken away from him. 27 But those mine enemies, which would not that I should reign over them, bring hither, and slay them before me.

The difference between these two parables is in Luke, verse 14 &27. You must understand that it is Israel Jesus is talking about, and that the people there hated and rejected Him, and their end is to be slain before the King (Jesus). Can you say destroyed, done away with, rejected. This was done in 70AD by the Roman army.

The Jewish people as nation did not carry God's command to witness to the world just as the man with one pound talent did not do as he knew his master wanted him to do. This is simple. Use what God gives you in the fashion that He dictates. You can say "make fruit". The problem was that Israel did not spread the word of God to the world and so is represented by the fearful man who hid His talent in the ground. The punishment is the same for both. To have taken away "even what you don't have" is to have your chance for salvation taken from you. You must reject Jesus, your chance for salvation, for it to be taken from you in the first place, and you will no longer any chance for salvation. This means that you on longer have a chance at what you had before you rejected Jesus, which is salvation.

This man (Israel) with one pound was saved and then rejected Jesus by not doing what he knew his master wanted, thereby; losing his salvation and any further chance at repentance. The first two men (the individual Jews who accepted Jesus and where saved) to receive talents or pounds of gold were rewarded because they were obedient to the king by doing what He commanded. Are you?

Matthew 27:46 And about the ninth hour Jesus cried with a loud voice, saying, Eli, Eli, lama sabachthani? that is to say, My God, my God, why hast thou forsaken me?

Mark 15:34 And at the ninth hour Jesus cried with a loud voice, saying, Eloi, Eloi, lama sabachthani? which is, being interpreted, My God, my God, why hast thou forsaken me?

I put this explanation in this study because it is so misunderstood and is the basis for a real dangerous and incorrect teaching in the modern church. What this should say is "for this was I spared"*. It is the cross Jesus was talking about. Check out the Greek and you will see the wrong of the translation used today. Like the prayer in the garden when He said, "take this cup from me, but not my will but yours". All this means is that he was praying not to be killed before He went to the cross. The Jews had tried to kill

Him 10 times before He went to the cross. Why would Jesus want to get out of the cross, it was what He came to do. The correct saying " for this I was spared"* also puts a lie to the teaching that Jesus was literally made to be sin in some manner or the other. I've never had any one explain to me by what process He was to be made a sinner. Or how, if He was made to be a sinner, He remained sinless, holy, and pure which He need to be for His sacrifice to be accepted by God the father as payment for the sins of the world.

* This comes from the ancient eastern (Greek orthodox) text translated by George M. Lamsa. This bible was written in Aramaic the Language of Jesus. The name of this bible is the 'Peshitta'.

Mark 1:14 Now after that John was put in prison, Jesus came into Galilee, preaching the gospel of the kingdom of God,15 And saying, The time is fulfilled, and the kingdom of God is at hand: repent ye, and believe the gospel.

Jesus came preaching that "the time was fulfilled". This literally meant that the time of the Christ was at hand NOW. The Jews understood this, and still rejected Him.

Mark 2:6 But there was certain of the scribes sitting there, and reasoning in their hearts, 7 Why doth this man thus speak blasphemies? who can forgive sins but God only? 8 And immediately when Jesus perceived in his spirit that they so reasoned within themselves, he said unto them, Why reason ye these things in your hearts? 9 Whether is it easier to say to the sick of the palsy, Thy sins be forgiven thee; or to say, Arise, and take up thy bed, and walk? 10 But that ye may know that the Son of man hath power on earth to forgive sins, (he saith to the sick of the palsy,) 11 I say unto thee, Arise, and take up thy bed, and go thy way into thine house.

Jesus uses this healing to show the Jews He was talking to that He was, and is, God who can heal, and most importantly forgive sins.

You cannot say that the leadership or most of the common Jews of that day did not know who and what Jesus was, but they where real confused as to what He came to do.

They wanted and expected a physical king and kingdom, which Jesus did not come to bring. This is also one of three times that Jesus forgives sin before He goes to the cross. Would he command us not to sin if we couldn't obey that command? I think not!

Mark 2: 21 No man also seweth a piece of new cloth on an old garment: else the new piece that filled it up taketh away from the old, and the rent is made worse.22 And no man putteth new wine into old bottles: else the new wine doth burst the bottles, and the wine is spilled, and the bottles will be marred: but new wine must be put into new bottles.

Luke 5:36 And he spake also a parable unto them; No man putteth a piece of a new garment upon an old; if otherwise, then both the new maketh a rent, and the piece that was taken out of the new agreeth not with the old.37 And no man putteth new wine into old bottles; else the new wine will burst the bottles, and be spilled, and the bottles shall perish.38 But new wine must be put into new bottles; and both are preserved.

Jesus is telling the Jews that the old covenant of the law of sin and death is to be changed to the new covenant of grace and love. A change that the leadership felt threatened by. They reacted to this perceived threat by killing Jesus who was their only hope.

Mark 2:23 And it came to pass, that he went through the corn fields on the sabbath day; and his disciples began, as they went, to pluck the ears of corn. 24 And the Pharisees said unto him, Behold, why do they on the sabbath day that which is not lawful? 25 And he said unto them, Have ye never read what David did, when he had need, and was an hungred, he, and they that were with him? 26 How he went into the house of God in the days of Abiathar the high priest, and did eat the shewbread, which is not lawful to eat but for the priests, and gave also to them which were with him? 27 And he said unto them, The sabbath was made for man, and not man for the sabbath: 28 Therefore the Son of man is Lord also of the sabbath.

The point I would like to make here is that Jesus was taking all of the old law that the religious leadership of Israel had instituted, and was making it null and void. He was changing things from the natural to the spiritual, and they saw this as a loss of power and a threat to their existence. Verses 27 and 28 show us, the spiritual Jews, that the Sabbath is not set on any one day. As long as you pick a day of the week, and set it aside to rest and worship God it's OK with God. Again Jesus' actions really made the leadership of the day upset with Him. They felt 'what right does he have to break and change the law' that they based their whole lives on. This was one more straw that hardened their hearts, and increased their fear horrendously.

He also told them exactly who He was.

Mark 4:24 And he said unto them, Take heed what ye hear: with what measure ye mete, it shall be measured to you: and unto you that hear shall more be given. 25 For he that hath, to him shall be given: and he that hath not, from him shall be taken even that which he hath.

Luke 8:18 Take heed therefore how ye hear: for whosoever hath, to him shall be given; and whosoever hath not, from him shall be taken even that which he seemeth to have.

Listen to the truth, repeat only the truth. What you do, truth or lie, will be charged to your account. This is what Jesus is telling the Jews of 2000 years ago and us, the spiritual Jew, today. Jesus is saying that He is telling them the truth, and if you don't listen you will be judged. This message was real relevant for the natural Jew and the nation Israel then as it is today for the whole world. They were judged in 70 A.D. The chance, for all people, for salvation goes away forever when you die, or at the Second Coming of Jesus. This chance is described in verse 18. Jesus told the Jews "I am the way and the light", "I am the bread of life", and many more statements proclaiming that salvation was now through Him. This salvation through Jesus is a new thing to the nation of Israel, and it is very different from the LAW that they had been obeying for 1500 years, and they are full of fear. Again what they did not have at that point, because of the rejection of Jesus after knowing full well who He was, a chance for salvation.

Mark 7:5 Then the Pharisees and scribes asked him, Why walk not thy disciples according to the tradition of the elders, but eat bread with unwashen hands? 6 He answered and said unto them, Well hath Esaias prophesied of you hypocrites, as it is written, This people honoureth me with their lips, but their heart is far from me. 7 Howbeit in vain do they worship me, teaching for doctrines the commandments of men. 8 For laying aside the commandment of God, ye hold the tradition of men, as the washing of pots and cups: and many other such like things ye do. 9 And he said unto them, Full well ye reject the commandment of God, that ye may keep your own tradition. 10 For Moses said, Honour thy father and thy mother; and, Whoso curseth father or mother, let him die the death: 11 But ye say, If a man shall say to his father or mother, It is Corban, that is to say, a gift, by whatsoever thou mightest be profited by me; he shall be free. 12 And ye suffer him no more to do ought for his father or his mother; 13 Making the word of God of none effect through your tradition, which ye have delivered: and many such like things do ye.

You, can see here that Jesus is showing how the Pharisees and scribes are not following God's law, but only giving "LIP SERVICE." They are teaching the doctrines of men contrary to God's doctrine, rejecting the true law of God. Holding up the traditions of men instead of what God would have them do. Disrespecting the word of God. Notice He calls the "Hypocrites". How can you believe that God would honor such people, even today, or hold them above all other peoples of the world, especially the "born again Christians" who do honor God's word and follow His dictates?

Mark 8:15 And he charged them, saying, Take heed, beware of the leaven of the Pharisees, and of the leaven of Herod.

Take heed and beware means "look out there's danger here"! The contrary doctrine of the Pharisees, and king Herod who supported the Pharisees, is poison to the believer of Jesus. If the leadership of the nation of Israel was spewing out the poison of man's doctrine, do you think God would honor them as a people and nation even to this day?

Mark 8:38 Whosoever therefore shall be ashamed of me and of my words in this adulterous and sinful generation; of him also shall the Son of man be ashamed, when he cometh in the glory of his Father with the holy angels.

Luke 9:26 For whosoever shall be ashamed of me and of my words, of him shall the Son of man be ashamed, when he shall come in his own glory, and in his Father's, and of the holy angels.

I hope you're not in this position, the same position National Israel was and is in today. Can you imagine? To be called ashamed of by Jesus! Is this not a rejection? Putting away of? Denial of? Casting off of? How many ways can I say it and get you the reader to believe that God "Divorced" the nation of Israel!!!!

Mark 12:1 And he began to speak unto them by parables. A certain man planted a vineyard, and set an hedge about it, and digged a place for the winefat, and built a tower, and let it out to husbandmen, and went into a far country. 2 And at the season he sent to the husbandmen a servant, that he might receive from the husbandmen of the fruit of the vineyard. 3 And they caught him, and beat him,

and sent him away empty. 4 And again he sent unto them another servant; and at him they cast stones, and wounded him in the head, and sent him away shamefully handled. 5 And again he sent another; and him they killed, and many others; beating some, and killing some. 6 Having yet therefore one son, his well beloved, he sent him also last unto them, saying, They will reverence my son. 7 But those husbandmen said among themselves, This is the heir; come, let us kill him, and the inheritance shall be ours. 8 And they took him, and killed him, and cast him out of the vineyard. 9 What shall therefore the lord of the vineyard do? he will come and destroy the husbandmen, and will give the vineyard unto others.

"A certain man", God, commissioned a group of people to do a job for HIM and when He sent servants to receive the end product, and they killed them. The "man" then sent his Son and they killed Him too. What should this "man" do to this group of people? What would you do? Replace them with other people that would and will follow your orders? This is what God did to the nation of Israel in 70 AD! Jesus is the son that was killed, and the servants who were killed were the Old Test prophets. The people who killed all these Prophets and messengers from God is the nation of Israel.

Mark 12:28 And one of the scribes came, and having heard them reasoning together, and perceiving that he had answered them well, asked him, Which is the first commandment of all? 29 And Jesus answered him, The first of all the commandments is, Hear, O Israel; The Lord our God is one Lord: 30 And thou shalt love the Lord thy God with all thy heart, and with all thy soul, and with all thy mind, and with all thy strength: this is the first commandment. 31 And the second is like, namely this, Thou shalt love thy neighbour as thyself. There is none other commandment greater than these. 32 And the scribe said unto him, Well, Master, thou hast said the truth: for there is one God; and there is none other but he:
    33 And to love him with all the heart, and with all the understanding, and with all the soul, and with all the strength, and to love his neighbour as himself, is more than all whole burnt offerings and sacrifices. 34 And when Jesus saw that he answered discreetly, he said unto him, Thou art not far from the kingdom of God. And no man after that durst ask him any question.

Mark 12:37 David therefore himself calleth him Lord; and whence is he then his son? And the common people heard him gladly.

You can see by these verses that there were some, even in leadership positions, who believed in the truth if God. Not all were hypocrites.

Mark12:38 And he said unto them in his doctrine, Beware of the scribes, which love to go in long clothing, and love salutations in the marketplaces,39 And the chief seats in the synagogues, and the uppermost rooms at feasts:40 Which devour widows' houses, and for a pretence make long prayers: these shall receive greater damnation.

Here we see a different attitude toward the scribes (lawyers), and toward the group as a whole. "Beware"! What does this mean? A strong warning stay away from, have no contact with, reject from your circle of friends. These are not good people, and they are in leadership positions. Do you think they are doing the will of God? Can you believe that God has rejected these people of 2000 years ago? Do you think that God will not, or has not rejected the same people today, be they Jew or Gentile?

Mark 14:48 And Jesus answered and said unto them, Are ye come out, as against a thief, with swords and with staves to take me? 49 I was daily with you in the temple teaching, and ye took me not: but the scriptures must be fulfilled.

You get the feeling that the leadership of Israel did not want the general population to know that they had arrested Jesus. Were they afraid of the common people? It certainly seems that way.

Luke 4:16 And he came to Nazareth, where he had been brought up: and, as his custom was, he went into the synagogue on the sabbath day, and stood up for to read. 17 And there was delivered unto him the book of the prophet Esaias. And when he had opened the book, he found the place where it was written,
18 The Spirit of the Lord is upon me, because he hath anointed me to preach the gospel to the poor; he hath sent me to heal the brokenhearted, to preach deliverance to the captives, and recovering of sight to the blind, to set at liberty them that are bruised, 19 To preach the acceptable year of the Lord. 20 And he closed the book, and he gave it again to the minister, and sat down. And the eyes of all them that were in the synagogue were fastened on him. 21 And he began to say unto them, This day is this scripture fulfilled in your ears.

This is an announcement to the people that He, Jesus, is the Christ. As you read the next few scriptures you will see the attitude of the people He just read the scriptures to. They tried to kill Him. This is real strong rejection. This attitude continued throughout Jesus' 3 1/2 years of ministry. Remember what Jesus said about being ashamed of them? Look up the word ashamed in the Greek.

Luke 5:20 And when he saw their faith, he said unto him, Man, thy sins are forgiven thee. 21 And the scribes and the Pharisees began to reason, saying, Who is this which speaketh blasphemies? Who can forgive sins, but God alone? 22 But when Jesus perceived their thoughts, he answering said unto them, What reason ye in your hearts? 23 Whether is easier, to say, Thy sins be forgiven thee; or to say, Rise up and walk? 24 But that ye may know that the Son of man hath power upon earth to forgive sins, (he said unto the sick of the palsy,) I say unto thee, Arise, and take up thy couch, and go into thine house. 25 And immediately he rose up before them, and took up that whereon he lay, and departed to his own house, glorifying God. 26 And they were all amazed, and they glorified God, and were filled with fear, saying, We have seen strange things to day.

Jesus announces again that He is the Christ and proves it by healing the man let down through the roof. They glorify God, but do they really believe? Why would they call this strange when they are familiar with healing from God through the priests in the temple?

Luke 6:39 And he spake a parable unto them, Can the blind lead the blind? shall they not both fall into the ditch?

Can the godless lead the godless to God? I doubt it. The Pharisees had given over God's rule for theirs, they were Godless. How could they lead Israel in God's laws when they made their own laws. They rejected God the Father and His Son the Christ. The only place they could lead anybody was to hell. The modern nation of Israel is in the same position. BUT "if" they change, and accept Jesus as the Christ, they would be fantastic leaders to bring the world to Jesus.

Luke 6:43 For a good tree bringeth not forth corrupt fruit; neither doth a corrupt tree bring forth good fruit. 44 For every tree is known by his own fruit. For of thorns men do not gather figs, nor of a bramble bush gather they grapes. 45 A good man out of the good treasure of his heart bringeth forth that which is good; and an evil man out of the evil treasure of his heart bringeth forth that which is evil: for of the abundance of the heart his mouth speaketh.

Good tree, bad tree, which do you think the Nation of Israel is? They rejected Jesus as the Christ and did not spread the word of God to the world, so which one is it to be? Good or Bad? You can not bring people to God by a bad example. Your heart can only be good or bad. And what is in your heart comes out your mouth. The Pharisees condemned Jesus with their mouths, where do you think their hearts were?

Luke 6:46 And why call ye me, Lord, Lord, and do not the things which I say? 47 Whosoever cometh to me, and heareth my sayings, and doeth them, I will shew you to whom he is like: 48 He is like a man which built an house, and digged deep, and laid the foundation on a rock: and when the flood arose, the stream beat vehemently upon that house, and could not shake it: for it was founded upon a rock. 49 But he that heareth, and doeth not, is like a man that without a foundation built an house upon the earth; against which the stream did beat vehemently, and immediately it fell; and the ruin of that house was great.

We as Christians understand that the rock of the foundation of our Christian life is Jesus! Our house stands firm as long as we do not undercut our foundation with sin. Now take a look at Israel, where is their foundation? Do you think on sand? I think so. They as a nation were washed away by the flood of the Roman Empire in 70 AD never to be back into God's good graces. Their house was completely destroyed. Their only chance, to this day, is to rebuild on the foundation of Jesus, which they can do any time they want to change their mind about Jesus as the Christ.

Luke 7:22 Then Jesus answering said unto them, Go your way, and tell John what things ye have seen and heard; how that the blind see, the lame walk, the lepers are cleansed, the deaf hear, the dead are raised, to the poor the gospel is preached. 23 And blessed is he, whosoever shall not be offended in me.

Jesus told this to the disciples of John the Baptist in public. Jesus did not keep secrets from the public. So all that were near heard what He said. Jesus is telling John that He is the Christ. This is one of the many times that Jesus told the people of Israel who He really was.

Luke 7:40 And Jesus answering said unto him, Simon, I have somewhat to say unto thee. And he saith, Master, say on. 41 There was a certain creditor which had

two debtors: the one owed five hundred pence, and the other fifty. 42 And when they had nothing to pay, he frankly forgave them both. Tell me therefore, which of them will love him most? 43 Simon answered and said, I suppose that he, to whom he forgave most. And he said unto him, Thou hast rightly judged.

Who do you think Jesus is talking about here? Do you think it is the Jews and the Gentiles? I think so. So who owes more? The gentiles who never had God, or the Jews who knew God but disobeyed Him, and claimed righteousness through the law. What did Jesus say: "I came for the sinner not the righteous".

Luke 11:29 And when the people were gathered thick together, he began to say, This is an evil generation: they seek a sign; and there shall no sign be given it, but the sign of Jonas the prophet.30 For as Jonas was a sign unto the Ninevites, so shall also the Son of man be to this generation.31 The queen of the south shall rise up in the judgment with the men of this generation, and condemn them: for she came from the utmost parts of the earth to hear the wisdom of Solomon; and, behold, a greater than Solomon is here.32 The men of Nineve shall rise up in the judgment with this generation, and shall condemn it: for they repented at the preaching of Jonas; and, behold, a greater than Jonas is here.

An evil generation, what a statement! This was a prevalent attitude in Israel, predominately among the leadership. Probably the only reason that they followed Jesus around was for food and entertainment. This is why He called them evil. Jesus tells how, and by whom, they will be condemned for their attitude. He also tells them that He, the Christ, is there and he is a whole lot better than Jonas was.

Luke 11:33 No man, when he hath lighted a candle, putteth it in a secret place, neither under a bushel, but on a candlestick, that they which come in may see the light.

This is just what the Jews didn't do, they hid the word of God from the world. In a sense they hid the light of God's mercy. This was in direct disobedience to God's will for the nation of Israel. If you were God would you be happy with this people? What is the one thing God demands of all who would be part of His family? Obedience to His commands, do Ya think? The nation of Israel "did it their way", and are now suffering for it.

Luke 11:37 And as he spake, a certain Pharisee besought him to dine with him: and he went in, and sat down to meat. 38 And when the Pharisee saw it, he marvelled that he had not first washed before dinner. 39 And the Lord said unto him, Now do ye Pharisees make clean the outside of the cup and the platter; but your inward part is full of ravening and wickedness.40 Ye fools, did not he that made that which is without make that which is within also? 41 But rather give alms of such things as ye have; and, behold, all things are clean unto you. 42 But woe unto you, Pharisees! for ye tithe mint and rue and all manner of herbs, and pass over judgment and the love of God: these ought ye to have done, and not to leave the other undone. 43 Woe unto you, Pharisees! for ye love the uppermost seats in the synagogues, and greetings in the markets. 44 Woe unto you, scribes and Pharisees, hypocrites! for ye are as graves which appear not, and the men that walk over them are not aware of them.

45 Then answered one of the lawyers, and said unto him, Master, thus saying thou reproachest us also. 46 And he said, Woe unto you also, ye lawyers! for ye lade men with burdens grievous to be borne, and ye yourselves touch not the burdens with one of your fingers. 47 Woe unto you! for ye build the sepulchres of the prophets, and your fathers killed them. 48 Truly ye bear witness that ye allow the deeds of your fathers: for they indeed killed them, and ye build their sepulchres. 49 Therefore also said the wisdom of God, I will send them prophets and apostles, and some of them they shall slay and persecute: 50 That the blood of all the prophets, which was shed from the foundation of the world, may be required of this generation; 51 From the blood of Abel unto the blood of Zacharias which perished between the altar and the temple: verily I say unto you, It shall be required of this generation. 52 Woe unto you, lawyers! for ye have taken away the key of knowledge: ye entered not in yourselves, and them that were entering in ye hindered. 53 And as he said these things unto them, the scribes and the Pharisees began to urge him vehemently, and to provoke him to speak of many things:54 Laying wait for him, and seeking to catch something out of his mouth, that they might accuse him.

Jesus is telling the Pharisees, scribes (lawyers) just what is wrong in their lives and how they have bastardized the word and intentions of God for Israel. He is saying that they are an anti-God system. The people at the dinner with Jesus now were looking for anything to use to get rid of Him once and for all. This shows how much they rejected God the Father, and now were going after His Son. These people were the leadership and their attitude was reflected by a great majority of the Jews, and still is today. As far as I can see this is cause enough for God the Father to reject and destroy the nation of Israel.

By the way, there is no great plan of salvation, separate from Jesus, anywhere in the New Testament. Some teach that the verses that say the natural branch can be grafted back in is that plan. This is a lie. The natural Jew today has the same chance that we, the rest of the world, have. It's called Give it up for Jesus! The vine is Jesus, who is the only way to the Father.

Luke 12:1 In the mean time, when there were gathered together an innumerable multitude of people, insomuch that they trode one upon another, he began to say unto his disciples first of all, Beware ye of the leaven of the Pharisees, which is hypocrisy.

Do I really need to explain this?

Luke 12:8 Also I say unto you, Whosoever shall confess me before men, him shall the Son of man also confess before the angels of God: 9 But he that denieth me before men shall be denied before the angels of God.

This is right in your face. It's real simple, either you are or you ain't of God. Did the Pharisees, scribes (lawyers) confess Jesus before men? I think not! As Jesus said: if you're not for Me you're against me! What a statement. It is as valid today as it was then. Where do you think the leadership of Israel was, for Him or against Him? What do you think it means to be denied before the angels of God? Can you say rejection, destruction, casting into outer darkness with weeping and gnashing of teeth, being tossed into hell?

Luke 13:6 He spake also this parable; A certain man had a fig tree planted in his vineyard; and he came and sought fruit thereon, and found none. 7 Then said he unto the dresser of his vineyard, Behold, these three years I come seeking fruit on this fig tree, and find none: cut it down; why cumbereth it the ground? 8 And he answering said unto him, Lord, let it alone this year also, till I shall dig about it, and dung it: 9 And if it bear fruit, well: and if not, then after that thou shalt cut it down.

This parable is pointed directly at the nation of Israel. The "man" is God the Father, the "fig tree" is Israel; "the dresser", the gardener, is Jesus. The year of digging and dunging is Jesus' 3 ½ years of ministry to Israel. Israel did not bear fruit; they did ignore the fertilizer added to them by Jesus' ministry for 3 ½ years! Israel was rejected and divorced by God for their rejection of Him and His Son Jesus.

To be "cut down" means the Nation and Temple of Israel were destroyed by the Roman army in 70 A.D.. Never -by the Grace of God the Father- to be rebuilt. If you think that God the Father ordained the establishment, in 1948, of the new Nation of Israel, and the future rebuilding of the Temple, you must ask yourself "have the Jewish people on a whole changed their attitude toward Jesus as the Messiah, and if not why would God reward this rebellious people with a new Nation and Temple? The Temple is another problem! As Jesus was the last and perfect sacrifice, would not a new temple and animal sacrifices be a slap in Jesus' face? Think about it and you will see the logic of this. There is and never was a prophecy in the New Testament of a new Nation or rebuilt Temple in 1948 or any other year. If you desire to trash the bible you can go to the Old Testament and bring up prophecy, that has been fulfilled, and make it say whatever you want about Israel! When Jesus said on the cross "it is Finished", He meant all Old Testament prophecy was fulfilled by Him.

Luke 13:24 Strive to enter in at the strait gate: for many, I say unto you, will seek to enter in, and shall not be able. 25 When once the master of the house is risen up, and hath shut to the door, and ye begin to stand without, and to knock at the door, saying, Lord, Lord, open unto us; and he shall answer and say unto you, I know you not whence ye are: 26 Then shall ye begin to say, We have eaten and drunk in thy presence, and thou hast taught in our streets. 27 But he shall say, I tell you, I know you not whence ye are; depart from me, all ye workers of iniquity. 28 There shall be weeping and gnashing of teeth, when ye shall see Abraham, and Isaac, and Jacob, and all the prophets, in the kingdom of God, and you yourselves thrust out. 29 And they shall come from the east, and from the west, and from the north, and from the south, and shall sit down in the kingdom of God. 30 And, behold, there are last which shall be first, and there are first which shall be last.

The straight gate is Jesus, and he is the ONLY way to enter into the kingdom of God period. This is for Israel as well for anyone in the world who wants to come to the Father in heaven. You must be sin free to enter the kingdom of God, this is done by entering in through the narrow gate (the only way is what makes it narrow), which is Jesus. It is his shed blood on the cross that makes possible the removal of sin from your conscience. This makes you sin free, which is the only condition for entry into the Spiritual Kingdom of God. Verses 28&29 are especially for the Jews. Jesus is telling the Jews that the kingdom of God will be given to the gentiles and that they will have no part in it, because of their iniquity. 'The last will be first" is the gentiles and "the first will be last" is the Jews. Remember Jesus said that he came to the Jews first, after they rejected Him the kingdom was given to the Gentiles.

Luke 13:34 O Jerusalem, Jerusalem, which killest the prophets, and stonest them that are sent unto thee; how often would I have gathered thy children together, as a hen doth gather her brood under her wings, and ye would not! 35 Behold, your house is left unto you desolate: and verily I say unto you, Ye shall not see me, until the time come when ye shall say, Blessed is he that cometh in the name of the Lord.

Here is the actual pronouncement of divorce on the nation of Israel! Jesus came to bring and confirm the New Testament covenant of the Spirit and Grace. The people of Israel, as a nation, rejected and even killed Jesus for doing God's will.

They had a history of rejecting God and all the prophets He sent to them with a call to repentance. Yes, on occasion they did repent, but for the most part they "did it their way", not God's way. Jesus was the last straw for them to finally "do it Gods way". They refused!

The word desolate is not a word I would want used about me, but here it is being told to Israel. Jesus also gives the conditions that MUST be met for the desolation to be removed from them. Jesus says that they will NOT see Him, "GOD", until they relent of their stubbornness. Do you think that modern Israel has relented and accepted GOD JESUS? Have they changed their stubbornness for willingness? I think not! Do you think God blesses the modern nation of Israel? Why would He? They still reject Him and His Son?

Luke 14:16 Then said he unto him, A certain man made a great supper, and bade many: 17 And sent his servant at supper time to say to them that were bidden, Come; for all things are now ready. 18 And they all with one consent began to make excuse. The first said unto him, I have bought a piece of ground, and I must needs go and see it: I pray thee have me excused. 19 And another said, I have bought five yoke of oxen, and I go to prove them: I pray thee have me excused. 20 And another said, I have married a wife, and therefore I cannot come. 21 So that servant came, and shewed his lord these things. Then the master of the house being angry said to his servant, Go out quickly into the streets and lanes of the city, and bring in hither the poor, and the maimed, and the halt, and the blind. 22 And the servant said, Lord, it is done as thou hast commanded, and yet there is room. 23 And the lord said unto the servant, Go out into the highways and hedges, and compel them to come in, that my house may be filled. 24 For I say unto you, That none of those men which were bidden shall taste of my supper.

This is the same as in Matthew 22:1-14 with a few differences, but the meaning is the same. The "MAN" is God the Father and the supper is the wedding feast of the Bridegroom who is Jesus. The first to be invited are the Jews. They promptly tell God not to bother them, that they are to busy. The "MAN" then invites all the people of the world to join Him in this meal. The "MAN" then rejects those who were to busy with their own affairs to bother to accept the invitation for the feast. This is also a pronouncement of divorce or rejection on the nation of Israel. They, the Jews, were called first just as the invitation for the feast went to them first, and the world second.

Luke 16:11-15 If therefore ye have not been faithful in the unrighteous mammon, who will commit to your trust the true *riches*? And if ye have not been faithful in that which is another man's, who shall give you that which is your own? No servant can serve two masters: for either he will hate the one, and love the other; or else he will hold to the one, and despise the other. Ye cannot serve God and mammon. And the Pharisees also, who were covetous, heard all these things: and they derided him. And he said unto them, Ye are they which justify yourselves before men; but God knoweth your hearts: for that which is highly esteemed among men is abomination in the sight of God.

Here is another example of Jesus telling the Pharisees that they were not worthy of God. The Pharisees put the praise of men and things of the world before the love for and obedience to God the Father. In verse 14 we can see just what the Pharisees loved then and today, whether they be Jew or Gentile.

Can you say Mammon instead of God? Is it any wonder that they hated Jesus? You can see how God feels about this kind of attitude.

Luke 19:32 And they that were sent went their way, and found even as he had said unto them. 33 And as they were loosing the colt, the owners thereof said unto them, Why loose ye the colt? 34 And they said, The Lord hath need of him. 35 And they brought him to Jesus: and they cast their garments upon the colt, and they set Jesus thereon. 36 And as he went, they spread their clothes in the way. 37 And when he was come nigh, even now at the descent of the mount of Olives, the whole multitude of the disciples began to rejoice and praise God with a loud voice for all the mighty works that they had seen; 38 Saying, Blessed be the King that cometh in the name of the Lord: peace in heaven, and glory in the highest. 39 And some of the Pharisees from among the multitude said unto him, Master, rebuke thy disciples. 40 And he answered and said unto them, I tell you that, if these should hold their peace, the stones would immediately cry out.

These verses tell us that not all of Israel hated and rejected Jesus, but the majority of the leadership and the people did hate and reject Him. Even at His entry into Jerusalem the Pharisees where trying to down play Him and His message.

Luke 19:41 And when he was come near, he beheld the city, and wept over it, 42 Saying, If thou hadst known, even thou, at least in this thy day, the things which belong unto thy peace! but now they are hid from thine eyes. 43 For the days shall come upon thee, that thine enemies shall cast a trench about thee, and compass thee round, and keep thee in on every side, 44 And shall lay thee even with the ground, and thy children within thee; and they shall not leave in thee one stone upon another; because thou knewest not the time of thy visitation.

Jesus is prophesying over Jerusalem, proclaiming the destruction that was coming to them in 70 AD. All this destruction that Jesus described is exactly what the Roman army did to Jerusalem. All this was hidden from the Jews because they chose not to believe that Jesus was the Christ.

Luke 20:17 And he beheld them, and said, What is this then that is written, The stone which the builders rejected, the same is become the head of the cor-

ner?18 Whosoever shall fall upon that stone shall be broken; but on whomsoever it shall fall, it will grind him to powder.**

We all know that Jesus is the "stone"; so did the Jews. This is a quote from the Old Testament. This is a warning to Israel, telling what will happen if they reject the Corner Stone. It is a warning to the rest of the world also. "Broken" or "ground to powder" is your choice just as it was and still is for the Jews, and everyone else in the world today. It seems to me that the Jews chose "ground to powder".

Luke 20:45 Then in the audience of all the people he said unto his disciples, 46 Beware of the scribes, which desire to walk in long robes, and love greetings in the markets, and the highest seats in the synagogues, and the chief rooms at feasts; 47 Which devour widows' houses, and for a shew make long prayers: the same shall receive greater damnation.

Jesus continues to warn against the corrupt leadership of Israel. He tells all who will listen that they, the leadership, will be and are condemned by their actions. Jesus was a threat to them, the leadership, by just calling them out in public. They were afraid that He would start a rebellion and take power away from them and rule as an earthly king. They were also afraid that Rome would step in and remove them from power for not controlling the Populace. So they removed the threat by crucifying Jesus, or so they thought.

Luke 22:52 Then Jesus said unto the chief priests, and captains of the temple, and the elders, which were come to him, Be ye come out, as against a thief, with swords and staves? 53 When I was daily with you in the temple, ye stretched forth no hands against me: but this is your hour, and the power of darkness.

This arrest was done in secret, the priests were afraid of the people. There were those who revered Jesus and they might have caused riots, which would have caused the Romans to take notice. Above all else the leadership of Israel did not want the hard eye of Rome on them, and the chance of them losing the power granted to them by Rome. Notice: the last part of verse 53, Jesus is equating the priests with Satan, and that is where the power comes from to take Him to the cross. Of course Jesus and the Father are allowing this to take place. In all reality Jesus and God the Father hoodwinked Satan, he thought he won by killing Jesus. The opposite is true.

Matthew 26:63 But Jesus held his peace. And the high priest answered and said unto him, I adjure thee by the living God, that thou tell us whether thou be the Christ, the Son of God. 64 Jesus saith unto him, Thou hast said: nevertheless I say unto you, Hereafter shall ye see the Son of man sitting on the right hand of power, and coming in the clouds of heaven. 65 Then the high priest rent his clothes, saying, He hath spoken blasphemy; what further need have we of witnesses? behold, now ye have heard his blasphemy.

Mark 14:60 And the high priest stood up in the midst, and asked Jesus, saying, Answerest thou nothing? what is it which these witness against thee? 61 But he held his peace, and answered nothing. Again the high priest asked him, and said unto him, Art thou the Christ, the Son of the Blessed? 62 And Jesus said, I am: and

ye shall see the Son of man sitting on the right hand of power, and coming in the clouds of heaven. 63 Then the high priest rent his clothes, and saith, What need we any further witnesses? 64 Ye have heard the blasphemy: what think ye? And they all condemned him to be guilty of death. 65 And some began to spit on him, and to cover his face, and to buffet him, and to say unto him, Prophesy: and the servants did strike him with the palms of their hands.

Luke 22:66 And as soon as it was day, the elders of the people and the chief priests and the scribes came together, and led him into their council, saying, 67 Art thou the Christ? tell us. And he said unto them, If I tell you, ye will not believe: 68 And if I also ask you, ye will not answer me, nor let me go. 69 Hereafter shall the Son of man sit on the right hand of the power of God. 70 Then said they all, Art thou then the Son of God? And he said unto them, Ye say that I am. 71 And they said, What need we any further witness? for we ourselves have heard of his own mouth.

John 18:19 The high priest then asked Jesus of his disciples, and of his doctrine. 20 Jesus answered him, I spake openly to the world; I ever taught in the synagogue, and in the temple, whither the Jews always resort; and in secret have I said nothing. 21 Why askest thou me? ask them which heard me, what I have said unto them: behold, they know what I said. 22 And when he had thus spoken, one of the officers which stood by struck Jesus with the palm of his hand, saying, Answerest thou the high priest so? 23 Jesus answered him, If I have spoken evil, bear witness of the evil: but if well, why smitest thou me.

Here Jesus finally tells them outright that He is the "CHRIST", and they refuse to believe despite all the evidence of healing, miracles, and authoritative teachings he did in 3 ½ years; plus the ministry of John the Baptist who proclaimed Jesus as the son of God. They had chance after chance to repent but chose not to. He also tells them He is their king and that He will sit on the right hand of God; which means that God has given all power to Him. The " high and mighty" of Israel understood this, and still rejected him in favor of Rome. What else could God do but reject them also? They gave God no choice but to destroy them. Jesus asks why they didn't arrest him in the temple. The leadership was fearful of the people who listened to Jesus, because they might riot if Jesus was arrested in the temple.

The destruction of Jerusalem and the Temple was done for several reasons:

The first was the rejection of Jesus and thereby the rejection of God the Father.
The second was to show that the law of sin and death was fulfilled.
The third that the kingdom of God was now a spiritual kingdom under the law of grace and love.
The fourth was to show, beyond a doubt, that no more animal sacrifices would ever be accepted again by the father.
The fifth to show that Jesus was the only way to the Father from then on.
The sixth to show that Israel was no longer a favored nation of God.

Jerusalem and the temple were destroyed in 70AD; this is one generation, or 40 years, after Jesus died on the cross and rose to glory. God the Father gave the nation of

Israel that one additional chance of one generation to repent and come back to Him! History tells us that they didn't repent. Subsequently the city and the temple were destroyed, and the Jews scattered all over the world; never to be made a nation, approved of by God, again. You must understand that salvation is only through Jesus' shed blood. The law of sin and death that the Jews lived under was fulfilled by the "new covenant of love and Grace", brought and confirmed by Jesus' work on the earth. See **Dan 9:26-27**. The prince in verse 26 IS JESUS. The Jews from the cross on had, and have, the same plan of salvation that the rest of the world has. It's called "JESUS". There is no other special plan of salvation anywhere in the New Testament exclusively for the natural Jew or anyone else today, or at the second coming of Jesus.

Luke 23:27 And there followed him a great company of people, and of women, which also bewailed and lamented him. 28 But Jesus turning unto them said, Daughters of Jerusalem, weep not for me, but weep for yourselves, and for your children. 29 For, behold, the days are coming, in the which they shall say, Blessed are the barren, and the wombs that never bare, and the paps which never gave suck. 30 Then shall they begin to say to the mountains, Fall on us; and to the hills, Cover us. 31 For if they do these things in a green tree, what shall be done in the dry? 32 And there were also two other, malefactors, led with him to be put to death.

What else can this be but another prophecy about the destruction of Jerusalem, the temple, and Israel as a whole? The green tree is when Jesus, in the flesh, and the Father was with them. The dried up tree is Israel left destitute without the temple sacrifices.

Remember the temple veil was ripped from top to bottom signifying that God the Father no longer resided there, that all sacrifices were no longer accepted by the Father for the forgiveness of sin, and that the way was open for all to come to God openly, not through a priesthood. For the Father to continue to accept the animal sacrifices would have been a slap in the face of Jesus and make His work on the cross null and void, and without effect. Can you see this?

John 8:53 Art thou greater than our father Abraham, which is dead? and the prophets are dead: whom makest thou thyself? 54 Jesus answered, If I honour myself, my honour is nothing: it is my Father that honoureth me; of whom ye say, that he is your God: 55 Yet ye have not known him; but I know him: and if I should say, I know him not, I shall be a liar like unto you: but I know him, and keep his saying. 56 Your father Abraham rejoiced to see my day: and he saw it, and was glad. 57 Then said the Jews unto him, Thou art not yet fifty years old, and hast thou seen Abraham? 58 Jesus said unto them, Verily, verily, I say unto you, Before Abraham was, I am. 59 Then took they up stones to cast at him: but Jesus hid himself, and went out of the temple, going through the midst of them, and so passed by.

The first blow from Jesus was that they didn't know God the Father. The second blow was that Jesus said He was from before Abraham, in other words God Himself. This was in a sense challenging the Jews concept of God and the law that they lived under. Some accepted this, but most did not. The hatred generated by Jesus' words led to the cross. The really upsetting thing, for me, is that Jesus came and delivered the truth to Israel. They knew it and still rejected Him. This is one of the ten times the Jews tried to kill Jesus before the cross for supposed blasphemy.

John 15:1 I am the true vine, and my Father is the husbandman. 2 Every branch in me that beareth not fruit he taketh away: and every branch that beareth fruit, he purgeth it, that it may bring forth more fruit. 3 Now ye are clean through the word which I have spoken unto you. 4 Abide in me, and I in you. As the branch cannot bear fruit of itself, except it abide in the vine; no more can ye, except ye abide in me. 5 I am the vine, ye are the branches: He that abideth in me, and I in him, the same bringeth forth much fruit: for without me ye can do nothing 6 If a man abide not in me, he is cast forth as a branch, and is withered; and men gather them, and cast them into the fire, and they are burned. 7 If ye abide in me, and my words abide in you, ye shall ask what ye will, and it shall be done unto you. 8 Herein is my Father glorified, that ye bear much fruit; so shall ye be my disciples.

As Jesus is the "true vine" He knows what each branch is doing. If you get into sin you will be cut off by the Father. The Jews can be grafted in, but only through Jesus. If you never "give it up for Jesus" you will NEVER be added to the Vine, and you will be cast out into the eternal fire of damnation. It's that simple. Do you think that the natural Jews in the Modern State of Israel are bearing fruit for the Father on the vine of Jesus? If Not, why would God honor them with a new nation?

John 16:1 These things have I spoken unto you, that ye should not be offended. 2 They shall put you out of the synagogues: yea, the time cometh, that whosoever killeth you will think that he doeth God service. 3 And these things will they do unto you, because they have not known the Father, nor me. 4 But these things have I told you, that when the time shall come, ye may remember that I told you of them. And these things I said not unto you at the beginning, because I was with you.

"They shall" is the Jews. Jesus tells the disciples what they can expect from the Jews, and this is because they, the Jews, do not know the Father in truth. Why would God bless and keep a people so full of hate and disbelief? Is it no wonder that God rejected them? Even here God was merciful toward the Jews in that He gave them one more generation (40 years) before He destroyed Jerusalem, the temple, and had the people scattered all over the known world by the Roman army in 70 Ad.

The names of natural Old test. Israel, and the New test. Spiritual Israel,

Old test. Israel:	**New Test. Spiritual Israel:**	
They were Jews	The Jews	Rom.2:28-29
They were Israel	The Israel	Rom. 9:6-9, Gal. 6:16
There were 12 tribes	The 12 tribes	Matt.19:28, Luke 22:30
		Acts 26:7
They had a temple	The temple of God	1Cor.3:16-17
They were Jerusalem	The Jerusalem	Gal.4:26, Heb: 12:22, Rev.3:12, 21:2, 21:12
They were God's nation	The nation	1Peter2:9
They had kings and priests	Kings and priests	Rev.1:6. 5:10
They were children promised	The children of promise	Gal. 3:29
They were Abraham's seed	Abraham's seed	Gal. 3:29
They practiced circumcision	The circumcision	Phil. 3:3

They were the elect of God	The elect of God	Col. 3:12
They were the people of God	The people of God	Heb. 4:9
They were a chosen generation	A chosen generation	1 Pet. 2:9
They were a holy nation	A holy nation	1 Pet. 2:9
They were a peculiar people	A peculiar(purchased) people	Titus 2:14, 1Pet. 2:9
They had a priesthood	A royal priesthood	1Pet. 2:9
They had their kingdom	Heirs of the kingdom	James 2:5
They had their city where God met with them	The city of the living God	Heb. 12:22
They were mount Zion	The mount Zion	Heb. 12:22
They had the Holy City	The Holy City	Rev. 21:21
They offered Sacrifices	We offer spiritual sacrifices	1Pet. 2:5

In Conclusion

First of all you must understand that all of these words of Jesus were spoken to the Jews of the old Testament nation of Israel, and are still valid for us today

Second, lest I be accused of teaching the "replacement of Israel", I will say that I am not! I am teaching, however, the completion, and fulfillment of God's plan for mankind, from the foundations of the world, brought and confirmed by Jesus for three and one half years ending on the cross, resurrection, and His rising to heaven. PTL._ God did not change who the Jews are, just how they get into the Kingdom. He opened up this glorious salvation to all the people of the world by Jesus' work on the cross.

The true, (God's), Nation of Israel is now a Spiritual Nation. We, as a, spiritual, saved people, no longer need to guided by the law as the OT Jews were, because we have been given the Holy Spirit Baptism to guide us into all things and all knowledge. We are spiritual citizens of a spiritual nation comprised of "all" who would go through Jesus the Christ to enter into this glorious kingdom of God. The entrance to this Holy Kingdom is not limited to any one group of people, but is open to all of the people of the world. The natural Jews and natural Gentiles alike. Remember there is only one gate and one narrow road to go through and walk on to get to heaven and that **is Jesus! Again He is the "ONLY WAY" to God the Father! No other religion on the earth can offer this removal of sin and a ride on the train to heaven to the one true Father God.**

This teaching has been done to counter the false teachings of special plans for the salvation of a separate people, the natural Jew. That the modern nation now called Israel is and was formed by God is a lie of Satan, but God did allow this new nation to be formed by man and Satan with a deceiving spirit. Do you really think God honored the modern Jews with a nation when they still reject Him and his Son Jesus. If you do you need a reality check.

Now it is up to you to decide whether or not you believe what these words of Jesus mean. You can make all kinds of explanations, but it seems to me that Jesus' words are very clear as to their meaning. My conclusion is that the Nation of Israel was destroyed, and the people scattered throughout the world for all time, just as the 10 northern tribes were, by God the Father for rejecting His Son as the Christ and thereby rejecting God the Father Himself. You might say it was the last straw in a long line of rejections by Israel.

There are many more verses that support this conclusion, but this study is only on the words of Jesus. **Ex:** Paul wrote: Who is the Jew? One who is circumcised of the flesh or one who is circumcised of the heart? He answers this by saying not of the flesh but of the heart. Can you find this verse? We as Christians are all Spiritual Jews in the Spiritual Kingdom of God. Now I will say it one last time: The modern day Hebrew can be saved, just as anyone else in the world, by accepting Jesus as the Messiah. There is no **other** "plan of salvation" in God's word exclusively for the "natural Jew"!!

The Anti-Christ, who, what, where and when

Daniel 9:20 And whiles I was speaking, and praying, and confessing my sin and the sin of my people Israel, and presenting my supplication before the LORD my God for the holy mountain of my God;

21 Yea, whiles I was speaking in prayer, even the man Gabriel, whom I had seen in the vision at the beginning, being caused to fly swiftly, touched me about the time of the evening oblation.

22 And he informed me, and talked with me, and said, O Daniel, I am now come forth to give thee skill and understanding.

23 At the beginning of thy supplications the commandment came forth, and I am come to shew thee; for thou art greatly beloved: therefore understand the matter, and consider the vision. ~Seventy Weeks and the Messiah

24 Seventy weeks are determined upon thy people and upon thy holy city, to finish the transgression, and to make an end of sins, and to make reconciliation for iniquity, and to bring in everlasting righteousness, and to seal up the vision and prophecy, and to anoint the most Holy.

25 Know therefore and understand, that from the going forth of the commandment to restore and to build Jerusalem unto the Messiah the Prince shall be seven weeks, and threescore and two weeks: the street shall be built again, and the wall, even in troublous times.

26 And after threescore and two weeks shall Messiah be cut off, but not for himself: and the people of the prince that shall come shall destroy the city and the sanctuary; and the end thereof shall be with a flood, and unto the end of the war desolations are determined.

27 And he shall confirm the covenant with many for one week: and in the midst of the week he shall cause the sacrifice and the oblation to cease, and for the overspreading of abominations he shall make it desolate, even until the consummation, and that determined shall be poured upon the desolate.

To understand Daniel chapter 9:20-27 is to understand what the Anti-Christ is not.
Verse 24 Tells us seventy weeks is weeks of seven years each (in this case equals 490 years). This is the prophecy that tells the nation of Israel when the Messiah will come, and the starting point is the Jews being set free from the Babylonian captivity. You will notice what will be done: 1- Finish transgression, 2- Make an end of sins, 3- Make reconciliation for iniquity, 4- Bring everlasting righteousness, 5- Seal up the vision and prophecy, 6- Anoint the most holy.

Let's look at these one at a time: 1- to end the sin or transgression of Israel for the sin of disobeying God by doing it their way for 1500 years of their history 2- to make an end of animal sacrifices for sin. 3- to bring people back into spiritual contact with

God, 4- the ability for us, the children of God, to walk holy and pure, without sin, and have eternal life with God by the removal of sin from our conscience through Jesus' shed blood, 5 the end and fulfillment of all old test prophecy and visions about Jesus coming as the Messiah, 6- the water and Holy Spirit baptism of Jesus that started His ministry on this earth. It can also be said the most Holy, along with Jesus, is the Church, the body of Christ.

Verse 25 tells us that Jesus will begin His work on the earth at 69 weeks or 483 years form the rebuilding of Jerusalem at the command of King Cyrus. The 70th is the final week of the 490 weeks of years prophcied by Daniel. Jesus was crucified 3 ½ years after He started His ministry as verse 26 tells us. The second half of the final week of years(3 ½) ended at the stoning of Steven. History tells us that Jesus was 30 years old, this is confirmed by the fact that the Jewish priests did not start their work until they were 30 years old. Notice that Jesus is called Messiah the Prince. This is the subject of all of these verses.

Verse 26 shows us that at the end of the seventy weeks the prince, who is Jesus, will be killed, not for himself, but for all the world. The people 'of the prince' (Jesus) is the Roman army that Jesus used to destroy the Temple and Jerusalem. **See Matthew 24:15-223 about the destruction of the temple and the City of Jerusalem.** Israel was divorced and destroyed by God for adultery to false gods and rejecting the Jesus the Messiah. The nation of Israel was scattered throughout the world never to be a nation again. God rejected Israel for rejecting Jesus. Do you think He had anything to do with the reforming of a still disbelieving Israel in 1948? Verse 27 is misunderstood and changed by man to make it fit their idea of end times and the Anti-Christ. Note the true subject of all of these verses is Jesus. It does not change back and forth from Jesus to the Anti-Christ. The phrases 'and he' is in reference to Jesus not the Anti-Christ. Notice what "he" is going to do; confirm the covenant, not as some say, 'make a covenant'. This change of words <u>from confirm to make</u> is used to prove that it is the Anti-Christ who will do what is said in verse 27. Here is what verse 27 really means: 1- Confirm the covenant: Jesus, by his work on the earth, brings the new law of Grace and love to the world, 2- the midst of the week (the cross): (3 ½ years), to cause the animal sacrifice to end, and sin to be forgiven by His blood. This three and a half years into Jesus' ministry is when He was nailed to the cross for all mankind, not just the Jews of the day.

The actual end of the 490 years is at the stoning of Stephen 3 ½ years after the cross. The Anti –Christ is not in Dan. 9: 20-27 as some teachers of end times would have you believe. That most damming evidence is the changing of the word 'confirm' to 'make' in verse 27. This changing of scripture is cause for a curse from God. The other evidence is the sentence structure and good grammar. The subject of these verses does not change from Jesus to the Anti-Christ. One other thing you must see is that these false teachers take the 'week' in verse 27 and transport it some 2000+ years into the future to some unknown point. They take this week, of Jesus' ministry, away from Jesus and give it to the so called Anti –Christ. This is a lie of Satan accepted by most of today's churches.

Daniel 7:8 I considered the horns, and, behold, there came up among them another little horn, before whom there were three of the first horns plucked up by the roots: and, behold, in this horn were eyes like the eyes of man, and a mouth speaking great things.

Daniel 7:24 And the ten horns out of this kingdom are ten kings that shall arise: and another shall rise after them; and he shall be diverse from the first, and he shall subdue three kings.25 And he shall speak great words against the most High, and shall wear out the saints of the most High, and think to change times and laws: and they shall be given into his hand until a time and times and the dividing of time.

Without going into a complete study of Daniel I am using these three verses to show, and you can see this in history, that the Anti-Christ system of Government and Religion started with the 'Holy Roman Empire' after the fall of the 'Roman Empire.' In verse 8 the little horn with eyes and a mouth is the end result of the fall of the Roman Empire and the beginning of the Anti-Christ religious system in the world. In verse 24 and 25 you see this Anti-Christ system described. This is the first place that shows that the Anti-Christ is not a single person but a system that is against Christ and the Father in all things. You can use a 'Halley's Handbook of the Bible' to show you the history spoken of in these verses. You will see in it the progression of Empires in history as given in the book of Daniel. You must also understand that anyone who is not in the Spiritual Kingdom of the Father God is a sinner and thereby a Anti-Christ. This includes all who have never come to Christ and those who have fallen away from Christ. I'll show the verses on this later in this study. Does not Jesus say if you're for me your not against me? Does not the opposite also hold true, if you're against me your not for me? What does Anti-Christ mean? Do you think against Christ? It also means to look like, to stand along side and be like a twin. An impersonator. Can you see this? A lot of you will say how is this possible that the 'Holy Roman Empire' (Catholic church) be Anti-Christ. Consider how many things that this so called Holy Church teaches that are against what the Bible teaches. Even the Catholic bible does not teach that you must call the priest 'father', that you must do penance for sins, confess your sin to a so called priest, pray in Mary's, or some saints name to get Jesus' attention, and on and on. If it's not in the bible how can you know it came from God and not some man? If it is cannon law it is made by man, how then can you trust it? Oh! By the way Purgatory is not in any of the teachings of Jesus or in the New Testament at all. There are two antichrist systems in this world :first is the religious system ,and second is the one world antichrist governmental system. If look around just a little bit you will see and understand this.

1 John 2:18 Little children, it is the last time: and as ye have heard that antichrist shall come, even now are there many antichrists; whereby we know that it is the last time.

As you can see in this verse that there are many antichrists not just one. The antichrists started to show up not long after Jesus rose to heaven. This verse also says we are in the last days, end times, also called the latter rain. All this started at the cross.

1 John 2:22 Who is a liar but he that denieth that Jesus is the Christ? He is antichrist, that denieth the Father and the Son.

This verse tells us that, as I said, any and everyone who denies Jesus is a antichrist. This includes all sinners, and Christians that fall back into even one sin without repenting. Are you guilty of just one un-repented sin or do you believe, as some churches teach, one sin doesn't matter. If you are guilty then you are Anti-Christ!

1 John 4:3 And every spirit that confesseth not that Jesus Christ is come in the flesh is not of God: and this is that *spirit* of antichrist, whereof ye have heard that it should come; and even now already is it in the world.

The antichrist is already in the world and there are many, many of them. I said above: sinners are the antichrists. Here you see if you don't confess Christ in your life you are antichrist. We are, as Christians, commanded to witness for Jesus Christ. If we don't we are in sin. Can you see this?

2 John 1:7 For many deceivers are entered into the world, who confess not that Jesus Christ is come in the flesh. This is a deceiver and an antichrist.

This is real clear. Deceivers (liars), all other religions, are not of Jesus, and are antichrist. All who are not for Christ are against Christ, thereby they are Anti-Christ. That there will be one Anti-Christ who sits on a throne in a 'new temple' in Jerusalem is a lie. Any teaching that includes this description of an antichrist is also a lie as you can see from this study. There is no place in the bible that says there will be just one antichrist in this world who will rule and reign. This false teaching is just wishful thinking by Satan, and the really sad thing is that Satan has gotten most of the Christian church today to believe this lie. Do you? Even after you just read the scriptures on this subject?

There are many parables on the desctruction that came upon Israel in 70 A.D., the fig tree is just one. See both studies on Israel.

A short study on sin

Ezekiel 18:21 But if the wicked will turn from all his sins that he hath committed, and keep all my statutes, and do that which is lawful and right, he shall surely live, he shall not die. 22 All his transgressions that he hath committed, they shall not be mentioned unto him: in his righteousness that he hath done he shall live.

In the above verses we can see the attitude of God toward sin. God literally says that the sins you have repented from are no more in existence and you are righteous before God in Heaven. Notice in verse 21 God says "he shall not die"; this is a spiritual death. This means that you ARE with and belong to God through Jesus the Christ as long as you don't fall back into sin. As God does not change and He, God, is not a respecter of persons, means that these Old Test. verses are as valid today as when they were first written.

Ezekiel 18:24 But when the righteous turneth away from his righteousness, and committeth iniquity, and doeth according to all the abominations that the wicked man doeth, shall he live? All his righteousness that he hath done shall not be mentioned: in his trespass that he hath trespassed, and in his sin that he hath sinned, in them shall he die. 26 When a righteous man turneth away from his righteousness, and committeth iniquity, and dieth in them; for his iniquity that he hath done shall he die.

When you sin you die spiritually! When you repent you are back on the road to heaven and the Father. Once you are saved the only way to fall away is to turn back to sin by your free will choice. Your answer then is to repent and God will forgive you no matter what you have done. The only exception to this is 'Blasphemy against the Holy Spirit', and this is only by a conscious choice to turn away from and reject God from your life totally. **(See Mat 12:31)**. This is the only sin unto death, all others are forgivable and will be forgiven when you ask from your heart. Remember, you can not have done anything so bad the God will stop loving you.

Hebrews 9:14 How much more shall the blood of Christ, who through the eternal Spirit offered himself without spot to God, purge your conscience from dead works to serve the living God?

From this verse we see and understand that when we repent and ask forgiveness, by the blood of Jesus, the sin that we just asked forgiveness for is wiped clean, removed from our conscience never to be remembered by God again. In fact you and Satan are the only ones who remember that past sins of your life.
Satan will bring them up to convince you that you are not forgiven, but this is a lie to get you to mistrust God the Father and to fall away from God and His Son Jesus. Remember this is a lie of Satan; your past sins are forgiven and gone forever. Again, God does not and will never bring them up to you, because He just chooses not have any memory of them. The one thing I would like to point out about **1 John 5:16** is that there is no specification as to any sin (other than Blasphemy against the H.S.) that can not be forgiven.

1 John 1:9 If we confess our sins, he is faithful and just to forgive us our sins, and to cleanse us from all unrighteousness.

I think most people misunderstand this verse. First of all it represents God's mercy in all His Glory. Did not Jesus tell the His disciples to forgive 70 times 7? This is an instruction to forgive every time. There is no limit on the number of times God will forgive; this includes us also in our attitude toward our brothers in Christ, or anyone for that matter. This means that you have available to you forgiveness from God the Father for any and all sins that you have committed as long as you ask from your heart, and you truly want to be forgiven. Also it means that God will forgive you as many times as necessary to get you to heaven, or when you learn to stop sinning as Jesus commands us to do.

The one last thing that needs to said is that Jesus' blood is sufficient for the forgiveness of "all" sins; to feel that His blood is not able to do so is to say Jesus' work on the cross was a waste of time. Did not Jesus say "it is finished"?

Penance is, absolutely, not necessary. This so called "paying for sins" that is given by the priests is a sin in and of itself, and is absolutely a slap in the face of Jesus.

By doing penance you are telling Jesus that He did not get everything done on the cross, and that your church is above the Holy Bible which was written by God through the hands of His obedient apostles and servants. Is this a position you want to be in?

A Joyful Marriage Fortress

By Terry Scerine

Building and Restoring Joy
Filled Marriages and Families
Tate Publishing *& Enterprises*

Printed here by permission

A Joyful Marriage Fortress
Copyright © 2009 by Terry Scerine. All rights reserved.

No part of this publication may be reproduced, stored in a retrieval system or transmitted in any way by any means, electronic, mechanical, photocopy, recording or otherwise without the prior permission of the author except as provided by USA copyright law.
Scripture quotations marked "kjv" are taken from the Holy Bible, King James Version, Cambridge, 1769. Used by permission. All rights reserved.
The opinions expressed by the author are not necessarily those of Tate Publishing, LLC.

Published by Tate Publishing & Enterprises, LLC
127 E. Trade Center Terrace | Mustang, Oklahoma 73064 USA
1.888.361.9473 | www.tatepublishing.com

Tate Publishing is committed to excellence in the publishing industry. The company reflects the philosophy established by the founders, based on Psalm 68:11,
"The Lord gave the word and great was the company of those who published it."

Book design copyright © 2009 by Tate Publishing, LLC. All rights reserved.
Cover design by Tyler Evans
Interior design by Joey Garrett

Published in the United States of America

ISBN: 978-1-60696-951-9
1. Religion / Christian Life / Love & Marriage
2. Religion / Christian Life / Spiritual Growth
09.03.

Dedication

This book is dedicated to my loving mother, Angelena (Boggio) Scerine, the unwavering support upon which my loving father, Richard T. "Curly" Scerine (1913–1979), stood, a marriage fortress that no man put asunder 'til death did they part.

Acknowledgment

A special thanks to my friends and fellow Christians Randy and Julie Jernigan, without whose confirmation, encouragement, and strong faith in our Lord and Savior Jesus Christ I may not have had the faith and courage to complete this book.

And a special thanks to Julie Jernigan in particular, without whose corroboration as a born-again Christian woman and wife, mature in God's Word, this book would not have been complete.

Table of Contents

- Foreword
- Introduction
- Prepare Yourself
- Our Purposes
- God Models Perfect Design
- God's Building Code for Marriage
- God's Plan for a Marriage Fortress
- Marriage Fortress Restoration
- Marriage Counseling
- The Enemy in Our Spiritual Battle
- Extreme Measures
- The Destruction of Dishonor
- The Evidence of Joy
- Epilogue
- Bibliography

Forward

My husband, Randy, and I have been married for thirty- five years. We were radically saved in 1983, are on fire for the Lord, and have been students of God's Word ever since. Long ago we both became convinced of God's perfect and infinite wisdom and his mighty and uncon- ditional love for us, his children. I am a disciple and lover of Jesus, and I'm convinced that his Word contains all the answers we need to the questions of life and all the solutions we need to the challenges and struggles of liv- ing a joy-filled life on this earth. In fact, when I pray, I pray God's Word. Psalms 138:2 says that he exalts his Word even above his name!

I met Terry Scerine at a prayer meeting about a year ago. He immediately struck me as a lover of God, a man of integrity, and a man with a resolute, unshakable will to do the right thing whatever the cost. I have come to love and admire him as a brother in Christ and a beloved friend. Terry came to me some time ago and asked me to read and critique his composition, the one now titled A Joyful Marriage Fortress, explaining that he needed the honest reaction and input of a married woman whom he considered to be openhearted to God's truth and asked me for any input I might have, good or bad.

He knew that I have been aware of the agents of Satan's spiritual battle against marriages and other Christian institutions for many years, been a researcherof such matters for a long time, and he knew that I try all information according to Scriptures in testing the spirit. In other words, if it can't be clearly substantiated in God's Word, then I hold no stake in it.

I was already well aware of the roles God has ordained for a husband and a wife, what he expects of a woman in marriage, and have been doing my best to be that type of wife to my husband for many years because I have a heart to please Jesus, my Lord and Savior. After carefully reading through A Joyful Marriage Fortress for the first time, my reaction was very positive— even though I felt convicted on some things. When I examined the things I felt convicted on (not wearing my wedding ring because Randy doesn't wear one—I now know that Randy doesn't wear one because most meat cutters don't wear one, just as my father never wore one; he was a meat cutter too) and my sometimes attitude of rising up and letting my inner Jezebel have its way.

I began to realize also that Terry's book was to me like the Word of the Lord was to King Josiah when he found the forgotten Word of the Lord after the Israelites got into rebellion to God and quit obeying him.

I realized that in the scriptures Terry presented— which I had forgotten—God spells out his perfect blue- print for an orderly marriage and family relationship. The "word of the Lord" regarding the marriage relationships has been lost due to society's "dumbing down" of men through the media and the public education system. But most importantly the Jezebel spirit has moved through the women's liberation movement and has left women refusing to submit to anyone and the men wondering how things got this way.

I believe that it is impossible to be submitted to Christ if a woman refuses to be submitted to her husband. The question is, bottom line, "Will we obey God or not?" Do we get to pick and choose only the parts of the Scripture we like to obey? Jesus said, "If you love me you will keep my commandments."

We are always serving someone; there is no gray area. We either serve the devil, or we serve the Lord. All I know is that God began exposing this Jezebel spirit to me four years ago and the reason Terry came into it is that he is the "writer." I don't care who would have writ- ten the book. With the scriptures, and the rest, the final result for me is that I love and esteem my husband more than ever. I believe God will and is using this book as a winnowing fan. And I know now more than ever that the Proverbs 31 woman is a woman after God's own heart, as is the 1 Peter 3:6 woman.

The author of this book, Terry Scerine, is really a nonessential in this whole story. He is just the person God used to write the book. It is up to us as women to repent if need be (as I did) and come into line with what God's Word says we should be. If we truly love God and are submitted to him, he is at work in us both to will and to work for his good pleasure (Philippians 2:13).

I think it is a positive sign that Tate Publishing, a leading Christian publishing company, wants to publish this book. This is the Lord's doing, and it is an awesome thing to behold God confirming his Word!

It is my urgent prayer, for the sake of marriages and children today, that God would move sovereignly in a mighty way to get this book into the hands of the mul- titudes who are suffering marriage problems. My prayer is that, as the people read it, God would quicken the truth of it to them by his Holy Spirit and that the read- ers, their marriages, and family relationships would be healed and made whole. To God be the glory!

Julie Jernigan

Introduction

"God doesn't call the equipped, he equips the called."
Unknown

We are all experts on our own experiences. In this regard, I am an expert on failed marriage with a minor in mar- riage counseling.

Jesus Christ is my Lord and Savior, and I am firmly grounded in nothing but the truth of God's Word, which is the only wise counsel. I'm convinced that it was the Holy Spirit who gave me the irresistible urge, and inspiration, to write this message.

I will be the first to admit that I am an unlikely candidate, by natural consideration, to carry forth a message such as this; but then I consider that God has historically used the unlikely for his purposes, perhaps because it brings him all the glory for the results, as he deserves. After all, if God can make a donkey prophesy truth, he can also use me to convey his truth. He uses us fellow believers to sharpen each other as "iron sharpens iron," and he uses the "foolish things of this world to confound the wise"; perhaps this is why he prompted me, as yet an unknown author, to convey this urgent message.

Still, why me? I can only guess. Among other things, though, I am a strong "left-brainer," a very logical and analytical thinker. By the gift of God, I've always naturally excelled at logical sciences, such as algebra, geometry, pre-calculus, physics, English grammar and composition, and psychology. Further, I've always wanted to know not only the "what's," but also the "whys" behind them.

I feel that if my own perceptions can't convince others, maybe the truth of Scriptures plus logic and reason will. This seems to be the way the Apostle Paul witnessed in the book of Acts. After all, our God is a God of order; he's the one who invented logic and created us with the ability to reason. I've found that God's Word stands as long as I don't try to alter it to fit my own understanding or agenda.

So it is up to you, the reader, to judge the source of my words. Everyone has his own opinions and conclusions; however, truth is not relative or subjective: the truth is not whatever I feel like believing or whatever I suspect to be true.

"The book of books is called the Holy Bible because it has a holy author and aims at a holy purpose, the production of holiness in its readers."
Daniel Steele

There is only one reliable truth; therefore, I have carefully supported everything in this book with scriptures themselves, along with logic and reason, with the true witness of my own experiences and observations, and with the testimonies of others.

My desire is to present convincing evidence of God's love and perfect wisdom for us, to the glory and majesty of our ultimate counselor, Jesus Christ. Specifically, I wish to present what I believe is the simplest and, in fact, the only surefire way of building and restoring marriages and families to fullness in Christ and to reach as many as possible as soon as possible with it.

Prepare Yourself

Have Ears to Hear

The following message, while it is virtually guaranteed to be a life-changing message for the better, is not for the wishy-washy or faint of heart. It's not for those with a buffet-style approach to God's Word, who feel they can take the verses they like and leave the rest. It may not give you a warm and fuzzy feeling at first, but if you will embrace it with a proper heart for God, a trust in him as the only source of true wisdom, and a dedication to his truth, it promises great results. Rather, God promises you great results, a truly joyful marriage fortress. And I know of the testimonies of many who confirm it.

The beauty of it is, it doesn't involve hard work and effort. Notice there's no workbook to buy and diligently work your way through in conjunction with it. No test questions to answer. No projects to do. All you have to do is read and be open to what God may tell you in it. Just let go of yourself and let God do the work in your heart. However, I would recommend journaling your results, because your faith may be increased considerably by it. "Being confident of this very thing, that he which hath begun a good work in you will perform it until the day of Jesus Christ" (Philippians 1:6, kjv).

Just for the fun of it, let's consider this hypothetical scenario: You're about to leave on a family fun trip. You're all in and ready to leave. You've started your car; but it's running very roughly and stalling, and you're trying to figure out why. You've tried everything you can think of and even called some people you know for their advice but to no avail, and your family is getting impatient. Then, when you've reached the end of your rope, this guy walks up and says, "Hi there! I see you're having trouble with your car, and I happen to be the engineer who designed it. If you will trust me and do what I say, we'll have're running like a top in no time!" What a godsend! He asks you to do this or that as he works under the hood, and you do it. After all, would you refuse? Would you ignore his advice? Next thing you know, you're all merrily on your way down the road on your exciting trip, enjoying your journey and so grateful that the expert came along.

So before you continue reading, dear reader, this is of utmost importance: pray and ask God for wisdom and discernment, to remove any spiritual blinders from your eyes, and to give you ears to hear the truth! Ask the Lord to soften and open your heart and grant you a teachable spirit. And most importantly, read carefully the Bible scriptures contained in this book (starting with these below), even those you may already be familiar with, because they are the only infallible, rock-solid truth, directly from the mouth of the expert:

> If any of you lack wisdom, let him ask of God, that giveth to all men liberally, and upbraideth not; and it shall be given him.
>
> James 1:5 (kjv)

> The fear of the Lord is the beginning of knowledge: but fools despise wisdom and instruction.
>
> Proverbs 1:7 (kjv)

Trust in the Lord with all thine heart; and lean not unto thine own understanding. In all thy ways acknowledge him, and he shall direct thy paths. Be not wise in thine own eyes: fear the Lord, and depart from evil.
Proverbs 3:5–7 (kjv)

Know the Author of Truth Who is our ultimate counselor? Jesus Christ is the one and only ultimate counselor, by way of his Word, by way of his Holy Spirit, and by way of his living example! He is the creator of all things (see below), including us; therefore, there's no one who knows us better than he does. He knows what makes us tick. He knows exactly what we need to live in freedom and joy, and that's what he wants for each of us.

There are certain religions and cults in the world that seek to rob Jesus of his deity. (Even atheists cannot deny the historical, non-biblical records confirming the life of Jesus.) They teach that Jesus was merely a prophet of God, or that he was merely a good teacher, or that he was merely a highly enlightened being. These beliefs are heresies, or non-truths. They're true about him but not the whole truth about him.

But even if these were the case, shouldn't they then still be willing to accept the fullness of his teachings, especially including those about who he is?

The truth is not whatever someone may suspect to be true; the truth is only what is clearly and plainly written in God's Word, and we must believe only what the Scriptures explicitly state and make no assumptions or implications about it. God does not deceive or lead us to be deceived, and he does not hide his truth from us!

God is the author of truth and has provided it to us because he wants us to know it and thereby know him.

This is what the Bible, the inspired Word of God, which has never been proven to be wrong in any way (though many have tried very hard), says about Jesus:

For unto us a child is born, unto us a son is given: and the government shall be upon his shoulder: and his name shall be called Wonderful, Counselor, The mighty God, The everlasting Father, The Prince of Peace.
Isaiah 9:6 (kjv)

In the beginning was the Word, and the Word was with God, and the Word was God ... All things were made by him; and without him was not any thing made that was made. ... And the Word was made flesh, and dwelt among us, (and we beheld his glory, the glory as of the only begotten of the Father,) full of grace and truth.
John 1:1–14 (kjv)

And without controversy great is the mystery of godliness: God was manifest in the flesh ...
1 Timothy 3:16 (kjv)

But unto the Son he saith, Thy throne, O God,
is for ever and ever ...
Hebrews 1:8 (kjv)

> For there are three that bear record in heaven, the Father, the Word, and the Holy Ghost: and these three are one.
> 1 John 5:7 (kjv)

> And God said, Let us make man in our image, after our likeness ...
> Genesis 1:26 (kjv)

The plain and simple fact is that Jesus Christ is God! Period. God the Father, God the Son, and God the Holy Spirit are all God: one in being. Though the natural mind of man cannot figure this out and accept it, it is never- theless the plain truth. And according to chapter one of the Gospel of John (above), Jesus Christ is the Word of God, and he made all that is made, including us.

He is the creator of all things and the source of the only real and reliable truth! He created us in his image and likeness, which makes him the definitive expert on human behavior.

Even among the non-Christian secular world of late, more and more experts in the field of psychology are admitting their realization that, if nothing else, Jesus Christ was the greatest psychologist of all mankind!

Our Premise

The following simple statements are the premise upon which we who believe in God stand, and upon which this book stands:

1. God is perfect love and goodness; there is no evil in him whatsoever. He does not deceive.
2. God created us and knows each of us perfectly.
3. God loves us perfectly and wants the best for each of us who belong to him.
4. God's Word gives us all the information we need so that we may live in joy and fulfillment.

"He that hath my commandments, and keepeth them, he it is that loveth me: and he that loveth me shall be loved of my Father, and I will love him, and will manifest myself to him" (John 14:21, kjv).

There is no doubt in my mind that those of us who truly love Jesus (and prove it to him by having a heart for him and for keeping his commandments) are heirs of his awesome promises! One who truly loves Jesus can be blessed with unquenchable joy in the midst of any human circumstances!

If you are a born-again believer in Jesus Christ, then you are a child of God and a member of the one true church, the body of Christ, and the following is true for you:

1. Our only true spiritual father is our Father in heaven:

> And call no man your father upon the earth:
> for one is your Father, which is in heaven.
> Matthew 23:9 (kjv)

perfect vessel into which God can freely pour out his blessings of protection, provision, and joy, as a proper witness to his wisdom and majesty, to the wonderment of the world.

Such a marriage fortress, complete with the bless- ings of God's promises for it, stands strong against the attacks of Satan to penetrate and infiltrate it.

And all these blessings shall come on thee, and overtake thee, if thou shalt hearken unto the voice of the Lord thy God.
>> Deuteronomy 28:2 (kjv)

2. Our only true teacher and master is Je- sus Christ, through his Word and his Holy Spirit:

But the anointing which ye have received of him abideth in you, and ye need not that any man teach you: but as the same anointing tea- cheth you of all things, and is truth, and is no lie, and even as it hath taught you, ye shall abide in him.
>> 1 John 2:27 (kjv)

But be not ye called Rabbi: for one is your
Master, even Christ; and all ye are brethren.
>> Matthew 23:8 (kjv)

3. Our only true shepherd and protec- tion, mediator, and counselor is our Lord and Savior Jesus Christ:

For there is one God, and one mediator between
God and men, the man Christ Jesus.
>> 1 Timothy 2:5 (kjv)

I am the good shepherd, and know my sheep, and am known of mine …
and there shall be one fold, and one shepherd.
>> John 10: 14–16 (kjv)

Our Purposes

I have set thee for a tower and a fortress among my people, that thou mayest know and try their way.
Jeremiah 6:27 (kjv)

Jeremiah was a man chosen by God to be his prophet, to prophesy (or to speak forth God's Word) among the people to try (or put on trial) their worldly ways.

A marriage constructed according to the design of God's instruction and model, built upon the solid rock of Jesus, is a fortress among people that glorifies him by putting on trial the ways of the world. Such a fortress is sanctified (or set apart) for his purposes, to exemplify to the world in so many ways God's perfect and limit- less love for us. Such a marriage fortress, built according to God's design, is a

Therefore whosoever heareth these sayings of mine, and doeth them, I will liken him unto a wise man, which built his house upon a rock
Matthew 7:24 (kjv)

And be not conformed to this world: but be ye transformed by the renewing of your mind, that ye may prove what is that good, and acceptable, and perfect, will of God.
Romans 12:2 (kjv)

Whereby are given unto us exceeding great and precious promises: that by these ye might be partakers of the divine nature, having escaped the corruption that is in the world through lust.
2 Peter 1:4 (kjv)

My purposes for this book are to:

- Exalt women by magnifying the crucial importance of their God-ordained purpose in a marriage and to encourage them to greatness in their role by illuminating the blessings of true freedom and joy available to them in it.
- Glorify God in his design for a marriage by care- fully examining the logic and reasoning of the ordinances of his perfect wisdom for us.
- Expose the very present and real spiritual battle being waged on families today; to expose Satan's motive, strategy, and weapons for disintegrating marriages and examine his agenda to infiltrate and capture the hearts of their children.
  - Illuminate the urgency, for the sake of the children, to fortify the protective covering of their parental marriage structure; to make the marriage a fortress of protection and provision against the attacks of Satan on their children's hearts.
  - Urge men and women not only to accept but indeed embrace the fullness of God's Word to husbands and wives and to consider what I believe is the only effective approach to building or restoring their marriage fortress to fullness in Christ.

- Urge biblical marriage and family counselors to carefully consider adopting the logical strategy presented herein that they may be prosperous in their efforts and produce good fruit in the marriages they counsel.

We were created by God to know him, love him, and glorify him. How in the world can we mere mortals glorify God in the eyes of others? By being living testimonies and witnesses of his almighty love and perfect wisdom, to magnify the glory of our Savior Jesus Christ.

How can we be living testimonies to him? How can we shine his light brightly in the darkness of our world? By exhibiting the blessings of joy and fulfillment that come from following his expert ways; by exhibiting the abundant good fruit that results from following his example and adhering to his perfectly wise and loving ordinances for us; by being a fortress of God in our present world, the enemy camp.

A Clear and Present Urgency

Marriages and families today are facing unprecedented challenges in these end times, and as those of us who know God's Word are aware, what they face ahead is likely to be even worse. They are suffering heavy tribulations at the hand of the enemy, and too many of them are in serious jeopardy. The divorce rate is staggering, even among evangelical Christians, and their children's hearts are being pummeled by the intense lure of Satan's world from every direction. "Wherein in time past ye walked according to the course of this world, according to the prince of the power of the air, the spirit that now worketh in the children of disobedience" (Ephesians 2:2, kjv).

We must be aware of and accept the fact that there is a very real spiritual battle being waged on the sanctified ground of families, and I believe it is ultimately for the hearts of children, and we must do everything we can to fortify the family unit against the enemy's attacks for their sakes. I believe one of Satan's prime objectives is to decompose the marriage structure, thereby disintegrating the God-ordained protective parental covering over their children, in order that he may gain unrestricted access to their children's hearts.

We should all know that Satan ultimately wants to take all of us down with him and see us destroyed! Jesus said of him:

And from the days of John the Baptist until now the kingdom of heaven suffereth violence, and the violent take it by force.
> Matthew 11:12 (kjv)

… He was a murderer from the beginning …
> John 8:44 (kjv)

… for the devil is come down unto you, having great wrath, because he knoweth that he hath but a short time.
> Revelation 12:12 (kjv)

We know the enemy's fate. It has already been sealed: "And the devil that deceived them was cast into the lake of fire and brimstone, where the beast and the false prophet are, and shall be tormented day and night for ever and ever." (Revelation 20:10, kjv).

Even among born-again Christian married couples and their children today, we see that Satan has been gaining ground in great strides, particularly since the early 1960s, once prayer was removed from our public schools here in the United States. When even a Christian marriage ends in divorce, God's ways are discredited in the eyes of the world; it is a very poor witness to the love, wisdom, and majesty of Jesus, and as a result his kingdom loses ground!

I present this very real scenario: A well-meaning Christian husband and wife who love each other and are committed to their marriage and family are struggling and losing the battle. Their marriage is without joy, and their attempts to shield their children from the lures of the secular world seem weak and futile. Their teens are strong willed and rebellious toward them and toward God. Sound familiar?

Now consider this: In a desperate last-ditch attempt to save their family, they seek biblical counseling. But once they've begun their counseling sessions, things have only seemed to get worse! They are in a downhill spiral, locked in a vicious circle, careening toward disaster, and its end will likely be destruction. Why is this? What's wrong with this picture?

In my opinion, the above scenario is happening too frequently (I have personally observed this in several cases), and this grieves me greatly because I'm certain that it shouldn't and doesn't have to be this way! It grieves me because it means that the devil, that vile, murderous, and destructive being, is pushing forward with great force!

Why are so many of today's marriages struggling so helplessly? Any number is too many! Why is their marriage structure and family, even those supposedly built on the solid rock of Jesus, still without joy and falling apart? This should never be! Why are even biblical marriage counselors ineffective in restoring many dysfunctional Christian families back to one that brings abundant joy to the family members and glorifies God and prospers his kingdom? It doesn't make sense!

To find our answers, first let's examine God's model of a perfect design for a solidly built fortress to find his wisdom in it.

God Models Perfect Design

How can any structure stand firmly and prosper for the glory of God and his kingdom? We know that its foundation must be Christ our rock, or it cannot stand. Again, as Jesus said, "Therefore whosoever heareth these sayings of mine, and doeth them, I will liken him unto a wise man, which built his house upon a rock" (Matthew 7:24, kjv).

But furthermore, how can any marriage structure itself stand firmly against adversities unless it is constructed on that rock according to God's full instructions? Any poorly built structure is bound to fall apart, even if standing on a solid foundation, especially when adverse forces are applied. We know this.

Let's start with a level setting of truth from God's Word, to establish our feet solidly upon a common ground of the truth. We who know God's Word should also know God's design for the headship of any organizational structure. It is the design that God not only models as an example for us but also ordains for us:

> But I would have you know, that the head of every man is Christ; and the head of the woman is the man; and the head of Christ is God.
> 1 Corinthians 11:3 (kjv)

> Wives, submit yourselves unto your own husbands, as unto the Lord. For the husband is the head of the wife, even as Christ is the head of the church: and he is the saviour of the body. Therefore as the church is subject unto Christ, so let the wives be to their own husbands in every thing. Husbands, love your wives, even as Christ also loved the church, and gave himself for it.
> Ephesians 5:22–25 (kjv)

From these two scriptures, which are clearly and explicitly stated, we derive not only the organizational structure of the headship of God himself but also of Christ's body of believers (the church) and of the marriages within it. The first scripture is a clear statement of fact, and the second clarifies the first by including clear and explicit ordinances to reinforce it. Furthermore, I conclude from these two scriptures that this is God's model of a proper and most functional design and can therefore be reasonably considered to be his model for the governing hierarchy of any purpose-driven organizational relationship:

God the Father is the head of Christ.
Christ is the head of his church.
Christ is the head of the husband.
The husband is the head of the wife.

There are several other scriptures throughout the Bible that clearly and plainly reinforce the above two scriptures, while appearing in the contexts of entirely different books of the Bible. I think it's clear how highly God exalts the significance of the marriage of husband and wife. He apparently considers it the greatest institution among men. I cannot recall any other organizational structure in scripture that is so often and so closely likened to the structure of the Father and the Son and the church. There is so much to be learned from so few words if we will only take the time to magnify and examine them!

I'd like to take a moment here to point something out. There are many who would like to believe that, for example, certain scriptures taken from Paul's letters to the Corinthians only apply to those of the church at Corinth. In my opinion, this is a convenient way for some to consider themselves as exempted from the direct application of certain scriptures to themselves. In other words, "Well, Paul wrote that to the Corinthians because they were blah, blah, blah. It doesn't apply to the rest of us today." Though we should never consider that any one scripture verse can be safely isolated from its context, I suggest that God's Word to us, though perhaps written to a particular sub-group of born-again believers in the body of Christ, apply as well to all of us in the body of Christ regardless of our geographic location or specific circumstances.

"If you believe what you like in the Gospel, and reject what you don't like, it is not the Gospel you believe, but yourself." - Augustine

> All scripture is given by inspiration of God, and is profitable for doctrine, for reproof, for correction, for instruction in righteousness: That the man of God may be perfect, thoroughly furnished unto all good works.
> 2 Timothy 3:16–17 (kjv)

Fortunately, in his perfect wisdom and love for us, God doesn't make us guess at these things. Why would he? Any good master who gives his willing servant a task will also provide him with all the instructions, direction, tools, reasons, and encouragement necessary for him to carry it out efficiently and profitably, right?

God not only gives us the ordinances of his design; he also models the examples of his design, as sort of a "how to" manual. That's why he said, "Even as Christ is the head of the church" and "the head of Christ is God." This is God's model of his design of providential government structure in all contexts when built according to his "building code." One is built upon the other, and together they form a solidly built structure that is sanctified to be used for his purposes, to the glory of his name. So now let's look at "the head of Christ is God."

The Submitted Heart of Jesus

When we carefully examine the construction of God's model by "reverse engineering" it (carefully taking some- thing apart to identify its components and how they have been assembled), we learn the "whys" for the instructions he has so lovingly given us. We find the solutions to our own human dilemmas, along with his precious promises that accompany them!

God the Father is the head of Jesus, his Son. Jesus is the head of his church. Jesus is also the head of the husband. The husband is the head of the wife. These are the materials necessary for God's design, but what about the assembly? If one element is missing, can the rest still be put together to function as well? If you remove any one of these elements, can the others still function well enough, even as a four-cylinder car running on only three cylinders?

Could God have carried out his plan of salvation for us without first being assured of having the perfectly submitted heart and support of his Son? Likewise, can a husband function properly in his God-given role with- out first having the willing support of his wife?

Just for grins, let's assemble those four elements together as though we're going to build the structure from the rock up: the wife is to submit to her husband (her head), and her husband (supported by his wife) is to submit to Jesus (his head), and they (the church) are to submit to Jesus (our head), just as Jesus is submitted to his Father (his head). Well built from the rock up! We don't build solid structures from midair down, and neither does God, I think, as we will see in the following example.

First, we see that Jesus illustrated his dedication and devotion to his Father by being baptized. As Jesus said, he was baptized by John the Baptist to "fulfill all righteousness" (Matthew 3:15, kjv). I love how John the Baptist, as soon as he saw Jesus approaching him for baptism, said, "Behold the Lamb of God, which taketh away the sin of the world" (John 1:29, kjv). John somehow recognized who he was right away! Then right after his baptism his Father spoke, "This is my beloved Son, in whom I am well pleased" (Matthew 3:17, kjv).

It has been said, and reasonably so, that it was this moment that Jesus began his ministry. Maybe I'm wrong, but it appears to me that once Jesus sealed his unwavering heart of submission, his Father was assured of his full support necessary for victory! Then they began their mission together.

(I know this is not necessarily literal, but I marvel at how the word submission seems to be so indicative of its true meaning. Sub, the prefix, means under or below, as in supported by. The purpose of the one in submission to another is a mission in itself to support the other so that the mission of such a team together can be accomplished.)

Anyway, right after his baptism, Jesus was "led up of the Spirit into the wilderness to be tempted of the devil" (Matthew 4:1, kjv) and was eventually tempted by Satan himself, not once, but three times! Even in what I imagine must have been a delirious state of mind after forty days and nights of fasting, Jesus won the victory over Satan's three powerful assaults on his heart, thus proving again his unwavering submission to his Father. If Jesus' heart was only weakly or conditionally submitted to God, do you think he would have won victory over Satan's three "shock and awe" strikes after forty days of fasting? And it's even important to remember how he did it: He quoted the Word of God. He won the victory by firmly supporting the words of his Father, his head!

You might be thinking, Well, yeah, but Jesus was God. This is true, of course, but now finish the sentence with: made flesh. I believe his fleshly human heart is evidenced by his fervent appeal to his Father just prior to his arrest and then by his cry on the cross:

> Saying, Father, if thou be willing, remove this cup from me: nevertheless not my will, but thine, be done. And there appeared an angel unto him from heaven, strengthening him. And being in an agony he prayed more earnestly: and his sweat was as it were great drops of blood falling down to the ground.
> Luke 22:42–44 (kjv)

> And about the ninth hour Jesus cried with a loud voice, saying, Eli, Eli, lama sabachthani? that is to say, My God, my God, why hast thou forsaken me?
> Matthew 27:46 (kjv)

I think that in these two events Jesus displayed what appeared to be a merely human heart of flesh. Otherwise, how could he have been a perfect model for us mere humans to follow? And he was tempted in the flesh by the temptations known of man. Without his having a human heart, could he have ever been tempted at all?

> For verily he took not on him the nature of angels; but he took on him the seed of Abraham. Wherefore in all things it behoved him to be made like unto his brethren … For in that he himself hath suffered being tempted, he is able to succour them that are tempted.
> Hebrews 2:16–18 (kjv)

Other Godly Models of Submission

I think it's significant that Peter, who seemed to be no particular rocket scientist or pillar of perfect faith (Jesus referred to the apostles as "ye of little faith" in Matthew 8:26 and 16:8) but whose heart was completely devoted to Jesus in childlike submission, was the one with whom Jesus had the following conversation:

> He saith unto them, But whom say ye that I am? And Simon Peter answered and said, Thou art the Christ, the Son of the living God. And Jesus answered and said unto him, Blessed art thou, Simon Barjona: for flesh and blood hath not revealed it unto thee, but my Father which is in heaven. And I say also unto thee, That thou art Peter, and upon this rock I will build my church; and the gates of hell shall not prevail against it.
> Matthew 16:15–18 (kjv)

And isn't it funny that Saul of Tarsus of all people, the zealous persecutor of Christians in service to the chief priests, was the one Jesus personally picked (and then changed his name to Paul) to spread his gospel to the Gentiles all over the earth? Why him? Was it because he was so zealous? And was he so zealous because of his unwavering heart of submission to his master, whomever that may have been? I think so.

> Then Ananias answered, Lord, I have heard by many of this man, how much evil he hath done to thy saints at Jerusalem: And here he hath authority from the chief priests to bind all that call on thy name. But the Lord said unto him, Go thy way: for he is a chosen vessel unto me, to bear my name before the Gentiles, and kings, and the children of Israel.
> Acts 9:13–15 (kjv)

A chosen vessel to bear his name! Wow! May we all know how it feels to be "chosen vessels" of our Lord Jesus to bear his name!

So I ask you, can it be that the wife's heart, like the examples of Jesus, Peter, and Paul above, is to be likewise devoted in submission to her husband in order to be the unwavering support upon which her husband can stand securely? Think of how difficult it is to try to do anything hands-free while standing on top of a rickety ladder. Furthermore, can it be that without this first, the husband cannot freely serve Jesus even by loving his wife as fully as he otherwise might?

We know that Jesus is our rock and anything not built upon him cannot stand. But I will show how and why a marriage and family structure falls apart unless it's built on that rock from the ground up according to the assembly procedure God modeled, beginning first with what I suggest is the most essential building material: a woman who has first resolved in her heart (in obedience to Jesus) to be fully devoted to supporting her husband with her unconditional honor and submission.

I'll put it more plainly: I liken the essential importance of a wife's role in a marriage and family to the essential importance of the role of Jesus in God's plan of salvation. In this the God-ordained role of the wife in a marriage is obviously highly esteemed and valued! What greater honor can one have?

God's Building Code for Marriage

The Key Ordinances

Now let's look again at the ordinances God gave us in Ephesians 5 to elaborate for us how we can emulate his perfect design in a marriage. In these two ordinances, he not only gave us clear instruction, but he also gave us his example to emulate with each of them. It was as if to say, "Do this, and this is how it's done." And, of course, we can trust that if it's how our perfectly wise and loving God does it, then it must be the thing to do, right? These are the two ordinances:

> Husbands, love your wives even as Christ also loved the church and gave himself for it. Wives, submit yourselves unto your own husbands as unto the Lord. (emphasis added)

First let's examine "Husbands, love your wives." The subject of love, and a husband's love for his wife, is a whole Bible study in itself that we should all do; but let me just say this: The word love in this command is not a feeling or emotion. God has commanded husbands to love their wives, and emotions cannot be commanded. I repeat, emotions cannot be commanded. The word love in this command is a verb, an action word, a determined choice of will, a willfully voluntary decision! We can very well choose to love (or to behave lovingly toward some- one), and by way of the good fruit of obedience to God with the right heart for him, the feeling of love will often follow one's obedient decision to love. And let's look at the rest of this verse, "even as Christ also loved the church, and gave himself for it." Christ suffered gruesome torture and death for his church, or those of us who are faithful believers in him. He gave his life for us. Need I say more? As Kay Arthur, in her book A Marriage Without Regrets, referring to John 13:1–17, explains:

> How can we observe our Teacher and Lord girding on a towel and washing the grimy feet of His disciples and not see that Jesus Himself modeled headship in a servant's role? He never ceased to be the head; but it was precisely because He was the head that He bent down and cleaned the soil from between dusty toes.

Again, this can be the subject of a study in itself. Christ's life was selflessly devoted in serving his Father entirely to his God-ordained purpose for the sake of us, his church; likewise, a husband's life must be selflessly devoted in serving Christ primarily to his God-ordained purpose for the sake of the well-being of his wife and family.

While a husband's role in a marriage is an appropriate subject for a book all in itself, and is not to be under- stated by any means, it is not to be the primary focus of this one, and as you read on, you will come to under- stand why. Remember that my first listed purpose for this book is to "exalt women by magnifying the crucial importance of their God-ordained purpose in a marriage and to encourage them to greatness in their role by illuminating the blessings of true freedom and joy available to them in it."

Now let's look at "Wives, submit yourselves unto your own husbands, as unto the Lord." First, let's clear up any misunderstandings about submission: submission is not servitude! Not by a long shot. These are two very different things. Submission, by definition, must be an entirely voluntary choice, while servitude is forced. Submission is a matter of choice, a determination of will:

> submission (noun): the action or fact of submit- ting; submissive (adjective): meekly obedient or passive; submit (verb): accept or yield to a superior force or stronger person; accept (verb): agree to receive or undertake; yield (verb): relinquish possession of (by these we see that it is clearly a voluntary choice)

> servitude (noun): the state of being a slave; slave (noun): a person who is the legal property of another and is forced to obey them (by these we see that this is not voluntary; it is forced)

Submission, by definition, which I'm also convinced is God's intention, is to be a willfully voluntary decision, the same as love. Submission is simply not to be confused with servitude! Just as God commands husbands to choose, or decide, to love their wives as an independently and voluntary act of obedience to Jesus, he commands wives to choose to submit to their husbands as an independently voluntary act of obedience to Jesus.

As Kay Arthur, in her same book, explains: God intends that all who are filled with the Spirit will gladly submit to one another and place themselves under whatever authority God has ordained. If you are a wife, that means that you will voluntarily place yourself under the authority of your husband.

I would like to expound more on this vast difference between voluntary submission and forced servitude, but I hope the rest of this presentation will be explanation enough. So let's just continue.

(Author's Note: I feel the urge to interject something at this point, before I lose some of you. Under no circumstances should anyone ever feel compelled, or even free, to do anything immoral or illegal. I consider this a given, and it has the full backing of God's Word.

Furthermore, my personal opinion is that no one is expected to tolerate, nor should they tolerate, any type of physical and/or sexual abuse, especially of children! I personally feel that there are some men these days who walk the earth with purely evil hearts, entirely given over to the lusts of the flesh. So I wish to qualify this book with this statement of my own: If a woman's husband poses a real and chronic physical or otherwise severely abusive danger to her or their children, all bets are off; she should do whatever it takes to remove herself and her children from such a situation immediately. As far as I'm concerned, this book only applies to a woman who is living with her husband under at least acceptably safe conditions for herself and her children. Please keep this precept in mind as you continue through this book.)

God is not our puppeteer, just as we are certainly not his. He has chosen not to be. He wants our love for him and our obedience to his ordinances to be entirely our free-will choice; otherwise, it wouldn't be love! We would just be his created puppets or robots, and puppets and robots that are incapable of making free-will choices are also incapable of love.

Just as God does not puppeteer us by instilling a "feeling" of love for him, he doesn't attempt to command a "feeling" of love in husbands for their wives or a "feeling" of submission in wives for their husbands. If God were to command feelings in us, then our obedience to him would no longer be our own free-will choice. By our nature, our "natural man," it is easy to follow our feelings, while it can be difficult to follow God's ordinances against our own feelings. "But the natural man receiveth not the things of the Spirit of God: for they are foolishness unto him: neither can he know them, because they are spiritually discerned" (1 Corinthians 2:14, kjv).

I'd like to take a moment to say something about what I call "blind trust." To me, blind trust is the type of trust I have in God, even against my own "natural man" understanding of things. Because of my wholehearted faith in God and because I've decided to believe whole-heartedly what he says in his Word about himself and his love for me, I have decided to have a trust in him beyond my own natural feelings, beyond all natural caution and reason, beyond all of my own understanding of things, and beyond what the world would otherwise have me do. Or at least I try to. He wants us to put our full trust in him; and our God is certainly worthy of it. The Lamb who was slain is worthy of it.

Blind trust, to me, would be like being blindfolded in a forest and having God tell me, in a booming voice from the sky, "Now, Terry, start running as fast as you can until I say stop," and then I do. Or like Jesus standing on the water in the midst of a storm and telling me, "Now get out of the boat and walk over to me." Peter was doing okay until he took his eyes off Jesus and lost his blind trust in him. Blind trust is a trust beyond fear and caution. I think of the faith of Abraham when God told him to sacrifice his precious and only son. There are many "interpretations" of this story among believers, but I like to think that Abraham just plain decided to have a blind trust in God. A no-holds-barred, 'throw all caution to the wind', reckless abandon, "If God says it, I'll do it" kind of trust. Romans 4:3 says, "Abraham believed God, and it was counted unto him for righteousness." I like the bumper sticker that reads, "God said it. I believe it."

Those of us who are truly saved love our Lord Jesus. Those of us who love Jesus have a heart to please him. We can please him by following him. We follow him by emulating what he does and by doing as he says. This is how we prove our love for him. He is our shepherd if we are his sheep.

I have to constantly ask myself, Who is my God? My own natural feelings, the lusts of my flesh, or my Lord and Savior Jesus Christ? When I choose to obey any feelings I may have that are contrary to what God would have me do, then I am obeying the lusts of my own flesh and have made myself my own god, and in this I am serving Satan.

To walk in the Spirit is to keep my own feelings in constant submission to God's Word. "Casting down imaginations, and every high thing that exalteth itself against the knowledge of God, and bringing into captivity every thought to the obedience of Christ" (2 Corinthians 10:5, kjv).

And the beauty of this is that God, in his infinite love and wisdom, encourages us to prove that we trust him and are faithful to him. As with all free-will obedience to his ordinances, our voluntary compliance is rewarded with blessings of joy, protection, and provision.

How the Ordinances Are Related

Husbands are to love their wives as Christ also loves his church and gave his life for her. Wives are to submit to their own husbands as unto the Lord. How are these two commands, or ordinances, related to each other?

In the same scriptural context that God commands wives to submit to their husbands, he also always commands husbands to love their wives. It is clear that they are both necessary as the ingredients for a healthy marriage; they are the essential building materials for a joyful marriage fortress.

But it is very important to note that each of these ordinances, while both equally essential, stand unconditionally independent of the other. They are not to be misunderstood as being interdependent or interrelated in any other way except to be both essential for a strong marriage: Husbands are to love their wives in obedience to the Lord. Wives are to submit to their husbands in obedience to the Lord. No ifs, ands, or buts. Each of these elements (or marriage-building materials) are to be present in individual submission to Christ, just as each building material of a house (such as lumber and shingles) that meet a certain standard of quality are to be individually present and correctly installed in the construction of a home. These are the minimum construction materials required for God's design of a solid marriage fortress, one that will glorify God the designer! Right now you may be thinking, We know this. This is not news. Now here is my crucial point; this is what I believe is a unique concept in building or restoring a marriage fortress: each of these individual elements are not only to be present, but also correctly assembled together as God has modeled for the construction of a solid structure, for a marriage and family to be built solidly, to be prosperous in glorifying

How They Are Not Related

Again, husbands are to love their wives as Christ also loved his church and gave his life for her. Wives are to submit themselves to their own husbands as unto the Lord. Each of these commands, while equally essential, stand unconditionally independent of the other in obedience to Jesus our rock, for the construction of a solid marriage and family fortress upon that rock.

In order to fully grasp the significance of these ordinances (what they mean), it helps to examine the contra- positive of them (what they don't mean). In this regard, it's important to note the fact that nowhere in God's Word is it taught or even implied that one can be considered as conditional upon the other.

They are never stated with conditions, such as "Husbands, love your wives as long as they are submissive" or "Wives, honor your husbands as long as they are honorable." And they cannot be considered conditional upon the other based on the order of their appearance in the context of scriptures, such as "Husbands, love your wives, and then your wives will submit to you." In fact, they appear in reverse order in different books. God carefully allowed for no misunderstandings in his Word when we diligently study it. God is such a genius!

And it cannot be misunderstood that it's acceptable for a wife to be the head of her husband or even for a wife to consider herself superior to her husband in any way. This should be obvious. A wife who assumes authority over her husband is entirely out of order, and this constitutes an "upside-down" design flaw in a mar- riage structure. There is not one single Scripture verse that could even be misconstrued to imply that this is acceptable or even tolerable. Not even close.

Neither should it be misunderstood that marriage can be considered an equal partnership. Again, not even close. This should also be obvious. In fact, equal partnerships are not a godly design for a providential government or headship in any context, not even in business, and for good reason. Equal partnership is a dysfunctional design for the headship of any organizational structure. Remember, God models perfect design.

In addition to the design he models, he also gave us plenty of clear instructions repeated often enough in scriptures to leave no room for doubt. They prevent any misunderstandings of "equal partnership" (wife and husband as co-heads) or "upside-down" (the wife as head of her husband) marriage design flaws.

Clarifying Scriptures for Wives

Now here are the reasons I am focusing primarily on God's commands for wives in this book: First, the freedom and ability of the husband to function properly and fully at his best in his God-ordained role of headship as a husband and father stand to be greatly hindered by the wife's improper function in her role, while the opposite is not true. Trust me. I will explain this.

First of all, any contention in the headship of any organizational structure or mission team most always takes place at the level of authority—never at the sub-ordinate level. Rarely, if ever, is there any contention for the subordinate role in any organizational headship. And any contention at the headship level is always initiated by the subordinate; therefore, contention is entirely within the subordinate's own control. Mutiny is never the idea of the captain of a ship.

And while authority, or headship, can be granted to someone in its entirety simply by the subordinate letting go and releasing it to him or her, the role of the subordinate can only be assumed, or owned, by the sub-ordinate voluntarily. Therefore, since any contention in a marriage always takes place at the position of authority, at the headship level, the presence of any contention (or the absence of it) is entirely within the control of the wife alone. No need to dwell on this principle now; I will explain it in more detail later. It's just to say that I have sound reasons for focusing on the role of the wife in this particular book. (Perhaps my next book will focus on the role of the husband, which is equally as crucial and deserving of special focus.)

For those reasons I present the following Scripture verses that reinforce and elaborate on the ordinances for wives. Please recall that my first listed purpose of this book is to exalt (or lift up and encourage) women in their God-ordained purpose in marriage. Also, please remember that these are God's words and God's design:

> And the Lord God said, It is not good that the man should be alone; I will make him an help meet for him.
> Genesis 2:18 (kjv)

> And Adam said, This is now bone of my bones, and flesh of my flesh: she shall be called Woman, because she was taken out of Man.
> Genesis 2:23 (kjv)

Unto the woman he said, I will greatly multi- ply thy sorrow and thy conception; in sorrow thou shalt bring forth children; and thy desire shall be to thy husband, and he shall rule over thee.
Genesis 3:16 (kjv)

But I would have you know, that the head of every man is Christ; and the head of the woman is the man; and the head of Christ is God.
1 Corinthians 11:3 (kjv)

For a man indeed ought not to cover his head, forasmuch as he is the image and glory of God; but the woman is the glory of the man. For the man is not of the woman; but the woman of the man. Neither was the man created for the woman; but the woman for the man.
1 Corinthians 11:7–9 (kjv)

Wives, submit yourselves unto your own husbands, as unto the Lord. For the husband is the head of the wife, even as Christ is the head of the church; and he is the saviour of the body. Therefore as the church is subject unto Christ, so let the wives be to their own husbands in every thing.
Ephesians 5:22–25 (kjv)

… the wife see that she reverence her husband.
Ephesians 5:33 (kjv)

Wives, submit yourselves unto your own husbands, as it is fit in the Lord.
Colossians 3:18 (kjv)

The aged women … That they may teach the young women to be sober, to love their hus- bands, to love their children, to be discreet, chaste, keepers at home, good, obedient to their own husbands, that the word of God be not blasphemed.
Titus 2:3–5 (kjv)

Likewise, ye wives, be in subjection to your own husbands; that, if any obey not the word, they also may without the word be won by the conversation of the wives … even the ornament of a meek and quiet spirit, which is in the sight of God of great price. For after this manner in the old time the holy women also, who trusted in God, adorned themselves, being in subjection unto their own husbands: Even as Sarah obeyed Abraham, calling him lord: whose daugh- ters ye are, as long as ye do well, and are not afraid with any amazement.
1 Peter 3:1–6 (kjv)

Now here's a very important point: just so that no one should be led to believe that the wife is to reverence her husband only if she feels that he's worthy of it or only if he is first perfectly submitted to Jesus, God carefully included this verse in the context immediately preceding the above excerpt from 1 Peter 3: "Servants, be subject to your masters with all fear; not only to the good and gentle, but also to the froward" (1 Peter 2:18, kjv).

Please note that the likewise in verse one above refers back to the immediately preceding context; in other words, "Likewise, ye wives, be in subjection to your own husbands … not only to the good and gentle, but also to the froward."

Also please note "ye wives, be in subjection to your own husbands; that, if any obey not the word, they also may without the word be won by the conversation of the wives." It's important to realize that this is a promise of blessings for a wife's subjection to her husband in obedience to the Lord!

Now to put the complete picture together, the following is the full context involving the above excerpts from 1 Peter, and it is awesome:

> Servants, be subject to your masters with all fear; not only to the good and gentle, but also to the froward. For this is thankworthy, if a man for conscience toward God endure grief, suffering wrongfully. For what glory is it, if, when ye be buffeted for your faults, ye shall take it patiently? but if, when ye do well, and suffer for it, ye take it patiently, this is acceptable with God. For even hereunto were ye called: because Christ also suffered for us, leaving us an example, that ye should follow his steps: Who did no sin, neither was guile found in his mouth: Who, when he was reviled, reviled not again; when he suffered, he threatened not; but committed himself to him that judgeth righteously: Who his own self bare our sins in his own body on the tree, that we, being dead to sins, should live unto righteousness: by whose stripes ye were healed. For ye were as sheep going astray; but are now returned unto the Shepherd and Bishop of your souls. Likewise, ye wives, be in subjection to your own husbands; that, if any obey not the word, they also may without the word be won by the conversation of the wives.
> 1 Peter 2:18–3:1 (kjv)

By these we see that it is especially important for a wife to be in subjection to a husband whom she may consider to be unworthy of it. And as a sideline, here's some more consolation and encouragement concerning the wife of a "froward" husband:

> Marriage is honorable in all, and the bed undefiled: but whoremongers and adulterers God will judge. Let your conversation be without covetousness; and be content with such things as ye have: for he hath said, I will never leave thee, nor forsake thee. So that we may boldly say, The Lord is my helper, and I will not fear what man shall do unto me.
> Hebrews 13:4–6 (kjv)

Just as there are scriptures for the husband to love his wife unconditionally, regardless of what kind of person she is, so there are for the wife to honor and submit to her husband unconditionally, regardless of what kind of person her husband is.

Just as God, in his Word, has commanded the husband to love his wife, God has also commanded the wife to love, reverence, submit to, subject herself to, and even obey her husband. Unless she believes her husband is "froward"? Only if she feels like it? Only once she's decided her husband is worthy of it? Only once he's earned it? No. There are no ifs, ands, or buts. There are no exceptions or conditions. This cannot be mistaken. And since our God is a God of order, you can be sure that he has perfectly logical reasons for this, along with the promise of his blessings that accompany it, as I will prove soon with evidence.

God's Plan for a Marriage Fortress

A Mission Team

What is God's purpose for a marriage union? Just as with all of us, I think it's safe to assume that God's primary purpose for a marriage is to know him, love him, serve him, and glorify him in it. But what is the primary mission of a marriage with children? To be the God-ordained providing and protecting covering over their children, to nurture and raise up children to know and love Jesus Christ as their Lord and Savior, and to serve him and glorify him!

Jesus voluntarily gave up his rightful place in heaven and became God made flesh for a purpose, and together with God the Father they formed a mission team to pro- vide us the only way to be reconciled with them. Without the fully submitted heart of Jesus, the Son of Man, for his Father, could they have carried out their mission to win the victory over Satan to save us?

Can you imagine what might have happened if Jesus' heart was only weakly or conditionally submitted to his Father, if he hadn't first purposed in his heart to keep his own fleshly feelings in submission to his Father's will? Could he have withstood the three "shock and awe" attacks of Satan in the wilderness (remember how he did it)?

Even if so, could he have then endured the extreme trials he knew he was faced with afterwards, knowing (obviously) how he would be so painfully tortured and crucified? Without the fully submitted heart of Jesus, how could the fortress of his relationship with the Father have withstood the incredible trials facing their mission together?

Likewise, without the fully submitted heart of a wife for her husband, how can the mission team of their marriage fortress withstand the incredible trials facing their mission together without falling apart?

There is no doubt in my mind that today's parents, especially in the popular culture of our society today, have an extremely challenging mission in raising children. Thanks to Satan's cleverly stealthy and deceptive tactics, the draw of the secular world on our children's hearts is irresistibly intense for them! Every element of the parental marriage fortress must be solidly intact to withstand Satan's "shock and awe" bombing raids to grasp the hearts of their children and prevent them from serving Jesus as their Lord and Savior! We are going to explore this in greater detail.

Blessings for a Solidly Built Fortress

God is not a mean, heartless dictator. He didn't just pick his commands and ordinances for us out of thin air to give us stuff to condemn us with, at least not in his New Covenant with us since Jesus "blotted out the hand writing of ordinances against us" in the mosaic law and "nailed them to the cross."

In his perfect love for us, Jesus has given us ordinances to follow so that we may avoid unnecessary heartache and pain and learn to live in joy; ordinances that, when followed, keep us from disconnecting our- selves from him, the source of abundant and everlasting life! We can show our Lord how much we love him by adhering to his ordinances in spite of our own thoughts, feelings, or understanding. Is this how we must "take up our cross" and follow him? After all, he took up his cross on the way to the destruction of his own flesh.

> I am crucified with Christ: nevertheless I live; yet not I, but Christ liveth in me: and the life which I now live in the flesh I live by the faith of the Son of God, who loved me, and gave himself for me.
> Galatians 2:20 (kjv)

> He that loveth his life shall lose it; and he that hateth his life in this world shall keep it unto life eternal.
> John 12:25 (kjv)

> For if ye live after the flesh, ye shall die: but if ye through the Spirit do mortify the deeds of the body, ye shall live.
> Romans 8:13 (kjv)

> But put ye on the Lord Jesus Christ, and make not provision for the flesh, to fulfil the lusts thereof.
> Romans 13:14 (kjv)

And the beauty of it is that our Lord and Savior has provided us with precious promises for our free-will obedience! I can't help but believe that, just as we love to bless our trusting and obedient children, God must love to encourage our victory over our own flesh with rewards for obedience. Among them he promises blessings of joy and good fruit for our obedience to him.

For this reason any marriage or family in which the husband and the wife willingly adhere to his ordinances for each of them and fulfill their God-ordained roles and purposes avail themselves to God's abundant blessings of protection, pro- vision, and, ultimately, joy!

"God is ready to assume full responsibility for the life wholly yielded to Him." - Andrew Murray

> If ye keep my commandments, ye shall abide in my love; even as I have kept my Father's commandments, and abide in his love. These things have I spoken unto you, that my joy might remain in you, and that your joy might be full.
> John 15:10–11 (kjv)

> For the kingdom of God is not meat and drink; but righteousness, and peace, and joy in the Holy Ghost.
> Romans 14:17 (kjv)

Remember that God, our Father in heaven, is the perfectly loving and flawless model of a father. Think of a loving father and a child who trusts him wholeheartedly. The child is obedient because he trusts his father. If the father tells him to do this or not to do that, the child obeys because he believes and trusts that his father loves him and knows what's best for him. And the loving father is always standing ready to shower blessings on the child for his obedience!

When we demonstrate our trust in God by our obedience to him against our own feelings, he is then free to bless us, to reward our obedience to him! We have his promise of blessings for our obedient victory over our own natural feelings and temptations of the flesh. Just as a loving human father loves to bless his trusting and obedient children, God our perfect Father must love to bless his trusting and willingly obedient children

I can't help but believe that he is always standing ready to protect and bless a marriage or family in which the husband and wife both comply with his design instructions for them!

True protection, provision, and abundant joy, avail- able to you from none other than the creator and master of the universe himself! What more could anyone want?

I personally know of the evidence of this in the testimony of the example of some, but unfortunately few, Christian families in which the marriage structure appears to be a solidly built fortress, built in full compliance to God's design. Here's the first example that comes to mind of a family I know.

The husband clearly has a heart of willing submission to Christ and of love for his wife and children.

The wife appears to have a heart of complete love, honor, and submission for her husband and outwardly supports and upholds him as her head and the head of their house- hold. She, as the helpmeet of her husband, seems to be the firm support on which he stands.

Their children, while still being children in every normal human way, are fully trusting of, and willingly obedient to, their parents. They seem non-rebellious, him and knows what's best for him. And the loving father is always standing ready to shower blessings on the child for his obedience!

When we demonstrate our trust in God by our obedience to him against our own feelings, he is then free to bless us, to reward our obedience to him! We have his promise of blessings for our obedient victory over our own natural feelings and temptations of the flesh. Just as a loving human father loves to bless his trusting and obedient children, God our perfect Father must love to bless his trusting and willingly obedient children

I can't help but believe that he is always standing ready to protect and bless a marriage or family in which the husband and wife both comply with his design instructions for them!

True protection, provision, and abundant joy, avail- able to you from none other than the creator and master of the universe himself! What more could anyone want?

I personally know of the evidence of this in the testimony of the example of some, but unfortunately few, Christian families in which the marriage structure appears to be a solidly built fortress, built in full compliance to God's design. Here's the first example that comes to mind of a family I know.

The husband clearly has a heart of willing submission to Christ and of love for his wife and children. The wife appears to have a heart of complete love, honor, and submission for her husband and outwardly supports and upholds him as her head and the head of their house- hold. She, as the helpmeet of her husband, seems to be the firm support on which he stands.

Their children, while still being children in every normal human way, are fully trusting of, and willingly obedient to, their parents. They seem non-rebellious, immune to the otherwise powerful draw of the world on their hearts, and are seemingly void of today's common child mental disorders (such as ADD, ADHD, or various other types of neuroses or other dysfunction). Though the family is not particularly wealthy financially, they seem to live comfortably and contentedly within their means and bear no signs of financial hard- ship. Their physical needs are amply provided for, and their marriage fortress is apparently an effective barrier against the enemy's attempts to grasp at the hearts of their children. Of course, I'm sure they still encounter trials, but it appears to me that they rely on their joy in the Lord and their freedom in Christ in dealing with them.

Now, in contrast to the beauty of the above example, let's take a look at the tragic reality of many marriages and families in our society today, even among Christians. Too many of them seem to be fraught with all kinds of struggles and tribulation. Frequent contentions and arguments between husband and wife, even screaming matches (or worse), and often in front of their children; adultery and infidelity; relentless financial hardship; rebelliously uncontrollable and wayward children and teens; spiritual buffeting of all sorts from the enemy— any or all of these are common traits of many families today.

Where is God's protection and provision for them? Why are so many of God's children, those who believe in Jesus and have put their faith and trust in him, suffering such heavy tribulation? And if it's this bad now and they're barely holding together, what if the tribulations they face ahead of them are even worse (which in these last days is very likely)?

I believe that God can only freely bless a marriage that exemplifies his design. I believe that he can only freely protect, provide for, and bless a marriage that's built in full compliance with his "building code" and carries his stamp of approval, one whose design glorifies him as the designer, one which testifies to God's design expertise! Remember how we can glorify God in the eyes of others? By exhibiting his blessings of provision, protection, and joy as the good fruit of our compliance with his ordinances. Jesus said:

> He that hath my commandments, and keepeth them, he it is that loveth me: and he that loveth me shall be loved of my Father, and I will love him, and will manifest myself to him.
>
> John 14:21 (kjv)

What awesome promises! I think we can be sure to be richly blessed when Jesus manifests himself to us, both in this life and in the next.

A Weak Fortress Cannot Stand

"Wrong attitudes in our lives will block the blessings of God and cause us to live below God's potential for our lives."- John Maxwell

If there are design flaws in the structure of a marriage fortress, can we still reasonably expect God to bless it and make it to flourish? If a marriage is built contrary to the "building code" of God's design for a marriage and family fortress, indeed why would he want to bless it and make it to flourish? As a testimony to rebellion against his ordinances? As a testimony to selfishness? As a testimony to Satan?

Here's some real and tragic evidence by the example of a Christian marriage in crisis that I know of, one that appears largely devoid of God's blessings of protection, provision, and joy, a marriage in jeopardy of falling apart and a family in peril, only one of several carbon-copy examples that I know of personally. I am aware that it's a very common scenario. Perhaps you, the reader, will think I am writing about someone you know personally as well.

The husband in this family has a heart of willing sub- mission to Christ and of love for his wife and children. The wife, though at least projecting a heart of willing submission to Christ in all other ways, admittedly takes exception with God's Word for wives. She apparently has little or no heart to honor and support her husband with her submission. She regularly undermines and usurps her husband's headship in their marriage and in their family. She contends with him frequently and often angrily reprimands him, not even as though he were a child, but as though he were an unruly dog. She occasionally beats him down with cutting and stabbing remarks against his character and against his manhood, making him to feel as though he is worthless as a husband and father. And she has done these things even in front of their children!

It is apparent that she considers herself superior to her husband, that she is in contention with him for the headship in their home (especially in the eyes of their children), and that she regards him often with con- tempt, if only subtly. She clearly has little or no heart of appreciation or honor for her husband. In fact, all things considered, it is safe to say that she despises (or has no proper regard for) him!

Regardless of the husband's sincere desire and best efforts to adequately provide for his family financially as the sole provider, they have been in a constant state of financial hardship for years. In fact, his attempts to provide for them seem almost supernaturally restrained from even reasonable financial gain. Regardless of his expertise, passion, and due diligence in his occupation, and regardless of the fervent prayers of many other Christians for his financial stability, he seems unable to realize consistent financial stability from it, and their bills and debts are a constant strain. He has felt at times that God is not only withholding his financial blessings from him but that God is actually preventing even the normal returns on his efforts that could reasonably be expected.

And their children have been rebelliously out of order. Regardless of their parents' attempts to shield them against the enemy's worldly influences, their children have succumbed to the intense lure of the ways of the secular world and have left home at as early an age as possible to "live their own lives" outside the covering of their parental structure over them, and this grieves the parents greatly. In fact, they reluctantly allowed their daughter to leave them even before she was eighteen, because she had become almost impossible to live with in her rebellion, and her destructive influence in their family had become almost intolerable. She is headstrong and wayward.

Can it be that the wife's disobedience to God's commands for her to love, honor, and obey her husband is the destructive flaw in the construction of this family's weak structure? Can it be that her rebellion against God's design for their marriage is the major contributing factor allowing these destructive forces to act upon their fam- ily? Can this be why God seems to be withholding his blessings of financial provision for the family and protection against the enemy's influence on their children?

I firmly suggest that it is. After all, if God were to bless the husband's efforts to provide for his family financially, then his wife with her rebellious heart toward him (ultimately toward Jesus) would also be blessed in it by default. Can this happen? Would God even allow his wife to be blessed in her rebellion?

Not only that—and this is equally as significant—I suggest that her rebellion is also a destructive influence on her husband's ability to function properly and fully in his God-ordained role as well, and I will prove this soon with convincing evidence.

But here's the real bottom-line tragedy in this all- too-common scenario: the bad fruit of a poorly built marriage structure is manifest not only in the joy-starved marriage but more tragically in the children God has carefully placed under its care. If the parents' marriage structure is constructed with weak (equal partnership) or upside-down (wife as the head of her husband) design flaws, then the children's protective covering is weak and vulnerable to the enemy, and the children are the innocent victims!

Therefore, I believe that it's absolutely imperative to start the construction of any marriage and family with the fully submitted heart of the woman to her husband first. And if you're a woman considering marriage and you're still reading this, I am very encouraged and excited for you and your future husband!

But while I know that this message is valuable as premarital counsel, I have a more immediate sense of urgency to help restore marriages that are falling apart already; not only for the sake of the hurting husband and wife but, even more importantly, for the sake of their children.

In his book Love for a Lifetime, Dr. James C. Dobson explains:

We all know that divorce has become the fashionable way to deal with marital conflict in the past three decades. Books such as Creative Divorce have described it as the start of a brand new life that was in the "best interest" of the entire family. But that is patently untrue. Divorce is devastating, not just for the children, but for their hurt and angry parents too. Women pay a particularly high price, even when they are the ones who opted out of the relationship.

Let me explain. There have always been irresponsible men who were unfaithful to their wives or abandoned their families. That is still going on and accounts for millions of broken homes today. But in my lifetime, marriages have begun to disintegrate for another reason. Women, encouraged by new freedoms and financial security, have shown a greater willingness to pull the plug. I have worked with many frustrated wives who seemed determined to obtain a divorce, not because their husbands were unfaithful or irresponsible, but because romantic love was missing from the relation- ship. These women expressed great anger and deep resentment toward husbands who were either unwilling or unable to meet their wives' basic emotional needs.

I would not minimize the distressing "soul hunger" that women so frequently describe, but I will say this: Divorce is not the answer to it! Those who seek that "solution" often jump from the frying pan into the fire!

So how do we go about restoring existing marriage and family structures that are weak, joyless, struggling, and even falling apart to the point of destruction? How can we empower and encourage husbands to consistently meet the emotional needs of their wives? How do we identify the root cause of their problems? How do we identify the first and most important step in an effective restoration process, one that will most assuredly produce the good fruit of restoration and healing?

Marriage Fortress Restoration

What about restoring failing marriages and dysfunctional families? They can certainly be restored! God can do any good thing that he wills to be done, and he can use any circumstances he wants to use! We can assume that it is not God's will for a marriage to be destroyed; on the contrary, we can be sure that it's God's will that every marriage be strong, joyful, and fruitful! And indeed, God can do most anything except to change a person's determined will to rebel against him.

But be careful of this: Even the best and most sacrificial intentions to restore a marriage, if poorly executed, can still be at least ineffective, if not downright destructive.

For example, you can believe you have the right manual and all the right tools to fix your car, but you must first be very careful to identify the root of the problem, then determine the correct repair strategy accordingly. If you haven't first correctly assessed the problem, your efforts will be in vain and could actually make your car worse. Need I say more?

Likewise, beginning in the wrong place to restore healthy function in a marriage or family could actually be counterproductive or even destructive. You could end up trying to "fix" the wrong thing first and make it worse.

I read once that someone asked Chuck Yeager, astronaut, test pilot, and first man ever to break the sound barrier, what he would do if he had a serious problem in the air and only had ten seconds to do something about it. His reply, as I recall, was, "I'd think about it for eight." Why? Because the correct action he would take to avoid disaster is entirely dependent upon first accurately identifying the root cause of the problem.

He was also known to say something to the effect that, "A disaster is always the result of the combination of two or more failures [or errors]." In other words, when a problem is encountered, doing the right thing about it will avoid disaster, but doing the wrong thing about it will result in disaster. I have pondered this theory for several years after first hearing it, and I have found that it applies in every circumstance. Here are some oversimplified examples.

While driving your car, someone pulls out in front of you (the problem, or the first error). If you are driving defensively (prepared to do the right thing about it), the crash is avoided, but if you fail to do the right thing quickly enough (the second error), a collision disaster results. Here's another: A small fire starts in a home (the first failure); no one in the house knows where the fire extinguisher is (the second failure), and they all watch helplessly as the house burns down.

And here's the most appropriate one: I've done some skydiving. On my third jump, my parachute opened with not just one but two malfunctions (the first failure). Remembering my training and the wise words of Chuck Yeager, I stayed calm and took the time to determine the root cause. Since one malfunction was a result of the other, if I had tried to correct the wrong one first (a second failure), it wouldn't have worked, and I probably would not have lived to tell about it. Once I was certain of which one I needed to correct first, the problem was easily resolved (no second failure), and disaster was averted! I enjoyed the rest of my ride and landed unharmed.

So in restoring a marriage fortress, where do we start? Let's consider this reasonable logic: Just as in attempt- ing to fully restore an old car or old house that is falling apart, there's a logical procedure one must follow to accomplish this. For a car you begin by removing the body from atop the chassis and setting it aside, then working first on restoring the integrity of the chassis (such as the frame, drive train, and brakes).

With a house we begin by restoring the integrity of the foundation, making it solid and level and square, then working our way up from there.

In all cases we start by restoring, or at least confirming the integrity of, the base, or the supporting member. Why? Because it's the most logically effective and efficient way. With a car even a perfectly restored body could be destroyed if its support is a weak chassis, as in a cracked frame or poor brakes. With a house even a perfectly restored building will likely be destroyed as its weak foundation gradually gives way under it.

God gave us the material list already (a husband sub- mitted to Jesus and a wife submitted to her husband in obedience to Jesus) and showed us his "video" of how he properly assembles a solid structure in preparation of his purpose for it: "First we started with my Son's heart of perfect devotion and submission to me; then we began our mission of salvation together." (not a direct quote from Scripture obviously but just my observation of the events in the Bible).

Likewise, in attempting to restore a marriage, we must also first start with the base, or the supporting member: the wife's heart of unconditional honor and submission to her husband.

However, it's not so simple. Only those who have ears to hear the truth can hear it, accept it, and actually embrace it, and embrace the Scriptures we must, for our own well-being. Unfortunately, this is seldom the case with a controlling, rebellious, or otherwise contentious wife. In the all-too-common pattern of blaming the man, many women today tend to assume that all their marital discord is primarily their husband's fault, and they have "itching ears" to be told so, to be vindicated and confirmed blameless.

> For the time will come when they will not endure sound doctrine; but after their own lusts shall they heap to themselves teachers, having itching ears; And they shall turn away their ears from the truth, and shall be turned unto fables.
> 2 Timothy 4:3–4 (kjv)

There is a greater enemy oppressing women with "itching ears" as such, which I am about to expose in the nucleus of this book ahead. For those of us who know our Lord Jesus and wish to be effective and profitable soldiers for him in this spiritual battle, we must also know the enemy! After the next chapter on marriage counseling, I will expose what I'm convinced is the real destructive force, the real reason for the itching ears of some wives, the real enemy in our marriages today.

Honor and Respect

I'm going to step up on one of my soapboxes now and interject a small nugget here. There is a common misconception in our world today. The misconception is that honor and respect must be earned to be deserved and must be deserved to be granted. While this may sound fine and dandy, it's wrong; in fact, it's upside-down. I find no evidence of this anywhere in God's Word. What I do find, though, is plenty of evidence to the contrary, not only in God's Word, but also in my own training and experience and the evidence I've observed through the years in human psychological behavior.

There is a dangerous epidemic of a lack of respect for authority in our society today, which becomes more prevalent with each new generation. And it is contagious. And this is not at all off the subject of this book.

Perhaps honor and respect are confused with trust. In the realm of human behavior, while we may initially choose to risk a certain amount of trust in someone, such as those with authority over us, our true trust in them must be earned. And even then we can only fully trust the one who is worthy of it; that is God. Any human being (because none of us are infallible) will possibly betray our trust or let us down in some way, sooner or later, regardless of their best intentions. But trust is a different subject; we were discussing honor and respect.

The fact is that where honor and respect are due, it is to be granted, whether deserved or earned or not. Honor and respect are action verbs, like love. One doesn't need to feel like it; they must simply decide to do it. One can choose to treat even a dishonorable person with honor and respect, and conversely, one can choose to treat even an honorable person dishonorably. From this I deduce that any honor and respect anyone receives is entirely granted to them by others either way. In other words, one is only respected or honored by that which is freely granted to him by another.

Besides, there is much to be said about the phenomenal effect that bestowed honor can have on a person, and we will be exploring this further.

Marriage Counseling

If you have a heart to help restore struggling or failing marriages and families to fullness in Christ and are led by God to do so, then may God bless you in your efforts! You are so desperately needed today! But please consider this: If you haven't correctly diagnosed the root source of the problem first, your efforts may make things worse. Best intentions alone do not automatically qualify some- one to perform such a critical and delicate mission.

And more importantly, don't be so sure that any counseling training you've received is true and trustworthy or that you've been properly trained. God's Wisdom, the Holy Spirit's leading, and your own discernment should not only be injected into any training curriculum; they should indeed supersede any training curriculum.

I may be willing to risk my life to disarm a ticking bomb, but if I haven't been trained properly in disarming bombs, I could very well not only sacrifice my own life but the lives of innocent others if I cut the wrong wire by mistake! Given a finite time before the bomb explodes, only a properly informed and prepared expert should be the one to attempt it. Either way, since there are many varieties of bomb designs, the focus of the first step should be to take whatever time necessary to be certain of which wire is the correct one to cut!

Counselors, consider the fruit of your past efforts. Have your counseling attempts always produced good fruit in a struggling marriage or family right from the start? Some of you might be thinking, Well, no, it got worse for them at first, but if they hadn't quit counseling, I'm sure it would have gotten better eventually, or, Well, it couldn't really get much worse, but it didn't seem to help much either.

Given a couple committed to each other and their family who, with open hearts and teachable spirits, would seek out biblical counsel for help (which I think are mutually inclusive elements), I think it's safe to believe that it should have helped things get better for them right from the start, no?

Why wouldn't it? Given these four ingredients: a well- meaning and loving husband, a well-meaning and loving wife, both committed to each other to the extent that they seek biblical counseling, and topped off with God's will to keep their marriage intact and joyful, which of them could be the weak ingredient? What do you think the problem might be? What's the weak link? How could this scenario not produce immediate and lasting good fruit?

If you are a trained and certified or otherwise credentialed biblical counselor, let me guess this: You are convinced with such great faith in the training you've received that you assume any lack of good fruit in your efforts to restore a marriage must be due either to your own personal ineffectiveness or to some influence beyond your control. Perhaps so, but perhaps not.

I suggest that whatever faith you may have in your training is to be questioned; your faith in it may indeed be misplaced. Though you may even be certified in some Christian counseling institute or training program, don't be so sure your training has been all 100 percent correct. It's natural to assume that the bigger and more widely accepted an idea is, and the more loudly it's proclaimed, the more believable and trustworthy it is, especially if you have a large investment in it, right?

Nevertheless, as Jesus has taught us, we can judge a tree quite accurately by the fruit it produces. Consider Satan for a moment. We know that he wants marriages destroyed and would want for us to feel hopeless in our efforts to restore them. So by this logic, is it safe to assume that he would put forth much effort to infiltrate and influence a marriage counseling agenda?

Now think of those throughout history that have single-handedly fought against widely accepted heresy and know this for a fact: There are any number of institutions, even Christian ones, that propagate erroneous or incomplete doctrines, teachings, or training; they're wrong regardless of how widely accepted and popularly trusted they may be. Though they may have nothing but the best intentions, beware of swallowing whole every- thing they may teach. Do not allow yourself to be blinded by whatever you have been taught by men!

> Cease, my son, to hear the instruction that causeth to err from the words of knowledge.
> Proverbs 19:27 (kjv)

> … even as there shall be false teachers among you, who privily shall bring in damnable here- sies, even denying the Lord that bought them, and bring upon themselves swift destruction.
> 2 Peter 2:1 (kjv)

Having a form of godliness, but denying the power thereof: from such turn away. For of this sort are they which creep into houses, and lead captive silly women laden with sins, led away with divers lusts, Ever learning, and never able to come to the knowledge of the truth.
2 Timothy 3:5–7 (kjv)

Can you imagine how a couple would feel if, in a last-ditch effort to save their marriage or family, they sought out Christian biblical counseling and still didn't receive the help they so desperately needed? How would they feel? Forsaken by God maybe? Unless I miss my mark, I think they would feel that their marriage was truly hopeless!

I adamantly urge anyone who attempts to help restore a failing marriage or family structure to first diligently gather all evidence of symptoms and carefully analyze them to ascertain the root cause. The first step in a marriage counseling strategy is the worst place to make assumptions, because the wrong assumption about the cause can render the rest of the efforts null and void, or worse.

It would be like assuming that the red wire in a ticking time bomb is the one to cut because that's what you've seen them do in movies.

The Wrong First Step

You may be equipped with the right information (God's Word) and even have some of what you believe is "expert" training, but if you've been trained to use some sort of standardized and questionably ineffective approach to marriage counseling, be prepared to throw it where it belongs: in the garbage! Given the complexities of the human psyche and the intricacies of human relational interaction, any standardized, one-size-fits-all approach to marriage counseling is at least foolish, if not down- right insane!

Some biblical marriage counselors that I am aware of have apparently been cookie-cutter trained to open their first marriage counseling session by telling the couple that the focus of their marriage counseling agenda will be on the husband, that they are going to start by "fixing" the husband first! Right now some may be thinking, Oh no, that's not how we put it! But I tell you now most assuredly—and here's the danger with it—that's how it can easily be taken by a woman who has "itching ears" to hear that their marriage problems are all her husband's fault! Again …

> For the time will come when they will not endure sound doctrine; but after their own lusts shall they heap to themselves teachers, having itching ears; And they shall turn away their ears from the truth, and shall be turned unto fables.
> 2 Timothy 4:3–4 (kjv)

What this first-blood assault on the husband does is to immediately vindicate a wife who already believes she is superior to her husband and is itching to be told that their marital and/or family problems are all her husband's fault! I may be stepping on the toes of many marriage and family counselors here, but the truth is nevertheless the truth; and sugarcoating it might only hide it from view. This misleading first impression of what may otherwise be good intentions sets the pace on a poor foundation. It is the first step in a wrong direction and serves only to reinforce the already subtle deceptions of Satan's agenda for women in a marriage and family!

Then the rest of the counseling efforts are essentially nullified, and an already struggling marriage can take a turn for the worse and end in destruction. And Satan, laughing, spreads his wings!

Indeed, we must be very careful not to suggest, even by implied assumption, that the husband is responsible to first come into obedience or that he is first to earn and deserve the headship in the home. This suggests to a wife that she is justified in her own disobedience to God's Word for her, that she is excused from her own obedience to God by the husband's failings!

It is destructive for a wife to be led to even unconsciously assume the attitude that I don't have to start honoring my husband until I feel he's become honorable, or I'll start honoring my husband as soon as he becomes the proper spiritual leader of our home or as soon as he becomes a proper provider or as soon as he starts loving me as he should. Such a wife actually despises God's Word for herself and is rebellious in her disobedience to God.

For this reason it is absolutely destructive to mislead a contentious wife into believing that her husband is primarily responsible for the problems in their mar- riage! It immediately satisfies the itching ears of such a woman, vindicating her and allowing her to rest assured that her husband is to blame for all the problems in their marriage and family and that she can just wait and pray for him to get "fixed" first! It sets the pace for her (and everyone involved for that matter) to focus all attention on getting him fixed first!

It's as if to say, "As soon as I'm satisfied that my husband has earned the headship in our home, I might let him have it." It's like running God's "assembly video" backwards.

It would be like trying to rebuild the home from the top down by first telling the husband to float himself as high as he can in mid-air, then telling the wife to install her support under him once she's satisfied that he's lifted himself high enough.

We Can Judge a Tree by Its Fruit

I have personally witnessed the bad fruit of this wrong counseling approach in one couple I know. After this first-blood assault on the husband in the beginning of session one, the husband and wife were both focusing their prayers and efforts on "fixing" him. Her attitude from then on was that she would be willing to start honoring and being submissive to her husband as soon as he got fixed and became worthy of it. Though she graciously attempted, at the prompting of the counselors, to modify some of her behavior in the meantime, the attitude of her heart, as it was established in the first session, was focused on his being fixed first. She (and everyone else involved) was waiting for him to become worthy of her honor. This marriage has now ended in divorce.

God never says or even implies that a wife's heart of honor toward her husband must be earned by him or that a husband must earn his headship in the family structure or even that a husband must first be acceptably in perfect submission to Jesus.

And I have seen this same bad fruit in another marriage with the same counseling team and the same trained approach. Fortunately, though, for them there's still time. The husband has wisely withdrawn from that counseling because it only seemed to make their marriage worse as well; however, because his wife's itching ears were satisfied in their first counseling session, the damage has already been done, and she remains resistant to the sound doctrine of God's Word for wives.

But I don't blame the wife entirely in these cases either. The buck doesn't stop here. There is yet another enemy in these marriages which influences this trained counseling strategy as well.

Here's a fact you can take to the bank: While there are always reasons for the wrong things we do, there are never excuses. Likewise, while there are never excuses for the wrong things we do, there are always reasons:

> For we wrestle not against flesh and blood, but against principalities, against powers, against the rulers of the darkness of this world, against spiritual wickedness in high places.
>
> Ephesians 6:12 (kjv)

There are reasons why this first-blood attack on the husband in each of these cases satisfied the itching ears of the wife and made her to feel vindicated by the counseling "experts." Here's the thing: I believe that their itching ears were not entirely their own fault; it is a result of other forces! And now I will finally expose what I'm convinced is the real destructive force, the real reason for the tickle in their ears, the real enemy in our marriages today.

For those of us who know our Lord Jesus and wish to be effective and profitable soldiers for him in this spiritual battle, we must also know the enemy! It is not enough to know the capabilities of the enemy's weapons; we must also know his strategy for deploying them so that we can anticipate his moves! And to know his strategy, we must know his objective.

The Enemy in Our Spiritual Battle

Satan's Prime Objective

> And from the days of John the baptist until now, the kingdom of heaven suffereth violence, and the violent take it by force.
> Matthew 11:12 (kjv)

> Be sober, be vigilant; because your adversary the devil, as a roaring lion, walketh about, seeking whom he may devour:
> 1 Peter 5:8 (kjv)

Satan's prime objective is to have full rein over us and to see us destroyed! But we Christians indwelled by the Holy Spirit who have hearts devoted to God and his Word are the remnant "resistance force" that remain in the enemy camp, the camp that became Satan's once he deceived Eve and led Adam to fall. Since then Satan has been the prince of the power of the air (Ephesians 2:2) and the god of this world (2 Corinthians 4:4). And he knows that he must take this ground by force in order to have supreme reign over us, because we obedient born-again Christians stand in his way!

He needs to raise up a generation rendered impotent against him and indeed devoted to him in order to edge out the resistance force by attrition! To this end, his end game is to infiltrate, capture, and subvert the hearts of our children to himself for his use so that his kingdom can march forward unhindered! And we know that he's making great progress in this end-run plan in our society today, as evidenced by the fruit in many of our younger generations today! Consider the violence uprising in our schools today alone. Consider the fact that, in this following verse, disobedient to parents is included in such a list:

> Being filled with all unrighteousness, fornication, wickedness, covetousness, maliciousness; full of envy, murder, debate, deceit, malignity; whisperers, Backbiters, haters of God, despiteful, proud, boasters, inventors of evil things, disobedient to parents, Without understanding, covenant breakers, without natural affection, implacable, unmerciful:
> Romans 1:29–31 (kjv)

But how is he getting the hearts of our children so forcefully in his grip? How can they be so effectively led into Satan's bondage by the draw of the world on their hearts today, regardless of our best godly intentions for them? Why are even Christian parents having to struggle so hard, in many cases losing the battle, to keep Satan's worldly influences from leading the hearts of their chil- dren astray?

Satan's Battle Strategy

Satan is not stupid by any means. He knows that he cannot freely assault and capture the hearts of children without first infiltrating their territory. And he knows he cannot infiltrate their territory without first disintegrating the God-ordained protective covering of their parental structure.

So based on that premise, this is his strategy: to first decompose the integrity of the parental marriage, thereby weakening their protective covering over their children so that he can then infiltrate their children's hearts with rebellion against authority and ultimately against God!

What weapons has he deployed to decompose our children's protective covering against his assaults? How has he managed to disintegrate our God-given force field against Satan's free access to our children's hearts?

Satan is surely a foremost expert on one thing: self-awareness, otherwise known as pride, and how it can separate us from God. He is the qualified expert on this because he has experienced it for himself, magna cum laude:

> How art thou fallen from heaven, O Lucifer, son of the morning! how art thou cut down to the ground, which didst weaken the nations! For thou hast said in thine heart, I will ascend into heaven, I will exalt my throne above the stars of God: I will sit also upon the mount of the congregation, in the sides of the north: I will ascend above the heights of the clouds: I will be like the most High.
> Isaiah 14:12–14 (kjv)

I, I, I. Satan, of all beings, knows how effective pride can be in leading us away from God. Our pride takes our focus away from God and redirects it to self. Pride is self-worship and is an element present to some degree in all of us except perhaps the most poor in spirit. It is ever present and ever destructive. About the time you think you've become pretty humble, it is your pride that is in effect.

Have you ever thought of yourself, Hey, I'm becoming pretty humble, or, I bet others see me as being quite humble? Come on, be honest. It happens to me at times; it is a constant struggle. Even false humility is pride. Whenever we stop to consider how humble we are, pride has once again reared its ugly head in us!

Let's carefully examine Satan's tried and true method of disintegrating the parental structure by studying his first appearance in the Bible in Genesis, when he defeated Adam and Eve in the garden of Eden. Note how he first appeared to Eve as a beautiful serpent, coming alongside her as her friend and ally and appealing to her self-awareness (pride):

> Now the serpent was more subtle than any beast of the field which the Lord God had made. And he said unto the woman, Yea, hath God said, Ye shall not eat of every tree of the garden? And the woman said unto the serpent, We may eat of the fruit of the trees of the gar- den: But of the fruit of the tree which is in the midst of the garden, God hath said, Ye shall not eat of it, neither shall ye touch it, lest ye die. And the serpent said unto the woman, Ye shall not surely die: For God doth know that in the day ye eat thereof, then your eyes shall be opened, and ye shall be as gods, knowing good and evil. And when the woman saw that the tree was good for food, and that it was pleasant to the eyes, and a tree to be desired to make one wise, she took of the fruit thereof, and did eat, and gave also unto her husband with her; and he did eat.
> Genesis 3:1–6 (kjv)

Satan first appeared to Eve as a beautiful serpent, came alongside her posing as her ally, and appealed to her sense of self (pride) by telling her, "Ye shall be as gods." Then she saw the tree as one to be desired "to make one wise." And it is obvious in this passage that she was not too confused to be completely unaware of God's one commandment to them concerning this tree; she clearly knew it well enough: "And the woman said unto the serpent … God hath said, Ye shall not eat of it … "

Now here's the important point at which I'm trying to arrive: notice that Satan didn't even attempt to directly and overtly attack Adam, Eve's husband and defensive covering of protection; he undermined Adam's authority by first deceiving Eve! It was like kicking the ladder out from under Adam, and then he fell.

And upon closer examination of this event, these most significant questions are raised: Why did she feel free to make her own decision on this without checking with Adam, her head, first, especially considering that he stood to be so directly and adversely affected by it as well? Why did she not at least refer the serpent to Adam for this major life- changing decision?

Clearly, his tried-and-true method of bringing the husband down is by first deceiving the wife! He sneaks in, disguised as her ally, like a wolf in sheep's clothing, and deceives her by appealing to her pride. It worked well for him then, on the first try!

He weakens the defensive forces (the husband, the head) by a stealthy rear-flank assault on its support (the wife)!

Satan's Weapons of Mass Deception

Now let's consider Satan's weapons. We know that he is subtle and deceptive. And we know that he is a counterfeiter. Since he cannot create his own devices (because he cannot create at all), he takes the things of God's kingdom and perverts them for his use in his kingdom of darkness. And we know that he can assume a pleasant form: "And no marvel; for Satan himself is transformed into an angel of light." (2 Corinthians 11:14, kjv).

It is apparent to me that from the beginning and throughout history, "decomposing agents" are among Satan's best weapons against us. A decomposing agent sneaks undetected into a system in which it can thrive and multiply and eventually take over, like a cancer. But here's the most dangerous part: it's undetected until the symptoms of its damage first appear. A decomposing agent is not detected until damage has already been done!

Once Satan successfully had prayer removed from the public schools in America, thus undermining God's authority over all of us, he was then free to launch what may be his most prized advancement in his stealthy mass assault on women, in disintegrating the parental covering and exposing their children. He has released the following two decomposing agents in mass quantity upon a well-prepared system, two weapons of mass destruction to deceive the hearts of women.

1. The Women's "Liberation" Agenda

In this modern American culture, nearly all our women today (yes, I said nearly all) have been heavily indoctrinated, or brainwashed, with the heresies of the women's liberation movement, or the feminist movement. Besides the homosexual agenda, I believe that this is one of Satan's most gloriously successful assaults on marriage and the family unit ever! Regardless of the reasons for its conception, it has since grown like a systemic disease to infect the whole fabric of our culture today, and it hasn't even stopped there. And though we may think we know why it started and what it's about, do we really? I don't pretend to be an expert on it, but I can clearly see the fruit of the tree.

In a culture now almost devoid of God's truth and so permeated by the heresies of the feminist agenda, what chance do women have for true liberation, to live in true liberty, the freedom in Christ that God intends for them? The enemy is such a clever and patient strategist! This strategy doesn't liberate them at all; on the contrary, it has brought them into bondage to him!

> While they promise them liberty, they them- selves are the servants of corruption: for of whom a man is overcome, of the same is he brought in bondage.
> 2 Peter 2:19 (kjv)

> For when they speak great swelling words of vanity, they allure through the lusts of the flesh, through much wantonness, those that were clean escaped from them who live in error.
> 2 Peter 2:18 (kjv)

The problem is that though it may have started out with what seemed to be a justifiable purpose, the bad fruit of the tree of women's "liberation" and feminism has ripened into the vastly prominent ideology that women are not only equal to men but are actually superior to men and that men are to be controlled and manipulated by their women! And this is more than coincidentally fertile ground for the ancient and very stealthy Jezebel spirit (below). Together their synergy makes them a potent force!

It grieves me whenever I learn of a wife whose heart is to be home managing her household and nurturing and raising her children but who feels ashamed that she doesn't have her own career outside their home. What grieves me about it is that our society has degenerated to the point where she should feel ashamed of it! What higher and more legitimate and challenging career or purpose can anyone have in this life than to raise children? And who better for it than their loving and nurturing mother? Yet when many women are asked, "So, what do you do?" they are often ashamed or embarrassed if their only honest reply is "I'm a homemaker." In my opinion (and I'm not the only one), there is no greater calling on earth than for a woman to minister first to her husband and children.

I am convinced that under Satan's current regime nearly all of today's women have been at least subliminally brainwashed into what I consider to be the women's liberation "cult" to believe, if only subconsciously, that they are superior to men—especially to their own husbands!

You see, the clever and patient beast doesn't assault with "shock and awe"; it would be too obviously evil to us. For example, he doesn't bother trying to force decent and well-meaning people to join satanic cults or to get on their knees and worship him, because it would be too obviously repulsive to them. Remember, he is a deceiver! He uses decomposing agents that are only obvious once the damage has already been done. He is a counterfeiter and can appear as "an angel of light." And as we know by the serpent's deception of Eve, he gains access into our hearts for the deployment of his stealthy weapons by first posing as a beautiful ally and appealing to our ever- present natural tendencies of pride and selfishness.

The feminist movement first appeared as an ally to women. Now we find that we are constantly bombarded by our pop culture media today with this destructive brainwashing: the wise and mature wife having to manipulate and control her stupid and immature husband! You know what I'm talking about, right? In fact, it's so common and predominant today that it has become almost invisible. The jokes have been passed around for years. If you watch television, you'll notice how many commercials and sitcoms promote the idea of the stupid and immature man being led, controlled, and manipulated by the wise and mature woman. I could name some I've seen, but I bet you are already thinking of some right off the top of your head. If not, then just tune your television to one of the major networks any evening for one hour (if you can stand it that long), and you will see it.

This very predominant message in our society indoctrinates all of us with the image that the husband is inferior to his wife. And Satan's agenda in this, I'm certain, is nothing other than to emasculate men in the eyes of women and children, thereby overturning their proper roles ordained by God! And sadly many men themselves are emasculated by being cut with it from all directions, not only in the popular media, but also in their own homes by their own loved ones.

If you're a man who is bombarded from all directions with messages that you are inferior because you're a male, then you will begin to believe it, and as the human psyche goes, your behavior will gradually emulate it. We all have a tendency to fit into the role that we're placed in by others. If any human being is told often enough by enough people that he is stupid and weak and irresponsible, if others are constantly regarding him according to only the shortcomings and weaknesses that they assume about him or his gender as a whole, if he is often ridiculed and slighted and treated as being only a little more valuable than the family dog, he will not only become convinced of it sooner or later, but worse, his behavior will tend to be consistent with it. It is a phenomenon of human behavior.

Men are not superior to women, and women are not superior to men! Not at all. But neither are we equal. Each gender is different from the other in markedly contrasting ways, not only physically, but also mentally and emotionally, because that's how God made us. God has obviously made men and women different from each other in more ways than just physical and for his perfectly good and perfectly wise reasons.

So God in his infinite wisdom has ordained the roles for each in the home according to the unique characteristics of each that he values so highly! In fact, God exalts women so much so that he commands husbands to love their wives as their own bodies and to love them as Christ loves the church! And I think it's safe to say that there is no greater love and that he exalts nothing on earth higher than his own body, the Body of Christ!

So it seems to me that God highly esteems women. Even so, while men and women are equally significant to him for their own unique attributes and neither is superior to the other in God's eyes, they are not equal. But the worldview of things has long ago departed from God's view of things.

Thanks, Homer and Marge Simpson, and you, too, Bart and Lisa, for your accurate icon of the decomposition of the sanctified ground of marriage and family in our society. Homer is a bumbling idiot, and Marge is the wise wife and mother who has to constantly reign Homer in, and even Bart and Lisa are both depicted as being much wiser than their father. Good-bye to the old black-and-white TV shows like Father Knows Best and hello to "Girls rule; boys drool."

2. The Jezebel Spirit

We've finally arrived at the nucleus of this book. Perhaps Satan's oldest and greatest operative in his war against the institution of marriage and family (besides the homosexual agenda) is the spirit of Jezebel! Jezebel first appears in the Bible in 1 Kings 16:31 and remains a prominent subject through 2 Kings 9:37. This is apparently when the evil spirit acting upon this woman Jezebel gained foothold and began marching forward through time. And her spirit is so significant that Jesus mentions her again in Revelation 2:20.

Much has been written about this deceptive spirit lately. Christ seems to be revealing the potent and wide-spread presence of this vile and destructive spirit among his body these days, and more and more Christians are becoming aware of her as one of Satan's most stealthy and effective "weapons of mass deception."

Read the following excerpts from Jezebel: Seducing Goddess of War, a book by Jonas Clark, and be amazed. He has much to say about how the evil spirit of Jezebel seduces and deceives women in our culture today and indeed in the whole world. In it he writes:

> Jezebel is a master manipulator who uses flattering words and smooth sayings to seduce your soul. She seeks positions of power, influence, favor and authority that allow her to control and advance her evil agenda.
>
> It is time to expose the methods of the spirit of Jezebel so that our generation can conquer her evil wiles.
>
> Jezebel targets those who are rebellious, weak or wounded and she knows how to use deep emotional hurts and wounds to mislead and exploit. Jezebel's aim is to pull people to her-self and away from those who can speak truth into their lives. She understands, thoroughly, the power of isolation as she actively searches out the fainthearted and seducible. She seeks to woo those who are being disciplined or corrected by leadership and those living in quiet, yet artful, rebellion. She targets others who resent authority, complain, backbite or gossip. She looks for recruits who will carry her message—those that will tap into her immoral spirit and transfer it to as many others as possible. In the wake of every Jezebel spirit is a life of chaos, confusion and instability that ultimately leads to broken homes, marriages, relationships, churches and utter destruction.

Francis Frangipane, in his book The Jezebel Spirit, also describes this spirit very bluntly and concisely:

> Jezebel is fiercely independent and intensely ambitious for pre-eminence and control. It is noteworthy that the name "Jezebel," literally translated, means "without cohabitation." This simply means she refuses "to live together" or "cohabit" with anyone. Jezebel will not dwell with anyone unless she can control and dominate the relationship. When she seems sub-missive or "servant-like," it is only for the sake of gaining some strategic advantage. From her heart, she yields to no one.
>
> Bear in mind that the spirit which produced Jezebel existed before its namesake was born.
>
> Look for Jezebel to target women who are embittered against men, either through neglect or misuse of authority. This spirit operates through women who, because of insecurity, jealousy, or vanity, desire to dominate others.

And in the book The Harlot Church System, Charles Elliott Newbold, Jr. seems to be describing a condition of the heart of many women in marriages today. Perhaps you, too, will recognize someone in this. He writes:

> The Jezebel spirit despises the authority of the man. She is driven to usurp the headship of her husband—taking over what God has given him to do. She answers for him, makes decisions for him, and manipulates him to get her way. She uses sex, crying, sulking, conniving, self-pity and threats to achieve what she wants ... Jezebel is driven by ambition and is characterized by the headship of the woman ... Women who usurp their coverings of headship open themselves up to deceiving spirits. Women who become the "power behind the throne" or in any sense begin to exercise authority over their husbands open themselves up to a Jezebel spirit. The headship of women is out of order and dangerous. It will lead God's bond servants astray.

It also appears that the spirit of Jezebel began operating on women's hearts already in the Old Testament, soon after Jezebel's introduction in 1 Kings. Read about Queen Vashti in Esther 1:10–22 (the following is a condensed version):

> On the seventh day, when the heart of the king was merry with wine, he commanded ... To bring Vashti the queen before the king ... But the queen Vashti refused to come at the king's commandment ... therefore was the king very wroth, and his anger burned in him. Then the king said to the wise men ... What shall we do unto the queen Vashti according to law, because she hath not performed the commandment of the king Ahasuerus by the chamberlains? And Memucan answered ... Vashti the queen hath not done wrong to the king only, but also to all the princes, and to all the people that are in all the provinces of the king Ahasuerus. For this deed of the queen shall come abroad unto all women, so that they shall despise their husbands in their eyes ... Thus shall there arise too much contempt and wrath. If it please the king, let there go a royal commandment from him ... And when the king's decree which he shall make shall be published throughout all his empire, (for it is great,) all the wives shall give to their husbands honor, both to great and small. And the saying pleased the king and the princes ... For he sent letters ... that every man should bear rule in his own house, and that it should be published according to the language of every people.
> Esther 1:10–22 (kjv)

This Jezebel spirit, which was apparently gaining force and momentum even then, already working in the heart of the queen Vashti, is a very definite, real, and potent enemy spirit today, one that thrives large in our culture. And the problem is that it remains largely unrecognized and ignored among even evangelical Christians as a prominent force acting in our society, especially among women these days!

But make no mistake: The spirit of Jezebel is real, and it is stealthy, and it is prominent. No one is immune, including Christians well versed in Scripture, because it is powerfully blinding and powerfully binding, feeding the already present will to exalt ourselves (pride) that most of us have! The spirit of Jezebel can be working not only in the heart of a wife in a dysfunctional family structure but also in the heart of a marriage counseling agenda.

The spirit of Jezebel is a real and present danger to be reckoned with in marriages, especially when there's any chance that the nature of the wife's personality can already perhaps be characterized as strong, controlling, superior, ambitious, self-reliant, and/or self-absorbed.

And here's my point: This spirit of Jezebel must be identified and dealt with first and foremost; otherwise, no other efforts to restore the marriage can have any effect.

And because this evil and vile spirit is so stealthy, one who is oppressed by it will likely deny it vehemently. Dear reader, you may be convinced that the spirit of Jezebel has no influence on you, but please consider this: If while reading any of this book so far, particularly any of the scriptures contained in it, you felt an anger welling up inside you, if you have not been able to not only accept but indeed embrace every Scripture verse so far, then this is a strong indication that the spirit of Jezebel may be oppressing you and holding you in bondage. And its end, if given free reign and not dealt with, is destruction. Meanwhile, at the very least, it will rob you of any freedom and joy you might otherwise have available to you!

Just as unforgiveness and bitterness withheld in your heart gives the devil a stronghold in you and you are held in bondage by it, so does the Jezebel spirit. Until you are rid of it and can embrace joyfully all the scriptures pertaining to God's ordained role for a wife, you can never live in the fullness of the freedom and joy of Christ.

Extreme Measures

An Urgency for Change!

The divorce rate in our society today has reached alarm- ing numbers! According to a recent article titled Study: Christian Divorce Rate Identical to National Average in The Christian Post dated April 4, 2008, Audrey Barrick writes:

> The Barna Group found in its latest study that born again Christians who are not evangelical were indistinguishable from the national average on the matter of divorce with 33 per- cent having married and divorced at least once. Among all born again Christians, which includes evangelicals, the divorce figure is 32 percent, which is statistically identical to the 33 percent figure among non-born again adults, the research group noted.1

Given the moral collapse of our society today and the greater tribulations ahead of us, I am convinced that there's a great urgency for change in marriages and fami- lies and in marriage/family counseling strategy! Otherwise, given a well-intentioned Christian wife and a well-intentioned Christian husband committed to each other and seeking counsel to bring joy and fullness into their marriage, how is it that even with biblical counseling their marriages seem unable to be restored?

I urge biblical marriage counselors, regardless of whatever training you've received, to seriously consider redirecting your first-blood attack away from the hus- band and to address first, rather, the essential necessity of the woman to resolve in her heart to unconditionally honor her husband.

And here's the logical reason why, as I've mentioned previously: Any power strug- gle, any contention in a marriage, always takes place for the level of headship, never for the subordinate role! A husband and wife will almost never contend with each other for the position of the wife's role. While many women today are already predisposed to contend for the headship in the home, no contention is required for her to assume her own role except the contention in her own heart against God's will, led by the spirit of Jezebel and the "cult" brainwashing of the feminist movement.

> But unto them that are contentious, and do not obey the truth, but obey unrighteousness, indignation and wrath.
> Romans 2:8 (kjv)

> It is better to dwell in the wilderness, than with a contentious and an angry woman. ... He that followeth after righteousness and mercy find- eth life, right- eousness, and honor.
> Proverbs 21:19–21 (kjv)

> A continual dropping in a very rainy day and a contentious woman are alike.
> Proverbs 27:15 (kjv)

Making Marriage Restoration Efforts Fruitful Without first deactivating these two potent weapons of decomposition in the female forces of the family, the fertile ground of the women's "liberation" movement in which the spirit of Jezebel flourishes, all other efforts to repair any dysfunction in a family will be for naught! And I consider that this decomposing force is passed down through generations in a family, as a familiar spirit.

Remember the interventions that were organized and performed in the 1960s and '70s to rescue loved ones from cults? In like manner, the potent forces of the women's lib cult and the spirit of Jezebel may call for a carefully planned and organized intervention to rescue a woman from these two binding weapons of Satan. An intervention like rescue mission may need to be performed to rescue the woman/wife/daughters of a family structure and deprogram them of any brainwashing and idol (self) worship!

Right now, some of you are thinking, But it's the husband's job to wash his wife with the Word. True, ideally, but the reality is that the husband cannot be the one to attempt this one, folks. For one thing, the husband whom the wife has already been brainwashed into believing is the "weaker vessel" and whom the wife may indeed despise holds no credibility or authority over her as far as she's concerned. Coming from her own husband's mouth, quoting God's Word for wives will carry no weight with her, except maybe to make her angry! It's a catch-22.

Furthermore, I don't recall ever reading any evidence in Scripture that would lead me to believe that it's the husband's job to somehow make his wife be submissive to him. In another excerpt from Kay Arthur's book, A Marriage Without Regrets, she explains:

> All right, you say, but should a husband force his wife to submit? Please note that the scripture tells a woman to subject yourself. The passage says nothing about husbands compelling their wives to submit. The apostle's only command is that a husband love his wife as Christ loved the church. Don't miss this because there are many who teach that it is the husband's "duty" to somehow bring his wife into submission. If that were true, God would command it, or Jesus would model it. But God doesn't command it—and Jesus certainly doesn't model it! Christ certainly commands the obedience of His bride, but He doesn't force it. It is the bride's choice (yours and mine as believers). If we're wise, we'll obey and reap the blessings. If not, we will feel the consequences—and they are devastating!

But God has still lovingly provided a timeless way, as seen in the Scripture verse below. He is such a genius! Such an intervention mission necessitates a special forces anti-terrorism operative. Only another woman (one of their own "superior" kind) whom the wife respects and reveres for her wisdom can possibly sabotage Satan's hold on her heart, if, in fact, she is herself blind to it or unwilling to address it:

> The aged women … That they may teach the young women to be sober, to love their husbands, to love their children, to be discreet, chaste, keepers at home, good, obedient to their own husbands, that the word of God be not blasphemed.
> Titus 2:3–5 (kjv)

Only such a woman (or better yet, two or more) empowered with the force of the name of Jesus Christ of Nazareth, armed with the weapons of targeted scriptures (including the ones already listed above), will be able to ultimately vanquish the spirit of Jezebel from working so aptly in a woman's heart and family structure. Without this first nothing else can work!

Now you may be thinking, But how can the wrong condition of a wife's heart toward her husband stifle or pre- vent his ability to perform functionally in his God-ordained role? Isn't that just an excuse or a cop-out for the husband's irresponsibility?

Well, that's partially correct: A husband's obedience to God to "love his wife as Christ also loved the church and gave his life for her" stands independently and unconditionally as well. However, he may very well have a heart to try his best to show his love for his wife, while at the same time being stifled in his ability to function fully in that role, as well as in his role of family headship, by his wife's lack of proper regard for him. I think we can all relate to how the disdain or apathy of others can cripple the best of us.

Many women, even without realizing the full impact they have, virtually emasculate their husbands by the lack of honor they have for them. The husband is rendered impotent in many ways by his wife's attitude toward him and by her words to him!

I will now explain this with sound principle and evidence.

The Destruction of Dishonor

The Principle of Aborted Authority

This is a sound behavioral principle: Responsibility with- out authority is a dysfunctional context. Therefore anyone who has a responsibility without the unconditional and uncontested authority to perform it is actually prevented from being functionally effective and will likely behave dysfunctionally as a result.

Insubordination deteriorates its authority and undermines the very foundation of the structure. And insubordination and rebellion can only be controlled from within the subordinate's own heart. Therefore, any husband whose wife hasn't first resolved in her own heart to unconditionally relinquish headship to him and honor him with her godly submission cannot function properly and freely in his own role, especially toward her!

I believe this is evidenced in the parable of the talents in Matthew 25:14–30. Jesus showed that the wicked servant's first mistake was that he despised (or had no honorable regard for) his master. Jesus carefully illustrated this in the wicked servant's opening remarks:

> Lord, I knew thee that thou art an hard man, reaping where thou hast not sown, and gathering where thou hast not strawed.
> Matthew 25:24 (kjv)

And his wickedly selfish and lazy heart toward his master was manifested in the fruit of his actions. He didn't lift a finger to prosper his master at all; he was only thinking of himself! He buried it to keep from being blamed by his "hard master" for losing it! It was his lazy way out of putting forth even the slightest effort to please his master, who scolded him for not at least putting it in the bank to gain interest. And that's why his master called him, "Thou wicked and slothful servant" (verse twenty-six) and then ordained his fate: "And cast ye the unprofitable servant into outer darkness" (verse thirty).

Why was he deemed unprofitable? Because he had no heart to please his master; his master couldn't count on his dedication to him and therefore couldn't count on his willing submission to help him prosper his kingdom! Could it be that with a proper heart for his master, even if he had at least tried and risked it and lost it by mistake, his master would have still invited him to "enter now into the joy of thy lord" (verse twenty-three) for at least trying?

And what do you suppose was Judas Iscariot's first mistake, whose selfish and greedy heart toward Jesus made him such a willing instrument for Satan's use and whose heart Satan ultimately entered and possessed?

A wife who has no heart for her husband, who habitually behaves insubordinately toward her husband, under- mining and usurping his authority over their household and family (especially in front of their children) actually stifles her husband from being profitable in his God- given role and is therefore much more than just a mere stumbling block to him.

Regardless of his best intentions, without her willing decision first to honor him unconditionally, he is actually prevented from functioning and behaving as he otherwise might, especially toward her. And he cannot control her insubordination, because he is rendered ineffective by her to even "earn" her devotion. It's a vicious circle: a spiral downward.

The "lord" in the parable of the talents apparently couldn't control the wicked servant's rebellious heart either. Isn't this evidenced by the servant calling his master a "hard man" to his face? Or did this illustrate that the master was perhaps really "froward" but was still worth honoring because he was indeed the master?

Remember that he wasn't so "hard" after all, as illustrated by how he invited his other two profitable servants to jubilantly share his joy with him! Indeed, maybe his faithful servants' hearts to please their master actually softened his heart toward them, encouraging his benevolence toward them.

No mission can be profitable when the head is rendered ineffective by the weak or nonexistent support of the subordinate.

Bad Fruit of Aborted Authority

This principle of responsibility without authority causing dysfunctional behavior is clearly evidenced all over our society today. It is evident not only in the dysfunction of many husbands and fathers but also indirectly in the rebellious attitudes and behavior of today's children.

Many children today are being raised by parents whose parental structure is upside-down. The children have repeatedly witnessed their mother undermining and usurping her own husband's authority. They witness their mother's power struggle for headship over her husband when they see her overrule his decisions; when they see her intentionally dishonor his feelings and wishes, sometimes lying to him or hiding the truth from him, and when they are repeatedly subjected to screaming matches between them, or worse!

Children, who are way more perceptive and astute than we give them credit for, from an early age repeatedly witness the weakness of their parental authority over them when they see the contention within it. They witness their mother undermining or even usurping her husband's headship in their home. They have been taught by their mother's example that it's okay to despise authority, seeing that their mother despises her own authority! We all tend to emulate the model of power.

In extreme cases they even witness their grandmother assuming headship over their father when the grand-mother reprimands him in front of them. God forbid! A grandmother who is naturally held in high esteem as a woman by her grandchildren is in a tremendously influential position and for this reason should never model headship over her grandchildren's father this way! It is safe to say that women who tend to usurp headship over their husbands have learned this dysfunctional behavior from their own upbringing. The acorn never falls far from the tree.

Furthermore, these days children are raised by parents whose hands have been tightly tied from performing their responsibility to properly train up their children, because their proper authority over their own children has been so grossly undermined by ungodly secular philosophies (such as Freudian philosophy) and by secular laws. The state can even usurp parents' sovereign author- ity over their children altogether by forcibly removing a child from them, based only on the word of the child! A parent can now very likely be arrested for properly spanking a child! And children all know these things better than any of us.

That's the biggest problem with this: Even though the state's police authority over parents started out with the justifiable purpose of preventing child abuse, the problem now is that children all know how they can abuse it. It's like giving a child a loaded gun with a hair trigger and suggesting to them to keep it aimed on their parents. In fact, they are such experts on how to undermine and usurp parental authority over them (learning it from their mothers) that they have become practiced in the arts of deception and manipulation, being fully aware of their ability to invoke police authority over their parents at any time for any reason whenever they feel "unjustly treated" by them. They know that through their ability to invoke the state's authority, they ultimately have sovereign authority over their own parents.

Further, thanks to parental structures weakened by upside-down or equal partnership designs and the cleverly deceptive satanic media, children have been easily deceived into being convinced in their hearts that they are superior to their own parents (and consequently adults in general) because the groundwork has already been laid by the "proof" they've seen that their mothers are superior to their fathers. How can they have confidence in their parental authority (and authority in general, for that matter) when they've seen that their parental structure is weakened by the ever-existent power struggle within it, and they know that their parents' authority is so weakened by their own authority over their parents readily available to them through the state?

Bart and Lisa Simpson, the icons for children these days, are both portrayed as superior to their father, Homer, and to their parents altogether.

In many cases parents fear their children and right- fully so. Under even normal duress from reasonable and healthy parental controls, children tend to have a rebelliously insubordinate attitude toward them, with an air of self-righteousness.

We all despise weak authority, because we cannot feel secure with it. And when we cannot feel secure about the absolute boundaries within which we are expected to function, it leads to rebellion and/or neuroses of all kinds, which manifest in neurotic behavior.

For this reason children understandably resent their parental structure's lack of sovereign authority over them because they cannot feel secure in it and so resent their parents for it. They can't wait to get away from their parents and "live their own life." Absent of any adequate authority over them, they might just as well live their own life. Their parental controls cannot provide any beneficial security for them; they only stifle what they have come to believe is their only dependable authority, which is their own sovereign authority over themselves!

More Bad Fruit

The bad fruit of aborted authority is also displayed in the apathy and indifference, and sometimes even destructive behavior, of some public school teachers toward the children they are helplessly responsible to teach. Both the teachers and the children are well aware that any authority the teacher might otherwise have over them to carry out this tremendous responsibility is virtually nonexistent! And they fear the children, with good reason. They can now only teach hoping that the children will feel like behaving properly and learning, because the teacher's hands are so tightly tied from administering any consequences for wrong behavior and attitudes.

And these days the teachers operate much without the support of the parents as well. There was a day when if a child had a conflict with the teacher, the parents categorically upheld the teacher, even if the teacher might have made a mistake. Now, however, the parents are more likely to blindly support the child against the teacher. Even many parents who demand excellence of the teachers to whom they have relegated (notice I didn't say delegated) their responsibility of teaching their children are the same ones who will proudly tell their children how they went in and "gave the teacher hell." Parents won't even support the authority of the teachers to whom they've relegated their own responsibilities.

These poor teachers have all the responsibility of raising our children with none of the authority to carry it out. No wonder so many children today just flat refuse to learn and their behavior in school is out of control and the teachers don't care. For their own sanity, and to avoid losing their jobs, they almost can't care!

And if you think about it, you have probably also experienced some situation, maybe at work, where you were given a certain responsibility but your authority to carry it out was repeatedly being usurped or undermined by one of your assistants. How did you function? Or per- haps you can recall a time when you repeatedly undermined your authority in a work situation. Did it make that person a better leader or a worse one?

The Evidence of Joy

Find Good Fruit, and You Find Good Counsel As evidenced by the good fruit of wifely obedience to God's counsel, many wives who have resolved in their hearts to independently obey God's Word to love, honor, and obey their otherwise "worthless and unloving" husbands, have actually uplifted and encouraged their hus- bands as a result, and as the blessed fruit of their obedience, their newly empowered husbands rose miraculously to deserve the honor! This should come as no surprise to anyone, because it is a well-known phenomenon of human behavior.

I know of the personal testimonies of several women who confess that their choice to obey Christ and honor their husbands unconditionally has had a phenominally posi- tive effect on their husbands' love for them. These testimonies are fairly well known. I recall one by Joyce Meyer. After the wife has deliberately resolved in her heart to unconditionally honor her husband by relinquishing all authority to him in blind obe- dience to God's Word, God has freely worked miracles in her husband's heart! Again:

For the unbelieving husband is sanctified by the wife …
1 Corinthians 7:14 (kjv)

Likewise, ye wives, be in subjection to your own husbands; that, if any obey not the word, they also may without the word be won by the conversation of the wives; While they behold your chaste conversation coupled with fear.
1 Peter 3:1–2 (kjv)

And the greatest benefit is that this produces good fruit not only in the husband but more importantly in the children too! They see by their mother's healthy and loving example that God-given authority is not to be considered conditional, not to be under- mined, and not to be usurped!

Now I will present to you the evidence of God's wisdom in all this with the follow- ing principle.

The Powerful Principle of Bestowed Authority Often we can train and encourage responsibility into the heart of a person simply by letting go of the authority to carry it out and bestowing that complete and unchallenged authority on them. Then, once they are secure in their authority, we can watch them bloom and rise to the occasion in their ownership of it and their desire to deserve it. If you think about it, you can probably remember seeing the positive effect of this. I know I've seen it.

This is a marvelous way of training up a child, for example, to learn responsibility and integrity. There are many well-written books on this principle; one of which I've read was Bringing Up Boys, written by Dr. James C. Dobson of Focus on the Family.

A godly wife is to bestow the honor and authority of headship to her husband. While a wife can willingly relinquish her husband's proper authority to him by sim- ply resolving in her heart to bestow it upon him, a hus- band cannot relinquish his wife's proper role of submission to her. A wife can bestow authority on her husband by sim- ply letting go of it herself, but a husband cannot bestow submission to his wife by sim- ply letting go of anything!

But there is often a fear associated with the letting go of anything, and I believe there's a fear at work here. The fear may be that, once given "full reign," the husband will become a mean and evil dictator, that relinquishing all authority to her husband will go to his head and make a monster out of him. While this can happen in men with naturally wicked hearts (who should then certainly be abandoned by his wife and children, and treated for mental illness, punished in court, exorcised of demonic possession, or "delivered unto Satan for the destruction of the flesh"), I am not aware of any danger of this happening in a well-intentioned husband or father with a good heart, especially not one who loves his wife enough to want to restore their marriage.

And incidentally, many people who don't have a heart for God tend to see him as a mean dictator, too, which is certainly not true!

Nevertheless, should a wife's heart toward her husband, or a biblical counseling approach to save a marriage, be based on a biblically illogical fear of making a monster out of an otherwise well-intentioned and loving husband by the wife's obedience to God's Word for her?

Maybe the wicked servant in the parable of the talents was afraid that his submission to his master would only encourage his master to be an even "harder man" toward him. But indeed, it appeared that the tendency was just the opposite: The honor that his two faithful servants bestowed upon him encouraged benevolence in him toward them! The devoted hearts of his faithful servants exalted him and lifted him up, and he invited them to "share in his joy"!

The following is my testimony of the good fruit evidence of bestowed honor.

The Good Fruit of Bestowed Authority

The principle of bestowed authority or bestowed honor is an amazing phenomenon. In a nutshell it's this: A per- son to whom authority is overtly and completely granted will generally feel compelled to earn and deserve it. It encourages the person to rise to the occasion! It makes them want to be a better person.

I have many fond childhood memories of my father employing this principle with me. And as I grew older and came to recognize exactly what he was doing when he did it, it still worked in me. But I knew it wasn't some sort of reverse-psychology trick. I knew in my heart that it was my dad's loving attempt to train me up to be a confident and capable adult.

And as an adult, I have personally experienced the good fruit of this principle in others. Many years ago as a young man, I was given authority over a large IBM account as the prime representative there, and I gave my utmost to deserve it. But despite my most diligent efforts, I found myself struggling to handle a two-man workload single-handedly and asked my manager for some assistance. To my disappointment he sent me a considerably older man who was considered somewhat lazy among our peers because he had a reputation of habitually arriving at work late, leaving early, and, with an indifferent attitude, doing as little as possible in between. Though he was a genuinely likeable man, he was considered to be ineffective in his work. I distinctly remember thinking, I ask for help, and he sends me this guy of all people.

But the day he came to me to be my assistant, his attitude toward me was clearly submissive. He said, "I'm here to do whatever you need." His words were genuine, and I knew it; and it immediately bestowed honor and authority to me. And my response to the honor he gave me was, "Here's the list of things that need to be done, and you can have first pick of whatever you'd like to do from it." Those first moments set the pace for our days ahead together.

After just a few weeks, much to my surprise, I realized that he was coming in early, staying late, and accomplishing much in between! Even when I had to leave him alone for indefinite periods, I would come back unannounced to find him not lazing around but happily busy. I found him not to be lazy at all but a very profitable assistant! Was it because I had such excellent leadership skills? No. It was because of his first words to me at our first meeting. The honest truth is that his initial honor toward me actually humbled me! And as a result, I simply felt compelled to return the honor he originally bestowed on me and we exalted and upheld each other in our respective positions. He honored me in my role of authority, and subsequently I honored him in his role of support.

If my leadership skills were indeed good, it's only because I was free to rise into my uncontested role of authority. In other words, I wanted to deserve the honor he had first bestowed on me. We proved to be a fit and profitable mission team, and in no time the account was right up to speed and running like a well-oiled clock. I often rewarded him in his efforts, defended his reputation among our peers, and made sure our manager knew how much I appreciated him. And we often reveled in our accomplishments and rested on our laurels together.

Can you see the striking parallels between the simple but real example of this team's structure in its mission and the structure of a marriage fortress in its mission?

Better Evidence of the Good Fruit

This is an even better example of the positive effect of bestowed authority. I was raised by well-intentioned parents whose marital and parental structure was formed and set before the women's liberation movement and our society's cultural rebellion against God. And they some- how both functioned quite well in their God-ordained roles, according to godly principles, without even necessarily realizing it!

My mother began her relationship with my father with the resolve in her heart that he was her head. She has recently told me this. She had purposed in her heart to bestow the headship in their home to him.

Even though my dad wasn't perfect by any means, my mom, under no circumstances, ever once attempted to undermine, much less usurp, my dad's headship in our home. And most certainly not in front of me! I never once witnessed a screaming match between my mom and dad. He was never made to feel challenged in his proper role in our home! My mother lovingly made certain that his authority remained securely unchallenged, especially in front of me, for my sake. And not uncoincidentally, he honored her and upheld her as his wife and my mother, and insisted on my highest honor and respect toward her at all times as well.

Recently, long after his death, I asked her if anything he ever did rubbed her the wrong way. She said, "Yes, sometimes. But then later, in private when you weren't around, I would speak to him about it." She would petition him in private, after the fact, with a quiet and gentle spirit. I think I can even recall the positive effect it had on him. And my mother was not otherwise a quiet and gentle person; she was quite strong, intelligent, self-secure, and self-sufficient, indeed meek in her own strength. Though she didn't always like what he did, she simply chose to unconditionally honor her husband regardless! Her sub- mission to him was by her free-will decision to honor him and bestow his rightful role of authority to him.

In fact, even whenever I complained to her about him, out of her love for me she supported him. She wouldn't allow me to speak disrespectfully about him to her, even in private. Her loving response to me, as I so vividly remember was, "He's not perfect, Terry. No par- ents are. But because he is your father, you are to have nothing but the highest respect for him! He loves you, and he is doing his best for you! Even if he makes mis- takes, I know he means only the best for you." I believed my mom, and I knew inherently that she loved me and would never lie to me. And she squarely and unwaver- ingly supported him in my eyes as he did for her. By her example I learned that respect for authority did not have to be earned, but merely bestowed as a free-will choice.

And the fruit is that my dad, securely supported in his role by my mom and me, functioned most always in a perfectly mature, loving, and compassionate way toward her and me. Even though he was known for having a strong and quick-tempered nature, he never once abused my mom or me. I only saw his temper flare toward me when my attitude was rebellious. Full reign didn't make him a mean and evil dictator. Not even close!

In fact, it was quite the opposite. Knowing what I know now about godly wisdom and sacrifice and remembering the many things my dad taught me in the way he dealt with and responded to my mother, me, and others, I am amazed at the profound godly wisdom he somehow had! Though he wasn't even a born-again Christian, he was a remarkably respectable and honorable husband and father and was well-respected by others for his solid integrity.

He was a great example of a loving husband and father. Did he make mistakes? Sure. Could a better man have done a better job? Sure. But I know that given his well-intentioned nature along with his assurance of my mother's unconditional submission to him, he did his best to deserve the honor that was bestowed to him in his position as head of our household! Unhindered by contention from her, he was free to rise to the occasion and fulfill his role.

He strove to deserve the honor he was already given. In fact, it seems to me that he rose way above what could have been naturally expected of him in many ways. I respect him for that, and I've always remained convinced of his devotion to us!

But more than anything, first and foremost, I respect my mother for her wisdom, fortitude, and consistency in bestowing the headship to him that I'm convinced encouraged and empowered him to give his best to deserve that honor: to be the best husband and father he could be!

Epilogue

I know that a husband's heart of proper love, honor, and dedication for his wife and children, in dedication to Christ, is essential to encourage his wife's willing heart of submission to him. I also know that a wife's heart of proper love, honor, and submission for her husband, in dedication to Christ, is essential to fully enable and encourage her husband's heart of love and dedication for his wife and children and to exalt him to excellence in his God-designed role.

I am convinced that the combination of these elements of a marriage fortress produces a synergy of limit- less potential. Given these ingredients, a marriage will be a richly fulfilling and satisfying joy-filled marriage fortress of provision and protection that stands tall and strong as a shining witness to the glory of our infinitely wise and loving Father in heaven and Savior Jesus Christ, a vessel of God's perfect design into which he can freely pour out the abundance of his blessings, and that he can freely use for his purposes.

But in attempting to restore a struggling, failing, or otherwise joyless marriage, as with disarming a ticking bomb, what's the correct and most effective course of action? I believe that all logic and scriptural evidence points toward first ascertaining the condition of the wife's heart toward her husband and her willingness to joyfully embrace all of the scriptures in God's Word pertaining to the wife. Once this is either confirmed or achieved, then the focus should switch to exhorting her husband's heart of love for her.

But not until then. Now that we are familiar with Satan's strategy and devices against marriages, we know where we must begin our damage assessment. The element of a marriage that we know the enemy targets for his first assaults must be the element that we go to first to fit and fortify. Then we can safely set about to correct and strengthen the rest, which may indeed also need it.

It is my greatest desire that you will embrace the fullness of God's complete and infallible wisdom for you and live your life in the fullness of freedom and joy in Christ.

Bibliography

Arthur, Kay. A Marriage Without Regrets. Eugene: Harvest House Publishers, 2000.

Clark, Jonas. Jezebel, Seducing Goddess of War. Hallandale Beach:Spirit of Life Publishing, 1998.

Dobson, Dr. James C. Love for a Lifetime. Portland: Multnomah Press, 1987.

Newbold, Jr., Charles Elliott. The Harlot Church System. Monterey: Ingathering Press, 1999.

Frangipane, Francis. The Jezebel Spirit. Cedar Rapids: Arrow Pub- lications, 1991

Endnotes

1 http://www.christianpost.com/article/20080404/study-christian-divorce-rate-identical-to-national-average.htm

CPSIA information can be obtained
at www.ICGtesting.com
Printed in the USA
FFOW02n2252110814
6739FF